Following Miss Bell

Travels Around Turkey in the Footsteps of Gertrude Bell

PAT YALE

T0062021

TRAILBLAZER PUBLICATIONS

First edition: 2023; reprinted 2024

Publisher
Trailblazer Publications
The Old Manse, Tower Rd, Hindhead, Surrey, GU26 6SU, UK
🖳 trailblazer-guides.com

British Library Cataloguing in Publication Data
A catalogue record for this book is available from the British Library

ISBN 978-1-912716-35-7

Text and maps © Pat Yale 2023

Photographs © Pat Yale 2023 (unless otherwise credited © GBPA:
Gertrude Bell Photographic Archive, Newcastle University)

Editor: Lucy Ridout
Cartography: Nick Hill
Layout: Bryn Thomas
Index: Jane Thomas

Printed in the UK by SRP (🖳 shortrunpress.co.uk, ☎ 01392-211909),
25 Bittern Rd, Exeter, Devon EX2 7LW

For Osman Nuri Diler (1961–2021)
and the memory of the mountain

Contents

Preface

*'The most exalted seat in the world is the saddle of a swift horse
and the best companion of all time is a book.'*
El Mutanabbi, quoted by Gertrude Bell in Nazlı's guestbook;
undated but probably July 1907

Towards the end of the nineteenth century, the artist, archaeologist
and statesman Osman Hamdi Bey was a leading light in Constantinople society. The coming of the Turkish Republic cast a shadow
over all things Ottoman, but in 2004 the sale of his painting *The Tortoise Trainer*, for what was then a record-breaking sum for a Turkish
artwork, signalled a revived interest in him. So when an Istanbul museum showcased the contents of his daughter Nazlı's guestbook, I
was eager to find out what famous names might be lurking between
its covers.

To my surprise, my eyes alighted on the autograph of Gertrude
Bell, best known of a band of British 'desert queens' famous for ex-

ploring the Levant in the years before the First World War. Born into
a wealthy family of industrialists
from the northeast of England in
1868, Gertrude travelled extensively in the territories that are
now Syria, Jordan, Iraq, Lebanon,
Israel/Palestine and Saudi Arabia
between 1905 and 1914. When war
broke out, her pioneering adventures in little-known areas of the
Middle East elevated her from amateur archaeologist and traveller to
go-to expert, the only woman in a
group of British former explorers
with experience of the region's
complex tribal politics. After the

© GBPA

Gertrude Bell, aged 26, between her
third and fourth visits to Turkey

7

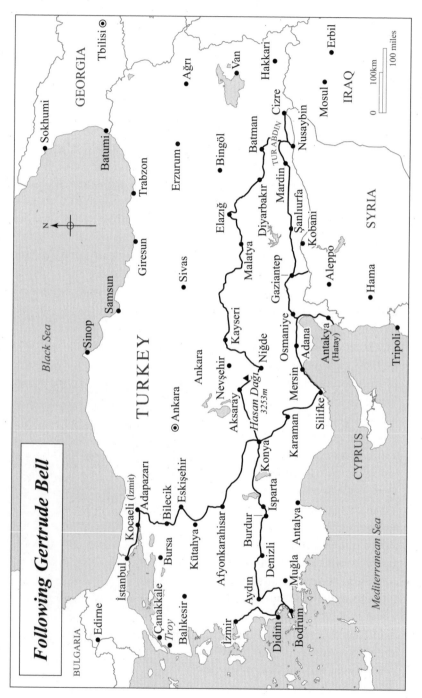

Following Gertrude Bell

war she settled in Baghdad where she came to be associated with the crude 'lines in the sand' used to conjure nation-states from the territory of the defeated Ottoman Empire. Later she would wet-nurse the inexperienced Saudi-born Prince Faisal as he made his stumbling first steps as ruler of the newly created Iraq.

Gertrude's, then, is a name more commonly associated with deserts than Aegean beaches, and, accordingly, for Nazlı's guestbook she selected a quotation from a revered Iraqi poet. But its presence there set me thinking. To have visited Osman Hamdi at home suggested a more than passing acquaintance with his family, which in turn implied a more than passing acquaintance with what was at that time still Constantinople.

Curiosity piqued, I turned to her letters and diaries and quickly learned that between 1889 and 1914 she had visited what is now the Republic of Turkey on at least eleven occasions. Between 1889 and 1899 a sequence of short trips had taken her to Constantinople, Bursa and Smyrna, as well as to the famous archaeological sites of Troy and Ephesus. In 1902 she spent a month exploring Smyrna and its hinterland, the experience marking, in Turkish terms, the turning point between Gertrude the tourist and Gertrude the explorer. That transition was completed in 1905 when she arrived in Turkey not in the relative comfort of ship or train but astride a horse, riding into Antakya (Hatay) from Aleppo on her way back from Syria and Palestine. Two years later Turkey itself formed the sole focus of a four-month overland expedition from Smyrna to Binbirkilise, a remote cluster of early Byzantine churches in the heart of Anatolia. Then in 1909 she rode into Cizre and across Turkey at the end of a long expedition through Syria and Iraq. Two years later and the border town of Nusaybin served as her entry point at the tail end of another months-long journey into Iraq and Syria. A premature farewell to Constantinople came in 1914 when she paused there briefly on her way home from a fraught expedition into what is now Saudi Arabia.

Despite these many visits and the fact that she had met both her friend and colleague Lawrence of Arabia, and the great love of her life, Dick Doughty-Wylie, there, Gertrude's time in Turkey has been largely overlooked. Yet the story was always hiding in plain sight. Her journeys had resulted in two books – *The Thousand and One*

Churches and *The Churches and Monasteries of the Tur Abdin* – that were wholly about Turkey, and another three – *Persian Pictures*, *The Desert and the Sown*, and *Amurath to Amurath* – in which it played a walk-on role. Pieces of the story cropped up in volumes of her letters published by her stepmother, Florence Bell, and her sister, Elsa Richmond. A sequence of articles on Cilicia and Lycaonia also appeared in the *Revue Archéologique*. The snag lay in the absence of one single book that pulled together all the threads. Plenty of foreign men had traversed the Turkey of the late nineteenth and early twentieth centuries and published accounts of their adventures. Gertrude was perhaps the only Western woman to have done the same thing at the same time, yet it wasn't until Newcastle University placed her archive online that the scattered pieces finally came together to reveal just how extensively she had travelled within the country, sometimes in the footsteps of renowned scholar-explorers such as Sir William Ramsay, sometimes – as in the Tur Abdin, where it can sometimes feel as if she has just walked out of the room – breaking new ground of her own. Her diaries revealed her climbing mountains (Cudi and Hasan) and rafting a river (the Tigris); they described her ventures in places as disparate as pre-Blue Cruise Bodrum and the Karaca Dağı, a region so remote that it is barely mapped even today; and they showed her at Binbirkilise, rolling up her sleeves as the first Western woman to dig for the past in the Anatolian countryside. Her letters oozed the gossip of late-Ottoman society. Her photographs immortalized all but inaccessible Byzantine ruins, some since lost to storm, quarrying or dynamite. They live on, rather touchingly, on the computer screens of local planning officers, cherished as the first known images of their domains.

The kernel of an idea began to seed itself. Cautiously, I marked onto a map all the places that she had visited on her different journeys. Then I joined the dots and stood back to admire an itinerary that kicked off easily in the comfort of Istanbul, then tracked down to Izmir on the Aegean coast before sweeping east across the heart of the country to dusty, neglected Cizre on the Syrian border and doubling back west to Istanbul via the basalt-walled stronghold of old Diyarbakır. Gertrude had ticked off archaeological sites as well known as Sardis and Aphrodisias and as forgotten as Blaundos and

Gertrude Bell's camp in front of the Ertokuş Han; 1907

Larissa; places as easily accessible as Konya and Eskişehir and as hard to reach as the Syriac monastery of Mor Augen. By amalgamating all her journeys and then retracing them, I hoped to find out how much had changed in Turkey and how much had stayed the same.

Boarding a bus out of Izmir in April 2015, I could never have imagined the casual way that politics would upend my plans as a mid-June election triggered the collapse of a peace process between the government and the Kurds. Turkey went into a tailspin. As I journeyed steadily further from the safe, tourist-favoured west coast towards the embattled southeast, the country's troubled past started to snap at the heels of its unhappy present. Only by keeping a low profile (and perhaps being a woman) could I keep going.

Most of my travel took place in 2015, but because of the fragile situation on the Syrian border I researched the Karkamış chapter first, in 2014, even though fighting in Kobani was underway. The ascent of Hasan Dağı had to await suitable weather conditions and was carried out belatedly in 2016.

Pat Yale
Istanbul, 2022

11

Gertrude's Spelling and Other Inconsistencies

Gertrude was travelling before Atatürk decreed that Turkish should be written in a modified form of the Latin alphabet instead of Arabic. She could read Arabic but must often have been transliterating the sound of place names without knowing how they should be spelt. It would have been churlish to attempt to correct the inevitable inconsistencies (and spelling mistakes) that arise in her diaries and letters.

After the switch to the new alphabet many names that were traditionally transliterated with a final 'd' swapped it for a 't' – so Ahmet replaced Ahmed, Mehmet replaced Mehmed etc.

Identifying unfamiliar settlements in Turkey is often complicated by toponyms that have changed multiple times over the centuries, either successively (in the west) or simultaneously and multilingually (in the east). Even the country's modern name is tricky since in Gertrude's day all the nation-states of the modern Middle East were part of the seamless Ottoman Empire with 'Turkey' as its heart. Like most, I've opted for convenience over consistency in the hope of making life easier for readers. So, modern names for the countries that emerged from the collapse of that empire and modern names for most settlements that feature in this book, with nods of recognition to the old or most common alternatives. Inconsistencies remain, however. I have, for example, chosen to use 'Constantinople' and 'Smyrna' in historic contexts and 'Istanbul' and 'Izmir' in contemporary ones, hoping that all four names are familiar enough to prevent confusion.

The Turkish Language

The Turkish alphabet varies slightly from the English one although this should not concern readers unduly. The most confusing difference is that the 'c' in Turkish is pronounced like a 'j' – so *cami* [mosque]' is pronounced 'jami' and *'caddesi* [road]' is pronounced 'jaddesi'. Two other differences to be aware of are that 'ç' is pronounced 'ch' as in church and 'ş' is pronounced 'sh' as in rush. The 'ğ' character is silent, so the name of the current president is pronounced 'Erdo-an', not 'Erdo-gan'. Alongside the familiar dotted 'i' Turkish has a dotless 'ı', but readers can largely ignore this. Every letter is pronounced in Turkish, so 'Söke' is 'So-ke', not 'Soak'. Finally, Turkish uses suffixes for many different reasons. One to be aware of is the 'li/lı/lu' suffix which means 'resident of' – so an Istanbullu is a resident of Istanbul, an Izmirli a resident of Izmir. I have omitted the dotted capital İ with which Turks write İstanbul and İzmir because the undotted version will be more familiar to English-speaking readers.

1

The First East

ISTANBUL

'In Constantinople there are almost as many dogs as there are Turks.'
Letter, 21 May 1889

'Hooooo.'

It's a sound to make the hairs on your neck stand on end. An unearthly sound, inhuman, dredged, it seems, from deep within the soul. To attempt to render it in words is futile not least because its nearest English equivalent is the sound made by a child playing ghosts in a bedsheet, which would be to inject a wholly inappropriate suggestion of levity into something quintessentially solemn. Better, perhaps, to think of the haunting 'woo' made by an owl crying out in the night.

Yet in Arabic there is no such transliteration problem. In Arabic the 'hoo' sound is a word that can be rendered as 'hu'. This 'hu' is the equivalent of the upper-case He of Christianity. But of course this He is not the Christian God but the Muslim Allah, and the elevation of the word into this spine-tingling sound speaks as profoundly of faith as that of a chorister's voice echoing around the vaults of a Gothic cathedral.

I've come to watch a troupe of whirling dervishes go through their paces in one of the waiting rooms at Istanbul's Sirkeci Station. It's a majestic, high-ceilinged space, the sort of space that was commonplace in the days before functionality and the need to remember heating bills eclipsed beauty in the design stakes. The lemony light filtering through the stained-glass windows above the quintet of elderly musicians only adds to the sense of this being a secular cathedral, a paean in stone to the glories of modern transportation.

Beneath the windows the musicians warm up their audience before the dervishes begin to rotate, their snow-white skirts, lifted by gravity, undulating around them as they rehearse a routine in which every step is ritualized and meaningful, and only the blood red of the rug carefully spread on the floor at the start of the performance then ceremonially gathered up again at the end injects any semblance of colour. Up swing the skirts, offering glimpses of white long johns, then back they drop again, twisting tightly around the dancers' legs before coming to rest again when they pause for a break. Those swirling skirts stir a breeze in the hall. It flickers across my ankles as I sit waiting for the eerie howl that I know will conclude the proceedings.

On a spring day in 1889 a young woman stepped ashore from the steamer that had brought her down the Black Sea coast from Constanza in Romania to the harbour of Constantinople. As her foot touched the cobbles, she took care to lift her skirt to prevent it from trailing in the dust, then raised a hand to her head to check that her hat had survived disembarkation. That young woman was to become the famous Gertrude Bell, archaeologist, writer and traveller extraordinaire, the woman who would turn herself into the kingmaker of Iraq and help delineate the boundaries of the modern Middle East. In the early May of 1889, though, she was merely Miss Bell, an unusually self-confident twenty-year-old tourist taking time out after sailing through a first-class degree in history at Oxford in the days when the university declined to grant their diplomas to even its most brilliant female students. Gertrude had been born into one of the six richest families in Britain, her family's wealth the product of the great iron, steel and chemical empire created by her grandfather, Sir Isaac Lowthian Bell. The visit to Constantinople was not her first foray overseas, but it did offer her a first thrilling glimpse of the Orient, where the haunting lilt of the muezzin's call, the nostril-assailing pungency of the rubbish-strewn streets and the crush of what sometimes seemed like all of humanity squeezed into the same place at the same time turned a page in a mental book hitherto focused on Europe, bringing the rest of the world leaping suddenly to life in all its vibrant variety.

Given the role that the Islamic world was to play in her life, it's ironic that Gertrude's first trip to Constantinople was a last-minute add-on to a more organized stay in Bucharest. A year earlier, the abrupt conclusion to years of study had left her rudderless. So when her uncle, the British Minister to Romania, invited her to waltz away the winter beneath Bucharest chandeliers she jumped at the opportunity. In the eyes of relatives, who had hoped it would rid her of her 'Oxfordy manner', that winter break had had a serious matrimonial purpose to it, and disappointment at its failure to throw up any suitor more promising than her blue-eyed cousin Billy might have been gnawing away at the back of her mind as the ship steamed down the Bosphorus to moor in Galata (now Karaköy). But as soon as it docked, all such thoughts would have evaporated. In the harbour tall ships with complex rigging jostled sailing boats with dhow-shaped lateens while a flotilla of gondola-like caiques darted in and out, their oarsmen bawling for customers. It was a first intoxicating glimpse of the East that must have been all but overwhelming for a young woman unaccustomed to frequenting so much as a Kensington art gallery unchaperoned.

As Billy and their new friend, the *Times* journalist Valentine ('Domnul') Chirol, stepped ashore beside her, Gertrude would have been swallowed up in a multi-coloured throng. Her eyes would have flickered over a sea of red fezzes as men crowded around her, pushing and shoving. Amid the crush she would have glimpsed the *hamals*, the porters struggling from the boats bent double beneath luggage; the *simit*-sellers, their trays of sesame-covered bread rings looped like quoits over wooden poles; the *şerbet* vendors bearing flasks of sugary drinks; the ragged *dilencis*, the beggars with their twisted limbs and whining voices; and the ubiquitous street curs, 'light yellow with longish rough hair', as she wrote home to her sister.

Spinning round, she would have been transfixed by the vista of Sarayburnu, the historic peninsula topped with Hagia Sophia, the Topkapı Palace and the Sultanahmet Cami, its rollercoaster silhouette of domes and minarets little changed to this day. Then Domnul would have been steering her into the Customs House, where she could smoke a cigarette while their bags were assembled and checked, and a horse and carriage procured to bear them up to Pera, the modern quarter on the hill above the harbour that had evolved to accommodate the city's European residents. They were heading for the Royal Hotel (on the Rue des Petits-Champs, today's Meşrutiyet Caddesi), which stood cheek by jowl with stately Pera House, then home to the British Embassy. The Royal was one of a cluster of new hotels to have sprung up in the space cleared by a conflagration twenty years earlier and it was in its plush and no doubt aspidistra-filled interior that she, Domnul and Billy would have put their heads together to plan their tour of the city.

Three years later, Gertrude returned to Constantinople on the Orient Express. I imagine her striding along the platform at Sirkeci Station, a young woman with green eyes and auburn hair, the chubby cheeks of college days newly streamlined to reveal a pointed nose and chin; a straight-backed woman of middling height whose love of fur and feathers played up a fragile prettiness that would not outlive the flattery of youth. No doubt that young Gertrude would have been thinking only of the mosques, palaces and bazaars dangled in front of her by her Murray's guidebook. Yet ahead of her lay a life of extraordinary accomplishment. For Gertrude was the consummate overachiever who had only to set her sights on something for it to become a success. This was a woman who would mature into so adept a linguist that she would translate the Persian poet Hafiz's *Divan* into English; so accomplished a mountaineer that a peak in the Swiss Alps would be named after her; such an expert in the little-known minutiae of Middle Eastern tribal politics that the British government would call on her services during the First World War. Later in life she would go on to found the Iraq Museum. By the time of her death she was so well known that her passing was announced in the House of Commons.

From a historian's point of view, Gertrude's most endearing characteristic was an addiction to putting pen to paper. Notes, letters, diaries, books, articles – hardly a day went by when she didn't pour her experiences onto the page as enthusiastically as any hyper-active blogger of today. From those scribblings we sense a youth spent in restless pursuit of a purpose. Rich, clever and successful she might have been, yet hand-in-glove with the public achievements went serial disappointments in her private life: love affairs that came to nothing, an enthusiasm for family that did not translate into starting one of her own. As I drain a glass of wine in the Orient Express Restaurant, I'm painfully conscious that I'm about to set off to retrace the footsteps of a woman whose life almost certainly ended in lonely Baghdad suicide.

★ ★ ★

By the late nineteenth century enough adventurous travellers were finding their way to Constantinople for an embryonic tourist trail to be emerging. Already there was a tick-list of places that all good visitors had to see, and top of that list, then as now, was Ayasofya.

Ayasofya had started life as a monumental Christian church, Hagia Sophia, the Church of Divine Wisdom, the present incarnation being the third church to occupy the site, its predecessors having succumbed to fire and riot. The third church was commissioned by the Byzantine emperor, Justinian, and for almost a thousand years it was revered as the greatest church in Christendom. But in 1453 the fall of the Byzantine Empire changed everything: after a six-week siege Mehmed the Conqueror cantered into the church, reined in his horse in front of the altar and commandeered the building for Islam. The youthful Mehmed decreed that the church should be converted into a mosque, and for the next five hundred years Hagia Sophia became Ayasofya (the Turkicized version of its name), its smoothly domed silhouette forever transformed by four flanking minarets from which the muezzin could call the faithful to prayer.

For the wide-eyed young Gertrude, St Sophia was 'the glory of Christendom ... the place of memories', but on her first visit in 1889 not only was it serving as a mosque but it was also Ramadan and she was able to witness one of the holiest days in the Islamic calendar there. On Kadir Gecesi (Laylat al-Qadr), the Night of Predestination, Allah is believed to have entrusted the first verses of the Koran to the Prophet Mohammed and angels are believed to descend from heaven carrying with them his plans for the coming year. All night long the faithful flock to the mosques to pray. From a vantage point in the western gallery once reserved for Byzantine noblewomen Gertrude gazed down through a shimmer of oil lamps as men prostrated themselves on carpets spread before the mihrab. 'The preacher's voice rolls out ... through arches and galleries and domes,' she wrote. '"God is the Light!" reads the preacher. "God is the Light!" repeats a praying nation, and falls with a sound like thunder, prostrate before His name.'

Since then, history has taken another turn. Convinced that it was the Ottoman Empire's failure to modernize that had led to its demise, and determined to secularize his new republic, Turkey's first president, Mustafa Kemal Atatürk, had Ayasofya decommissioned as a mosque. No longer could Christians or Muslims worship in it; the great church-mosque was to become a museum. Now, daily armies of tourists pour over the rutted threshold of the Imperial Gate once reserved for the emperor. I yearn to share their enthusiasm, to gaze up at the dome that was for so many centuries the largest in the world with reverence, but the selfie-sticks that have replaced the conquerors' swords are an irritant. Ditto the wall of scaffolding elbowing its way into the nave. It took less than six years to build the church, but it's taken more than three times as long as that not to complete its restoration.

To refresh the experience I've enlisted the help of Trici Venola, a forthright, Los Angeles-born graphic artist and high-school-history dropout, who came to Turkey in 1999, fell under the spell of Byzantium and has made it the work of her later life to sketch every last crumbling window-frame in greedy detail. Trici has no time for the irksome present; like a wife blind to her ageing husband's paunch, she still sees Hagia Sophia as it was in its Byzantine heyday. Straightaway she leads me to the end of the southern gallery where what looks from a distance like a group of portrait paintings dissolves, as we near it, into thousands of tiny glittering tesserae, mosaic depictions of the Empress Zoe and the last of her three husbands paying homage to Christ. The daughter of Constantine VIII, Zoe (c.978-1050) lived a life as colourful as the mosaics: betrothed to a Holy Roman Emperor, who expired before the nuptials could take place; belated marriage to a cousin; suspicion of involvement in his murder; remarriage to a likely co-conspirator; exile to the Princes' Islands; return to reign as joint empress with her sister, Theodora; third and final marriage at an age when most of her contemporaries were dozing in the Byzantine equivalent of bath chairs. Scrutiny of the mosaics reveals that the male head has been tweaked several times as artists rushed to revise the spousal image.

Trici gazes at Zoe with an affection born of long acquaintance. 'People say that she was ugly, but really she was lovely right into old age. You can even see that she was wearing make-up. She ended up queening it over all of them.'

But the trump cards up Trici's sleeve are the hidden crosses. In Zoe's day Hagia Sophia was a place of prayer sanctified by a thousand crosses: on the walls, on the columns, on the doors. Today they would seem to have vanished as completely as the Christian worshippers and it takes an artist's eye to see differently. For the crosses are not quite as lost as it might appear, and the way to find them is to spend hour upon meticulous hour with sketchpad in hand, looking, seeking, seeing.

In the women's gallery our fingers trace indentations once filled with jewel-encrusted crosses levered out by looters either in 1204 when the Fourth Crusaders laid waste to the church or in 1453 in the three days of looting permitted before Sultan Mehmed called a halt. On the balustrade overlooking the nave seemingly simple decorations conceal more crosses, hatching indicating where the arms were prised out to leave just the stems. There are crosses on the back of the Gates of Heaven and Hell. There are crosses peeking from under the ceiling frescoes. There are crosses on the plinths of the pillars. There are even crosses etched into the columns, crosses we can only find by running our hands up and down them like blind women reading braille. As we amble out through the great bronze door sequestered from a Hellenistic temple in Tarsus (more crosses, of course), I realize that I've barely noticed the crowds nor felt the need to glower at the scaffolding. Through Trici's eyes I've recovered some of the sense of wonder felt by Gertrude when she first stepped inside Hagia Sophia more than a hundred years ago*.

Ramadan, the month of dawn-to-dusk fasting, is the time when Islam most manifests itself to outsiders, and for a young woman born in the north of England and with almost no prior knowledge of the religion to have arrived in Constantinople just then must have been life-changingly revelatory. 'Not only is every true believer forbidden

*In July 2020 Ayasofya was once again converted into a mosque. The scaffolding has finally been removed.

to eat during the prescribed hours, but nothing of any kind may pass his lips; he may drink nothing, he may not smoke,' she wrote in her first published book, *Persian Pictures*, adding that

> these rules ... fall heavily upon the poorer classes, who alone preserve them faithfully. Porters carrying immense loads up and down the steep streets of Pera and Galata, caiquejis rowing backwards and forwards under the hot sun across the Golden Horn and the swift current of the Bosphorus, owners of small shops standing in narrow, stuffy streets and surrounded by smells which would take the heart out of any man – all these not one drop of water, not one whiff of tobacco, refreshes or comforts during the weary hours of daylight.

But alongside the deprivation she also witnessed the anticipation preceding *iftar*, the communal lighting of cigarettes and sipping of water that marked the end of the day's deprivation:

> The tables in front of the coffee-shops are set out with bottles of lemon-water and of syrups, and with rows and rows of water-pipes, and round them cluster groups of men, thirstily awaiting the end of the fast ... [Then] the sunset-gun booms out over the town, shaking minarets and towers as the sound rushes from hill to hill, shaking the patient, silent people into life. At once the smoke of tobacco rises an incense into the evening air, the nargilehs begin to gurgle merrily, the smoke of cigarettes floats over every group at the street corners, the very hamal pauses under his load as he passes down the hills and lights the little roll of tobacco which he carries all ready in the rags about his waist.

Then, with the eating and drinking out of the way, it was time for the exuberant night-becomes-day festivities.

> From that hour until dawn time passes gaily in Constantinople, and especially in Stamboul, the Turkish quarter. The inhabitants are afoot, the mosques are crowded with worshippers, the coffee-shops are full of men eating, drinking, smoking, and listening to songs and to the tales of story-tellers. The whole city is bright with twinkling lamps; the carved platforms round the minarets ... are hung about with lights, and, slung on wires between them, sentences from the Koran blaze out in tiny lamps against the blackness of the night.

In the Grand Bazaar, Ramadan even incommoded shoppers: 'all the sleepy old Turks were undoing their bales of carpets looking as if they had had a tremendous night of feasting, and had rather an ache of the head after it'. The visit was, in any case, a daunting experience:

'the crowds jostle you, the shopkeepers, throwing aside Oriental dignity, run after you and catch you by the sleeve, offering to show you Manchester cottons and coarse embroidered muslins'. Elbowing my way through the congested alleys of the modern bazaar, I glimpse her ahead of me, bargaining for rugs and rose essence, running a hand over porcelain and silk. Importunate shopkeepers are kept at bay by the swish of a skirt and an imperious glare.

The Constantinople of around one million inhabitants that greeted Gertrude in 1889 was the faltering capital of the Ottoman Empire, its glory days under the Mehmeds, Selims and Süleymans all but forgotten as its problems multiplied. The monuments of the great architect Sinan still harked back to the days when the Ottomans were feared and respected in equal part, but by now they had become something of a mockery, sticking-plasters of tile and marble obscuring a reality of potholed streets, ramshackle housing and poverty-stricken people. Already Tsar Nicholas I had coined the humiliating 'Sick Man of Europe' nickname to describe an empire so in hock to the Western powers that an office to administer taxes that would go straight to paying off its debts to them loomed over the waterfront at Eminönü. One by one the outer provinces were shearing off from the periphery, sending waves of destitute refugees pouring into the city to jam the courtyards of the mosques.

Presiding over this dismal situation was a sultan very much for the times. Abdülhamid II had succeeded to the throne in 1876, replacing his brother, Murad V, who had been deposed on the grounds of insanity after a reign of only ninety-three days. Their uncle, Sultan Abdülaziz, had died in mysterious circumstances, perhaps at his own hand, perhaps at that of another. Not altogether surprisingly, Abdülhamid was consumed with paranoia and had retreated uphill from the waterside Dolmabahçe Palace to the more readily defensible Yıldız Palace, which was ringed with walls and undercut with tunnels – the architects who had designed it were said to have been executed to prevent them from revealing the plans.

It had taken the new sultan a mere two years to dispense with the constitution imposed on him at his accession and he had neutralized the modernizing grand vizier, Midhad Paşa, by exiling him to the outer reaches of Arabia. But while Abdülhamid certainly had reason to fear some of the politicians still surrounding him, this was a sultan who saw enemies even in his own people. It was impossible for him to completely avoid appearing in public, but such unwelcome occasions had been whittled down to little more than the weekly *Selamlıks*, when he would venture out from the palace to take part in Friday prayers.

Gertrude struck lucky with the sultan, hurrying down to the Galata Bridge to watch him process over it in his carriage on his way to the abandoned Topkapı Palace, a ritual performed at the midpoint of Ramadan when his role as caliph required him to pay homage there to the Prophet's robe and standard. The man she glimpsed through the crowd was already middle-aged, his pinched and wary face dominated by darkly watchful eyes and a Black Sea beak of a nose. The caliph of all Islam he might be, and the man who held at least theoretical sway over the deserts through which she was later to travel, but, like all the sultans since his grandfather, the reformist Mahmud II, he was dressed not in romantic kaftan and turban but in prosaic frock coat and trousers. 'I expect he shivered with fright the whole time,' she wrote with the casual callousness of youth.

At the tail end of a round-the-world cruise, Gertrude returned to Constantinople in 1898, this time rushing to see the city's new archaeology museum, brainchild of Osman Hamdi Bey, who had not only helped excavate the intricately carved Alexander Sarcophagus from a necropolis in Sidon but had overseen its transportation to the Ottoman capital to form its centrepiece. Mistakenly believing this to be the actual tomb of Alexander the Great, Gertrude gushed over its rendering of the Battle of Issus, in which the Macedonian had routed the Persians: 'As one looked at the battle scene one wondered why all was silent and why no din of battle rose from that conflict. The dead lay under the horses' feet with exquisite heads thrown back and arms outstretched or doubled under them and over the top of them rode the conquerors striking and slaying the hooded Persians.'

That night she stayed in the Hotel Bristol on the Rue des Petits-Champs (Meşrutiyet Caddesi). Long since refashioned to accommodate the Pera Museum, the building hints at another link to Gertrude. Osman Hamdi Bey was not just an archaeologist and museum-maker but an artist too, and the Pera houses his masterpiece, *The Tortoise Trainer*. As I ponder the image of a turbaned man with a flute behind his back gazing at tortoises grazing on lettuce leaves, it's hard not to imagine him showing it off to her, paint barely dry on the canvas, in the book-lined study of his Kuruçeşme *yalı* just before she lifted her pen to inscribe El Mutanabbi's words in his daughter's guestbook.

★ ★ ★

By the end of the nineteenth century a visit to the whirling dervishes was already de rigueur for Constantinople tourists. Gertrude duly popped in to watch them in their Galata *tekke*, although on a day when a frenetic sightseeing schedule left no energy for recording what she saw. It was a deficiency compensated for by a British contemporary, the young Dorina Clifton, who had grown up in a *yalı* at Kandilli and left a lively description of the performance in her *Romance of the Bosphorus*:

> Mounting an old winding wooden staircase to a balcony overlooking the circular hall, we caught sight of the dervishes sitting cross-legged in a semicircle on the floor. There were about thirty of them, of all ages, wearing flowing robes made of thick snuff-coloured material and tall conical turbans. In the centre of them sat an aged dervish who wore the distinctive green turban which proclaimed him to be a direct descendant of the Prophet Mahomet, and a pilgrim who had visited the Holy City of Mecca. With stately measured steps the dervishes followed each other round the hall with their hands tucked inside their wide-sleeved cuffs. For a moment they halted … they kissed each other's hands, crossed the big toes of their feet, then stood erect while they prayed and waited for the religious spell to descend upon them … after a while a shiver passed over the bodies of these devout men, as if the earthly spirit were released from the human frame, whereupon lifting their arms and slowly spreading them outwards the dervishes one by one skimmed spinning over the ground … The ritual continued until the dervishes, completely exhausted, fell into trances and lay on the floor senseless.

Before returning to England, Gertrude stocked up on Turkish delight in the one Istanbul shop that is still in the same business on the same site today. Ali Muhiddin Hacı Bekir's sweetshop has been selling *lokum* since 1777 when the original Hacı Bekir concocted a sultan-pleasing soft candy. In a nineteeth-century watercolour by Amadeo Preziosi, Hacı Bekir appears as a roly-poly Father Christmas of a man with tight-pleated turban in place of floppy cap. As Mehmet Bey hands over a sample he indicates a cauldron perched in a fireplace behind a wooden counter just as in the painting. 'Rosewater,' he replies when I ask what flavour Gertrude might have purchased; certainly not the Johnny-come-lately pomegranate variety he's given me.

Those initial brief visits to Constantinople left an indelible impression on Gertrude. 'The first east one comes to is so enchanting,' she concluded. 'I feel that I could stand from now till next week at the end of Galata Bridge and watch the people pass and never be bored for one moment.'

2

The Topless Towers of Ilium

BURSA–ÇANAKKALE–TROY

'Delighted to see minarets and veiled women again'
Diary, 1 May 1899

On her first visit to Turkey Gertrude crossed the Sea of Marmara to visit Bursa, then Brusa, a town 'almost entirely untouched and unmodernised. One sees nothing but Turkish dresses in the streets, Turkish houses closely latticed, Turkish eating shops with curious foods in them.' Her sights were set on buying some of the silk that was already popular in Europe, and it was an elderly Turk sitting cross-legged at his counter in 'the street of the silk merchants' who snared her custom. Caught up in the schoolgirl-crush phase of adoration for everything oriental, she lingered over details of the leisurely shopping experience that was once so quintessentially Turkish. 'We might have been paying a morning call,' she wrote as coffee and nargiles appeared before them. Only after the cups had been drained was 'the subject of silks … broached and set aside again as unworthy of discussion'. Then casually, as if showing off the exhibits of a private museum, the shopkeeper spread embroideries before his guests for them to admire. Only belatedly did he pull down a roll of silk and wait for them to enquire what else he was hiding. And then the real wonders were spread out to tempt the women: 'There were muslins woven with tinsel lines, coarse Syrian cottons, and the brocades for which Brusa is famous, mixtures of cotton and silk woven in small patterns … yellow on white, gold on blue, orange on yellow.'

When at last their choices had been parcelled up, they mounted donkeys to return to the hotel, Gertrude reflecting, as so many have done in the century since, that although she had almost certainly paid over the odds for her purchases it had been worth it for 'the pleasure of a delightful afternoon spent in the old Turk's company'.

The Murray's *Handbook* recommended that visitors to Bursa should try out one of the town's *hamams*, the bathhouses that guaranteed public hygiene before the advent of private plumbing. In *Persian Pictures* Gertrude wrote that 'the hot steam of the sulphur springs diffuses a drowsy warmth through the atmosphere', but the passage is problematic, for the rather stiff woman that I'm getting to know through her diaries hardly strikes me as someone likely to have stripped down to her smalls in a public bathhouse. The words have a generic quality, as if describing something seen rather than experienced. Missing is the masseuse, for example. Missing, too, the Turkish women who would surely have shared the steam with her. The answer lies in a letter to her mother: 'We wanted very much to see the inside [of the hamam] so Mr Block* promptly went in, discovered an old Turk in the furthest room, bundled him out of the water and into a towel and led us through in triumph.'

In the suburb of Çekirge the Eski Kaplıca (Old Baths) sit in a dip across the road from the Hotel Anatolia, brutalist successor to the more elegant Hotel d'Anatolie where Gertrude stayed. It's tempting to assume this must be the *hamam* of her description. But in *Persian Pictures* she described the bath as lying 'a little to the east … in fields which vine and olive share with irises and great scarlet poppies.' Photos of the Çekirge Square of the 1890s show a crush of carriages completely at odds with such rusticity. Those of the sixteenth-century Yeni Kaplıca (New Baths) are more promising. Here are cypress and plane trees. Here are women strolling along a country road. Here is a camel train plodding past the bathhouse, a little donkey at its head. A residential suburb has since engulfed the *hamam*, but the stately Sinan-designed building with its soaring dome still welcomes male bathers. With no Mr Block to expel them for me, I sneak back after hours and plead with the caretaker. Ahmet is slooshing the last soapsuds off the *göbektaşı* but ushers me into a residually steamy chamber containing a pool. Running a finger over blue tiles that still suggest Ottoman distinction, I can all but hear Block lecturing Gertrude on the Roman roots of the *hamam* while she fantasized about 'Turkish youths [swimming] in the hot water of the sulphur springs while through the mist the sunlight glimmers down on them from the windows in the dome'.

*Sir Adam Block (1856-1941), who became chief *dragoman* at the British Embassy

Bursa residents liked to boast that their town had a mosque for every day of the year and Gertrude raced round as many of them as a short visit permitted. She also inspected 'the old walls which resisted the Turkish invaders, but are now in ruins'. Those walls still enclose the Hisar district, a bijou enclave of old Bursa perched on a rock in the centre of the modern town. In a plane-tree-shaded park I find women reclining on the grass having a girly get-together with picnic baskets, samovars and a brazier just steps away from a gap in the wall that sealed the city's destiny. The story of the conquest of Constantinople in 1453 gets a regular airing, but the earlier conquest of Bursa from the Byzantines in 1326 is less celebrated, even though it too involved a lengthy siege as Osman Gazi, the first of the Ottoman sultans, and his son Orhan battled to breach the walls. Finally Orhan forced a way through near the Fethi Gate and his army poured in, kettledrums pounding, white flags fluttering in the breeze.

Just outside the walls, Gertrude paid homage at the mausolea of Osman and Orhan on a plateau once occupied by the Byzantine monastery of the Prophet Elijah. During the siege Osman is said to have gazed across in awe at the sunlight bouncing off its silvery dome. Having made Orhan promise that if he died before the town fell he would bury him beneath that dome, Osman duly passed away just days before Bursa was vanquished. Orhan then laid him to rest inside the monastery, which survived until an earthquake destroyed it in 1855. Eight years later Sultan Abdülaziz commissioned new tombs for father and son. Embedded in the floor, the tesserae of an opus sectile pavement are the last reminders of a Byzantine monastery so lovely that it won a battle-hardened sultan's heart.

★ ★ ★

On her way to Constantinople for the fourth time in 1899, Gertrude stopped in Çanakkale on the Dardanelles planning to visit Troy with her father. According to the Murray's *Handbook*, 'Mr Frank Calvert, the American Consul, is a great authority on the local antiquities, and would, no doubt, give all travellers, who are properly introduced, any information they may require before going into the interior.' Nowadays, when the consulates of Western nations in the

Middle East seem more like besieged fortresses than places of welcome, it's hard to believe that at one time travellers were actually referred to them for run-of-the-mill travel information. But in the late nineteenth century a consul was a kind of economic and cultural attaché with added legal and translative responsibilities, such grab-bag duties often carried out in tandem with the business affairs needed to boost their meagre stipends. In today's Turkey most countries maintain a consul in Istanbul to supplement the work of the ambassador in Ankara. Before the First World War, however, British consuls cropped up all over the country: in Çanakkale, in Konya, in İskenderun, wherever there was sufficient trade to justify it.

By the time of Gertrude's visit Frank Calvert was the man undertaking the multifarious consular tasks in Çanakkale. The youngest son of Anglo-American parents, Frank seems to have arrived there around 1845 and was soon assisting his older brother Frederick, the then British consul, the pair of them living companionably in a neo-classical seafront mansion.*

In 1874 Frank himself became both American consul and acting British consul. A quiet, unassuming bachelor, he was also one of life's losers in the fame game. Of all the place names of classical history, Troy's has echoed most loudly down the ages thanks to the heroic exploits described in *The Iliad*'s account of the Trojan War. Strangely, despite the romance of its name, the precise location of Troy had been forgotten. There was no second Ephesus, no great collection of theatre, stadium and temple, marking the spot in the Troad. Instead, for much of the nineteenth century, archaeologists of varying degrees of expertise scoured the hinterland of Çanakkale, trying to cajole its reluctant topography into compliance with Homer's words. As the local consul, Frank Calvert threw his home open to these dreamers and became himself an enthusiastic amateur archaeologist. Troy was generally thought to lie in or around the small settlement of Pınarbaşı. However, in 1847 the Scottish journalist Charles Maclaren concluded that a mound at Hisarlık was more likely to cover its remains. Shortly afterwards, Frank and his brother bought the land on which half of the mound stood, and he began trial excavations.

*In 1912, an earthquake reduced Calvert's house to a ruin; the remains were demolished in the 1940s, although part of the garden survives as a public park.

Then along came Heinrich Schliemann, a self-taught German businessman keen to use his fortune to make a name for himself as an archaeologist. Lacking the funds to excavate Hisarlık on his own, Calvert went into partnership with Schliemann, failing to foresee the danger of being sidelined from a successful enterprise. Time and again Schliemann trumpeted the discovery of Troy prematurely before finally hitting pay dirt when he unearthed a cache of gold jewellery. This he promptly dubbed Priam's Treasure, before smuggling it out of Turkey behind Calvert's back. When it went on display at the Victoria and Albert Museum in London in 1877 it was as much a hit with the public as the British Museum's *Treasures of Tutankhamun* exhibition a century later. Schliemann was made. Calvert was history.

By the time Gertrude met Frank he was already seventy-one, white-haired and bespectacled, 'very friendly, a beautiful old man'. I imagine him greeting her at his front door, then conducting her round the hall where items from his private archaeological collection were displayed. But time was tight and already the carriage she and her father were to take to the ruins would have been waiting. Off they clattered across the Troad, which was, on a late-spring day, thick with corn and dotted with shepherds and their flocks.

Like any expensively-educated visitor from late-nineteenth-century England, Gertrude arrived at Troy mulling over the famous Menelaus-Helen-Paris love triangle that sparked the Trojan War. No doubt Calvert would have advised her how to recognize what were by then called the walls of Priam's Troy, but the site remained largely incomprehensible. She mentions the 'great paved ramp', still one of its most readily identifiable features, but found the mound 'covered with the debris of the excavations ... [and] the Acropolis covered with a confused mass of ruins', slim pickings from which to conjure the heroics of Homer's saga. Instead, she let her imagination spread its wings, claiming that the 'steep mounds of earth left to show the depth of the excavations ... look as if they were the topless towers of Ilium'. It must have been a relief to turn her eyes to the 'great pyramidal funeral mounds' believed to cover the remains of the war heroes Achilles and Patroclus; to the serpentine coils of the Scamander (Büyük Menderes / Meander) river; and to the twin islands of

Tenedos (Bozcaada) and İmbros (Gökçeada), anchored in the cerulean sea.

That night Gertrude stayed in Thymbrae, the Calverts' white-washed farmhouse near Çanakkale, where valonia oaks were cultivated for tanning and dyeing. There she admired photographs of the excavations as well as the Greek vases that Frank had unearthed. Irish writer and Çanakkale resident Catherine Yiğit drives me to Thymbrae, which is still a base for farming, albeit now on an industrial scale. The results are disappointingly predictable. We drive to the entrance. We approach the security guard. We plead to be allowed to walk around the grounds. We listen as he phones a distant decision-maker. Back comes the inevitable answer – no. In a fit of impotent fury, I scramble up the embankment beside the road and peer through a gap in the wall. I see a lawn with sprinklers playing on it. I see Gertrude strolling across it, bending to smell a rose, listening to the clatter of storks' bills, dreaming of a decent dinner. Then a security guard strides towards me and it's time to leave.

3

Shopping like a Native

IZMIR

'You should see me shopping in Smyrna – quite like a native, only I ought to have more flashing eyes.' Letter, 3 March 1902

In December 1899 Gertrude sailed from Marseilles to Jerusalem, stopping off in what is now Izmir. But of course when she first set foot on the Kordon promenade there was no Izmir, the big, pushy, defiantly Turkish city of modern times. Instead there was *'gavur* [infidel] Smyrna', a cosmopolitan trading town where Greek residents easily outnumbered Turks and where the quayside echoed to the sounds of voices raised in English, in Greek, in Armenian, in Judaeo-Spanish, but above all in French. This was a town that was sometimes called 'the Pearl of the Orient'. Typical tourist-office guff, I'm inclined to assume, but at the end of the nineteenth century there was truth to the hyperbole. For the waterfront on which Gertrude's excited eyes would have come to rest was every bit as lovely as the shores of the Bosphorus, lined with elegant stone buildings housing consulates, shipping companies, banks, insurance offices, sports clubs, theatres and offices. The hotels had carriages parked in front of them, and horse-drawn trams trundled past the doors. Presiding over it all, providing the perfect backdrop, loomed Mt Pagus, with the ruins of Kadifekale (Velvet Castle) encircling its summit.

Like all travellers arriving in a new country, Gertrude would have been fretting about the formalities to be got through before she could relax. Fortunately, she had contacts to smooth her path. As she gathered her skirts about her, she could see a man waving furiously. Oscar van Lennep was a scion of a Dutch trading family that had been based in Smyrna since the early eighteenth century. Gertrude had made his acquaintance on a boat trip from Piraeus to Constantinople. Now he was waiting to whisk her off to stay with his family. Her friend Domnul had also written ahead to alert the then British consul to Smyrna, Henry Arnold Cumberbatch, so that he could send a *kavass* (bodyguard) to ease her passage through Customs. The great-grandfather of today's *Sherlock* actor, Benedict Cumberbatch, Henry was to become a firm friend with whom Gertrude would go jaunting in the surrounding countryside.

Smyrna was at that time one of the few towns in Anatolia where visitors could stay in proper hotels as opposed to the *hans* designed for travelling salesmen and their animals. The most impressive were arrayed along the Kordon, with pride of place taken by the grand hotels Kraemer and Huck. But for Gertrude it was the smaller Hotel de Ville, on the quayside with a peerless sea view, that ticked the right boxes. On her first visit it was merely somewhere to grab lunch and freshen up. Later, however, it would become so firm a favourite that, on finding it full in 1902, she preferred to squat in the linen room rather than seek greater comfort elsewhere.

If only I too could have rocked up at the Hotel de Ville and ordered lunch, I think, but, like the Kraemer and the Huck, Gertrude's hotel was left a smouldering ruin by the Great Fire of Smyrna in 1922. Instead I check into the Antik Han on rundown Anafartalar Caddesi, near the bazaar. It's clean, it's quiet, it offers a laundry service and there's çay on tap in the dining room. But the really big plus is that it was built in 1857, which means that I can imagine Gertrude's carriage clip-clopping past it.

Rarely wide enough for two cars to pass, Anafartalar Caddesi is an unexpected slice of 1990s' Turkey surviving into the 2010s. On a chill April day with the rain beating down relentlessly, I wander along it, marvelling at the contrast between the grand indicators of a more opulent past and the dreariness of the much-diminished present. On the steps of the once-three-star-now-no-star Paşa Konağı Hotel a trio of young African men stare gloomily out at the downpour. They're amongst the first of what started as a trickle and is about to become a flood of refugees hoping to make their way to Europe via the Greek islands. Today is not going to be their big day though. Under dripping awnings grim-faced Syrians mutter into their mobiles, probably coming to much the same conclusion.

Izmir is a secretive city, lumbered with a history in which the glorious victory over the Greeks that it wants to celebrate sits uneasily atop the cataclysmic destruction of the past that it knows is so unattractive to visitors. On the surface everything seems upfront and open. Every shop, every restaurant is festooned with images of the city in the good old days of Smyrna; only pictures of the Great Fire are conspicuous by their absence. But there's no way to understand modern Izmir without first getting to grips with that conflagration. This was no Great Fire of London, no accident sparked in a bakery that wrote off much of the medieval city. Instead the Great Fire of Smyrna remains a hotly contested act of war, almost certainly started deliberately and thus hard to discuss without the conversation itself becoming inflamed.

On 9 September 1922, at the end of the Turkish War of Independence, the Turkish troops led by Mustafa Kemal (later Atatürk) rode in triumph into Smyrna, which had come to resemble a giant refugee camp as terrified Greeks from the surrounding towns and villages forced their way into it, seeking sanctuary from the approaching army. They had good reason to be fearful. Not only had the Greeks, with the tacit support of the British, invaded Turkey in 1919 in the aftermath of the First World War, but they had wreaked havoc on those self-same towns and villages as they fought their way to within sight of Ankara before the Turks managed to force them back again.

It was after this rout that the fire broke out. The details are mind-boggling. Watching from a ship in the harbour, a *Daily Mail* journalist reported that on 13 September the fire ran in an unbroken wall for two miles; the flames rose in 'jagged, writhing tongues' a hundred feet into the sky; it took nine days to extinguish them. Some half a million citizens found themselves hemmed in on the quayside by fire and the baying mobs; with nowhere left to run many fell, jumped or were pushed into the sea. Old Smyrna never recovered from the blow.

Close to the waterfront is what should be the Central Park of Izmir but is instead an expanse of unkempt greenery, known officially as the Kültürpark and unofficially as the Fuar (Fairground). It's a pleasant enough space with the sound of great tits calling in the trees, but the rain is tipping down again and the fallen blossoms of the paulownia trees are dissolving into a slippery brown sludge on the grass. Inside the gate I find a plaque commemorating the words of a former Izmir mayor, Dr Behçet Uz, as he laid the park's foundation stone in 1936. It was being built, he said, on the site of the '*geniş yangın* [extensive fire]'. Nearby, the nineteenth-century Greek Orthodox church of Aya Vukla has been restored to serve as a concert hall. Here too the '*büyük yangın* [great fire]' is acknowledged.

There's no dispute about the fire then. The tricky business comes in agreeing on how it started. In the tourist office the changeable weather has left Gürfem Hanım feeling poorly. She's swaddled in a shawl against the unseasonal chill and struggling to cope with a phone that rings incessantly even as she's doing her best to run through with me a collection of images of old Izmir that show smoke billowing over the harbour. Calm, polite and unfailingly helpful, her feathers ruffle only slightly when I mention blame.

'It doesn't make sense to say that the Turks did it,' she sniffs. 'Why would they burn their own country? It's not logical.'

The trouble is that there are many contemporary eyewitness statements that attest to the Turks having set the fire. Besides, if logic were the touchstone, then it would hardly have made much more sense for the Greeks to burn precisely the parts of the city in which they and their Armenian co-religionists lived. The fact remains that the one part of town that suffered almost no fire damage was the Turkish quarter.

Smyrna actually started life at Bayraklı to the north of the Gulf of Izmir, but, according to the geographer Pausanias, it was refounded further south after Alexander the Great, snoozing beneath a tree in front of the Temple of Nemesis on Mt Pagus, was visited in a dream by two goddesses who advised him to rebuild there instead. After consulting the oracle of Apollo at nearby Claros, the great warrior was told: 'Those who live on Pagus beyond the sacred Meles [the modern Yeşildere] will be three or four times happier than before.'

Who could have resisted such a promise? The fact that Alexander may not even have visited Smyrna does little to spoil the story.

Because the port straddled the easiest sea route from Europe to the Middle East, Gertrude ended up visiting Smyrna on four separate occasions and on one of them she ascended Mt Pagus. It was a sunny spring day with anemones in flower and the fruit trees bursting into leaf. The summit offered her a spectacular view over the city and the gulf, with the smaller town of Cordelio (today's Karşıyaka) shimmering on the horizon. Slithering downhill in front of her would have been the red-tiled roofs of the Greek quarter. Her photos feature long stretches of the castle's outer wall and towers, their stones since borne off as building material.

But time has not stood still on the hilltop. Since the fire and the expulsion of the Greeks, a second wave of transformation almost equally dramatic has swept over Izmir. Inside the ramparts of Kadifekale I come across a shantytown of huts, their walls held together with scraps of carpet and old advertising hoardings, smoke billowing through holes in their corrugated-iron roofs. Each turns out to house a kitchen, the space inside almost completely filled by a *tandır*, the ceramic oven encased in a mud-brick frame as is typical of southeast Turkey. In one of them I find Harbiye, a cheery woman from Mardin, a mother of nine with no husband to support them. The youngest, five-year-old Fırat (Euphrates), toys with a mobile phone while his mother flattens pats of dough between her palms, then presses them against the oven walls using the cut-off sleeve of a denim jacket as an oven glove. From time to time a dough pat tumbles from the wall. Down she bends, right into the oven, to retrieve it.

Fighting between the government and the PKK* in the 1980s and 90s sent a tsunami of people fleeing from southeast Turkey, leaving no western conurbation unaffected. Like Istanbul, Izmir saw its population skyrocket as migrants, particularly from Mardin and Diyarbakır, flocked there in search of, if not exactly a better life, at least a less militarily frightening one. Everyone here seems to be from Mardin: the hotel receptionist is from Mardin, the man who serves

*Partiya Karkeren Kurdistane (Kurdish Workers Party), a designated terrorist group in Turkey and abroad.

my coffee is from Mardin, the man who sells me a *kumru* sandwich
of cheese, tomato and sausage, is from Mardin. Many of the newcomers settled on the slopes of Kadifekale, throwing up the sort of
slum dwellings quaintly called *gecekondus* (built-overnight homes)
in Turkish. Now some have been forced to move on again as the authorities clear the slopes to create parks more attractive to cruise
tourists. The upside of the slum clearance is that it has uncovered
the remains of the ancient theatre for which Gertrude searched in
vain.

★ ★ ★

Eşrefpaşa Caddesi cuts across Anafartalar, bisecting it at the point
where the town's once thriving Jewish community used to live. To
the west of Eşrefpaşa is Kemeraltı, Izmir's sprawling bazaar, the area
of Smyrna most popular with nineteenth-century visitors, who rev-
elled in its un-European atmosphere. Gertrude came here to shop for
lokum and sip Turkish coffee, something that is once again all the
rage with young Izmirlis, who flock to the streets around the Kı-
zlarağası Hanı to down chewy hits of caffeine brewed straight into
the cup. In a pop-up coffee shop down a side street velveteen prayer
rugs serve as tablecloths while rugs on the wall feature stags at bay.
The proprietor is from Ömerli, near Mardin. He's a city man through
circumstance, wistful for the countryside, who ticks off the seasons
back home on his fingers – June cheese- and yoghurt-making, September grape-harvesting – as he serves me a demi-tasse of coffee
with *lokum* nibbles. It's a relief to discover that if I take a quick hit,
then chase it with the *lokum*, I can almost persuade myself that I'm
enjoying it.

In a letter to her mother Gertrude described the bazaars as 'delightfully Oriental and of enormous size' and went on to offer what
might still pass as a fair description of its deepest corners: 'Here and
there you come out of the narrow covered streets into a square court
surrounded by some old khan, the walls of it dating back to Genoese
times and the deep verandahs housing a motley collection of Armenian antiquity dealers, Turkish counting houses, store rooms, baths
and heaven knows what.' But then there were also 'bales of dried
fruit lying everywhere, ready for shipping'. To her mother she joked
that she was shopping 'quite like a native, although I ought to have

more flashing eyes'. In an aside, she dismissed as 'horrors' the souvenirs snapped up by visiting friends of the Cumberbatches.

At the outset of a daunting journey into the interior in 1907 she stocked up at the Anglo-Oriental Stores, which must have gone up in flames in 1922. I comb the bazaar for my own trip, snapping up fabric for trousers, which a tailor speedily runs up for me; browsing for a sunhat; and combing through countless shoe shops in search of suitable sandals. The trousers trail in the dust when I try them on, so I rush them to another tailor on Anafartalar. He looks almost as ancient as his shop, which is so minuscule that there's only room inside it for him, his sewing machine, the cutting counter and me. The friend who'd been sharing an ice cream with him backs hastily out of the door lest the business be lost.

Back in the nineteenth century, every autumn brought caravans of three or four thousand camels lumbering over the humpbacked Kervan Köprüsü (Caravan Bridge), bearing produce from Manisa to the port at Smyrna. The Murray's *Handbook* rated the bridge highly. It is, it declared, 'the scene where the Turk terminates the labours of the day; and on Sundays is the centre of attraction to Christians. Numerous coffee-houses are here erected on the banks of the Meles; and the scene is rendered animated and picturesque from the beauty and variety of the costumes of every country here assembled.' It was at Caravan Bridge Station that Gertrude waited for the train to Ephesus, sharing the platform with 'a little gazelle eating cigarette ends'. On her return she reported the street 'ill paved, muddy and crowded' and 'almost impassable for enormous camels, each string with its tiny donkey leading'.

Quiz a random passer-by on an Izmir street today and it's unlikely that they will have heard of the Kervan Köprüsü, let alone be able to pinpoint its location. In the tourist office Gürfem Hanım rings the map roughly where she thinks it stood. With no more than that to go on, I alight in a downpour from Izmir's light-rail system at Kemer, the old Caravan Bridge Station, and soon find myself lost in the grim urban poverty of modern Yeşildere. First I head east; then I head west. 'Watch out for thieves,' shout the skulk of dejected *zabitas* who try and fail to help me. 'Welcome to Hell' reads the message scrawled above one of the bridges.

After several hours of fruitless searching I'm dripping wet, exhausted and have more or less given up on finding the bridge when some last flicker of hope leads me to ask a young man grilling chicken in a makeshift kitchen on a highway beside the river if he knows where it was. To help him I flash up a picture of it after a rebuild. To my surprise his eyes light up.

'*Abla*,' he says, 'you're standing on it!'

The bridge lies hidden beneath a tarmacked modern usurper, with traffic lights and lampposts taking the place of the willows, and lorries that of the camels. I wander down to the river for a closer look and find an old-fashioned teahouse, the sort of place that lives for its elderly male clientele, the sort of place where glasses freeze in mid-air along with the conversation should a woman dare to enter. Accordingly, there's an awkward moment as I cross the threshold. Then out rushes the owner from behind his tea urn, all smiles, and a door is thrown open at the rear. I step through it. And there on the far side is the Caravan Bridge. A smooth arch has taken the place of the lovely old humpbacked version, but a room has been set up to welcome history lovers who can loll on cushioned banquettes while admiring it. Etchings of the original grace the walls. Plastic water lilies float around a plastic fountain in the middle of the room.

The years between Gertrude's first visit to Smyrna in 1899 and her second in 1902 were formative ones. On her first visit she was still just a tourist with her sights set on Ephesus, a young(ish) woman who had grown up in hidebound Victorian society, who had been presented to Queen Victoria at a 'coming out' ball and been forced to endure three seasons of ballroom banalities in the hope of securing a husband. But Gertrude had grown up in a household influenced by the liberal ideas of John Stuart Mill, including his contention that a woman, as much as a man, had a right to be a Person with a capital 'P'. For most turn-of-the-twentieth-century women, being a Person meant little more than getting married and having children. For Gertrude, conscious as she reached the end of her twenties that this was a future likely to elude her, it was vital to find another way to define herself. A winter in Tehran in 1892 had led her to translate Hafiz and pen *Persian Pictures*, her first travel book. But writing and translating could not entirely fulfil her. By the time she arrived in Smyrna for a month-long stay in 1902 she had discovered another outlet for her boundless energy, performing feats of daring in the Alps that made her a legend in mountaineering circles. Writing home, she boasted of the fact: 'I am a Person! And one of the first questions everyone seems to ask is "Have you ever met Miss Gertrude Bell?"'

By then she had also completed the first of her great expeditions into the desert, roaming across the areas that now make up Israel, Palestine, Syria, Lebanon and Jordan. Her third visit to Smyrna in 1907 was at the start of an expedition deep into the heart of Anatolia. By the time she stepped ashore there for the last time, all her major expeditions were behind her, including her journeys along the Euphrates and the Tigris. She also had four more published books under her belt: two more works of travel literature, *The Desert and the Sown* and *Amurath to Amurath*, and her two books on the Byzantine heritage of Anatolia, *The One Thousand and One Churches* (with Sir William Ramsay) and *The Churches and Monasteries of the Tur Abdin*.

It was a very different Gertrude, then, who stopped off to visit her friend Edward Whittall on her way back to England in May 1914. The news was grim, he told her, as a nationalist governor attempted to relieve the Greeks and Levantines of their businesses. But for all the palpable anxiety, few could have foreseen the horror that lay ahead. As she stood on the deck, hands resting on the rail, looking back at Smyrna, Gertrude could never have imagined that within the space of just eight years everything she knew and loved there would vanish, friends scattered to unknown 'homelands', buildings consumed in a blazing inferno.

4

The Mediterranean Race

BORNOVA–BULGURCA–DEĞİRMENDERE

'They called themselves English and American and what not and carried strings of amber beads and we all talked broken English.
'Letter, 6 December 1899.'

I arrive in Bornova in wisteria season. Violet-coloured blossoms tumble over the entrance to a house where Liszt once gave piano lessons to a young Englishwoman. More blossoms cascade down the facade of the Kafe Pi, where students from Ege University gather to snap selfies. A floral fragrance and the busy hum of bees permeate the atmosphere.

It's Easter and I've come to this eastern suburb of Izmir to visit the pretty little Anglican church of St Mary Magdalene. Inside, I get a shock. What looks from the outside like a rococo folly of a Greek temple, the sort of thing commissioned by rich men to add interest to their country estates, turns out to pair a baroque barrel vault and neoclassical pilasters with a set of stained-glass windows clearly shipped from England. The congregation is less than a dozen strong, and the priest arrives belatedly from presiding over an earlier service in downtown Izmir. We sit down. A young man positions himself beside the organ and starts cranking it up like an old-fashioned car with a flat battery. We stumble our way through a hymn. It's not easy to observe what's going on because a laser beam is shining out towards us. After several unexpected pauses I start to wonder if perhaps the priest is suffering from dementia. The service over, an elderly woman takes one of the two Turks present to task over the glare. Only then do we learn that in his rush to get here the priest had left his glasses behind. Hence the blinding light. Hence the awkward pauses.

The old lady has a definite air about her. Could she, I wonder, be a descendant of the Whittalls, with whom Gertrude had stayed in Bornova on several occasions? It turns out she's Daphne Aliberti, wife of Enrico, scion of a prominent local family. 'Why does everyone always want to know about the Whittalls?' she demands. 'My mother [herself a Whittall] said that they were very dull people!'

Off she goes to her delightful and no doubt wisteria-draped mansion mere steps from the church, leaving me to take a closer look at the windows. Identifiable by their tiny wheatsheaf insignia as being from the Kempe workshop, several are dedicated to members of the Whittall family as are some of the plaques on the walls. Dull they may have been, but the history of Bornova is impossible to imagine without the Whittalls.

On her first visit to Bornova – then Bournabat – in December 1899, Gertrude stayed with the van Lennep family. What is now just a suburb of Izmir was then a separate settlement that had developed as a refuge from the outbreaks of plague that intermittently ravaged the port. From 1866 a rail link to Smyrna had enabled Bournabat to expand into a dormitory for wealthy merchants; Gertrude records a pleasant fifteen-minute train ride through orange groves to reach it. I arrive by metro and am delighted to discover that, although it was decommissioned in 1996, the original Bournabat Station still survives, a café now occupying the waiting room. Once upon a time the platform would have bustled with activity in the rush hour; catching the early evening train back from Smyrna Gertrude commented that it was full of business men – 'I might have been spending the day at Clarence* instead of Ephesus!' Most of the men she was introduced to claimed to be 'English and American and what not', yet ran amber beads through their fingers like Turks and spoke in broken English. In *Paradise Lost*, Giles Milton records that every family had its assigned seats on the train. Woe betide anyone foolish enough to sit in the wrong place.

On her first night Gertrude stayed with the van Lenneps in their Bournabat house. Unlike many of the surviving mansions, their home was very simple: it was 'cold and pretty uncomfortable', she wrote in her diary, and the 'cooking [was] shocking, most of the crockery of various sets'. As for heating, she records the family spending the evening 'round the Pandour or tambor or whatever it

---

* Home to her father's factory in Middlesbrough.

is, a wooden table covered with a quilted cloth and a brazier inside [tandır]'.

It was the van Lenneps who introduced Gertrude to the Whittalls in 1902. Born in Liverpool in 1791, Charlton Whittall had arrived in Smyrna as an eighteen-year-old and had gone on to found a company that became the biggest exporter of locally grown figs and raisins. In terms of wealth, the Whittalls were to Smyrna what the Bells were to Middlesbrough; their house in the centre of Bournabat was so impressive that it was known simply as the Büyük Ev (the Big House). It was Charlton who commissioned the Church of St Mary Magdalene in 1857.

Charlton married Magdalene Victoire Blanche Giraud, cementing an enduring relationship with a second wealthy Bournabat family of French extraction and big in the carpet trade. Their son James married another Giraud Magdalene and it was their son, Herbert Octavius, whom Gertrude met at the van Lennep farm in 1902 and with whom she later stayed. 'The house is a great big place with high enormous rooms,' she wrote to her mother, adding in her diary that the cypresses on the lawn were planted in the shape of a cross, marking the site of what had once been a monastic garden.

Today the Büyük Ev serves as the administrative centre of Ege University and visitors still approach it via a grand marble staircase. Inevitably the interior has been hacked about to create offices, but much of the original layout survives and in an upstairs room I'm shown a Victorian fireplace of cast iron and marble that would have looked perfectly at home in the Bells' Redcar house. Perhaps it's not surprising, then, that as I glance out of the window I can almost feel Gertrude standing beside me, admiring the cypresses while clapping her hands together to warm them against a chill that not even a roaring fire in the grate could dispel.

James Whittall had died before Gertrude's visit. Not so his seventy-nine-year-old wife Magdalene, 'the old mother of the tribe'. Married at fifteen, Magdalene had borne twenty children and acquired a reputation as a bit of a harridan, although she rallied to kiss her English guest. Next door, Gertrude was introduced to Herbert's brother, Edward, a cultivator of wild Turkish tulips, one of which, the fiery orange *Tulip whittallii*, was named after him.

Of the Whittall family properties, she wrote: 'The big gardens touch one another and they walk in and out of one another's houses all day long gossiping and laughing.' It was, she concluded, as pleasant a life as could be imagined.

Rubbers of bridge, games of patience, croquet on the lawn - to read Gertrude's Bournabat diaries is almost to forget that she was writing them in Anatolia rather than the north of England. But the van Lenneps and the Whittalls were members of a curious subset of Turkish society, the European immigrants to the Ottoman Empire who came to be known as Levantines, and it was here that she observed their distinctive lifestyle in all its contradictory detail.

The Levantines serve as a reminder of how rarely foreign communities completely integrate into local life. By the time of Gertrude's visit, the van Lenneps had been living in and around Smyrna for two hundred years, the Whittalls for the best part of a hundred. Mention of the *tandır* oven suggests a token adaptation to local ways, but in most other aspects of life the Levantines seem to have been as content to cling to the habits of their ancestral countries as third-generation Turks in the Kreuzberg of today. Old photographs show the Whittalls posing on the steps of the Big House. Their clothing is precisely that of late-Victorian Liverpool.

This lack of integration arose in part from human nature and its preference for the familiar but also from the way that the Ottoman Empire was administered. Since the earliest days European traders had strong-armed the sultans into granting 'capitulations' that allowed them in effect to govern themselves. Later Ottoman society was subdivided into *millets*, separate communities whose rights and duties were defined by their religious affiliation. Consequently the different nationalities that made up the Levantine community were used to having things their own way. No need to queue in the Ottoman post office, for example; the British, French and Germans all had their own mail services in Smyrna, just as they had their own police stations and churches. There was little incentive for the Levantines to worry about integrating into Turkish society; nor was it expected of them. Smyrna has often been described as one of the most cosmopolitan cities of all time. Reality was actually a set of different communities leading separate lives side by side in separately delineated parts of the city.

It was the pick-and-mix speech of her new friends that most struck Gertrude. On first meeting Oscar van Lennep's wife, she queried the origins of a woman who spoke French to her friends and English to her children. Then in a letter of December 1899 she wrote gleefully: 'I have found out the nationality of my hosts – they belong to the Mediterranean race. It speaks no language though it will chatter with you in half a dozen; it has no native land though it is related by marriage to all Europe, and with the citizen of each country it will talk of his compatriots and itself as "we"; it centres round no capital and is loyal to no government though it obeys any.'

A longer stay in 1902 refined her perception of the van Lenneps:

> They talk no tongue properly – Greek the best, I expect; English with the funny little clipped intonation of the Levant and French very fluently and very uglily ... Mr V.L. is Dutch by nationality, but he has never been to Holland [and] speaks no Dutch among his many languages ... He is strongly English over the S. African war – indeed you might call him English if you cd call him anything.

The Levantines may have been a mixed-up bunch of people, but that didn't stand in the way of their ability to turn a buck in Smyrna. Indeed, by the time Gertrude crossed paths with them, theirs were the brains and money behind almost all the city's main commercial enterprises, including the banks and insurance companies. At the pinnacle of all the commerce sat the Whittalls and the Girauds, their fortunes intertwined.

The Gertrude Bell of popular imagination will always be associated with sand dunes and great heat, with tribes and wilderness and solitude. However, the letters she wrote from Smyrna show her to have been just as happily at home in a very different environment. For when she wasn't staying at the Hotel de Ville or putting up with the Whittalls in Bornova, Gertrude headed out of town to stay on what sounds like a modern experimental farm run by the van Lenneps at Malkacık deep in the countryside around Bulgurca.

Malkacık Farmhouse, near Bornova, where Gertrude stayed on several occasions.

'He has 20,000 acres,' she wrote of Oscar van Lennep's farm, some of it sublet to another Levantine Dutchman, the young Baron van Heemstra, a distant ancestor of Audrey Hepburn. Van Lennep himself she describes as a Micawberish character, forever coming up with new money-making schemes that rarely came to anything; during one visit he was pursuing the fantasy of developing a manganese mine on his land. At the same time he was another keen amateur archaeologist, busily excavating a tumulus that he hoped would reveal the treasures of the kings of Colophon. Gertrude was soon rolling up her sleeves to join in, writing home lightheartedly to request £2,000 to finance a proper excavation.

Mr van Lennep had 'the whole Tower of Babel in his village'. Alongside the resident Greeks were the Albanians who arrived on the farm each winter and were organized by the early equivalent of a gangmeister who paid them pathetic wages and fed them only bread 'in consequence of wh[ich] they are half starved'. The Albanians were helping Mr van Lennep excavate the tumulus but were so hungry that when he offered them extra cash they pleaded instead for extra food.

More intriguing was what she had to say about the tribal people living on the van Lennep land. Gertrude would go on to become an expert on the tribes of Arabia, but before the First World War even the Smyrna hinterland was pretty tribal. On a freezing March day, when snow had already fallen, Gertrude visited a gathering of Tahtacıs, 'a very curious race, the original inhabitants of the country'. They were, she said, woodcutters with a distinctive costume of their own. Later she wrote that 'they have a religion apart though they conform outwardly to Islam and are ruled by priests called Karabash who come travelling around and settle all disputes. They hold yearly religious gatherings in their churchyards.' She wound up with a vivid description of a Tahtacı wedding: 'The bride is paraded through the village covered with a lot of rags and a red cloth on top with flowers and muslins over it. She rides a horse on which a nice carpet is laid and whoever lends the horse takes the carpet or saddle bag.'

The Tahtacıs remain enigmatic. They were, and still are, Alevis, members of a minority sect that, while Muslim, shares some features with Christianity and shamanism. Despite Gertrude's suggestion that they were indigenous Turks, they are more likely to have been Turkmens who followed Tamerlane into Anatolia in the fourteenth century. Their greatest claim to fame is that when Mehmed the Conqueror was planning his assault on Constantinople it was Tahtacıs who built the wooden ships that were dragged over the hills and down into the Golden Horn.

Gertrude and Mr van Lennep also rode out to a remoter part of the farm to call on some *yörüks* (nomads), 'tenants of his, if you can call the inhabitants of a tent a tenant'. In later life Gertrude would meticulously classify the Arabian tribes, but even as a younger woman she had a filing cabinet of a mind, carefully itemizing the subdivisions of the local *yörüks*. They were ruled, she wrote, by *beys* (lords) and operated a system of crop rotation. Those working on the van Lennep land used his animals and tools, in return for which they received a quarter share in the produce, a system quite as feudal as that of medieval England. Her description of being served coffee with flat bread and butter in a *yörük* tent of black goats' hair reads as a taster for her later encounters with the Bedouins. 'It was an entertaining tea party,' she wrote to her mother.

Identifying the site of the Malkacık farmhouse isn't easy. Best local guesses place it near Bulgurca, south of Izmir, but long before the bus stops, I'm having my doubts.

A modern village of small concrete houses shielded from the sun by fruit trees, Bulgurca is the sort of nondescript settlement travellers normally whizz through, barely noticing it. Shopkeeper Şaban rushes me to the teahouse and sits me down with the local men, where conversation about the farm doesn't get off to a promising start since no one can understand my interest in somewhere that no longer exists. Malkacık? No, there's nothing left of it. When the Tahtalı Dam was completed in 1998 we were forced to abandon our old homes and move here, they tell me. Now only the minaret of the old mosque sticking up from the water of the reservoir marks the spot.

That seems to be that. But it's not every day that a stray foreigner fetches up in Bulgurca and suddenly the mood shifts and everyone starts to take an interest in the quest. A young man opens his phone and circulates a photograph of the old farmhouse. Conversation livens up as *çay* drinkers juggle the names of every conceivable property that might have been Malkacık.

Finally: 'You need Ali,' Şaban announces, and the young man reverts his phone to its original purpose and summons the community's most senior member to join us. While we wait for him, I translate Gertrude's diary entries for the *çay* drinkers. She would come to Develiköy Station, I say, and then proceed by horse cart to Bulgurca. That brings a smile to the face of Nihat, the oldest person at the table. 'Oh, the mud,' he laughs, and chops at the top of his thigh with the side of his hand.

Then Ali appears and we run through the introductions. Ali is eighty-eight, but no one would guess it from his upright posture and on-the-ball attitude. He hails from a family that arrived here from what is now Thessaloniki after the *Mübadele*, the Turkish name for the enforced exchange of populations with Greece brought about in 1923 by the Treaty of Lausanne at the end of the Turkish War of Independence.

Ali studies the picture. 'It's the Kerim Bey Farm,' he says firmly, and everyone else nods and agrees that in that case it's definitely under the water.

'Let's take a look anyway,' suggests Şaban and minutes later he and Ali and I are on our way to the reservoir. There we stare out over the water and ponder the half-submerged minaret, a finger jabbed accusingly at the heavens.

'My house was just beside it,' says Şaban. 'Ali's was nearby.'

A silence falls.

'*Vah, vah* [What a pity],' sighs Ali, and I begin to regret our coming here, having obliged him to look again, perhaps for the last time, at the site of his childhood home.

★ ★ ★

Mehmet Dincer's house is the last but one in Değirmendere before the start of the track leading up to the remains of the ancient Ionian settlement of Colophon. I've bumped into Mehmet outside Cumao-vası Station in Izmir, where we were both twiddling our thumbs while waiting for our bus driver to finish his *çay*. An escapee from Istanbul, Mehmet lives the good life here with a pair of cats and a dog for company, and a garden full of fruit trees – apple, pear, persimmon, plum and peach.

Değirmendere, he tells me as he hands me a pear, used to be the hub of local life, able to support not just two pharmacists but ten local butchers' too. Then in 2002 a bypass shifted the focus north to Menderes. Now the pharmacies and butchers' shops are mere memory.

He points me to the path up which Gertrude rode on a nag and I follow her on foot through stands of asphodel that reach to my chin, passing olive trees as tightly entwined as the lovers who have etched their initials into their trunks. Some three thousand years ago this may have been the site of a prosperous town with a vibrant commercial life, but now nothing moves here except jays flashing blue and white through the trees, tiny lizards skittering from my footsteps and a solitary tortoise making a meal of the grass.

I emerge eventually on a plateau with, to one side, a small Muslim shrine ringed with white stones. Gertrude had believed this to be the site of the lost palace from the days when Colophon was prestigious enough to merit a king. But after its sacking by Lysimachus in the third century BC the city went into a slump from which it never recovered and its inhabitants moved south to Notium, the old port city near modern-day Ahmetbeyli, which, in time, co-opted the Colophon name. Of its once lofty walls nothing remains. Scraps from the houses and temples lurk unnoticed in Değirmendere's drystone walls.

Back in his house, Mehmet is waiting to greet me with an apple deftly peeled in one strip and passed over on the tip of a knife. Together we amble back to the centre of the village, past a mountain stream cascading into the gutter. Sometimes coins are washed down here, he tells me; sometimes even small pieces of ancient jewellery. We dine together on *köfte* (meatballs) and *piyaz* (white beans) in a 'garden' fenced with torn meshing. Dust-caked lightbulbs and a plastic chandelier hang from the ceiling. Yet the food is delicious, the meat sourced straight from the owner's farm.

It's my final day in Bornova and I've been invited to lunch by Brian Giraud, one of the last descendants of a family that once ruled the roost here. Bournabat's Levantines valued their privacy and hunkered down behind high walls that made it impossible to guess what lay behind them. The address I've been given brings me to a nondescript gate in just such a wall. I push it open and it's like stepping through the back of the wardrobe into Narnia, except that this Narnia is a little piece of England transposed unexpectedly to Asia Minor.

Behind the gate lies a stunning garden with lush lawns, rock-fringed lily ponds, a wisteria-draped pergola and even a miniature lake. Only slowly does it dawn on me that this was Edward Whittall's garden, the very place where Gertrude had strolled with the renowned botanist, admiring his tulips and tapping him for tips on propagation.

With Brian and his British-born wife Vanessa I sit down to chat in the shade of the trees that ring the lake. The great-grandson of Edward Whittall, Brian has made it his life's work to maintain the precious garden that now serves as a venue for society weddings. As we talk, with a dog or two circling in hope of titbits, it's almost impossible to believe that I am not in England, that Brian's family have really been living here for two centuries. The muddled language that had so struck Gertrude has given way to standard English and in every superficial way Brian seems entirely British. But as we discuss the problems of the church down the road I'm struck by the way in which he exudes the contradictory air of being both deeply rooted in Turkey and at the same time faintly beleaguered, as if even now he can't be entirely sure of his place here, the unenviable fate of all immigrants even several generations removed.

Vanessa takes me into their house, an elegant two-storeyed villa with a wide veranda, so that I can admire a modern-day Levantine home. And there, gazing down the length of the wooden dining room table, I spot two portraits. 'Brian's ancestors – Charlton and Magdalene,' says Vanessa, and at once I remember a passage in one of Gertrude's letters:

> In the dining room, here are all the family portraits, bad as pictures but most interesting as types. On one side the grandfather of Mr Whittall ... a stern old man in a smock, and all his sons and grandsons flanking him. On the other side his wife, a Venetian, one of those Venetians who lived in Constantinople and were driven out by the Turks and settled first in Crete, then in Athens, then here; and her mother who was an Italian, a Capo d'Istria, both women wearing a semi-Oriental costume; and their men folk in 18th century clothes.

'They're copies,' Vanessa says apologetically, but it doesn't matter. I've been inside the Big House. I've seen pictures of the Whittall ancestors just as Gertrude did in a house I know that she visited. It's enough. I can leave Bornova satisfied.

5
Alone with History and the Birds
LARISSA–KEMALPAŞA–KARABEL PASS

'The anemones were out on the castle top and the plum trees in the plain and every hedge was full of violets.' Letter, 7 April 1907

'Larissa!' announces Mesut the taxi driver triumphantly.

We've come to a stop in a car park in front of a small shopping centre featuring branches of Burger King, the downmarket A101 supermarket, and the far ritzier English Home.

'And the ruins?' I ask cautiously, since I don't see anything remotely ancient in the vicinity.

'Ruins?'

'Yes. Larissa *örenyeri*.'

'Well, this is Larissa. Larissa Alışveriş Merkezi [Larissa Shopping Centre]!'

While staying in Smyrna, Gertrude used trains to get close to many of the archaeological sites in the vicinity. This was Anatolia's first great Railway Age, when tracks were rapidly being laid to ease the movement of trade goods from the interior to the coast. In 1858 the British had started work on a line from Smyrna to Aydın, while a second line via Manisa to Cassaba (Turgutlu) opened in 1866. The location of the stations often dictated the itineraries of visitors to Smyrna, since even if the journey had to be completed in a carriage or on horseback, at least the major part of it could be done in the comfort of a railway compartment.

In 1902 Gertrude set off to explore the ruins of Larissa, then being excavated by Swedes and Germans. From Menemen she hired a carriage as far as the Hermus (Gediz) river, where she crossed by ferry and continued up to the acropolis on foot. My journey had gone just as smoothly as far as Menemen, now a stop on Izmir's suburban train service. There I'd bumped into Mesut, a hyper-enthusiastic taxi driver married to a Russian. Larissa? Yes, of course he knew it, and off we'd rushed at the speed of a startled lizard, racing past the pottery-sellers of Menemen and on up the main road towards Foça. Where we'd ground to a halt in this car park.

As I start to splutter, Mesut twists round to stare at me, seemingly astounded that I didn't actually plan to pay a taxi driver to bring me to a roadside Burger King in the middle of nowhere. I pass my map to him. I point out Larissa and the symbol for an ancient monument. His expression is blank.

'Is it at Haykıran?' he asks, naming a village I've never heard of.

'Well, I thought it was at Buruncuk …' I begin, but already he's reversing the car and hurtling back the way we came. Fortunately, he's game for tracking down this hitherto unheard-of archaeological site, because it's safe to say that it's hardly advertising its where-abouts. Again and again we consult random youths and tractor drivers, all of whom shake their heads emphatically.

'We'll find it, we'll find it,' Mesut says, full of seemingly mis-placed confidence. Finally we flag down a *dolmuş*, whose driver is prepared to concede that there is indeed an archaeological site near Buruncuk. Up the slope behind it, he says.

Ten minutes later we're climbing a hill that, from a distance, hardly looks as if it will be covered in ruins but does at least have a battered yellow interpretation sign at the bottom to confirm that we've reached the right place. After an unusually long, wet winter, the slope is thick with asphodel and with villagers plucking a form of *diken* (thistle) that is great eaten with lemon and olive oil appar-ently. Around us stand the remains of circular buildings that I pre-sume to have been windmills, given the slowly rotating turbines now besmirching the skyline. Then we chance upon Hüseyin, a diminu-tive shepherd with four dogs who race towards us barking.

Hüseyin looks as if he's somehow managed to shrink in the wash, his clothes – wellington boots, corduroy trousers and jacket – all seemingly designed for a much larger man. But he walks these hills with the mastery of one who's known them since childhood, gliding along in front of us as we stumble over the rocks in his wake. He shows us all there is left to see of Larissa and explains how the acrop-olis was quarried for stone to build Eski Buruncuk (Old Buruncuk) further down the hill. When this, in turn, was abandoned after an earthquake, the villagers landed up by the highway, the old stones of Larissa left behind in the walls of their sheep pens.

Passing by in the early 1950s, that other great British traveller,

Freya Stark, mentioned the existence of a polygonal wall at Larissa that is still visible today. But why, she asked dismissively, 'should one climb, when so little worth hearing seems ever to have been said or thought about Larissa?' It's true that very little is known of the settlement, which is generally listed as a Pelasgian site, tantamount to an admission of ignorance on the part of the writer. However, Gertrude had been given a letter of introduction to Johannes Boehlau, the German archaeologist in charge of the dig, who would, as they wandered round, have filled her in on the scraps of information available: namely, that the site probably dated back to around 700 BC and that hoped-for evidence of earlier Mycenaean settlement had proved elusive. In a letter home she wrote of her joy at having been able to spend a 'peaceful afternoon with someone who thought of nothing but temple walls and mother goddesses!'

It's hard to take seriously a town with as Monty Pythonish a name as Nif. Perhaps not surprisingly then this industrial extension to the northeast of Izmir has renamed itself Kemalpaşa after the great wartime leader who freed this part of Anatolia from Greek occupation, Mustafa Kemal Atatürk. Gertrude travelled to Nif on her third visit to Smyrna in 1907, hoping to examine a Hittite carving called the Sesostris. Keeping her company on the day out were Henry Cumberbatch and his wife, Helene. The three of them set off by horse cart on a pleasant spring day but soon ran into trouble negotiating rocks brought down by a recent storm. Her photograph shows the occupants of the carriage rugged up like extras from *Doctor Zhivago*. In all, their short journey from Smyrna took four hours.

My own could hardly have been more different. At Bornova I board one of the frequent minibuses that head this way, with the conductor hanging out of the door and yelling 'Kemalpaşa!' at every passer-by in the apparent belief that if he shouts it loudly enough and often enough they'll abandon whatever other plans they might have had for the day and opt instead to go in search of the Sesostris.

We roar out of town along a dual carriageway past scenery of the urban-nightmare variety: soaring concrete struts for a new flyover, earthmovers marshalled for action, then factories, factories and yet more factories. Plastic, paper, chemicals, foodstuffs – they're all made here and no doubt the pay is regular and welcome. But alas for the beauty of the early twentieth century. What became of the plum and peach trees that Gertrude noted? And what of Kavaklıdere, once a vista of grape hyacinths and anemones, now a mess of earthworks?

I'm feeling crabby, then, by the time I roll into town and spot scaffolding still encasing what Gertrude called the Palace of Andronicos (I Komnenos). That same scaffolding had been there some years ago. All the energy that should have gone into the restoration seems to have been expended instead on wrapping the palace in a disfiguring metal box. That achieved, the workers appear to have packed up their tools and departed.

This is particularly frustrating given that the palace is a rare reminder of the period between 1204 and 1261 when the Latin leaders of the Fourth Crusade had driven the Byzantine emperor into exile. Two branches of the imperial family then set up rival courts, one in Trabzon at the eastern end of the Black Sea, the other much closer to the capital in İznik. It was this latter branch, the Lascarid family, who built themselves a summer palace in Nif, and it was here in 1254 that one of them, the self-proclaimed Emperor Vatazes, died and was buried.

I stomp away disappointed. But the sun is out and high above the ugly little town I spot the remnants of a castle. A passer-by mimes the twisty-turny route through the back streets that will bring me to the ruins. And, oh, is it worth the climb! Within minutes modern Kemalpaşa is behind me. The castle rides high on shoulders of emerald green grass embroidered with daisies and buttercups; there's such a sweet scent of meadow that I half expect to see the cows of Gertrude's day happily munching their way across the fields. The walls of the castle and its towers are cracked and broken but happily untouched by the hand of any restorer. Layers of Byzantine tile still sandwich layers of Byzantine stone. I'm alone with history and the birds.

The path winds round the shattered keep, and the higher I climb the more the vegetation closes in until at last I feel that I'm literally walking in Gertrude's footsteps in a little piece of Anatolia that hasn't changed at all since 1907 when she wrote: 'I could have shut my eyes

Henry Cumberbatch, British consul to Smyrna, and his wife Helene travelled to Nif (Kemalpaşa) with Gertrude Bell in 1907.

and thought it Switzerland.' The gnarled old olive trees, their trunks trussed with rope-like lianas, remind me more of Greece, although there are drystone walls up here too, an unexpected echo of the Cotswolds. I emerge on a country road, the sort of road a taxi driver would assure me was *'berbat* [awful]' and should be replaced immediately with a dual carriageway. Slowly, quietly it leads me back into town via the rural reality of suburban Kemalpaşa. Cockerels are crowing, hens dustbathing in the sun. A white kid goat is so newly born that its knees quiver beneath it. I can see the black stick of the umbilical cord still sticking out from its navel. I may be the first human being it's seen.

Gertrude and the Cumberbatches lodged for the night with a local Greek, sharing their beds with 'all the fleas and bugs in the world'. In the morning they were off again, this time with an entourage of guards, guides and hangers-on for fear of a local robber called Çekerci. His name was on everyone's lips, she wrote, although he was unlikely to be caught, 'for he murders everyone who gives information against him'. Fortunately, they reached the Karabel Pass on what is now the road to Torbalı without incident.

There, thirty metres above the road, Herodotus had recorded the existence of a carving that he believed to be of an Egyptian pharoah called Sesostris. However, since Sesostris (probably Senusret III) never penetrated this far into Anatolia, the carving is more likely to depict King Tarkasnawa, ruler of the obscure state of Mira and a vassal of the Hittites, hence Murray's huffy renaming of it as the Pseudo Sesostris.

I'm pleased to see that steps still mount the steep hillside to the carving. Up I start enthusiastically, only to find that, just as with the would-be palace restorers, the energy of the step-layers has quickly exhausted itself; after eighteen risers the path reverts to its natural state, an obstacle course of uneven purple stones jutting out at crazy angles from deep red mud. As I slip and stumble, I imagine the agile Gertrude in her long skirt, holding it up with one hand while using the other to steady herself on branches, the Cumberbatches following in her wake, glancing up aghast at her increasingly muddy hemline.

The carving is set into a rock of such a harsh grey that for one awful moment I think the original has been replaced with a copy. Not so, however, and no doubt by now it's even more weathered than when Gertrude inspected it, for, try as I might, I can't make out the Greek graffiti she recorded. The life-sized carving shows the king side-on in the style so typical of the time. He has a bow hooked over his right shoulder and a spear clasped in his left hand. His shoes curl up becomingly at the toe and he wears a pointed cap and gangsta-style baggy shorts. Gertrude found the remains of a second incomplete carving and I scramble about for a while in the hope of finding it. But there's a surly sod of a taxi driver waiting for me and the thought of his unsmiling countenance hardly encourages prolonged investigation. Not that it matters anyway. The second carving, it turns out, went the way of road building in the early 1980s along with the two Luwian inscriptions that accompanied it.

6

On the Tourist Trail

SOMA–BERGAMA–MANİSA–ALAŞEHİR–BLAUNDOS

'I walked up to the top of the hill by a paved road which was the road of the Attalid kings and rutted by their carriage wheels.' Letter, 6 March 1902

In the cemetery at Soma what immediately strikes the visitor is the piston-like repetition of the same date. Then you notice the ages of the dead; that the men commemorated were all remarkably young. On their own those two details are enough to suggest some terrible tragedy even without the signposts that point to this cypress-ringed corner of the cemetery. 'Maden Şehitliği Gider', they say: this way to the Mine Martyrs Memorial. For, like Aberfan in Wales, Soma is one of those unhappy towns where time once stood terrifyingly still. Wives and mothers, sons and daughters, all waited in dread for news that they must have known would be bad. It was May 2014, and an explosion in a mineshaft had sparked a fire underground. Of the men who had been working there only half would get out alive. By the end of the rescue effort 301 bodies had been recovered.

On a coolish April day almost a year later, men from the local authority are busy framing the burial plots with black marble. Miners to whom little attention was paid in life are being honoured in death even while their families continue to battle for compensation. The scale of such a disaster cannot be concealed. A trickle of people will continue to visit the graves. Best that they're seen to be treated respectfully.

Necdet, the taxi driver, pauses to snap one of the graves on his phone. 'I knew him,' he says. 'He had two jobs. He worked in the mine, but he was also a taxi driver. I'd had *çay* with him just ten days before it happened.'

We drive back to town in some agitation. 'Without the mines Soma would be nothing,' he mutters. It's hard to argue with that conclusion and therein lies the tragedy of the situation.

★ ★ ★

Although the Murray's *Handbook* included a mention of the nearby ruins of ancient Apollonia, dreary Soma might strike the modern traveller as rather an odd place for Gertrude to have visited. It did, however, have a station, which made it the perfect starting point for a day trip to Pergamon followed by a round-trip expedition through Manisa and Sardis to Alaşehir and Blaundos, and then back to Smyrna.

Inland from the coast, Soma was not the sort of place to have had a proper hotel in 1902, so after taking almost all day to crawl there in the train from Smyrna, Gertrude stayed the night with a Mr Laussiki, 'a very affable station master, Greek but speaking French', who accommodated her splendidly. I, on the other hand, put up at a hotel so unaccustomed to lone foreign females that the weaselly woman in charge takes my identity card hostage, demands payment upfront, then pops her head out every time I open my bedroom door, not so much to see if she can help but to check what I'm getting up to. Necdet, too, recovers from his grief swiftly enough to charge a vastly inflated fare for the trip to the cemetery. I'm not particularly sorry to see the back of Soma.

In the morning Gertrude set off for Bergama in a horse-drawn carriage. It was market day, she wrote, and they trundled past villagers heading into Soma to convert their onions into cash as well as 'peasants ploughing with bullocks and buffaloes'. Having already mastered French, German, Italian, Farsi and Arabic, she whiled away the bumpy ride to Bergama in a tussle with Turkish, a language she thought of as 'singularly beautiful and flexible' even if it ultimately defeated her. Finally, after a wearying four and a half hours on the road, she spotted the acropolis of Pergamon soaring up above the 'pretty modern town of Bergama set in fruit trees and cypresses', a description that might come as a surprise to the modern visitor arriving at the bus station and having to endure the long haul into town via a never-ending canyon of concrete high-rise apartment blocks. Fortunately, the canyon eventually dissolves into old Bergama, a warren of narrow streets lined with old stone houses, most of them built for the town's pre-1923 Greek population.

A Greek named Mr Sophianos whisked Gertrude off to inspect the Kızıl Avlu (Red Courtyard), an enigmatic brick pile that she was

Remains of the theatre of Pergamon at Bergama; 2015

told was a bathhouse although it was actually a shrine to the Egyptian gods. In a howling wind, they struggled up the steep slope to the acropolis, Mr Sophianos no doubt relieved to be able to cry off early to go to a wedding. Left with the *dragoman* (interpreter), she pressed on up to the wreckage of the altar of Zeus; a scatter of ruins marking the site of the palaces of the Attalid kings; and 'the highest and narrowest' ancient theatre of them all.

There was just time to snatch tea and biscuits chez Sophianos before settling back into the carriage for the return to Soma. 'Most magnificent sunset,' she wrote: 'the whole floor of heaven red and gold which faded into a grey cold sky like the fading of the glories of the Attalids'.

★ ★ ★

In the middle of a Manisa roundabout a statue of a robed man crouches protectively over a pestle and mortar, his turban askew as if to imply all the head-scratching that had gone into concocting his magical potion. It commemorates Merkez Efendi, without whose efforts the town would rarely see a visitor.

The story winds back to 1540 when Hafsa Sultan, the mother of Süleyman the Magnificent, was laid low with a malady that proved resistant to all conventional treatments. Then up popped a local pharmacist clutching a life-saving elixir made from forty different ingredients. Süleyman's mother made a miraculous recovery and the rest is the curious history of *Manisa macunu*, a fudge-like paste tossed once a year to half the assembled population of nearby Izmir from the roof of the Sultan Medrese by men dressed in faux Ottoman finery.

No doubt Gertrude would have turned her nose up at such frivolity. In any case she had arrived in Manisa with an introduction to an Armenian named Mr Gagossian, who was waiting to show her the town. The Gagossians hailed from Bitlis in the southeast, where they had 'suffered during the massacres' of 1895. Some of the family had emigrated, but this particular branch had headed for Manisa, where they lived in the American Mission, inside the *haremlik* (family part) of the old Karaosmanoğlu Palace. According to Gertrude, the Karaosmanoğlus were local lords of wealth so immense 'that they themselves could not number it'. They had, she learned, lorded it over Manisa until the start of the nineteenth century and their home was 'a beautiful place with deep balconies and fountains and lovely woodwork, all empty and falling into decay'. There she was accommodated in a room 'completely furnished with Bibles, hymn books, texts, a portrait of a dead Armenian lying on his bed in dress clothes – everything except my bed which is entirely absent!'

Together, Mr Gagossian and Gertrude toured the town's sights, including the Sultan mosque complex which forms the centrepiece of today's *macun* festivities. Like medieval monasteries, such complexes tended to be walled-in worlds, seemingly self-contained even though they actually formed the sociable heart of their communities. But the separate buildings that make up the Sultan complex are dotted about a magnolia-shaded park. In a dip behind the *hamam*, from whose chimneys smoke still billows, sits what was once the *bimarhane*, the hospital for the mentally ill. Today it houses a museum detailing early Islamic medical practice. Mannequins weave baskets, listen to soothing music and undergo eye surgery so gruesome that a notice advises parents to cover their children's eyes. But in 1902 the hospital was still very much in business. 'I saw the men and women in separate courts wrapped in white felts and kept behind bars like wild animals,' wrote Gertrude.

A young man named Selman approaches. I expect him to refute her words, but instead he points to a length of chain attached to the wall. 'It's symbolic now,' he says. 'But, yes, people were chained up, although outdoors where they could sit in the sun.' He's so chirpy and keen to be helpful that I don't have the heart to ask if her suggestion that newcomers were beaten to frighten them into good behaviour was also true.

Not far from the Sultan Cami a path leads uphill to a mosque whose courtyard whispers of a time much earlier, of a place much further to the east. The Ulu Cami is a work of the *beylik* period, a troublesome time in Anatolian history between the collapse of the powerful Selçuk Sultanate of Rum, with its capital in Konya, and the clean-sweep takeover of the Ottomans. The *beys* were powerful warlords who established regional fiefdoms all over Anatolia. Manisa was the capital of the Saruhan Beylik. The eponymous Saruhan is said to have snatched the city from the Byzantines in 1313 by sending ahead a flock of goats with candles between their horns, thereby tricking his enemy into believing his army much bigger than it really was. It was his grandson, İshak Çelebi, who commissioned the mosque.

The Ulu Cami's courtyard resembles an architectural car boot sale, showcasing a plethora of columns either taken from an earlier church on the site or filched from lost structures of what was once Magnesia ad Sipylum. Inside, Gertrude admired the wooden *mimber*, as fine a piece of medieval woodwork as survives outside a museum. But today is not my lucky day. A trio of worshippers leaving the mosque cast a suspicious look at me, then hurry away. When I try the door, they've locked it firmly behind them.

Mr Gagossian was eager to show Gertrude a bulbous rock formation that the Manisans call the Ağlayan Kaya (Weeping Rock) but that the residents of Magnesia ad Sipylum believed to be the petrified re-mains of Niobe, the Greek woman foolish enough to boast about her fourteen children, comparing her own fecundity favourably with that of Leto, the beautiful Greek woman who was the lover of Zeus and had given birth to the twins Apollo and Artemis. The punish-ment for such hubris was appalling. It wasn't enough for Apollo to murder her sons and Artemis her daughters, but Niobe herself had to be turned to stone, the stream that once cascaded from the rock the never-ending tears she wept for her lost children.

Gertrude was much taken with the rock, describing it as 'high up and very old, [Niobe's] body bent over her knees looking down with a blank featureless face. You can see her knees and the tops of the arms and the breasts, all else but 2 wings like the arms of the seat is too disfigured.' Personally, I struggle to 'see' Niobe. Mostly I can see what looks like a nose so pointed that it would be better described as a beak, as if Niobe were an angry eagle gazing out over Manisa. Time seems finally to have dried up her tears.

In the hills above the rock one of Turkey's largest dervish com-munities once flourished. As I approach their *tekke*, a wave of envy washes over me. Gertrude had visited it as a still living, breathing component of local life. I, on the other hand, must amble around an-other museum while listening to women barter for dervish-themed fridge magnets by the door. The 'felt-hatted dervishes sitting in their cells as comfy as possible' were driven out as part of Atatürk's drive to laicize his new republic (the *tekkes* were all closed in 1925). The only dervishes visible now are of the strictly mannequin variety.

Today's Manisa is so defiantly modern that it's easy to overlook the fact that it ever had a history unless you come for the *macun*-tossing festivities when suddenly the Ottomans are the only show in town. But why, the passing traveller might ask, are the Ottomans so im-portant to Manisa? What was Sultan Süleyman's mother doing here in the first place?

The answer lies in a quirk of early Ottoman governance. Together with Amasya in Central Anatolia and Trabzon on the Black Sea, Man-isa formed a triptych of towns to which the sons of the sultans were sent to hone their governing skills. Knowing that, you start to sense an absence. Where, you begin to wonder, did those princes live?

Gertrude wrote that her search for Niobe passed over 'where Sultan Mahmud's great palace and gardens were – now empty ground with a factory at one corner'. That palace was the Saray-ı Amire, template for Topkapı, its foundations laid by Murad II, its walls and towers raised by his conquering son, Mehmed. The palace lives on in the details of a sixteenth-century miniature and in a description by Evliya Çelebi, the seventeenth-century Ottoman traveller. Alas, the gilded pavilions and shady porticoes have long since given way to the concrete nothingness of a square sprawling out behind the town hall. The factory has been revamped to serve Manisa kebabs to the locals.

Freya Stark regarded Gertrude as overrated, claiming that she 'never … stayed anywhere long enough to get to the heart of things'. As regards the Gertrude of the Baghdad years, it's a comment that reads like sour grapes, but of her younger tourist incarnation it was not, perhaps, so wide of the mark. At Sardis, for example, she had time to do little more than snatch a quick look at the temple to Kybele/Artemis, before shinning up the hill behind it, skirting nomad tents and fetching up on a plateau 'red with anemones' from which she could observe the mountain top, 'knife edged … and fallen down in debris below' and 'the great plain where Croesus was defeated' by the Persians in 546 BC.

She had arrived by train from Manisa chaperoned by a Mr Hatton, a 'rotund and cheerful' railway worker who continued with her to Alaşehir, where an invitation to stay with the Sarandides family trumped that from the stationmaster. The Sarandides lived in what she called a 'regular Greek sort' of house, 'the door opening onto a hall with the Salon and its row of brocade covered chairs and sofa and the dining room at the end'. But homestay tourism was something of a mixed blessing. The night before she had moaned to her family that her host had 'five of the nastiest little children you ever saw'; now she recorded that she sat in a circle with the Sarandides 'conducting a most laborious conversation in wh[ich] we repeated the same platitudes over and over again … the amount of times that we said that spring was the pleasantest season of the year and the Turks robbers would surprise you!' When asked what time she'd like to dine, she 'replied with decision Now', after which they shared an 'enormous dinner of many courses, of each of which I was obliged to partake'.

Today it's a rare visitor who makes it to Alaşehir, the ancient Philadelphia, despite its advertized appeal to Bible aficionados as one of the Seven Churches of the Revelation. There was a little more to see in Gertrude's day, when she reported climbing the hill to inspect traces of a theatre and stadium. But the main sight, then as now, was the clumpy ruin of the church, no more, really, than 'two great piers of masonry' and the faint outlines of frescoed saints' heads, even more spectral now after the passage of a further century.

From the hillside Gertrude surveyed the Byzantine city walls 'which could be clearly seen all round'. A stretch of that wall still survives, but whereas in 1902 she could describe the town as 'shrivelled somewhat' within the walls, now it has thrown out tentacles in every direction, with the result that most of what remains of the wall can only be tracked by dogged pursuit through garages, gardens and backyards until at last it heaves a sigh and abandons the struggle to survive just shy of the main square. To my disappointment I'm unable to find that part of it supposedly built by Tamerlane in which the bones of local Christians were visible. No one I ask will admit to knowing anything about it, whether through genuine ignorance or embarrassment it's impossible to tell.

Before returning to Smyrna Gertrude was determined to visit the remains of ancient Blaundos, accessible from the station at İnay, near the modern village of Süleymanlı. There being no other option, she and Mr Hatton passed the night in adjoining sleeping cars on the train, he rising early to conjure a miraculous breakfast of bacon and eggs. Then, at the first break in the rain, they set off on a ninety-minute trek to the ruins across bleak and empty countryside.

As my taxi bumps along the road from Uşak, I picture her striding through the fields, head bowed against the wind, boots slithering in the mud. The reward would have been what even today comes as a delightful surprise. For Blaundos is simply breathtaking, completely forgotten yet absolutely glorious, the remains of its buildings – presumably much less extensive now than in Gertrude's day, when *yörüks* were busy dismantling them – scattered in picturesque disarray across a headland amid daisies and dandelions. The most striking structure, a putative administration block, looks, in its ruinous state, like a lost piece of jigsaw placed upright. The canyon ringing the headland is pockmarked with tombs.

The site is as much of a discovery to Mehmet, my Uşak-born taxi driver, as it is to me. He's completely enraptured, snapping away promiscuously while I struggle to make sense of rusted signboards. Gertrude confessed to knowing nothing about Blaundos 'but what I have seen today', although the simple building style suggested a date of around 200 BC. Despite the dismal weather it was an inspirational expedition: 'Some day I shall come and travel here with tents, but then I will speak Turkish, which will not be difficult and I will take only a couple of Turkish servants with me.'

7

Ephesus Quite to Ourselves

EPHESUS

*'There were a few shepherd boys high up on the hills but otherwise
it was all solitary and most beautiful.'* Letter, 9 April 1907

Just behind the arches of Selçuk's storks'-nest-studded aqueduct a
small stone building occupies a rare square of lawn. It looks rather
like a clubhouse on a manicured English bowling green, and it
houses the Café Carpouza, a name that quietly immortalizes a little
piece of early tourism history. The café is all that survives of the Ephesus Huck Hotel, a branch of the Grand Huck Hotel that graced
Smyrna's quayside. In the late nineteenth century the Ephesus Huck
was one of two hotels built to accommodate visitors arriving in Ayasuluk (modern-day Selçuk) by train. The other was the Frenchified
Hotel Ephesus, which was owned by a Mr Carpouza, whose picture
hangs on the wall of what was once the rival hotel, his own establishment having been demolished in the 1980s. The photo shows Mr
Carpouza as a grown-up Billy Bunter. Everything about him bulges;
it's hard to imagine how he could have got through a day without
popping the buttons of his waistcoat. A postcard shows him amid
the ruins of Ephesus, sitting astride what resembles a yoga ball but
is actually a slice of ancient column. He looks like an old-fashioned
wobbly man.

   In 1862 a station on the branch of the new Izmir to Aydın railway
opened in Ayasuluk, injecting new life into a settlement on its
deathbed. Inland from renowned but ruinous Ephesus, Ayasuluk
had grown gradually as the great Roman city's harbour silted up and
its residents moved away from the malarial lowlands, taking refuge
on the hilltop now occupied by a castle. But once Smyrna and Scala
Nuova (Kuşadası) took off as ports, Ayasuluk lost its raison d'être.
Passing through in the first half of the nineteenth century, the French
traveller Charles Texier reported just a handful of families hunkered
down amid the ruins. Then came the train and suddenly things were
looking up again. European travellers had always been interested in

Ephesus, as much because of its associations with St Paul as for its Roman glory. Then in 1869 John Turtle Wood, an English architect employed to design the stations for the new railway line, stumbled on the remains of the Temple of Artemis (Diana), one of the Seven Wonders of the Ancient World, and promptly gave up his job to excavate them. Ultimately his efforts revealed little more than waterlogged foundations, but, as in the case of Troy, a veil of romance hugged the memory of the temple, guaranteeing the ruins top-billing with every history lover arriving in Smyrna.

Mr Carpouza, Gertrude Bell's guide in Ayasuluk (Selçuk); c1907

The new hotels received an even bigger fillip in 1891 when the remains of a small Byzantine building on the slopes of Bülbül Dağı (Nightingale Mountain) were identified as the last home of the Virgin Mary, as seen in a dream by a German nun who had never set foot in Turkey. Ephesus became the single biggest tourist attraction in late-nineteenth-century Asia Minor and Mr Carpouza was the man on hand to take care of its most illustrious visitors. It goes without saying that Gertrude Bell was one of them.

Met by Mr Carpouza at the station on a cold, grey day in 1899, Gertrude described him as 'a fat and smiling person cut out by nature for his profession'. She stopped briefly for refreshment before striking out on a whirlwind walking tour of the sites. Off she strode along the then main road to Scala Nuova, bypassing the great aqueduct that used to supply drinking water to the families living inside the castle and marching through the 'tumble-down village' to the Gate of Persecution, 'built out of older buildings with a bit of frieze over the arch'. The gate led into the Basilica of St John, commissioned by the Emperor Justinian in honour of the Apostle John, who was believed to be buried there. From the basilica she gazed up at the castle that had once been the centre of Ayasuluk. Then she paid a duty call on the 'few marble blocks, overgrown with thorns and pampas' that survived of Turtle Wood's Artemisium. 'Poor Diana of the Ephesians,' she wrote. 'I wish she had left a little more of her greatness behind for me to see. She has had a bad time of it, poor dear.'

Mr Carpouza had arranged for ponies to follow Gertrude and now she mounted one to continue along the Via Sacra (Sacred Way) to Ephesus itself. Approaching from the north, she made a circuit of the site, clambering up the cyclamen-studded tiers of seats in the theatre while Austrian archaeologists looked on. Then she marched along the road to the harbour, mulling over St Paul's failed mission to convert the locals: 'It is curious to think of St Paul landing there, with the shining, gorgeous Greek city in front of him, walking up the colonnaded street and the marble steps to the theatre at the end, and being hissed off the stage before the piece was finished.' But monuments that are today's biggest attractions eluded her: the Library of Celsus still lay in pieces, and the terraced houses, with their evocative Pompeii-style frescoes, were still waiting to be dug out of the silt.

Back at the hotel an impressive spread awaited the weary explorers – 'an excellent lunch … which the fat Karpouza, a god of feasts he is, dealt out to us with a liberal hand'.

On a return trip to Ephesus with Mr van Lennep in 1902 it was 'the beautiful columns taken from [the] Artemisium – the fellows of those in St Sophia' in the ruins of the fourteenth-century İsa Bey Cami that bewitched Gertrude, sparking a dig at the Ottomans: 'I wonder why the Seljuks were such artists and builders and the Osmanlis could never lay one stone on another. Everywhere where the Seljuks have passed they leave mosques and medressehs and khans of most splendid work but the Osmanlis leave only the ruins of what they found.' But her attribution was not quite correct. In reality the mosque, with its soaring, striped marble portal, frilly window-frames and utterly un-Turkish floor plan, had been commissioned by the youngest son of the founder of the Aydınıd Bey-lik, and the architect entrusted with the task had been Ali ibn al Di-mashki (Ali, son of the Damascene), whose blueprint was almost certainly the Great Mosque of his home town. It would be another three years before Gertrude would ride into Damascus and see its inspiration for herself.

A mere five days later she was in Ephesus again, this time with Edward Whittall and his family. Together they rode up to St Paul's Prison, then walked along the winding city wall, which offered a 'magnificent view ... all Ephesus lay spread before us, the Asiatic and the Greek town and the whole valley of the Cayster down to the sea'. There was one last visit with the van Lenneps in 1907, when for the first time the weather was on her side: 'The place quite empty in the sun. Perfectly delicious.'

That last visit formed the start of her great expedition to Binbirk-ilise in the heart of Anatolia. To get in the mood she turned down the chance of a bed in Mr Carpouza's hotel, opting instead for a night under the stars. 'Camped on the hill above the aqueduct,' she wrote in her diary. 'Extremely happy.'

I, however, am in a quandary. I've arrived in Selçuk on a particu-larly busy Easter weekend when the town is also gearing up to cel-ebrate the annual Children's Holiday. I know I should follow Gertrude round the ruins of Ephesus, yet, after multiple visits in my guidebook-writing days, I can't quite make myself do it. The mere thought of the holiday crowds added to the usual crush of visitors bussed in from the Kuşadası cruise ships makes my heart sink. Then inspiration hits. I'll retrace her steps along the city wall instead.

For that you need Özgür Çağdaş, I'm told, and I'm directed to a shop in the town centre where I find said Özgür, slender, youthful, trimly bearded and a whizz when it comes to the wall. Up onto his computer screen he pulls a map dating back to the 1890s. On it he traces the line of the wall, tossing out snippets of information as he goes. When doubt flickers across my face he reassures me that the walk is 'easy', a doddle, anyone can do it sort of thing.

Özgür volunteers to drop me off close to St Paul's Prison. We turn off the main road beside the ruins of what were once lime kilns nestling in a field of artichokes. It's a wonderful spring day, hot but not too hot, the sky clear, the slightest of breezes just getting into its stride. I set off with the proverbial spring in my step. What can possibly go wrong, after all, when I have the remains of the wall to guide me?

For the first couple of hours I hike either on top of or alongside the wall. This had been erected in the late fourth century BC by Lysimachus, a crafty general who 'persuaded' the locals to move to Ephesus from their original settlement on the hillside in what is now Selçuk by blocking their drains so that sewage flooded their houses. The original wall stood to a height of ten metres and ringed what would be the new city for a distance of almost ten kilometres. Now it is for the most part mere stubby ruin. 'Magnificent Greek fortifications in the best style,' Gertrude had written: 'dressed stone without mortar much in the style of the Colophon walls'. The word 'Colophon' should have set alarm bells ringing. Those walls had, after all, completely vanished.

But for the time being I'm in my element, congratulating myself on having escaped the crowds. In front of me the hillside is ankle-deep in wildflowers, the delicate little yellow and violet ones outclassed in colour by splashy red anemones and in height by giant fennels. I divert for a quick look at the 'prison' building that just might have held St Paul after local silversmiths rebelled against his preaching, seeing it as a threat to their trade in tacky Diana trinkets. I take a peek over the far side of the wall and find it much more overgrown, not to say much windier. That, too, should have given me pause had I but had my wits about me.

On I trek, very chipper, until eventually I find myself looking down on one of the miniature lakes that Özgür had pointed out on the map. Round its edge I can see little fishermen's huts, then beyond them, as if looking down from the basket of a hot-air balloon, the harbour road running up to the curve of the theatre at Ephesus, straight as a die. In the distance I can make out modern Selçuk reclining against the hill with the castle neatly crowning it. This is Ephesus as it's almost impossible to imagine it, I think. Silence. No guides bellowing dates at disinterested clients. No risk of losing an eye to a selfie stick. Up here I'm quite alone. Just me gazing down on those spectacular ruins.

The ruins of Ephesus from its ancient city walls; 2015

In passing, Özgür had mentioned a fallen stretch of the wall and, sure enough, I eventually come to a field of broken stones across which I scramble, still high on history and glibly assuming that I'll pick up the wall again on the far side. Except that I don't. On the far side, what had been open hillside transmogrifies into thicket, a tangle of scrub oak and prickly undergrowth that I can only penetrate by folding myself in half. Insofar as there was ever a real path up here, there certainly isn't one now. What's more the dense tree cover makes it impossible to pick out the wall.

I flounder around trying to distinguish some sort of track or some way of getting close to the wall again, but only succeed in getting more and more lost. I can feel the day starting to draw in. Perhaps it would be wiser to turn back, I think. Except that I can't do that either because by now I've wandered round in so many circles that I can no longer find the way back. Unlike Gertrude I have not taken the precaution of going on an orienteering course at the Royal Geographical Society. And, unlike Gertrude, I'm up here completely alone, which had felt heavenly just an hour earlier but is beginning to feel potentially hellish now that the sun is starting to set.

Eventually, more by luck than judgement, I find myself back beside a solid stretch of wall with the remains of towers still punctuating it. I climb to the top of a tower and scan the terrain ahead of me. It doesn't look remotely promising. I climb down again and drop to the far side of the wall, but by now the wind is gusting so ferociously that it's hard to stand upright.

Retreating to the tower, I ponder an unpalatable set of options. Darkness is closing in rapidly now and with every passing minute that I don't come up with a plan it's becoming increasingly dangerous to be on my own here.

Finally it dawns on me that I may end up having to call out the emergency services. Did you bring a satnav, they are likely to ask, or did you bring a compass? Admitting that I left home with neither is going to be – well, embarrassing doesn't begin to describe it. There's nothing left to do. With a sigh, I reach into my pocket, pull out my mobile phone, dial Özgür's number and outline my predicament.

'Where are you?' he asks.

'At the highest point of the walls,' I say with more confidence than I actually feel.

'Wait there. I'll come and get you,' he replies.

Never were five words more welcome. Never was I happier, a mere half-hour later, to see a distant red blob sharp-focusing into T-shirt shape as he climbs up to meet me from the Selçuk end of the walls. I'm almost whimpering with gratitude, too relieved to be rescued to worry about the indignity of having had to ask for help.

Only when I'm safely back in the hotel do two things strike me. We 'scrambled down to the port', wrote Gertrude, which suggests a) that the walk wasn't terribly easy even in her day and b) that she had descended before the point where the wall had collapsed. I'd assumed that the schedule of the train back to Smyrna had left her time to walk only part of the way. It's just as possible that a whispered word from the wise Mr Carpouza had persuaded her to retreat.

8
Crossing the Meander

SÖKE–PRIENE–MILETUS–DIDYMA–LAKE BAFA–SELİMİYE

'It's very laborious being the careful traveller and I don't think I do it well either.'
Letter, 3 May 1907

'Can you direct me to the Şehitler ve Gaziler Parkı?' I ask the receptionist in my Söke hotel.

A look of panic creeps across his face. It's reminiscent of the one that had crossed the faces of the Uşak taxi drivers when I'd enquired about visiting Blaundos.

The man turns to a friend who's hammering away at the computer. He shrugs. 'No,' they intone. 'There isn't one.'

'I think it may have had a big factory in it once?'

A smile as of the sun coming out after rain. 'Ohhh! For-bes Parkı!' they say, pronouncing every letter carefully and placing the emphasis on the second syllable as is the way in Turkish.

I nod. 'Yes, that sounds like it,' I agree.

Out comes a piece of paper. Out comes a pen. Minutes later and I'm striding across the marketplace in what is an unnecessarily shabby little town and heading for the Kemalpaşa neighbourhood, where, sure enough, a sign over the park gate reads 'Şehitler ve Gaziler Parkı [Martyrs and Veterans Park]'. Not that it's a park to write home about. Broken-backed seats of concrete and wood sit in a semicircle facing a war memorial. The ground is strewn with litter. The best one can say of it is that it's an interlude of greenery amid relentless concrete.

The loss of the factory is a shame since it would have served as a reminder of an industry, once as vital to this area as coal was to Newcastle, that now survives only in the past tense. Once, this part of the Aegean offered the perfect conditions for growing liquorice, an 'ugly unsociable plant' according to Freya Stark, but one that attracted the attention of William Forbes, scion of another powerful Levantine family. Sometime in the mid-1850s he and a fellow Scot opened a factory to refine the liquorice roots for use as flavouring in American cigarettes. Old postcards of Söke show its tall chimneys lording it over the skyline.

In the April of 1907 Gertrude was shown round the factory, recording in her diary that it was the largest such enterprise in Turkey. A liquorice factory might seem an unlikely attraction for a thirty-nine-year-old woman with her sights set on the archaeology of Asia Minor. But Gertrude had just helped her stepmother Florence prepare *At The Works*, a report into working conditions in her father's factory at Port Clarence in Middlesbrough. Factories were in her blood, production figures a staple of family conversation over drawn-out winter evenings.

She passed the night in 'a very clean and comfortable' hotel, even though the bill was 'rather exorbitant', an odd complaint given her family's wealth except that her father had always instilled thriftiness in his offspring. As to its location, she offered no clues. But by now I've wised up to the essential role that railways played in the early history of travel in the Aegean hinterland. The obvious place to start looking, then, has to be the station.

I head out there on a Sunday morning, when the streets of Söke are as silent as an English suburban library. The station stands in a chichi part of town with a pleasant park, much cleaner and better maintained than that of the Martyrs and Veterans. On one side stands a fine old Greek mansion midway through transition into a museum. Could that have been it, I wonder?

The door is locked so I wander into the station, where a quartet of local men are breakfasting at a platform café. I down a coffee. Then I approach the café owner. 'That house across the park – was it once a hotel?' I ask him.

'Oh no,' he says. 'It was always a private home.'

That appears to be that, but just as I'm turning away I hear one of the breakfasters calling after me – '*Hanımefendi! Hanımefendi!*' Foreign faces being almost as rare in Söke as in Bulgurca, he'd asked the owner what his unlikely inquisitor had wanted. Now he's keen to be helpful. 'There *was* once a hotel near here,' he says. 'It was called the Erol Palas. Zeki Acem will have a photograph. I'll give him a call.'

'But it's Sunday. I can come back tomorrow.'

Muhtar Zeki Acem recovers the image of Hotel Priene at Söke; 2015

'*Boş ver* [No matter]. I'll call him anyway.' And the next thing I know, I'm in a bus speeding towards the Atatürk neighbourhood, where I find Zeki Bey waiting for me as if it were perfectly normal to be summoned from home on a Sunday morning to show photographs to a complete stranger.

Zeki Bey is a remarkable man. As the bus pulls up I see him standing on the pavement chatting to his friends, a man in his seventies wearing a black fedora that gives him the slightly louche look of a leading man from a Yeşilçam* blockbuster of the 1950s. Zeki is the neighbourhood *muhtar* (headman) and at once we set off to his office, where ballot papers are neatly laid out ready for the upcoming general election. The walls are thick with photographs of old Söke, the shelves heavy with books, files and other evidence of a busy life. But from my point of view the most important thing about Zeki is that he turns out to be the living repository of Söke's history. On his computer are stored hundreds of old photos of the town, the snag being that he has filed them under the names of the people

*Yeşilçam was the nickname given to the early Turkish film industry after an Istanbul street with many film studios.

who donated them, resulting in much chin-stroking and many false positives before at last he can call up a picture of the Erol Palas. I peer over his shoulder. It clearly post-dates the founding of the Republic and hence Gertrude's visit.

But Zeki is not a man to admit defeat. We chat about Gertrude's travels and I translate what she wrote about Söke and the factory for him. 'From here she went on to Priene,' I wind up.

Priene! It's the trigger he was waiting for. Once again Zeki scrolls through those files while I peer over his shoulder, wringing my hands and hinting at the urgent need to devise a storage system more accessible to outsiders without which it looks as if the history of Söke will soon be irretrievably lost. Then up on the screen pops a picture of the Hotel Priene. It's a fine stone building with a pedimental roof, just the sort of place that might have felt entitled to charge exorbitant prices. What's more it stood in the Kemalpaşa neighbourhood close to the factory. This must be where Gertrude stayed then, although disappointingly it is no more. Zeki and I are as thrilled as if we'd run the Istanbul marathon. At the door we shake hands and go our separate ways.

The altercation over the hotel bill out of the way, Gertrude trotted south from Söke to Priene, where, having returned the horses with the owner's son, she climbed the hill to the ruins to explore a 'magnificent place', the ancient town 'spread out like a map with the broad flooded Meander' below her.

I'm thinking of that broad, flooded Meander as I follow her up the hillside in glorious spring sunshine, which means that I'm certainly not looking down at my feet and certainly don't see whatever it is that whips out from nowhere and bites me. There is a brief moment of freedom from pain such as one experiences after shutting one's finger in a door. Then, wham, my foot is convulsed in agony, throbbing, stinging and generally obliterating all further thought of the Meander.

In the ticket office the young site custodian, Melis, is as good as her mellifluous-sounding name and rushes to daub ammonia on my toes. I tell myself it must be doing some good, although the pain is still excruciating. In any case, being British, I find the embarrassment at making a scene almost equally excruciating, so I thank Melis profusely and hobble on to the ruins, there to plonk myself down, doubled-up in agony, on a capital that has probably been sitting undisturbed for more than a millennium.

At Priene it's the dramatic hillside location together with the way that nature interacts with the fallen masonry that so enthrals the visitor. Gertrude mentioned the great city wall and the Temple of Demeter. Worse, from my point of view, is the fact that she also mentioned the acropolis that rises sheer behind the temple. Up she went, ever energetic, along a 'winding path cut in the face of the rock, in many places a rock hewn stair'. I read these words with dread. There may indeed be a 'splendid view', but I've already had one mishap and am reluctant to risk another, which is what I'm sure will happen if I try and follow her up there. Instead, I content myself with inspecting the delicate little theatre with its lion-footed front-row seats, then duck into the reclusive remnants of a Byzantine church still with its ambo (pulpit) intact.

Gertrude spent the night in a house used during the digging season by the German archaeologist, Theodor Wiegand, who had initiated the excavations at Priene and whom she had bumped into, quite fortuitously, on the platform at Ayasuluk. The house turned out to double as a hotel owned by the same rapacious individual with whom she'd sparred over the bill in Söke. In the village I spot a gracious two-storied wooden building near the start of the path to the ruins. There's nobody home to make enquiries so I waylay a passer-by. 'I wonder if you know anything about this house?' I ask her.

'Yes, it belongs to the Germans.'

Which is good enough for me.

★ ★ ★

In a time characterised by eye-wateringly expensive statement bridges it's hard to imagine quite how big an obstacle to transport a river could once have been, especially if it was a river with a wide and marshy delta as was the case with the Meander (Büyük Menderes). To get from Priene to Miletus these days is a drive too short to mention. But at the turn of the twentieth century you still had to cross the delta, which was no swift or easy matter.

Gertrude had been assured that it was a mere half-hour's ride to the ferry, and Wiegand had supplied her with a *kavass*, an all-purpose bodyguard-cum-manservant, to accompany her. In reality it took almost three times as long as that to pick their way over the boggy ground to the landing stage, and when they finally arrived there was still another hour of hanging around in the cold and wet to endure before a vessel finally appeared. 'It was the smallest and rockiest boat,' Gertrude wrote, and, since she had all the luggage for her journey into the interior of Anatolia with her, 'an unfortunate Turkish boy who wanted to cross with his dog had to remain behind'. Almost at once the boat ran aground and it was lucky that the water was not particularly deep since its passengers had to jump out and help refloat it. The crossing was rough, she recorded, and rendered even more wretched by the rain that started to fall again before they reached the other side.

No sooner did she reach Miletus than she ran up to the theatre to lunch in the shelter of its galleries. The 'greater part of the excavations [are] under water', she wrote, and in her photos it looks as if the sea is lapping gently at the bottom of the theatre's tiered seats. But, water or no water, she was still able to whip round the bouleuterion (council chamber), the great baths of Faustina, and the Delphinion, the temple to Apollo that was the starting point for the Kutsal Yolu, or Sacred Way. Paved and decorated with marble lions and statues of members of the Branchidae family, the temple's plutocratic priest-custodians, the Sacred Way ran eighteen kilometres across country to the great oracle in Didyma. Every year as the first leaves unfurled to announce the start of spring, the residents of Miletus would indulge in three days of town-based revelries before setting out on a pilgrimage along it.

The site is still waterlogged, but now it has also fallen prey to an algae infestation so that the stones around the lake look as if they're draped with fishing nets. I admire the Triton monument erected in honour of Pompey the pirate-slayer in 63 BC. I admire the Temple of Serapis. Then I scramble up to the top seats of the theatre and reflect on the curious fact of this one port town having given birth to so many of the greats of Greek philosophy – Thales, Anaximander,

Anaximenes – as well as to Isidore, one half of the architectural partnership behind Hagia Sophia's awe-inspiring dome.

Despite her tight schedule Gertrude managed to snatch a quick look at the İlyas Bey Cami, an early-fifteenth-century mosque built in the era when this part of Anatolia was governed by the Menteşe Beys. Grateful for the safe return of a wife who had been cap-tured by Tamerlane, İlyas Bey

İlyas Bey Cami at Miletus; 1907

commissioned an exquisite building whose carvings look vaguely Mughal. Once it stood half-buried in undergrowth, with purple irises pushing up through cracked courtyard flagstones. It was almost absurdly charming. But in 2013, I'd arrived to find that restorers had been at work. The undergrowth was gone. So too were the irises. In their place had come a glistening white and crack-free pavement. The gate was guarded more zealously than the Central Bank, but at least it was still open. Now the guards are gone, the gates padlocked. Disappointment hits like a punch in the gut.

A small settlement inland from the brash beach resort of Altınkum, Didyma is dominated by the ruins of a vast temple to Apollo that was once home to one of Asia Minor's most widely consulted oracles. Here, sitting astride a vaporous spring, a priestess dispensed prophecies in return for cash. Like the great Temple of Artemis at Ephesus, the original Apollonion had burnt down; it's the remains of a replacement dating from 334 BC that survive today. Unlike at the Artemision, though, its soaring columns still stand high enough to suggest its original splendour. What's more, the intricate carvings ringing their bases testify to the top-notch workmanship invested in the rebuild.

Where else to stay, then, than at the Oracle Pension, whose veranda sits right beside the ruins? It's such an archaeology-y place, I think, so perfect for whiling away the evening over stories of the cryptic messages dispensed by the priestesses to the credulous. I imagine sitting on that veranda with a book open and a glass of wine beside me. I imagine discussing the route of the Sacred Way with other history-loving guests. Sadly, the owner has other ideas. 'We don't open until May,' he tells me, as if only a fool could have hoped otherwise, which leaves me nowhere to go but the Medusa House next door, whose owner is soon bending my ear over plans to launch boat rides all the way up to the ruins of Miletus.

I've arranged to meet the blogger Natalie Sayın, who lives in nearby Didim and has agreed to walk along the Sacred Way with me. We'll be doing so in contraflow to Gertrude, who took the boat from Akköy to Panormos, the old port of Didyma, and then trotted along it on horseback.

Natalie and I take the bus to Akköy, midway between Miletus and Didyma, where we meet up with Erkin İlgüzer, a guide of half-Greek and half-Bulgarian extraction. He's waiting for us in what was once the local *bakkal* and is now a small art gallery, along with multiple hopeful street dogs. Since Erkin is going to be leading our trek the dogs anticipate excellent walkies. He, however, has other ideas. As we set off down a cobbled back street five dogs tag along behind us. '*Eve git* [Go home]!' Erkin shouts at them, but they thump their tails and press on. Out we walk, into the fields, with three of them still behind us.

The great plus to the Sacred Way of today is that it runs across flat, open, waymarked countryside. Except that most of the waymarks have fallen down. From time to time it's possible to pick out huge cut stones lying in the grass that must have formed part of the original paving, but without Erkin we would soon have been hopelessly lost. Still, it's a splendidly sunny day, perfect for a stroll. The wildflowers are as thick on the ground as a pile carpet and I think of Gertrude pausing occasionally to press unfamiliar specimens between the pages of her diary.

Midway along, we pause for lunch beside a deep stone water tank into which a dog hurls herself with relish. It's only when we finally stumble back onto the main road near Mavişehir, the resort built over the old Panormos, that I understand why the dog-loving Erkin was so determined to prevent the pack from accompanying us. Because now we need a bus to get us back to Akköy and the one thing you can be sure of is that very few Turkish bus drivers are going to welcome dogs into their vehicles, especially dogs of the wet street-mongrel and unleashed variety.

Gertrude used Akköy as her base for exploring the local ruins, putting up at the excavations house with Wiegand, then in charge of the dig at Miletus.

'You want the Alman Kulesi [German Tower],' says Erkin. We're strolling round the village, a sleepy backwater that is about to become positively somnolent with the opening of a new bypass, and he's pointing out to me the ways in which the buildings of the past were designed to suit the lives of the time. 'See how the corners have been smoothed round so that the packs on the camels' backs wouldn't catch and tear,' he says. 'See how the stone houses were built with little gaps in the walls. Birds would nest in them and feed on the flies. All the windows were placed to catch the breeze and avoid overlooking the neighbours.'

He points out the site of the lost Church of Aya Yorgi (St George): 'Once the Greeks left it was turned into a tobacco warehouse. Then someone thought they could warm it by lighting a fire and removing stones from the dome to let the smoke out. Of course it came crashing down.' But this is a story of equal-opportunity destruction. We wander past the concrete *düğün salonu* (wedding hall). 'The old Ottoman mosque was also turned into a tobacco store. Then they pulled it down to build this,' he says sadly. And the tobacco? 'Oh, that finished about ten years ago.'

Erkin waves me off up the road to the Alman Kulesi, a short walk above the village. There's no one about except some distracted sheep-shearers, so when I come to a gate I ignore the padlock and hop straight over. And there on the hillside, poised to take advantage of a splendid view over the Menderes valley, I find neat stone bungalows fronted with shady verandas grouped around a fountain half-hidden in roses, a slice of tidy Teutonic paradise.

Just not quite as abandoned as I'd assumed though. Out pops the custodian, Ahmet, who looks initially wary of a trespasser, then perks up and invites me to drink çay with his wife. He's been looking after the site for thirty years, he tells me. The archaeologists would come back in August every year once the tobacco harvest was in and there was spare labour available. Now the tobacco has gone the way of the liquorice. A few locals have turned their hands to olives, but most have succumbed to the touristic pull of Altınkum.

Like Erkin, Ahmet is of Bulgarian extraction, but although his own life had offered only limited opportunities, his three children face a much brighter future, one at university, another at high school, a third studying in a *dersane* (crammer), the same Turkish Dream success story that is a commonplace in conversations with taxi drivers countrywide. The çay glasses drained, he unlocks a workshop to show me a photograph of Wiegand, a fine-looking man with trim moustache and high-necked collar. Waving goodbye, I remember Gertrude's description of the outlook: 'The theatre [of Miletus] wonderfully lighted. The great waters of the Meander, the Priene hill with the chain of mts behind it and to the N[orth] east Mt Lat[mos].' For once modernity has held back on the casual process of uglification. But for the faint wisp of a mist I could be admiring exactly the same view today.

From the bluff above Lake Bafa glittering water stretches seemingly to infinity. Offshore, the remains of Byzantine monasteries that look like miniature castles cling to rocky islets. Down below, the rock-cut tombs of the mysterious Carians poke up from the shallows, their lids gone, their contents rifled. From time to time a little egret flaps by, a white pennant against the silvery-blue. Not surprisingly, one of the most beautiful settings in all of Turkey gave rise to a slither of Greek mythology that is either very romantic or ever so slightly creepy, depending on your viewpoint. For it was in a cave on the shores of Bafa that the moon goddess, Selene, was said to have spotted a handsome sleeping shepherd boy called Endymion. Smitten by his good looks, Selene pleaded with Zeus to put him into an eternal sleep that would preserve them undimmed. How this equates with the belief that she then went on to bear him fifty daughters is unclear.

It's easy to understand how the shimmer of the moonlight reflected on the silent waters of the lake could have conjured fantasies of celestial romance. Turn one's back, however, and this is a landscape more suited to a battle of the titans. Looming on the horizon are the Beşparmak Dağları (Five-Fingered Mountains, Mt Latmos), their jagged peaks a saw slicing at the sky. Beneath them, supersized granite boulders with sides as smooth as footballs litter the ground as if teams of irate giants had gathered here to shout abuse, then hurl rocks at one another.

Standing inside the keep of a Byzantine castle, I eye the tiny lakeside settlement with affection. The village of Kapıkırı is a rarity in modern Turkey in that it has managed to avoid the ravages of concretization. This is still a place where chickens scratch in the dust by the roadside and where lone villagers steer quartets of cattle home from the fields as the sun goes down. It's noisy in the unobtrusive farmyard way, a constant buzz of bleating, braying, crowing, gobbling, mooing and cooing. Around the village the remains of simple Aeolian structures blend so perfectly with the boulders that it's often hard to tell where boulder ends and ruin begins.

Up on the hills, square towers still punctuate the line of the city walls of ancient Herakleia ad Latmos. The theatre is hunkered down in a field, barely the shadow of a shape, with fragmentary seats half-buried in grass. The council chamber hides in a backyard whose owner smiles and proffers an embroidered tablecloth as I scramble up to inspect it. In the 1950s a schoolhouse was constructed along one side of the ancient agora, but it too is now history. No longer is the schoolmaster the village kingpin, the go-to person in times of crisis. Now economy – and better educational opportunities – dictate that village children be bussed to the nearest town to be educated en masse. Peering through a cracked window, I see only sad abandoned blackboards, sad abandoned desks.

Gertrude passed this way in 1907, riding across from Akköy, a gruelling eight-hour haul even with the stunning scenery to distract
her. Her diary is hazy about her route, but since she wrote that Mt
Latmos was 'always opposite' it's fair to assume that she traversed
the lake's southern side, so bypassing the boulders and the legend
of Endymion. It was very empty countryside, she noted, a world of
olive trees and red-roofed olive presses; and 'all the world [was]
Muslim', a striking change after the ostentatiously multiracial
coastal settlements with their churches, mosques and synagogues.
Surprisingly, she opted not to pitch camp amid the bee orchids but
instead pressed on to Mendelya, the modern Selimiye, a little further
south.

There she passed the night in the home of a local baker, which
was 'about the first house of the village'. But Selimiye has grown
exponentially and, with no idea where to start looking, I head for
the teahouse, where the seniors agree that there was once a bakery
in the upper part of the village. Vague directions centre on the Ab-
dülfettah Ağa Cami, a cute little work of the last years of the eighteenth century, its capacious porch supported by strong stone
capitals, its shoe rack lined with wooden clogs. I pass a happy hour
or so admiring the gracious old houses in the surrounding streets.
They are built of stone; they have wooden shutters; they have
sweeping pantiled roofs and soaring brick chimneypots, none of
which has saved them from being abandoned in favour of stripped-
down modern apartments. In front of one particularly fine specimen
whose upper storey sports an undulating loggia I encounter a semicircle of women stirring a cauldron of rice, a treat for a young man
about to start his military service. Nearby, storks are tending their
nests while a child chants, 'Leylek, leylek, leylek var [There's a stork,
stork, stork]' as her mother and grandmother no doubt did before
her. According to Gertrude, storks had been nesting near the home
of her hospitable baker; given that they return to the same spot
every spring, these might be descendants many times removed of
the same birds.

Finally I round a corner and find myself facing a crumbling *han*,
its tiled window-frames a throwback to Byzantium, its topknotted
gateway mirroring those in nearby Muğla. The *han* is derelict, but

as I turn away I spot a large serving hatch sliced out of a wall. I pop my head through and, astonishingly, find that it's a bakery. Or at least it was a bakery, since it too is now derelict. Then I catch on the breeze the mouth-watering aroma of fresh bread. I turn another corner and there's the Dadaş Fırın (Bakery). Tradition is tenacious in Turkey and it looks as if there has been an unbroken habit of baking on or around the same spot for more than a hundred years. Inside the modern bakery, women are sliding loaves out of the oven on long wooden paddles. A man sidles up to me. 'I'm the boss,' he says cheekily. 'We don't usually need so many workers. Just on market day. The rest of the time I head out to Bodrum for the beach, sleeping, the girls …'

Of her accommodation Gertrude wrote that 'people below were making a bonfire which flickered into my room and a muezzin [was] watching from the minaret'. I've found a mosque of a suitable age. I've found people cooking over a fire. I've found bakeries old and new. Circumstantial it may be, but I walk away happy that I've identified the right area. Ballpark anyway.

9

From Exiles to Oligarchs

BODRUM–IASOS–MİLAS

'I rowed across the bay and walked over the isthmus…then I walked and rowed back.'
Letter, 18 April 1915

'What Turkey needs is a blue plaque system!'

Thus proclaims Marion James, a friend bumped into unexpectedly while we were both exploring Bodrum Castle. Now we're sitting on the waterfront, peeking out through the palms at a glorious line-up of wooden *gület*s with her friend Charlotte McPherson and local journalist Chris Drum Berkaya. We're a jolly little multicultural gathering of Westerners – two Brits, an American and an Australian – all of us long-time residents of Turkey, and Marion's comment has been sparked by Chris pointing out what was once the Pasha's Palace, the sea-facing home of Atlantic Records founder Ahmet Ertegün. Amid Bodrum's full-on opulence its discreet simplicity struggles for attention. In any case Bodrum has Cevat Şakir Kabaağaçlı, the famous Fisherman of Halicarnassus, to celebrate. Plus it has the Liberace-lookalike crooner Zeki Müren. They may not qualify for plaques either, but the fisherman merits two busts and Müren a terrifyingly large statue that looms over the eastern bay. Between them, they are as many dead celebrities as a town so overwhelmingly preoccupied with the present can handle.

The Bodrum I've come to is a Bodrum of outdoor chandeliers and mosaic-encrusted tree trunks, a Bodrum of cacophonous nightclubs and oligarchic yachts that dwarf everything around them. But it's also a Bodrum that seems ambivalent about its beauty, the very thing without which the modern celebrities for whom the chandeliers are hung would not come, yet at the same time the very thing that stands in the way, in the form of pesky conservation regulations, of all-out rampant development. The traditional little whitewashed houses with their upturned eaves and discreet windows, each placed just high enough up the slope from its neighbour to leave their view unimpeded, are still hanging on in the town centre, but on the outskirts the usual concrete is running riot, albeit dressed up in whitewash, albeit pinned down kicking and screaming to two storeys. The town has the feel of a frisky pony barely prevented from bolting by a determined rider.

The odd thing really is that Bodrum should exist at all. For in Gertrude's day it was not in Bodrum that the wealthy itched to build their villas but in nearby Güllük, then Kuluk, where the Whittalls of Smyrna kept a summer home. Bodrum was swampy and malarial, cut off from the rest of the country. It was a place where meagre livings were scraped by diving for sponges rather than by opening headline-grabbing restaurants. Right into the 1920s it remained a place of exile. Fisherman Cevat Şakir Kabaağaçlı may have won his laurels by coming up with the prototype Blue Cruise, but he was also a convicted parricide, not quite the all-round good guy his tree-hugging, tourist-friendly image might suggest.

Bearing Bodrum's isolation in mind, it's astonishing to find that Gertrude even made it here in 1907. It's true that desire to see the ruins of the famous Mausoleum of Halicarnassus would have exerted a strong pull. But the actual mechanics of reaching what was then little more than a village would be unimaginable to the hordes of modern tourists who are whisked in air-conditioned buses from the airport to their hotels and back again each summer.

An invitation from the Whittalls was enough to ensure that Gertrude would make it to Bodrum. From Selimiye she had ridden south to Milas, where she swapped horses and pressed on down to Güllük. There the Whittalls supplied her with a boat, and a boatman named Mustafa, who guided her first to the ruins of ancient Iasos. It was 'very romantic landing below the rock in the old port guarded by a Byz[antine] tower', she wrote. I, however, must content myself with the long and winding bus ride to a village revelling in a tongue-twister of a modern name, Kıyıkışlacık, where the remains of an old Graeco-Roman settlement sprawl across an isthmus. Since Gertrude's visit the 'indistinguishable ruins' have been clarified – there's a dear little bouleuterion, a stretch of wall that once enclosed a Byzantine fort, and an agora so self-assured that I half expect to see chiton-clad women strolling around it. But of the theatre there's no sign, the stones having been shipped to Constantinople for reuse, as

Mustafa explained apologetically. On the hill above the harbour the walls of a castle built by the Knights Hospitaller are studded with large stone lily pads that turn out on closer inspection to be the salami-sliced drums of columns presumably hauled from a redundant temple. The Byzantine tower still stands in the sea, where it probably served as a lighthouse.

In the loneliness of Iasos my unexpected appearance triggers massed disorder. Jewel-coloured goldfinches rise from thistles in twittering clouds of indignation. Iridescent flies briefly vacate cowpats, then settle straight back down on them once I'm gone. Cats starved of affection come flying through the air to greet me as I clamber up to the necropolis that Gertrude described as resembling 'a small city'. Even a man sunning himself with a newspaper over his face leaps to his feet in embarrassment as I pass.

Gertrude regretted not having walked as far as what looks like a bell tower but may have been a lookout post where dues could be collected from travellers. Buried amid the reeds nearby, I find a sunken pool with a spring bubbling up inside it. It's a Hekate kind of place, I think, a place to dream of oracles, of magic, of secret get-togethers beneath a full moon. Then the bus comes rattling down the road to return me to the prosaic reality of Milas.

Ever the early riser, Gertrude continued south to Bodrum as 'the stars [were] just beginning to pale' the next morning. There followed a six-hour sea crossing that carried her round the island of Tarandos (Salıh Adası) and down into a place she called Durranda.

Here I rub up against a problem that is to repeat itself intermittently. Writing at the start of the twentieth century, Gertrude used the place names then current in Anatolia. Since then, however, there have been several waves of place-name tampering aimed at Turkifying the country: in 1916, when the Young Turk Enver Paşa sent out an edict that all non-Muslim place names should be changed; on Atatürk's watch after major Kurdish rebellions; and again in 1957, under Adnan Menderes, when an estimated twelve thousand villages were renamed. Most places of archaeological interest have a classical name as well as a successor Turkish one, so ancient Herakleia has become modern Kapıkırı, as Iasos has become Kıyıkışlacık. Like other Western writers before her, Gertrude was most at home with the classical names, and most such dual identities are well known. Minor changes in place-name spelling are also easy to decipher: Budrum for Bodrum, for example. The toughest nuts to crack are the name changes applied to the smaller settlements of the least historic interest. In such cases the most failsafe remedy is to wait until one arrives in the vicinity of the puzzle, then call on the knowledge of a villager sufficiently grizzled to remember the original name.

But now Durranda has me stumped. No one I speak to in Bodrum can recall such a name; nor do I strike lucky on the Peninsula. It's Chris Drum Berkaya who persuades me that it must have been somewhere near Torba, on the north coast, where the Bodrum Peninsula narrows to its thinnest point. Given that Gertrude walked from Durranda to Bodrum, she must surely have opted for the line of least resistance. In her diary she noted that there was 'no town [there] but a kahweh [teahouse] by the sea and through the rich land scattered houses'. Durranda, then, must have been at most a hamlet. If it was indeed at Torba, then every trace of it is now buried beneath the modern seaside resort.

From the hills above Durranda Gertrude gazed down on Bodrum, 'lying in its curve with the Castle of St Peter standing out in the middle'. In those days the castle was an active prison and to visit it required special permission, hastily granted, from the startled *zabita*. From the walkways between the towers she stared down into the courtyard and saw 'all the prisoners walking about'. No doubt amongst them there must have been the odd hardened murderer, the odd determined thief, but many of the men she saw would have been prisoners of conscience, guilty only of using words that offended the sultan. In any case, the castle's days as a prison were drawing to an end. In 1915 the French bombarded the harbour in front of it and the prisoners were transferred elsewhere. In 1925 the Fisherman of Halicarnassus started off on the three-month trek from Ankara, where he had received a custodial sentence for a second, essentially political, offence. When he finally reached Bodrum it was to find that no one had thought to report the prison's demise to the authorities in the new capital. Rather than return him to Ankara, the police found him a small local house to live in. Merely being exiled to Bodrum was regarded as punishment enough.

It took Gertrude some time to locate the site of the mausoleum, the burial place of the Carian king, Mausolus of Halicarnassus, that had been one of the Seven Wonders of the Ancient World. This was hardly surprising. Even after excavation there's little more than a large hole in the ground for a modern visitor to admire; by the time Gertrude found the spot, the English archaeologist Charles Thomas Newton had already shipped back to the British Museum everything of interest that he had found there in the 1850s, including the remains of giant statues of Mausolus and his wife that are believed to have topped the tomb.

Nor was Newton the first person to have raided the ruins. The friezes that he sent back to England had been embedded in the walls of the castle, suggesting that it was the Knights Hospitaller who had removed them as they prepared to build their fortress in the early-fifteenth century. The town's other ancient relics haven't fared much better. On the hillside above the tomb, Gertrude inspected the ruins of a theatre now severed from the lower town by a ferocious highway. She also mentioned the remains of a temple unknown to me. 'Let's go and look for it,' suggests Chris, and off we trot, scurrying through the back streets of Bodrum and past the stumpy Doric columns that mark the site of the agora. Soon we're edging along a drainage channel, then hanging left into a car park. It's not a promising location, squeezed in between the highway and an ad hoc rubbish dump, and I can feel my spirits start to sag. Still, with Chris striding ahead of me and an enthusiastic street mutt trailing behind, I double-back beneath the car park and there, sure enough, acting as a support for it, is a corner of the lost Temple of Mars.

'Look how beautifully the stones fit against one another,' Chris purrs, and in the dying light of evening she runs her hand down them as if caressing the face of a lover.

Before King Mausolus laid the foundations for Halicarnassus, the inland city of Mylasa (modern Milas) served as the Carian capital.

Passing through it in 1907 Getrude found horses for hire in unexpectedly short supply. The Murray's *Handbook* gave a five-star rating to the pleasures of riding around Turkey:

> There are three modes of travelling in the East. The most agreeable and comfortable is that adopted by a Turkish gentleman. It consists in having several native servants, tents, and one's own horses or those hired from a katerji [muleteer]. The speed is slow, the caravan rarely accomplishing more than 20 to 25 m[iles] a day. The tents are pitched in the evening, near some running stream or some pleasant gardens. The provisions, either brought from the last resting-place, or purchased in the village near the night's encamping ground, are cooked near the tents, and your servants spread your carpets, prepare your pipes, and mix your sherbets. This mode of transport ... commands the most respect, enables the traveller to see and learn most, and causes him least fatigue and annoyance.

It was, however, silent on the fatigue and annoyance that would result should no horses turn out to be available. Luckily for Gertrude, horse procurement was a task she could delegate to her Man Friday, Fattuh, while she sped off in search of the Gümüşkesen, an elaborate marble tomb then standing in empty countryside but now the centrepiece of a small park* where old men come to snooze in the sun while their grandsons use it to perfect their climbing skills. The tomb is presumed to be the burial place of a local grandee who died some time in the second or first century BC, although its inscription is long gone along with the remains of the grandee. What makes the Gümüşkesen so special, though, is its pyramidal roof, which some believe makes it a model in miniature for the lost mausoleum.

The Gümüşkesen in Milas; 1907

On the outskirts of Milas, Gertrude noticed a 'fine ruined castle on the hills', presumably Beçin Kalesi, seat of the Emir Menteşe, the founder of the Menteşe Beylik, who had, like the Byzantines before him, chosen to build his fortress on a rocky plat-

---

*The park has since been requisitioned for a museum. At the time of publication, work on it had been halted.

form offering reassuring views of movements on the plain below. No doubt at the forefront of his mind was the recent defeat suffered by the powerful Selçuks at the hands of the Mongols at Kösedağ in 1243, a defeat that had resulted in the splintering of their empire and the creation of myriad regional *beyliks* just like his own.

In a condensed telling of Anatolian history all complications are ironed out in favour of a simple linear narrative in which the Greeks and Romans were followed by the Byzantines who were followed by the Selçuks who were followed by the Ottomans, the long lead-in culminating triumphantly with the founding of the Turkish Republic in 1923. It's a version that works fairly well on a national level but breaks down rapidly at the local one. All over the country monuments intrude speed bumps that insist on greater complexity. The Sesotris carving near Izmir, for example, with its hint of the Hittites in the Aegean, or the Lascarid Palace in Kemalpaşa recalling a time when not one but two exiled Byzantine emperors vied for possession of the throne. The Menteşe Beylik is another such complication, seemingly so remote from modern Milas yet perhaps not quite as remote as one might assume.

I pass a pleasant evening in a hotel, shelling peas on the balcony with the owner's wife. The entrance is just steps away from a trio of pastel-painted houses that look as out of place amid the high-rises of Milas high street as a tower block would look amid the ruins of Beçin. They're detached houses with gardens, two storeys high, with steps up to the front doors and wooden shutters, the sort of houses that might look more at home in a Budapest suburb, which is not, as it turns out, that surprising, since they were built in the 1930s by a Hungarian architect. Nearby stands one other detached house, its garden awash with roses. It's the prettiest of the group and behind it lies a suitably pretty story. For the house was built in 1927 for his French wife, Marie Suzanne Dugenie, by Murat Salih Menteşe, one of the last members of a family that could trace its ancestry back to the thirteenth century. Madame Menteşe died in 1976 but the couple's initials still link arms affectionately in the wrought ironwork of the gates, a faint reminder of a dynasty whose name was once feared in these parts, some five and a half centuries after the Ottomans descended on Beçin to boot it out.

10
In Brigand Country
ESKİHİSAR–ALABANDA–AYDIN
'It's not all beer and skittles, travelling, you know.' Letter, 6 May 1911

After a night rendered wretched by mice running across her pillow, Gertrude was keen to be on her way at first light. Now at last she was heading into the interior of Anatolia, leaving behind every last trace of tourism and Levantine commerce. Now she would ride across the countryside accompanied at all times by her faithful manservant, Fattuh. With the wind roaring 'like the very devil', she headed over Aksivri Hill on 'the most beautiful road in the world', arriving eventually at Eskihisar (Old Castle), near the small modern town of Yatağan.

Like all good friends, Gertrude and I sometimes have our disagreements and Eskihisar is a case in point. Perhaps weary from her sleepless night, she dismissed it immediately as a 'miserable little Moslem town', whereas I adore the Ottoman settlement that grew up around the ruins of ancient Stratonikeia and long to have been able to stroll its cobbled streets, gazing into its small shops, perhaps pausing to buy a pastry in the days when it still teemed with life. Alas, that can never be because the Eskihisar that Gertrude visited is no more, its residents having been relocated to new concrete homes in nearby Yeni Eskihisar (New Old Castle) when a lignite quarry opened in 1983. Now the streets are silent but for birdsong and I can only imagine the village women in their floral *şalvar*, spreading middle-aged bottoms perched on borrowed chunks of Roman masonry carefully positioned beside their front doors.

In Eskihisar all the elements for residential beauty congregate in perfect harmony. Everything, from the cobbled streets to the ruined temples to the houses, was constructed from local stone. The mosque is of wood and stone. So is the village teahouse. And everything is shaded by giant plane trees, natural umbrellas as lovely in autumn when their leaves are brown and crumbly as in spring when they're sprouting and green. Gertrude was guided around by a 'cheerful party' who showed her a gateway set in the wall, presumably the northern entrance to Stratonikeia, in front of which a long stretch of flagstoned road has since been uncovered. He also showed her the platform of the bouleuterion, where she noted the 'Moslem patterns carved on it, the cypresses etc,' that have survived undamaged until today. Oddly, she didn't mention the striking gymnasium with its curvy outer walls that must surely have been visible with the now vacated village houses facing it.

Elated, I sit down in the teahouse and strike up conversation with its owner, Dursun. He lives in Yeni Eskihisar, he starts off, his family having moved there when he was twelve. That's as far as he gets before my taxi driver butts in. He's a nice enough soul, but way too full of himself, the sort of man who insists that his passengers admire his credentials whether they want to or not. Nothing will do but that I listen to his reminiscences of his days as a driver for the local mayor and inspect his multiple press cards. I grind my teeth in irritation as Dursun vanishes into the café, taking with him his memories of the living village.

★ ★ ★

I'm planning to stay in Yatağan, a town seemingly named rather bloodthirstily after a dagger although more probably after a boat of that name owned by the Fisherman of Halicarnassus. Gertrude, however, headed for the village of İleina, now the small town of Turgut, accompanied by her 'delightfully cheerful' Armenian Catholic Man Friday, Fattuh, a muleteer from Aleppo who knew 'every inch of ground from Aleppo to Van and Baghdad' and was always ready 'to cook my dinner or push a mule or dig out an inscription … and to tell me endless tales of travel as we ride'. Today, a thermal power-plant looms over the road to İleina/Turgut, hinting that I should expect another Yeni Eskihisar, a place devoid of a past. Instead, the walls of the İlyas Bey Cami turn out to be stippled with ancient masonry, inverted Greek inscriptions testifying to how what had once been precious had come, by the fourteenth century, to be regarded as mere building material. Wooden shutters and tall brick chimneys distinguish the houses of the back streets. Carmine snapdragons splash colour against their whitewashed walls. A stream trips musically past front doors.

At İleina Fattuh bumped into Jamil Bey, a swashbuckling brig-and-hunter and friend from Aleppo, who, by chatting up the local lord, Tahir Ağa, secured them lodgings in 'the best house in the village'. The most obvious candidate for his house is a newly restored *konak* (mansion) with stone-built living rooms and a wooden upper gallery. A banner flops across the padlocked gate, showing off Osman Hamdi Bey's *The Tortoise Trainer*. From this bolthole, Hamdi Bey had excavated the remains of the temple to Hekate at nearby Lagina in the 1890s.

At the teahouse in the main square I cast around for the oldest men present, then strike up a refrain that is to become so routine that I almost wish I could record it: 'Hello. I wonder if you could help me. Just before the First World War there was an Englishwoman who was travelling around Turkey on horseback taking photographs. I'm following her travels. Her diary says that she stayed in your village. At Tahir Ağa's house. I wonder if you know where that might have been?'

Clicking *okey* tiles beneath a grape arbour, the seniors take a few moments to recover from the shock of this female invasion of their male-only space. But once they've unruffled their feathers they confer briefly and nod their heads. 'It's the Osman Hamdi Bey Konağı,' they agree.

'Does anyone have the key?'

'You'd have to go to Yatağan for that.'

Their words are promising if hardly conclusive. But wherever it was that Gertrude actually stayed, her diary provides a glimpse of the rough justice that pertained in the remoter outposts of the early-twentieth century Ottoman Empire. In the middle of the night, Jamil Bey brought a 'notorious' bandit armed with a Martini rifle and revolver back to the house for lack of any more suitable lock-up. But his triumph was short-lived, Fattuh admitting later that Tahir Ağa had offered Jamil money to let the brigand go – 'and no doubt he would [let him go], martini and revolver and all, for as Fattuh said he got no pay probably and he must live'.

In the morning Gertrude strolled to Lagina with Tahir Ağa and Jamil.

There she found the shell of a temple dedicated to Hekate, the mysterious deity of dogs, witchcraft and ghosts. The rites of Hekate were normally conducted at junctions where three roads came together; nowhere in Asia Minor other than at Lagina has a built temple to her cult come to light. Gertrude's party found the site 'all overgrown with brush wood', but I'm greeted by the magenta splash of a Judas tree in blossom beside the remains of the propylon, the monumental gateway erected in the first century. The propylon is in much better shape than the great temple, whose friezes Hamdi Bey had shipped to Constantinople for his new museum. The marble pavement looks as if some indecisive giant had scrunched up an unsatisfactory letter, then changed his mind and tried to smooth the creases out again. The actual culprit, as ever in these parts, was an earthquake.

The beauty of Eskihisar comes from the intricate blending of ancient and (relatively) modern with a modicum of help from nature in the shape of the glorious plane trees. In contrast Lagina's beauty lies in the exquisite interplay of marble columns and an unspoilt pastoral landscape with soft blue hills rolling away into the distance. Great tits call to each other from the poplars. Blackbirds shrill out throaty warnings. Lizards scuttle from my shadow. There's nobody here to share the loveliness. As I leave, I disturb a pair of turtles copulating on the stone rim of an ancient pond as no doubt turtles have been doing for the last two thousand years.

The road between Yatağan and the small town of Çine to the north tracks the route of the Çine Çayı, the old Marsyas river, through some of Turkey's most extraordinary scenery. Gazing out of the bus window at huge smooth-sided boulders faintly reminiscent of the Dartmoor tors in England, I entertain myself with a game of fantasy I-Spy. I spy piled-up stone frisbees. I spy dolmens. I spy Easter Island statues. And all the time I yearn to be Gertrude, riding along with her 'ragged and very cheerful muleteers and … equally cheerful and ragged boy', pausing to admire the ancient aqueduct that used to supply Alabanda (modern Araphisar) with its water. A picture of that aqueduct adorns the wall of my hotel, but the receptionist finds himself suddenly busy when I enquire as to its whereabouts. The İncekemer aqueduct, it turns out, vanished beneath a reservoir when the Çine Dam opened in 2010.

At first sight Gertrude was no more taken with Araphisar than she had been with Stratonikeia. 'A miserable little hamlet', she wrote, where she might have been forced to camp had it not been for Jamil, who cajoled 'a charming old Turk' named Hacı Salih Efendi into providing her with a house to herself – 'barring fleas'.

Affection for *The Tortoise Trainer* has elevated archaeologist Osman Hamdi Bey's name into one of the best loved of late Ottoman history. Hamdi Bey excavated not just in low-lying Lagina but also high on the mountainside at Nemrut Dağı in the middle of the country. But a love of archaeology was something that ran in the family and here at Alabanda it was little brother Halil Ethem who called the shots, digging up a section of what is thought to be the agora as well as a hillside temple which he believed to be dedicated to Artemis but which is now thought to be the shrine of Zeus Chrysaoreus.

Bumping into a latterday Hamdi Bey from Aydın University, I grill him over the absence of signs of life in the village – there's no teahouse, for example, let alone a shop.

'Only the old people are left,' he explains. 'The young are all gone. To Bodrum. To Aydın. To Muğla. They don't come back. If they want to get married, there are no women who will come and live here. There's no work, only farming, and who wants to do that?'

It's a story I hear repeated all over Turkey, a story of the pell-mell emptying of villages, leaving them as glorified old-people's homes, waiting rooms for an empty future. In Gertrude's day perhaps eighty-five per cent of Anatolians lived in villages, a figure that has now been inverted. Even the reassuring claim that around twenty-five per cent of the population still lives in villages is deceptive since it fails to mention the age of those hanging on. Unless something changes, the rural Anatolia of the 1900s is on the verge of eradication.

The Gertrude who headed on from Araphisar to Aydın was a completely different Gertrude from the wide-eyed tourist of her first visits to Turkey. By now she was an experienced desert traveller and in 1907 her sights were set on exploring little-known corners of Anatolia. There would be no more trains until she reached Karaman, so it was as well that she had more or less grown up on horseback. She had already kicked the Victorian custom of riding side-saddle and her long skirts had been replaced by ankle-length culottes with a modesty panel that dropped demurely when she dismounted. The riding, then, was no great challenge, but to get to Aydın her party needed to cross the Çine river, no easy matter in April when the river was at its widest. 'We crossed in a buffalo waggon, leading the horses,' she wrote. At the old Gyroba, now Eski Çine, there was no carriage available to carry her on to Aydın, so she simply switched horses and rode on until they came once again to the even more formidable barrier of the Meander that had caused such delay near Miletus.

It was as they approached the ferry that she stumbled on one of the grimmest encounters of her Turkey travels. By the roadside she saw a young girl guarding the body of a dead gypsy from feral dogs while her brother (presumably) walked back to their village to seek help. The ferry operators refused to carry the body across the river without the family's permission. 'We cd do nothing,' Gertrude wrote sadly.

Even with the rivers behind them, the onward journey was hardly plain sailing. On the far side of the Meander they found the road 'swamped' and had to 'ride by an old paved road through deep mud and rushing water'. What's more, whenever a camel train heading for Aydın passed they had to abandon the path altogether and 'plunge into the mud'. It was dusk before the little party finally trailed into Aydın, where she was forced to take a room in a 'dirty khan' opposite the station.

The *hans* (or khans) were the urban equivalents of the great caravanserais, the semi-fortified waystations that had dotted the country since at least Lydian times. The Selçuk sultans had modernized them and formalized a system that guaranteed travellers free bed and board every few hours' ride along the main trade routes. Even inside the cities such munificence continued. It was a system that endured into the modern era, vanishing only as cars rendered stabling redundant and hotels evolved to meet demands for greater privacy and comfort.

The Murray's *Handbook* was blunt about what to expect:

[Khans] are large buildings surrounding a court, in the centre of which is usually a mosque or fountain. The rooms are small, generally opening upon a galley above ... but they never offer any further accommodation than a clean mat. On the traveller's arrival, a key of the bare and unfurnished apartment allotted to his use is delivered to him ... the first thing to do before entering his room is to have it well swept, cleansed and supplied with plenty of water ... The gate of these khans closes soon after sunset ... Though these khans are chiefly occupied by travelling merchants, still strangers from all parts of the world ... may lodge in them gratuitously, and nothing is expected on their departure but a small payment to the Khanji, or innkeeper.

Given such limitations, Murray's strongly advised tipping a local to provide alternative lodgings. Until now, Gertrude's connections had guaranteed better beds, but, with no alternative presenting itself in Aydın, it's easy to imagine the stir that would have been caused by the arrival at the *han*'s gate of a fine foreign lady with her baggage of books, crockery and fold-out bath, unheard-of indulgences in a place catering exclusively for the needs of men.

Gertrude had come to inspect the remains of Tralles, the original settlement overlooking the modern city that perches on a platform amid olive groves and poppies. Hamdi Bey had put in digging time here too, but she had little to say about the ruins, her enthusiasm dented by the sort of hiccough with which modern travellers who forget to charge their phones will sympathize: her camera-bag turned out to contain only exposed film, making it impossible to record her visit.

Aydın itself is relentlessly modern, the centre another long canyon of shop-cum-apartment blocks, the oppressive concrete dominance barely softened by the palm trees tripping down the median strip. This is a town that suffered terribly in the aftermath of the First World War as first the invading Greeks and then Turks intent on revenge rampaged through it, vanquishing almost everything that was old. It would be easy to visit the city and leave again believing that its past had been obliterated. On the quiet, though, bits and pieces do still live on, in particular the delightful small complex around the Cihanoğlu Cami that Gertrude called simply the 'stucco mosque'.

It's here that I bump into a man whose parents must have been more than usually enthusiastic about their neighbourhood to judge from his place-particular name: Aydın Cihanoğlu. He's standing on the steps leading up to the mosque that overlooks its delightful fountain and encircling medrese. By Turkish standards this is a new mosque, only built in 1756, but Gertrude's photos reveal that by 1907 it was already showing its age, the stucco peeling away to expose the brickwork of the portico, weeds pushing skywards from the roof of the şadırvan (ablutions fountain). To admire the baroque flourishes inside the mosque itself she had to approach the chief dervish at the local *tekke* for the key.

Now all is new and restored and impressive again. Aydın is standing on the steps and, mistakenly assuming him to be the imam, I linger to share my enthusiasm with him. But: 'No, I'm not the imam,' he says in surprise. 'I'm the English teacher at the medrese.'

Chuffed to be able to give it in English for a change, I launch into my habitual explanatory spiel: 'Before the First World War there was an Englishwoman who was travelling around Turkey on horseback taking photographs. I'm trying to follow her journey …'

Aydın's face lights up. 'Ger-ter-ood!' he exclaims.

Out of the blue in this most unlikely of places I've bumped into the first Gertrude fan of my journey, and the next thing I know I'm being rushed into the medrese with promises of çay.

Our conversation gets off to an awkward start since Aydın is convinced that Gertrude and Agatha Christie were great friends. 'Her husband was an archaeologist in Iraq,' he insists as a look of doubt crosses my face.

Simultaneously we reach for our phones and fire up Wikipedia/Vikipedi. No, we agree, there's nothing to suggest that they would have met; Max Mallowan did indeed start digging with Leonard Woolley at Ur in 1925, by which time Gertrude was living in Baghdad, but he didn't meet his crime-writing wife-to-be until 1930, four years after Gertrude's death.

With that misunderstanding out of the away, Aydın asks the question that has always troubled him as a man brought up in a world where women rarely ventured anywhere unaccompanied. Namely, 'Did she really travel alone?'

'She was certainly the only woman in her party and the only Westerner. But she always had her manservant, Fattuh, to put up her tents and cook for her, as well as a local *kavass* and guide and perhaps a couple of muleteers too.'

Then it's my turn for the questions. 'Is the *tekke* still standing?' I ask.

'No, it was closed in 1925.'

'But sometimes the building survives?'

'No, it was completely torn down.'

'Well, what about the *han* then? She says that she stayed in a *han* near the station. Would that have been the Zincirli Han?' (This being an imposing, recently restored building in the back streets that looks as if it's about to reopen with craft workshops and cafés in place of the camel stables.)

'Probably. But this was a main trade route so there were three or four small *hans* here then.'

We move on to the history of Aydın itself, skirting round the contentious and destructive peri-Republican period. 'There's something I don't understand,' Aydın says. 'She talks about the remains of churches at Tralles. But surely it was a pagan site?'

I explain to him how in the post-Roman period Tralles became the seat of a Byzantine bishopric, then he explains to me how the town was relocated to its current position and renamed Aydın after the Aydınıd dynasty that held sway here after the Selçuks.

At this point the conversation starts to dry up. Aydın is a notoriously humid city and, with the promised *çay* having somehow failed to materialize, I can feel sweat trickling down my back and pooling round the waistband of my trousers. I stand up to say my farewells and we pose self-consciously beside each other for photographs. With a grin I pull on the straw hat bought in Izmir but rarely worn. 'You are the new Gertrude!' Aydın laughs, 'And in a hundred years people will read your book and follow you too!'

11
Claudius the Chippendale
APHRODISIAS

*'The town must have been distinguished above all other places for the
elaborate beauty of its architecture.'* Letter, 24 April 1907

In 1958 a thirty-year-old Turkish Armenian photographer named Ara
Güler was sent to Aydın to take pictures of the opening of the new
Kemer Dam. On the way back his driver risked a shortcut and soon
they were hopelessly lost in the countryside. 'Then I saw a light,' he
told a reporter. 'It was a teahouse. We went inside and there were
men playing games. They were lit by lamps. Gradually my eyes grew
accustomed to the dark and I could see that there were no tables. In
place of tables there were just the capitals of columns. They were
playing dominoes on them.*'

The two men had stumbled upon the tiny village of Geyre, south
of Nazilli, and in the morning Güler took haunting black and white
photographs of the villagers, who lived in and around the remains
of Graeco-Roman Aphrodisias, a city that took its name from the li-
centious cult of the goddess, its big selling point in ancient times. For
romantics those photographs, weaving together the distant and the
more recent past, have an almost incomparable allure. Here, beneath
a vast plane tree of aching antiquity, two bearded men in flat caps
and baggy overcoats sit cross-legged on a marble bench whose dol-
phin-shaped armrests would have been carved almost two thousand
years before they were born. Here, in front of the village teahouse,
the uneven wooden struts of a portico balance on upturned capitals
that must have been borrowed from a temple. Here, men press olives
into basins scooped from ancient marble while women stir their
pekmez (grape molasses) in an open sarcophagus oblivious to the
weeping women carved along its side.

Almost at once old Geyre's days were numbered; three years
later, serious excavation of the site began and the villagers were

---

*Translated from Erman Ertuğrul's report in *Arkeofili*, 16 March 2015.

moved away. Güler is often credited with having discovered Aphrodisias, although the French traveller Charles Texier had made drawings of it when he passed through in 1864. A French railway engineer named Paul Gaudin had also carried out tentative excavations in 1904–5 during the extension of the Smyrna–Aydın railway to Denizli. Soon afterwards, Gertrude headed east to visit the site, hiring a private train compartment to carry her from Aydın to Kuyucuk, where it doubled as her accommodation for the night, then rising at dawn for the seven-hour horseback ride south to Geyre. It was a strenuous journey which nonetheless took her through pretty countryside where the 'pomegranates [were] putting on their russet dress'. Later, though, the cultivation dropped away, and she commented on the 'scantiness of the population and the laziness of those people that there are. One rides for hours over beautiful well watered country without seeing an inch of ploughed ground.'

Through the windows of the bus from Nazilli I note not only that cultivation seems to have picked up but that its nature has completely changed, with plastic polytunnels for strawberries thrusting out in all directions. As the bus glides to a halt, a tractor-drawn trailer sits waiting to convey visitors to the ruins. With a snort that could hardly have been outdone by Gertrude herself, I turn my back and stalk off down the road.

Arriving 'tired and hungry' after her long ride, Gertrude headed straight for the shattered ruins of the Temple of Aphrodite, where she settled down for a picnic lunch. From a perch on a fallen capital, I soak up the view that would have greeted her. Looming on the horizon is Topçambaba Dağı, the ancient Mt Cadmos, its summit as snowy now as it was a hundred years ago. Between it and the ruins the landscape unrolls in a palette of greens – ivy, acid, emerald and jade.

Gertrude wrote lyrically of Aphrodisias, describing the ruins as 'some of the most beautiful in A[sia] Minor ... the town must have been distinguished above all other places for the elaborate beauty of its architecture; every doorway was covered with scrolls of fruit and flowers with birds and beasts entwined in them, every building was crowned by a frieze, Artemis and her maidens chasing the stag through garlands of acanthus, Victories spreading their wings round the capitals'. But the conversion of the temple into a church towards the end of the fifth century makes it hard to decipher what remains. Only the soaring columns hint at the temple's immense size and superiority.

Aphrodite is famously the goddess of love, whose birth from the sea foam was so memorably depicted in Botticelli's *Birth of Venus* that her image in the popular imagination will always be that of a naked woman with one arm raised to hide her breasts while the other trails locks of corn-coloured hair across her pudenda. In thus portraying her, Botticelli was continuing a tradition that can be traced back to the fourth century BC, when the Athenian sculptor Praxiteles created two carvings of the goddess, one clothed, the other naked, the naked version ending up on a plinth high on the hillside at Knidos in the far southwest of Caria. Inland Aphrodisias was very far from Knidos both geographically and culturally. When the Christians completed their takeover of the site they made sure to destroy the cult statue of the goddess from the temple. Later archaeologists made a curious find in the walls of the replacement church. There, treated as so much building rubble, they found a headless, armless statue of Aphrodite. But for all the Christian fear of the cult, this was an Aphrodite bearing no resemblance at all to the shapely goddess of Praxiteles or Botticelli. This was no naked Aphrodite, the personification of female beauty. Instead it was a crowned and veiled Aphrodite wearing a robe so stiff and densely woven that it revealed no more of her figure than the mackintosh of a Turkish matron. This was an Aphrodite, in fact, who more closely resembled the statues of Kybele / Artemis uncovered at Ephesus, evidence of the portmanteau nature of Graeco-Roman religion in which the cults of the conqueror were blended with those of the local pantheon, in this case giving rise to an Aphrodite born of Kybele, the Mother Goddess, just as surely as the Artemis of Ephesus.

Gertrude's ride round the ruins took her past the remains of a huge bathhouse paid for by Hadrian and down through the strung-out agora, marshy then as it still is today. From there she ascended the hill that conceals the theatre from the agora before trotting down a colonnaded street to the Sebasteion and back past the tetrapylon to the remains of the silent stadium. But she arrived too soon to marvel at what are the greatest treasures of the modern site, the sculptures from the Sebasteion, the temple to the Roman emperors reincarnated as Olympic deities. For it was only in 1979 that archaeologists trowelling through mud at its base uncovered the carvings that had once covered its facade, a panoply of reliefs tracking the ancestry of the early emperors back via Hercules to the great Aphrodite herself. To a modern eye the sculptures present a startling celebration of male nudity, with Claudius in particular tossing his cloak into the air like a Chippendale bringing his act to its triumphant conclusion. But it was only female sexuality that fired up the zealots. Such masculine exhibitionism left them unmoved.

By the time Gertrude was through with the sightseeing, it was too late to ride back to her comfy Kuyucuk train carriage. Instead, she lodged at the local *han*, in a 'tiny room separated by a rough wall of planks from 30 or 40 muleteers and camel drivers ... It was quite empty however and I put my camp bed in and was as happy as possible. One wall was all window – I closed half of it with a shutter when I went to bed.' Through that window she could watch the villagers unloading camels, boiling eggs in earthenware pots and saying their prayers on an outdoor platform. Entranced by the romance of it all, she strolled out once more to relish the sight of the great temple ruins bathed in moonlight. Then she returned to her bed, where 'no number of talking, smoking muleteers could have kept me awake'.

12
Moustaches and Marsyas
LAODİKEİA–PAMUKKALE–DİNAR

'..the calcareous falls of the stream over the rock very curious.'
Diary, 24 April 1907

April in Turkey can be an unforgiving month. Waking at dawn, Gertrude could already hear the sound of rain beating down on the roof of the Geyre *han*. A weaker mortal might have decided to take a day off from travelling. She, however, insisted on saddling up for the long ride back to Kuyucuk. For much of the way heavy rain lashed down and at one point they came upon a camel sucked so deep into the Meander mud that only hump and head were visible. Beside it a woman stood helplessly wringing her hands. 'We could do nothing,' wrote Gertrude.

By the time they arrived back at the station they were drenched. Nothing daunted, Gertrude paused only for a quick change of clothes before arranging to have her private carriage steam eastwards as far as Goncalı, the railhead for the ruins at Laodikeia, which she reached just as dusk was starting to fall. In the curious way of travel in Turkey she immediately bumped into an old family friend, the military historian Professor Henry Spenser Wilkinson. It was 'grey and cold', she wrote in her diary, so they did little more than take a quick turn around the ruins, noting the twin theatres and the ghostly outline in the grass of what was once one of Asia Minor's lengthiest stadiums, before retreating to dine together and catch up on all the news.

Unlike the Laodikeia of the early twentieth century, which amounted to little more than heaps of rubble, the Laodikeia of today is addictively attractive, a posterchild for what can be done to re-create a lost city. Over many years as a guidebook writer I've watched archaeology students painstakingly piecing together hundreds of tiny fragments of mosaic and marble, and stared in amazement as cranes were used to heave tumbled capitals back onto lofty columns, the 'left a bit, right a bit' adjustments rendered so much harder when

Travertines at Pamukkale; 1907

the marble to be realigned weighs not much less than a bear. The western theatre lacks the drama of Bergama's, not least because most of its seating was shattered by an earthquake towards the end of the fifth century. But at midday, in the utter silence that falls when the workmen down tools for a communal lunch, I could swear that I hear its Roman audience stirring to life again: the jabber of Latin as families search for their places, the swish of tunics as they're folded into cushions against the stony chill. As I wander towards the exit, a little owl stares down from a realigned architrave. Its look is nothing short of scornful.

Anyone who has ever spent long months travelling overland will remember those days when nothing seems to go right: the mattress is lumpy, the soup cold, the weather lousy, the locals unfriendly. Hardy as she undoubtedly was, Gertrude was nonetheless just as prone to such off-days. Unfortunately one of them was the day she had set aside for exploring Pamukkale, pictures of whose glistening white travertines beckon from modern travel agency windows countrywide. Rising before dawn, she was soon crossing swords with a 'roguish innkeeper' who tried – and failed – to overcharge for her horses. A 'misty drizzle' blighted most of the morning, and she was succumbing to a cold, brought on no doubt by the soaking endured on the way back from Aphrodisias.

From Goncalı it was a one-and-a-half-hour ride to Pamukkale, where she arrived to find the travertines, the 'calcareous falls of the stream over the rock', shrouded in mist, robbing her of the chance to appreciate a hillside naturally decorated with pools of turquoise water cupped in basins of snow-white calcium. 'Very curious' was her perfunctory brush-off. Of the extensive ruins of Hierapolis, the ancient spa town on the plateau above the travertines, she commented only on the 'imposing' bathhouse, the friezes that once formed the theatre's backdrop, and the necropolis where, on such a doomed day, she searched in vain for a particular tomb.

It's drizzling again when I reach Pamukkale, so I take refuge in a café beside the newly created lake beneath the travertines. There I bump into Ali Tak, who's hanging about in a way that suggests he's something of a fixture. Ali is one of that curious band of men who have convinced themselves that longer is better in the moustache stakes. Accordingly, he sports a version so extended that it conceals his upper lip then ripples out beyond his cheeks into rat's-tail extensions that he has wound round and tied up like parcel string above his panama hat. He's wearing a white suit, a red cravat, blue-tinted glasses and a ring on every finger, a get-up that gives him the air of an Elvis impersonator gone bad. I eye him from a distance, before steeling myself for a chat.

Ali is a hangover from the hippie days. He's sixty-five and hails from the small town of Çivril, where he would have fitted in about as well as one of the sultan's eunuchs. Like many Turks of his vintage who work on the fringes of tourism, he carries around a dog-eared notebook full of accolades and fading Polaroids, every one of which he longs to share with passers-by. 'This was me when I was twenty-five,' he says, showing off a picture of a perfectly ordinary young man with a perfectly ordinary length moustache. By the time he turned sixty-three, though, a belated mid-life crisis had set in and the moustache had blossomed to one and a half metres in length. Now he assures me that it's a full two metres long, a Guinness World Record of some sort.

With difficulty, I unglue myself from Ali, then head off to walk to Hierapolis. To protect the delicate travertines shoes must be removed, and walking barefoot over the calcium crust feels like tiptoeing through finely crushed seashells then crunching down on sole-shredding gravel. I picture Gertrude in the rain, gloomily removing her boots and stockings to paddle in water the temperature of a tepid bath, the rain soaking through her blouse. But her reward was to have witnessed the travertines in the days when the water flowed freely, before it had to be carefully corralled to ensure that at least some of the pools would match up to the hype. Her photos show them softly steaming. She's alone in the landscape, a luxury routinely available to early-twentieth-century tourists, entirely lost to those of a century later.

Much has happened at Hierapolis since Gertrude's hasty visit. In 1907 the great second-century bathhouse stood in ruins, and the theatre was in a parlous state, its seats cracked, its *skene* (stage backdrop) reduced to rubble. Now it has been splendidly restored, and, from what would have been the equivalent of the gods, I gaze over it to the village of Pamukkale, not so much as a glimmer in a developer's eye back then. On the hill behind me St Philip is believed to have been crucified upside down for the crime of converting the local proconsul's wife to Christianity sometime around AD 80. It was not until 2011 that the remains of his tomb were uncovered amid the ruins of a church nearby.

Later, Gertrude retreated to her train carriage to spend a quiet afternoon with a book. She had planned to visit the remains of Colossae, an ancient city to which St Paul may or may not have written a letter, but the strain of an intense month of travelling was about to catch up with her. 'Very ill in the night, pains, sick and faint,' she recorded in her diary. Fattuh nursed her with tea and a hot-water bottle, but even though the Honaz Dağı (Mt Honaz) behind Colossae looked 'quite splendid' from the train window, she was forced to concede the need to rest. And so she sat back and no doubt reflected on what she had already seen on her long journey as the train puffed on via Acıgöl to Dinar, the ancient Apamea-Celaenae, where, to her delight, she found 'an excellent little inn ... kept by a charming old Greek fairy godmother Marigo Cubic', just what the doctor would have ordered.

I, on the other hand, find the Grand Akdeniz Hotel, which is as unaccustomed to foreign female guests as was the hotel in Soma. They try hard here, offering a laundry service and thereby lifting spirits that have taken a nosedive from the dreariness of its back-of-a-car-park location. But on my way out to explore I make the mistake of leaving my key at reception. When I return it has vanished. I must have taken it with me, the receptionist insists. Mysteriously, it later reappears in someone else's bedroom. No explanation is forthcoming.

Aydın, Denizli, Dinar. All these towns that straddle the course of the Meander have suffered dreadfully at the hands of modern developers. Photographs of old Aydın and old Denizli show narrow streets lined with lovely wood-and-stone houses, their upper storeys jutting so far out that neighbours on opposite sides of the street would have been able to exchange knitting tips with only the slightest of raised voices. Gertrude's photos depict Dinar as similarly attractive, its flat-roofed houses top-heavy with wooden verandas, its streets prettily cobbled. But in 1995 an earthquake wiped out almost anything of historic interest. There's nothing left to suggest immediately that this was once a place of great splendour, an oasis watered by the sources not just of the Meander but of the Marsyas, the İncirli Suyu and the Ilıca rivers as well. Here, at a vital transit point between the Aegean coast and the Anatolian interior, the Persian king Xerxes built himself a palace in the early fifth century BC; then, as the century drew to an end, his grandson Cyrus created a splendid hunting lodge too. Xerxes and Cyrus were military men whose route was followed by that best known of all military men, Alexander the Great. It was only with the coming of more settled centuries and the growth of importance of Constantinople that Apamea-Celaenae started its long decline into the slumber of today.

With the exception of flowers, Gertrude rarely evinced much interest in the natural world, so I'm surprised to find that while in Dinar she took time out to track down the source of the Meander. In the morning I set off at a brisk pace, hoping to do the same thing myself. It's a sunny day, with delicate white poppies brightening the fields, and I'm soon walking along the banks of what I'm sure from its width must be the Meander. Pretty soon though my spirits are once again flagging as it becomes obvious not only that I won't be able to find its source on my own but that I won't be able to find any of the other sites mentioned by Gertrude on my own either. The sight of rusting exercise machines standing unused amid a patch of weeds sends me scurrying back to the centre just as the town's tannoy system stirs itself to announce the imminent coming of the Sixth International Marsyas Culture, Art and Music Festival. This brings me up with a start. In Greek mythology Marsyas was a satyr who had the audacity to claim that he was a better flute player than Apollo. For such hubris the punishment was extreme and revolting. Marsyas was flayed alive inside a nearby cave and his skin nailed to a tree, hardly an event, one would have thought, to merit immortalization with a cultural festival.

I have one last stab at finding my way around unassisted.

'I wonder if you could point me towards the ruins of Apamea?' I ask the hotel receptionist.

'What, the Apamea Restaurant?' is his discouraging response.

With a sigh I head for the town hall, where the tourism folk are busy preparing for the festival. I'm directed to a man who might be able to help me, but, 'You need Mehmet Özalp!' he counters immediately. And so it is that I find myself in the book-filled offices of a diminutive lawyer whose skin emits a yellowish aura as if he's been pickled in tobacco. He's a John Grisham, small-town type of lawyer, I think, sitting behind his desk in a somewhat forlorn quest for business in a town where crime and criminality must be passing rare. On the shelves behind him rest statuettes of the forces that guide him: the predictable scales of justice and the less predictable Marsyas. But Mehmet Özalp is as much the living embodiment of Dinar's history as Zeki Acem is of Söke's. I outline my venture to him and at once he's all action.

'This is what we'll do,' he says and reels off a list of the sights of Dinar as he ushers me through the office door and locks it behind us.

'But what if someone has a legal problem?' I stutter, this being Friday around noon.

Mehmet Özalp in his Dinar office; 2015

'*Boş ver!*' he says, that wonderful Turkish phrase that can mean anything from what of it, or it doesn't matter, to let's just leave it, shall we?

We head towards a beat-up old car that hardly suggests legal business is booming in Dinar. 'We'll go to the station first,' he tells me.

I hadn't initially realized just how much of my travel time was going to be taken up with examining the cute little stone-built stations of early-twentieth-century Turkey. But Gertrude was a woman who made the best of whatever transport options presented themselves. Horses? Fine. Even camels when nothing else was available. But where there was a nice comfortable train to be used, then, like any other sensible traveller, she (or rather Fattuh) was first in the ticket queue.

As we near Dinar station Mehmet points out roadside railway lodgings. 'The hotel would have been there,' he says, although there's no sign of it now. In any case he's keener to show me the hidden treasures of the station itself. Embedded in the wall, a carved hand clasps the folds of a toga, a last reminder of a local with the wherewithal to finance a memorial. Then there's the drinking fountain installed by the Ottoman Railway Company in 1892. 'Look more carefully,' Mehmet insists, and I see that the back incorporates a Latin and Greek inscription alerting the twin-tongued people of Apamea to a new 365-day calendar to commence henceforth in January.

Mehmet is clearly wasted on the law, I think, as we roar off – insofar as his car is capable of roaring – in search of the acropolis of Apamea, where Gertrude had examined the remains of an early Byzantine church. Leaving Mehmet to enjoy the fifty-first smoke of the day, I follow a dirt track up the hill and emerge beside the foundations of the sanctuary, the only recognizable feature in a confusion of tumbled masonry from which the forlorn posts of a gateway jut up at incoherent angles. Gertrude's soon-to-be digging partner, Sir William Ramsay, had recorded a theatre at Dinar, the remains of which eluded her. When Mehmet points them out, the reason becomes obvious, for the theatre of Apamea is a homeopathic structure rendered down to the mere memory of a building; I can make out the curve of the *cavea* cut into the hillside, I can just about piece the last remaining stones into a seat or two, but that's it. Ditto the stadium: a five-layer-deep slice of seating not much longer than a banqueting table, half-buried in grass, surviving miraculously within metres of a busy road junction.

As we drive around town I piece together snatches of Mehmet's life story. Born in Dinar, he was sent to a boarding school in Antalya before qualifying for a place at Istanbul University's Faculty of Law. But when his father died prematurely Mehmet was forced to return to help support his family until eventually the municipality agreed to pick up his fees as their own future lawyer.

'Is there much crime in Dinar?' I ask, anticipating a negative response.

'Oh yes,' says Mehmet brightly. 'Theft, drugs ...' Why, Dinar is a veritable hotbed of bad behaviour.

We're pulling to a stop before a murky fishpond. In her diary Gertrude had mentioned 'Ramsay's Laugher and Weeper', which she assumed to have been the source of the İncirli Suyu river. 'Wrong!' retorts Mehmet. 'This is Ilıca, the old Terma, and this is the true Laugher and Weeper.'

He then proceeds to recount a story second only in repulsiveness to that of Marsyas. In the days of Apamea, he says, there was a king who wanted to discover the source of the Ilıca stream. Accordingly, he summoned three seers, two of whom told him what he wanted to hear: that the source was at Pınarbaşı. The third, however, begged to differ. The source was at Sandıklı, he claimed. Assuming that the man was lying, the king had pins pushed into his eyes to blind him. But, unlike Apollo, he came to regret his cruelty. When he asked how he could make amends, the poor man said: 'This water has been the reason for my eyes becoming blind. Make two eyes here and let this water always flow as warmly as my tears.' The penitent king then installed the twin-arched outlet that still stands at the back of the pond, forever afterwards known to the locals as the Laugher and Weeper.

Gertrude was taken to look at the Düden stream, the source of the Meander river, and reported that 'the marshy source ... lies in an amphitheatre of ... bare hills'. Mehmet assures me that it has since dried up and rushes me instead to Suçıkan Park, where water cascades down a rockface and into a duck pond that forms the centrepiece of a popular picnic spot. Here he has established an ethnographic museum housed, in the Turkish way of things, in an outsized building completely concealing the cave behind it where, according to the myth, poor Marsyas was robbed of his skin. By now, like Gertrude, I'm beginning to muddle my Marsyas river with my Meander, so it's a relief to head on to the true source of the İncirli Suyu, where a much scruffier, far less popular tea garden has grown up around another small pool. Mehmet and I sit down and order çay. While we're waiting I glance at the wall behind him. And there to my amazement is a reproduction of Gertrude's photograph, taken on 26 April 1907, with Fattuh standing beside the pool in completely unspoilt countryside. 'Subject of Photo: Fettah (sic)', it says, and, 'Photographer: Gertrude Bell'. For the first time on my journey I've come face to face with a memorial to Gertrude in the most unlikely of locations.

13

Into the Turkish Lake District

BURDUR–SAGALASSOS–EĞİRDİR

'I don't suppose there is anyone in the world happier than I am or any country more lovely than Asia Minor.'   Letter, 28 April 1907

From Dinar Gertrude was prepared for a long ride across country to Konya, but already a fractious retinue of muleteers and baggage handlers was proving hard to control. Hoping for an argument-free canter into Burdur, she sent most of them ahead to prepare a campsite, while she herself took the slow route there via Uluborlu. The peach and plum trees were in blossom, storks were nesting on every lofty perch, swallows were circling in the sky above her. To the south of Lake Burdur the mountains retained their crusting of snow, but it was a 'delicious day, sunny … quite hot for a few hours'.

After eight hours of riding with just a brief break for lunch, Gertrude rounded the east end of Lake Burdur ('bitter salt it is and very blue'), dropped down into the town of the same name and headed straight for the *han* in search of coffee. There she signed up the *han*-keeper to show her the delights of Burdur, which amounted, he assured her, to three churches and a dried-up spring.

Today, the heart of historic Burdur is marked by a clumpy clock-tower. Built in 1942, it replaced an earlier model felled by an earthquake in 1914. The devastating tremor flattened almost all the houses and killed some thirty thousand people, and I'm thinking about it as I perch on a stool in a dusty nearby shop stuffed full with sacks of wheat and flour. I've come here with Mehmet Bedel, the director of Burdur Museum, and his friend İsmail, it having become apparent after a quick stroll around town that I have no more hope of finding Gertrude's churches on my own than I had in Dinar of finding the source of the Meander. Luckily for me, business in the museum seems about as slack as business in the Dinar law centre, so here the three of us are, taking up all the available space in the shop, while Mehmet calls the history-loving former mayor on his speed-dial.

'Take this down!' he instructs me. 'Two storeys. Wooden. With a courtyard. Tayarın Hanı.'

The old *han*, it seems, used to stand on the site of the modern town hall, and in all likelihood it's there that Gertrude would have found her helpful *han*-keeper. Then Mehmet asks about the three churches.

'There were four of them,' the ex-mayor insists and proceeds to reel off their locations.

Only the first church is remotely recognizable now. Gertrude had described it as a basilica with a small apse and an open narthex, a description that matches the Kavaklı Kilise, a cookie-cutter church, one of hundreds that went up all over Anatolia in the 1830s after the Ottoman law prohibiting the religious minorities from building new places of worship was abolished. There was a school there, she wrote in her diary, but by the 1970s that had given way to a cinema, according to Mehmet, whose expression grows wistful as he recalls the screenings of his childhood. The church is about to become a natural history museum. Within weeks it will echo with children's voices again.

Fate has been less kind to the three other churches, all of them wrecked by the quake and long since torn down. On one site we find a car park. Another church became a school and then a military base; its plot is now empty. The third stood, we conclude, where there is now a small garden beside an apartment block.

Mehmet waylays a man emerging from it. He looks to be about forty. 'Do you remember a church here?' he asks him.

'*Valla, bilmiyorum* [Well, I don't know],' says the man in typically uninquisitive Turkish style.

'It would have been here in 1907 ...'

A look of panic crosses the man's face. '*Valla, abi,* I wasn't alive then!' he exclaims and we can see him thinking, oh no, they're going to come here and rebuild that church and take my apartment away from me.

Back at the museum, Mehmet, İsmail and I run through our discoveries. We may not have seen much of what Gertrude did, we conclude, but we've certainly had a bit of fun in the trying. Then Mehmet opens a drawer and pulls out a small flute called a *sipsi*. He raises it to his lips. Despite its tiny size it emits a screech not unlike bagpipes. On his computer he plays a video of himself cutting reeds from beside the lake, then whittling them into the shape of the pipe. It's a craft he learned from his father, a craft he's passed on to his sons.

★ ★ ★

Gertrude passed a wonderful night at her campsite, where 'the sun went down very red over the lake', but her presence threw the local authorities into a tizzy. Time and again she was visited by individuals who begged her not to sleep in the 'wilderness' and to instead take up residence in their 'fleay houses'. When she told them that she was planning to ride on in search of the ruins of ancient Sagalassos all hell broke loose. No, she couldn't do this, they assured her, 'because of the snow and the mountains and I don't know what'. Fattuh was terribly scornful. 'What sort of soldiers are these? They fear the cold and they fear the mountains and they fear the rivers – perhaps they fear the rabbits and the foxes.'

In any case the naysayers had reckoned without Gertrude's determination. In the morning she was on the road by six, riding hard over mountains and through valleys until, after four and a half hours, she reached Ağlasun, where the village was, then as now, 'full of worked stones from Sagalassos'. Then '[we] climbed and climbed till I thought no town could ever have been built so high', until finally she arrived at the remains of a settlement built by the mysterious Psidians.

Unlike Gertrude I need vehicular transport to reach Sagalassos, which means hanging about in a *lokanta* until the last lunchtime *pide* has been served and its owner can career-swap to taxi driving. A silent man, keen for my *kuruşes* but less keen on what he must do to earn them, he drops me off at the main entrance on another of the days when I'm full of envy for Gertrude. She had ridden down rather than up to the site, coming out 'suddenly into the theatre, the cavea half full of snow'. How wonderful that would have been, I think, to stumble on the ruins almost without warning and see them spread out below you with not another living soul in sight. Even better, the spring rain had spurred a swift flowering of bulbs. A blue mist of crocuses and scilla softened the landscape, a mesmerizingly beautiful sight.

Like everywhere else in these parts, Sagalassos was battered into submission by earthquakes. The theatre may be clear of snow when I climb up to it, but the *skene* looks tossed about as if by a titanic playwright spurred to rage by a scathing review. I sit down at the back and gaze out in wonder. The warlike Psidians always picked eyrie-like locations for their settlements, Termessos, near Antalya, a city that even Alexander couldn't conquer, being the prime example. But Sagalassos could certainly give it a run for its money, the steepness of the site and the soaring mountain backdrop giving it an air of impregnability even today. Scrambling out over the fallen stones, I'm delighted to find a copy of Gertrude's photograph of the snow-filled orchestra posted in front of the theatre as if she were laying claim to it as her own.

But the story of modern Sagalassos is a story of water and the imaginative decision to set in play again the monumental Roman fountain that presides over the central forum and would still have been lying in pieces in Gertrude's day. Trailing a hand in the water and gazing up at the replica statues now adorning it, I feel again that same fleeting, hair-standing-on-end sense of the presence of the living Romans as in the theatre at Laodikeia. I see a matron, portly and weary, carefully putting down a basket of vegetables, then leaning in to scoop water over her face. I see two senators, scrolls in hands, pausing to chat to each other, the thunderous sound of falling water camouflaging the content of their conversation. Finally, I see a child climbing up, cupping his hands, taking a drink, then running back through the forum and out to play with his friends.

With a long ride to Isparta still ahead of her, Gertrude could only linger at Sagalassos for a few precious hours. Then up she went, through 'a little crick in the very top [of the mountains] – we call such things roads in Turkey'. Fattuh had gone ahead to scout out a campsite and had found one at the edge of a vineyard above the town, looking towards Eğirdir. There she settled down for the night, freezing out those figures of authority who came calling with yet

Ruins of the theatre at Sagalassos; 1907

more words of discouragement. She was in her element. To her mother she wrote of the 'excellent beauty of my camp ... I don't suppose there is anyone in the world happier than I am or any country more lovely than Asia Minor.'

That happiness was marginally diminished by a dawn visit from the local military commander, intent on learning her plans. I rub up against a different snag. My first choice of hotel is full. So is the second. So is the third. Only then do I start to notice the abnormally large number of young people milling about on the pavements. Turns out I've arrived on the weekend of the sporting equivalent of the Glastonbury Music Festival except that rather than camping out in leaky tents the sports lovers are occupying hotel rooms. All of them. Even those in the highest price brackets.

Cursing, I hop on the bus to nearby Eğirdir, only to encounter the overflow from Isparta already filling its best beds. Which is how I come to find myself as the clock hits ten crawling into a pension that regards the provision of toilet paper, let alone breakfast, as a luxury.

★ ★ ★

Of course everything looks better in the morning. While Turkey's Lake District may indeed boast many lakes, most of its towns are some way inland from their shores. Only Eğirdir sits slap-bang beside the water with a backdrop of mountains doubling down on its beauty. Gertrude may have been an experienced horsewoman, but even so it must have come as quite a relief after the gruelling ride from Burdur to Isparta to be able to trot quite comfortably along the flat road leading into Eğirdir. 'Very lovely with the Aghlasun D[ağı] dropping straight down into the lake and the town clinging to its side,' she wrote.

Having left Fattuh to pitch camp on the eastern edge of town, where Lake Eğirdir peeled back far enough to leave space for their tents, Gertrude walked back into the centre to examine its monuments. This is one of those rare and magical moments when time seems to have come to a complete stop. Mostly, even when I manage to identify the buildings she saw, they have been much knocked about over the intervening century. But here in the heart of Eğirdir lurks a secretive little hollow that will forever be the Middle Ages. Steps lead down into a courtyard. To the right stands the Hızır Bey Cami, to the left the Dündar Bey Medrese, still retaining the capitals carved with angels with their 'heads broken off' that she noted.

On the far side of the square a detached minaret sits above the gate leading out in the direction of the castle, still 'much ruined, only the towers of the gate and the walls on either side remaining'; her photographs show water reaching the base of the walls before the land in front of it was reclaimed for a highway. Here she went in search of a boatman to take her to Yeşilada (Green Island), the larger of what were at the time two islands completely cut off from the mainland. How wonderful it must have been, I think, to be rowed across that lake then, with only the squawks of the seagulls and the splash of the oars dipping in and out of the water for company. I, on the other hand, have to speak very firmly to Eyüp, my fisherman-turned-boatman, before he'll accept that I really don't want to circle the island to the accompaniment of a Tarkan golden oldie.

Time may have stood pleasingly still at the Hızır Bey Cami, but on Yeşilada it will always be the 1970s in the least appealing of ways. Until 1923 this was an island almost entirely populated by Greeks. After the population exchange forced them out a dejected silence fell over their abandoned homes. Then the tourist prospectors moved in, ringing the island with a concrete palisade of pensions. Yet behind that screen there still exists a pretty village, a provincial take on Istanbul's Büyükada. But where Büyükada's wooden houses bestow come-hither looks on their visitors, their Yeşilada equivalents glower from behind a coating of *saç*, the tinplate nailed onto crumbling facades to stop them from disintegrating.

Gertrude found two churches on the island. The first, Hagios Stephanos, was 'merely a square with a dome and an apse built out', but before 1923 it had been the focus of an annual pilgrimage, and, across from it, she noticed an *ayazma*, or sacred spring. Standing in an overgrown dip with some loose stones in the bottom, I half-manage to persuade myself that I can hear the sound of running water. In a nearby garden a man is hoeing vegetables.

'I'm looking for the *ayazma*,' I call to him.

'*Abla*, you're standing in it,' he calls back. 'But it dried up years ago.'

A more curious absence is the church of Hagios Theodoros. I walk around the tiny island, then I walk around it again, but there's absolutely no sign of a second church. What there is, however, is a small, roughly circular park in front of what was once the local school. Not a single identity-clinching stone survives, but instinct insists that the church must have occupied this dominant position looking straight over the lake. An elderly man with more bristles on his chin than teeth in his mouth is chatting to two visiting Istanbullus. I wait for a gap in the conversation, then cut in to ask about the church. Yes, he confirms, this was where it used to stand. Then he launches into an anecdote about Hagios Stephanos.

'The patriarch came from Istanbul for a visit,' he says. 'It was packed with people praying and there was lots of music, so I thought it would be all right to dance' – at which point he mimics something reminiscent of the hornpipe – 'but someone called the police and they came and chased me away. Said I was a nuisance.'

As for the *ayazma*, which locals regarded as a cure-all for sickness, the man sneaks a sly smile. 'My grandfather asked the Greeks why they brought their children there and that's what they said. But some of them still died anyway, so I don't know …'

For most of the next day Gertrude's party rode northwards around Lake Eğirdir, sometimes following a road in the making, sometimes diverting into the foothills in search of obscure churches and inscriptions. But, as the day wore on, the baggage train fell further and further behind, especially after one of the horses tumbled into the water. The plan had been to make it to the top of the lake by evening, but their schedule had slipped so badly that instead they set up camp in front of the Ertokuş Han, a Selçuk caravanserai dating back to 1223. Her photographs show an idyllic setting beside a picturesque ruin just inland from the water. Gertrude wrote in her diary that she took a dip in the lake. The photos show Fattuh stirring the cooking pots while she bathed.

Alas for Ertokuş though. The walk from the main road starts off full of promise, a cobbled path speckled with poppies running past a stone farmhouse whose owners stare boggle-eyed at me as if I was a reincarnated Selçuk warrior. All around cluster the apple orchards that are the pride of Eğirdir. But then I reach the *han* and find that it has been restored, a euphemism for effectively rebuilding it and then installing all the tacky, atmosphere-destroying paraphernalia of modern tourism: steps, lampposts and a ticket office. But there are no tourists here, so the ticket office is closed and there's a padlock on the gate. Weeds are pushing up through the natty new terracing. It takes me five minutes to circle the exterior, seething silently throughout.

14

The Road Less Travelled

YALVAÇ–LAKE EĞİRDİR–KİRELİ–EFLATUNPINAR

*'I was riding my new horse which was as wild as a hawk and
as timid as a lizard.'* Letter, 7 May 1907

At the back of the site of ancient Antioch in Psidia a curved wall of
rock is pierced with a line of square holes that would once have held
the beams supporting the roof over a semi-circular portico. Here, it
was thought, there once stood a temple to Men Askaenos, a god associated with a moon cult that can be traced all the way back to
Mesopotamia.* Like the Kybele-like clothed Aphrodite of Aphrodisias, Men is a reminder of the ancient beliefs that held sway in Asia
Minor in the remotest past. At the same time the remains of the Au-
gusteum, a temple to the Roman emperor in his deified form that
was built right in front of it, are a reminder, like the Sebasteion, of
the way in which all these local gods were eventually subsumed into
the pantheon of the conquerors.

But it's not the echoes of prehistory that attract such visitors as
make it to Antioch in Psidia these days. Instead, most of them come
in search of reminders of St Paul, who, with St Barnabas, passed
through the town in AD 47 on the first of his missionary journeys to
Anatolia. Paul is believed to have preached to the Jews in the local
synagogue on more than one occasion, apparently with enough success for a church to have been established in the town. Ultimately,
though, the locals took against him, as the Ephesians were also to
do. The odds are high that he was subjected to a punishment beating
before being ejected from the city.

Walking around what Gertrude called 'a very fine site', I'm struck
by how little survives of what was once a flourishing settlement on
the main military route to Konya. The great temples, the marketplace, the theatre, the bathhouses, the monumental fountain, even
the walls, all have been reduced to little more than foundations on

*Sir William Ramsay later identified the site of the temple to Men six kilometres
east of Antioch in Psidia.

which tiny lizards sunbathe. Yet the reason is familiar. In her diary Gertrude reported that 'all the big stones have been carried away [from Antioch] to Yalovach and the people were digging out and carrying away still more'. To judge by the walls of the Devlethan Cami in nearby Yalvaç, that quarrying habit must already have been well established by the fourteenth century; the mosque's window-frames reveal a magpie's nest of marble offcuts presumably purloined from the site.

With black-headed buntings and blue-grey nuthatches hopscotching ahead of me I wander round the ruins, hoping to find either the synagogue or the church dating back to St Paul's time. The remains of the church are probably buried beneath what came to be known as the Great Basilica, which may itself have stood above the old synagogue, but the Antioch expert Sir William Ramsay, the man with whom Gertrude was to work at Binbirkilise, believed that it stood beside the much smaller central church. It's while reading these conflicting opinions on the interpretation boards that I start to feel irritated on Gertrude's behalf. Ramsay is regularly referenced. So is Cornish-born Francis Arundell, a chaplain in Smyrna who penned two books on the ruins of Asia Minor. But of Gertrude's visit there is no mention, despite her having been one of the very few Western women to venture so far into the interior in the early twentieth century, battling her way against clinging mud and drenching downpour in conditions almost unimaginable today.

Yalvaç is the modern reincarnation of Antioch in Psidia, and beneath the giant plane tree, said to be 1,200 years old, that forms the centrepiece for a collection of much loved teahouses I sit down to reread Gertrude's diary. What a shock her presence must have been to the locals in this out-of-the-way spot is immediately apparent. In the ruins of Antioch she reported 'great plagues of little boys' bothering her, and even in the town she was soon 'terribly plagued by the people who followed me in crowds'. Luckily, *çay*-drinking at the Çinaraltı teahouse is too enjoyable for anyone to bother plaguing me and I'm left in peace to study an extraordinary description of the northeast corner of Lake Eğirdir.

Ramsay had asked Gertrude to try and identify an ancient site beside the lake where every September pilgrims were said to celebrate Mass in a cave. Trotting along the shore, she eventually came to a place where 'the rocks drop down steeply into the lake' and where there was 'a great natural arch some 15ft high through which glistens the blue water of the lake'. Spotting a cave nearby, she scrambled up and found a slab that looked as if it might have been a sacrificial stone belonging to a time before Christianity when this would have been a shrine to 'Artemis of the lake ... a Psidian deity rebaptised by the Greeks'.

All this was exciting enough, but then, spotting an offshore island that no other Western explorer had visited, she pressed on around the shore until eventually at Gaziri she found three fishermen 'with a very old and smelly boat' prepared 'for an infinitesimal sum' to row her through the 'immensely tall reeds' to reach it. 'Densely populated with snakes', Hoyran Adası (the ancient Limenia) turned out to be ringed with Byzantine walls enclosing the remains of a shrine to that same Artemis of the lake. In the water she spotted a stele with a carving of a woman holding up waterskins. Keen to record any inscription, she waded up to her knees in the lake and tried to scrub it clean, 'but the slime floated back and finally I gave it up and came out very wet and more than a little annoyed'. Ever a glass-half-full kind of a gal, she nonetheless wrote home enthusiastically that 'now we know that it's there and someone can go and fish it out'.

I put the diary down and inspect my map. Clearly I'm going to need a particularly patient driver of the non-clock-watching kind. I wander up the road to the taxi rank and throw out a few feelers. Tokmacık, I say, and Kumdanlı; the Tırtars and Afşar. Then I watch the drivers' faces carefully. At first there's the usual look of panic – who is this foreigner who doesn't want to be taken to Eğirdir? But as they begin to realize that I can speak Turkish they start to relax, whereupon mayhem breaks out. Men snatch the map from me and shout at each other about possible routes. At one point someone even vaults over the wall from the neighbouring tea garden to join the melee.

The man who emerges from all this sparring with the dubious honour of escorting me around the lake is Hüseyin, a dapper little man in a buttoned-up cardigan who has taken up taxi-driving in his retirement. Our first stop is Kumdanlı, where Gertrude camped after her visit to the island and where we make ourselves known in the local teahouse. Kumdanlı is a pretty village with many houses constructed from *kerpiç* (adobe) and finished off with wooden verandas. The old mosque, too, had been a *kerpiç* beauty with a single unobtrusive minaret. In the modern way of things the bombastic new one is concrete with a soaring tinplate dome and double minarets.

In Kumdanlı, Gertrude had been eager to inspect stones described by Ramsay that mentioned an enigmatic clique of second-century anti-Christians called the Society of Those Who Showed the Sign. In one house she was shown an inscription overlooked by Ramsay and 'took a rubbing, to the surprise and joy of the inhabitants'. But in a letter to her mother she chided herself for not finding as much as she had hoped for – 'There are probably lots of things that I don't see because I don't know how to look.'

I explain about the stones to the elderly men in the teahouse and they look suitably bemused. Then the most venerable of them, clad in a woollen bobble-hat shaped like a fez manqué, pipes up. 'Yes, I remember those stones. They took them away to the museum.'

We drink a *çay*. Then we drink another. Time has always moved at snail's pace here and Gertrude described a priceless encounter to her mother:

> The barber's shop is as you know the fashionable lounge and there (Fattuh) found the Kaimakkam (district governor), the Binbashi (local military leader), the Imam (priest), the Kadi (local judge) and a few more all sitting together. In the afternoon I go to the Konak: the Kaimakkam, the Binbashi, the Imam, the Kadi etc are still all sitting together drinking coffee and smoking. An hour later comes a message…that the Kaimakkam, the Binbashi etc wished to call on me, so up they came, 6 of them, all in a serried row and sat in my tent and drank more coffee and smoked more cigarettes. It's my private conviction that that's all they ever do, any of them, and they all do it together every day. They appear to have given their advice collectively as regards the hiring of a cart for my luggage and even the buying of candles and rice, so today they have been unusually busy. I've bought another horse… in this transaction I did not seek the advice of the Kaimakkam, the Binbashi, the Imam or the Kadi.

Earlier travellers had reported the presence of all sorts of noteworthy inscribed stones in the lakeland villages, and for three days she used maps made by Heinrich Kiepert, a German geographer who had made several visits to Asia Minor in the 1840s, to seek them out. Her hope had been to supplement the maps with the local knowhow of a soldier despatched from Eğirdir to guard her. However:

> Our intercourse is confined to something like the following:
>
> Me: Where does this road go to?
>
> He: Effendim I do not know.
>
> Me: What is the name of that village?
>
> He: Effendim I could not say.
>
> Me: How far is it to so and so?
>
> He: Effendim I have not been.

Fortunately my driver is more on the ball, so on we press to Tokmacık, where she found fountains 'full of old stones' and an inscription embedded in the mosque wall. To my delight it's still in situ, a pyramidal piece, probably the apex of a Roman tombstone, curlicued flowers hemming its edges.

Hüseyin stares at it. 'This mosque is very old,' he says with the complete lack of chronological sense so common in Turkey (it was actually built in 1889). The imam nods along with him, shelving the astonishment he must surely be feeling at having a foreign woman show such interest in his out of the way mosque. Collecting himself, he presses on me boiled sweets he has no doubt been hoarding for years against just such an unlikely visitation.

With the light fading we press on. Then, without warning, my head starts to pound. For some time Hüseyin has been urging me to add to our itinerary the village in which he grew up, where he claims there's a stone that I'll love, but suddenly his words are hammering my ears, the oncoming headlights stabbing my eyes. It was somewhere in the vicinity that Gertrude felt obliged to write to her mother that 'it's very laborious being the careful traveller' and suddenly I know exactly how she felt. All I want is to get back to the hotel and lie down, preferably with a damp cloth cooling my forehead. But Hüseyin has been so good and patient with my unlikely requests that I don't have the heart to snub him.

And it's just as well that I don't because to my amazement it's in Kurusarı, the very last village we pass through, the one that didn't even feature on my list, that Hüseyin directs his headlights at a mosque wall and I see embedded in it an undamaged gravestone complete not just with an Ancient Greek inscription but also with crude carvings of a man and his wife.

'We didn't know the inscription was Greek,' says Hüseyin with a laugh. 'We thought it might be Russian.'

To have stumbled on an unexpected inscription is a very Gertrudey thing to have done and I just wish there was time to do her justice and take a rubbing. I feel like hugging Hüseyin, but, since to do so would be to wreak havoc on propriety, make do with beaming at him instead. I thank him. I ask about an after-hours pharmacy since it will be late by the time we return to Yalvaç. In the hotel I collapse onto the bed, convinced that my head is throbbing too much for sleep. When I wake up again, it's gone eleven and all the restaurants are closed. Not that I care. Hüseyin's gravestone alone more than makes up for the loss of a supper.

How could anyone who has grown up with motorways truly imagine the hardship entailed in travelling long distances in the days before proper asphalt surfacing? Even if there were no roads, one tends to think, there would surely have been perfectly viable tracks. But in Turkey, where there were hardly any all-weather roads well into the twentieth century, the sources are unanimous. Mud, they wail. Thick mud. Cloying mud. Glutinous mud. Mud that could, as Gertrude had witnessed, swallow an entire camel as easily as a snake swallows a mouse.

On her travels from Smyrna in 1907 fortune had generally smiled on Gertrude, but east of Lake Eğirdir that good fortune ran out. By the time she set out from Yalvaç on the road south to Beyşehir, she was already weary from days of riding around barely mapped countryside, camping in villages with barely edible food and berating herself for failing to record inscriptions whose locations proved impossible to identify. It was bad luck, then, that the very next day should be one on which the heavens opened and she found herself stuck north of Lake Beyşehir in Şarkikaraağaç (Karagach), 'a miserable little village with a few Roman stones and Greek inscriptions'. Absolutely nothing remained of the past prosperity suggested by its *han*, in which she bedded down despite its being 'crowded with bugs and fleas'. For the second time in the space of a few weeks she was unwell; a bout of indigestion had left her 'feeling a dog'. Fattuh attributed her pain and his own swollen eye to the 'heaviness of the air' at Yalvaç, while Gertrude was more inclined to attribute their ailments to 'the toughness of the chicken' on which they had been obliged to dine in Kumdanlı.

The *araba* (cart) carrying her baggage had also broken down, forcing her men to return to Yalvaç in search of a replacement. 'I had always been told by the authorities on the subject that that was the proper way to travel in Asia M[inor]. Now I know it isn't,' she complained. There were no baggage horses to be hired in Şarkikaraağaç, so Gertrude left Fattuh to wait for a replacement cart and rode on to Kireli, only to learn that the replacement had also broken down and a third cart was needed. By the time it arrived, Fattuh had managed to haul the second one out of the mud with the help of water buffaloes. When he finally caught up with her in Kireli, he was triumphantly leading not one but two replacements.

Such adversity cast her into an uncharacteristically bleak mood. To her mother she wrote that Turkey was:

> a melancholy land, in spite of its lakes and mountains … You leave the bright and varied coastline that was Greece, full of vitality, full of the breath of the sea and the memory of an active, enterprising race, and with every step into the interior you feel Asia, the real heart of Asia. Monotonous, colourless, lifeless, unsubdued by a people whose thoughts travel no further than to the next furrow, who live and die and leave no mark upon the great plains and barren hills – such is Central Asia, of which this country is a true part.

Kireli she dismissed as 'another miserable little hole'. I hop out of the bus there, hoping to find the *han* in which she'd lunched, and my first impression of the high street is that 'miserable little hole' might still be the best way to describe it. Unable to see anything of the slightest age or interest, I head for the teahouse to enquire about taxis. From here Gertrude had pressed on in search of a spring sacred to the Hittites at Eflatunpınar. Her route ran via Çukurkent, Yenice and a village called Munafer, but the mention of Munafer provokes only puzzled looks and an outbreak of headshaking. Mustafa, the proprietor of the local alcohol outlet, listens to my story, then breaks the bad news that taxis in twenty-first-century Kireli are in as short supply as baggage-carrying carts in the early twentieth.

'But if you can wait until 2 p.m.,' he says, 'I'll run you round myself.'

In the interim his friend Mehmet passes by and finds himself pressganged into joining the expedition. Mehmet and Mustafa are chalk-and-cheese friends. Mehmet had been a teacher of Turkish literature. Even in late middle age, with his belly pushing out the buttons on his shirt, he still sports a thick and foppish flop of steel-grey hair; in his youth he must have been quite a catch. Mustafa, on the other hand, is short and stocky with the sort of tight-packed physique that ought to denote a prize-fighter when he's actually a pussycat of a man. Appearances aside, they are united in their devotion to the old ideals of the Atatürkist Cumhuriyet Halk Partisi (the Republican People's Party or CHP), in particular to women's rights and the strict separation of religion from government.

Mehmet and Mustafa have a few suggestions for Munafer's identity and we plough doggedly on, chasing a chimera, as one by one they turn out to be non-starters. Their last toss of the dice is a village called Köşk that straddled one of the old Silk Roads, where we come upon a man named Ali Parla sifting through sacks of flour in the sun.

'You wouldn't happen to know where Munafer is, would you?' I ask in a flat tone suggesting little hope of success.

A smile flashes across his face. 'Ah, Munafer! It was my village,' he says. 'I grew up there.'

I lean out of the window and explain about Gertrude. 'She says that she stayed in a *misafir odası* [guestroom] in Munafer,' I wind up.

'Oh yes, we were very hospitable,' he says. 'We used to have a lot of *misafir odası*. Sixty of them!'

Then the story he had probably been saving up to impart to a passing stranger all his life comes tumbling out. 'The people of Munafer had a quarrel with a neighbouring village,' he says. 'Then one day they all went to a wedding in another village. While they were gone their enemies came to Munafer and burnt it down. There was nothing left. That's why my family had to come here. I was three at the time.'

He's sixtyish now, which means that this episode, if it actually happened, would have taken place in the mid-1950s. Yet even in 1907 Gertrude reported that Munafer 'looked so ruined that I thought it at first deserted till I was set upon by dogs'. She also got off on the wrong foot with a Munaferli. With no more idea where Eflatunpınar was than we had had about Munafer, she sought directions of a local woman, who sent her off on the scenic – and very muddy – route. By the time she returned, a storm had soaked her to the skin. What joy it must have been, then, to arrive and find 'my things ... set out in the most charming oda and the horses are lodged ... below me ... In the smallest village one is always the best lodged.'

With Ali Parla's directions ringing in our ears we press on, confident now of finding Munafer. Gertrude had described it as 'completely surrounded by swamps'; what we find is a glade featuring a succession of ponds, beside one of which two young men have settled down for a picnic and perhaps a puff on something illegal. Despite their disappointment at having their retreat invaded by three middle-aged Munafer hunters, they rise to the occasion in true Turkish style, conjuring extra çay glasses and divvying up the köfte they're grilling over a wood fire.

While the çay is brewing we stroll around the ponds and find huge foundation stones half-hidden in the long grass that confirm the past existence of a settlement. The youths point us towards its mosque, and we follow their directions half-heartedly along a muddy ridge before concluding that they, like Gertrude's Munaferli, are probably telling us what they think we want to hear. The tea, sipped in the leafy shade of a pond, tastes as good as the finest Darjeeling. It's as if we've stepped into a Constable watercolour transposed to deepest Anatolia.

Back in Kireli it turns out that Mehmet's shop occupies the site of the *han* in which Gertrude had lunched. It was demolished in the 1960s apparently. 'It was a lovely building, huge, with a garden,' a passer-by sighs.

★ ★ ★

With no *han* in Kireli and no *misafir odasi* left in Munafer, I continue south to the small town of Beyşehir in search of a taxi to Eflatunpınar. In Turkish Eflatunpınar means Plato's Spring, a rather unlikely moniker given its distance from the big Graeco-Roman settlements of the coast. But Plato (Eflatun) has passed into Turkish folk memory as a generic wise man whose name somehow attached itself to a spring which rises here before flowing into Lake Beyşehir. The site must have been especially important to the Hittites, who glorified it with a huge stone screen resplendent with effigies of solar deities. As Gertrude rode towards it she would have seen what looked like the soaring stone backdrop for a Wagnerian opera abandoned in bleak and lonely moorland. Despite torrential rain, she waded into the water to photograph the details. 'And so we came to the earliest record of what was probably the earliest trade road in the world and the forerunner of the Roman road, and here the clouds broke upon us in thunder and lightning and hail and rain and I saw the four Hittite kings, carved in massive stone, against a background of all the fury of the storm,' she wrote.

15

The Unlikely Romance of Konya

KONYA–KİLİSTRA–KARAPINAR

'My best friend is a dancing dervish.' Letter, 13 May 1905

In May 1907 Gertrude finally rode into Konya after a five-week cross-country journey from the Aegean. It will have been with a profound sense of relief that she checked into her first proper hotel room in weeks – I imagine her shutting the door, tossing her hat on the table, bending to unfasten her boots, then throwing herself down on the bed, relishing the feel of a real mattress beneath her back at last. The hotel was 'the best in Asia, on my honour', she wrote to her father.

Gertrude arrived in Konya remembering Celaladdin Rumi, the Mevlana, whose great work of thirteenth-century mystic poetry, the *Mesnevi*, she had read during her youthful stay in Persia. Off she rushed to pay homage at his tomb beneath its high-drummed turquoise dome. To her father she wrote that the visit was 'a real pilgrimage for I know some of his poems and there are things in them that are not to be surpassed'. The dome was 'bluer than heaven or the sea', while the tomb itself was surrounded by 'rich and sombre Persian enamel and lacquer, and on either side of him are rows and rows of the graves of the chelebis, the Dervish high priests and his direct descendants … and over each is the high felt hat of the order with a white turban wrapped round it'. The setting was charming, she wrote, 'like all Tekkiyas, with a garden and stocks and pansies blooming in it'. She admired the two 'dancing halls', although the authorities turned down her request to be allowed to view a carpet on which they claimed that Rumi had prayed. 'To my mind,' she concluded, 'the whole quiet air was full with the music of his verses', where now it is full with the haunting refrain of the *ney*, the flute associated with the dervishes, that lingers like the song of the skylark.

This was her second visit to the city, the first having been in 1905 when she had been introduced to the cravat- and pince-nez-sporting Julius Harry Löytved-Hardegg, the then German consul in Konya. The Konya of the early 1900s was a small town of just fifty thousand inhabitants with a glorious history behind it as the erstwhile capital of the Selçuk Sultanate of Rum but a much-diminished present in which it served as a distant dumping ground for those who had fallen foul of the sultan. Now it stood on the threshold of a step-change in importance. Plans were afoot to lay a railway all the way from Berlin to Baghdad, a project espoused by Kaiser Wilhelm II as a way to circumvent the British and get at the oil wealth of southern Iraq. In 1896 a standalone railway line had been constructed from Ankara to Konya; in 1903 work began on extending it as part of this much more grandiose scheme.

A Beirut-borne Dane turned naturalized German, Löytved was despatched to Konya in 1902 to watch over German interests. With too little to occupy his time, he soon turned his attentions to Konya's treasure trove of Selçuk mosques and medreses, and in particular to the handwoven carpets that still covered their floors. When Gertrude met him in 1905 he was thirty, seven years her junior, and she quickly became friends with him and his wife Grace. However, it was not a friendship that would have met with the approval of Osman Hamdi Bey back in Constantinople. Löytved was implicated in the smuggling of many precious artefacts from Konya to Berlin, eventually spurring Hamdi Bey to draft legislation criminalizing such removals.

The Löytved-Hardeggs lived in a house overlooking Alaadin Tepe, the artificial mound on which the Selçuks had built a huge mosque and palace complex. In the Alaadin Cami Gertrude homed in on the mismatch between its two wings, reasoning (erroneously) that it must have started life as a church since most of its columns were Byzantine. But it was an even more perplexing curiosity nearby that most intrigued her. Constructed in the ninth or tenth century, the tiny church of St Amphilokios had been converted into a *mescit* (Muslim chapel) before having a clocktower added to its roof. It wasn't just its higgledy-piggledy architecture that was eye-catching. By the thirteenth century the church had, like the Hittite site at Eflatun-pınar, acquired an association with Plato; visitors believed that it stood over his grave, which was said to secrete a holy oil. Passing through in the 1830s, the French traveller Charles Texier could still sketch out an obvious Byzantine church, but by 1907, when Gertrude raised her lens to it, it would have been hard to say with confidence what it was. In 1921 church, *mescit* and clocktower were demolished. Not a trace of them now survives.

★ ★ ★

Guided no doubt as much by Löytved as by her Murray's *Handbook*, Gertrude made a quick circuit of all Konya's other Selçuk remains – the İnce Minare Medrese, the Karatay Medrese, the Sırçalı Medrese and the Sala bin Atta Medrese. Their intricate

Lost Church of St Amphilokios in Konya; 1907

artistry inspired her to write that 'the domes and mihrabs are a glory of priceless tiles, the windows and the gateways a miracle of delicate carving'. But the buildings were crying out for attention: 'all are falling into ruin – have long since fallen,' she wrote, 'for the Ottoman govt is just as indifferent to Muslim traditions as it is to Greek, Roman or Christian'. In passing, she commented on the 'queer tombs … with stone walls and pointed brick roofs', the *kümbets* that ambush history-lovers as they stroll between the town's determinedly modern apartment blocks. Perhaps Lötyved also showed her the cute little Beyhekim Cami, whose wonderful turquoise-tiled mihrab was sneaked to Germany in an act of vandalism often attributed to the consul.

My much less dubious equivalent of Löytved is Nurettin Özkan, a local archaeologist who takes time out from watching over what is being uncovered during excavations for an extension to the tram to take me on a tour of the back streets in search of pre-First World War Konya. This is something of a wild goose chase in a town not much given to sepia-tinged nostalgia. Grudgingly, it accepts the need to big up the Selçuks in the interests of tourism, but of the mansions that once housed the consulates of the great powers, for example, only the French one still survives, reconditioned as a finishing school for local girls.

Nurettin leads me up the hill to visit the mosque and the military tea garden that now occupies the site of St Amphilokios. Then down we go again, circumnavigating the base of the hill along a newbie of a main road. Running parallel to it is the demoted older road, Mimar Muzaffer Caddesi, where still today a handful of disconsolate Ottoman houses cling to life, praying that a sugar-daddy will find them before the wrecker's ball. But Löytved's house is gone. Gone, too, is the hotel with a garden that was once kept by the Swiss missionary, Fraulein Gerber. On Mevlana Caddesi Nurettin points out the site of the old Ottoman Bank, a 'sort of social centre for all Konia' where Gertrude had listened to the grievances of the city's lonely exiles. The space is now occupied by a Türkcell office. It's slim pickings for architectural historians of the early twentieth century.

Later I head for the Archaeological Museum in search of a stone lion that once stood on the hill near Löytved's house. There's a lion beside the entrance, but since the angle of its paw doesn't match with Gertrude's photograph, I venture inside to be introduced to another local archaeologist, who is ensconced in a room quite as dusty as the reputation of his profession. Given Löytved's behaviour, it's perhaps not that surprising that Westerners enquiring about historic artefacts are viewed with suspicion; I'm not invited to take a seat until I have proved my bona fides by running through the names of anyone who is anyone who might ever have crossed my path. Even then a Kemalist-tinged air of suspicion hovers over our exchange. 'Why didn't you take a Turkish name when you became a citizen?' I'm asked. When the subject of the British Museum is raised, I realize I'm wasting my time. There are apparently 'many' lions in the storeroom but none that I am going to be allowed to see.

Modern Konya has a reputation as a dour and conservative city, a place where the drinking of alcohol is almost as reprehensible as murder. Not, then, a place one would readily associate with romance. But before heading back to Constantinople in 1905 Gertrude wrote rapturously of dining on the balcony of the Löytveds' home 'with Konia all mysterious under the moon – the mosque domes and the ruined citadel tower and the double peaks beyond … Konia will remain thus in my mind'. Little could she have guessed that two years later it was to be here that she would meet Dick Doughty-Wylie, the great love of her life.

Charles Hotham Montagu Doughty-Wylie, commonly known as Dick, was a soldier with a list of military achievements as long as his name. Born in Suffolk, he had joined the army in 1889 and never looked back during a career that took him to India, Sudan, Somalia and South Africa before landing him in Konya as British consul in 1906. Doughty-Wylie was the nephew of Charles Montagu Doughty, whose *Travels in Arabia Deserta* was never far from Gertrude's side. He had been married for the last three years to Lilian Adams, commonly known as Judith.

Dick Doughty-Wylie, the British consul in Konya, and his wife Judith in their Konya garden; 1907

Gertrude's first encounter with Doughty-Wylie took place over a Konya dinner table and the photographs she took of him in the garden of the British Consulate hardly suggest a dreamboat. On the contrary, with his slimline suit and straw boater worn at a rakish angle he looks less like a war veteran bearing the scars of numerous military encounters and more like a spiv on his way to the races, an unlikely spouse for the overdressed woman posing beside him. In other pictures he is simply bald and middle-aged, very far from a conventional Romeo. But what Gertrude saw was 'a charming young soldier … a good type of Englishman, wide awake and on the spot, keen to see and learn'. Later Doughty-Wylie was to recall her 'walking in covered with energy and discovery and pleasantness'. The spark was there from the start.

Theirs was to be a slow-burn romance, kindled beneath the Konya moonlight but only flaring into reckless passion after Sultan Abdülhamid was ousted from the throne and Doughty-Wylie metamorphosed into a hero who had saved hundreds of Armenians from almost certain death. Given that he was married, theirs could only be a furtive affair conducted almost entirely by mail. There were brief meetings in London and in her grandfather's house at Rounton in Yorkshire, and by January 1914 Dick was professing love quite as gushingly as Gertrude. Their last encounter took place at his London home in February 1915. But with no prospect of a wedding ring, the woman who had braved deserts and faced down the jailers of Hayyil proved unable to shake off the ingrained inhibitions of her Victorian upbringing. Her last letters to her beloved Dick reek with regret that, in failing to consummate their relationship, she had almost certainly turned her back on her last chance of a family life of her own.

I have no luck tracking down the site of the old British Consulate where they met. Nurettin thinks it may have been near the Kadı Mürsel Cami off Mimar Muzaffer Caddesi, where a fetching wooden house with red roses rambling round its eaves catches my eye. Just down the road a large church once stood over a catacomb beside the Sırçalı Medrese. Nearby a fountain inscribed with the Greek word for fish indicates that we're in what was once the Greek quarter. I imagine Gertrude strolling through it with the Doughty-Wylies, silently wishing the kindly Judith elsewhere. It's the closest I'm going to get to them.

★ ★ ★

Gertrude first arrived in Konya at a time when even the heartland of the Ottoman Empire was fracturing. Having listened to nothing but complaints about the government as she travelled around the desert regions, it must have been surprising to hear Löytved defending Abdülhamid, totting up his legacy in terms of new roads and railway lines, all achieved, he claimed, without recourse to the public purse.

I, too, have arrived in Konya in interesting times, just two weeks before a general election in which the governing Justice and Development Party, or AKP, will be seeking a third term in office. With its tidy streets and kilometre upon kilometre of factories, Konya is a town that explains the party's success. While it might not be the residence of choice for a free-thinking liberal, for a member of Turkey's fast-growing conservative middle class the city offers a dream of urban comfort and security with plentiful housing and jobs, spotless streets and money to spare for innovative projects such as the flashy new Science Centre. Today's Konya is also the constituency of Prime Minister Ahmet Davutoğlu, whose face gazes down on us from all over town. Poor Davutoğlu is somewhat lacking in the charisma stakes. Like him or loathe him, the president, Recep Tayyip Erdoğan, whom he replaced as prime minister in 2014, is a man with charisma in spades. He's also a man with a considerable physical presence; when he strides on stage to greet a crowd, he stands head and shoulders above the men detailed to guard him. What's more, he has the physique and carriage of the footballer he was in his youth. Davutoğlu, in contrast, exudes an air of chalk dust. He's a man designed by nature to be a teacher with leather patches on the elbows of his jacket. Nor does it help that those in charge of poster production have highlighted his lower lip so that it looks as if it has been rouged. The smile he bestows on us comes across disconcertingly like a smirk.

Before leaving Konya, I treat myself to a date-flavoured ice cream in a shop entirely devoted to the fruit, a favourite snack of the Prophet. The life-sized model camel that used to take up much of the interior has been ejected along with the colourful old shop facia, replaced with a tasteful but woefully dull local-authority-decreed version in brown and gold as Turkey, once a byword for a the-only-rule-is-that-there-are-no-rules kind of society, turns at speed into a culture of top-down-dictated conformists.

An election battlebus trundles past, half-heartedly pumping its message into the stale air of a safe seat. The slogans are relentlessly upbeat. The government has been in power for thirteen years and has plenty to shout about. 'We Can Go to University in Our Head-scarves' screams one poster. 'We Make Our Own Tanks Now' boasts another. The election is a battle for voters' memories. In Burdur the MHP (Milliyetçi Hareket Partisi or Nationalist Action Party) had been struggling to remind the electorate of the government's failings. 'Remember Soma', it said, and 'Remember Those With Unpayable Credit Card Debt'. But in Konya such reminders would be pointless. As Davutoğlu's face sails past on the side of the bus I glance at the women sharing the bench with me. Their faces wear a beatific look of absolute adulation. 'Our boy,' they are clearly thinking.

★　★　★

I head south from Konya with Mustafa Korasan, a taxi driver very satisfied with his life, his son a vet, his daughter married to an engineer, two apartments waiting to host his upcoming retirement. At Kilistra a row of what look like petrified organ pipes frame a ridge of basalt rising abruptly from the plain. Cut into the ridge is a village with a long history of troglodytism, its soft rock hollowed out to create houses, stables and storerooms. The interiors of the abandoned homes fascinated Gertrude: 'Nearly all have sort of divans along the walls,' she wrote, 'many, a deep niche like a fireplace, but no opening for smoke'. A local guide showed her a domed church sliced out of the rock as cleanly as if with a pastry cutter. Then, in pouring rain, the local bigwig Şakir Ağa accompanied her up nearby Alisumas Dağı so she could measure and photograph the two ruined Byzantine churches on its summit. Back in Kilistra two potential guestrooms were rejected – 'perfectly disgusting ... above stinking stables' – before a 'charming' room materialized on the roof of the *ağa*'s house, which she described as 'no more nor less than a cave ... the horses are lodged in the big vaults of it. You go in from the top climbing and burrowing down.'

In time the Kilistralıs abandoned their caves in favour of conventional homes in neighbouring Gökyurt. But now that village too is on its last legs, abandoned by all but the elderly, its wood-and-stone houses with fetching oriel windows slowly disintegrating. Şakir Ağa's name rings no bells with two men hefting straw in a backyard. Nor do they recall their houses ever having been accessible via the roofs. Tradition claims that St Paul paused to pray in Kilistra and grudgingly they point me in the direction of the cave-church most strongly associated with the apostle. I wade knee-deep through a meadow of daisies, lured by a fancy-pants facade of rock-cut blind arcading. There's nothing fancy pants about what lies behind it though – just a bare-bones rock chapel with a barrel-vaulted ceiling cloaking an illustrious history.

The road east from Konya carried Gertrude to Karapınar along a road 'as level to the horizon as it was level under my feet. It looked like an immensely wide floor made ready for some splendid spectacle.' Now poppies and newly-planted Judas trees frame fields of yellowing wheat that stretch to the horizon.

I arrive just as Friday prayers are ending. There's a clatter of walking sticks on cobbles as old men hobble away from the Sultaniye Cami, a susurration of voices as the teahouses fill with thirsty worshippers, the rasp of keys turning in locks as the shopkeepers return to their businesses in the bazaar. Arriving here in 1907, Gertrude observed that it was possible to see the minarets of the mosque long before riding along the main road which 'runs through it from nowhere to nowhere'. She was very taken with the mosque, which had been built for Sultan Selim II in 1566, noting the elaborate metalwork of the door and the striped marble of the mihrab. Most of all, though, she admired the 'huge carpet ... rolled up in one corner. It covers the whole mosque and is said to be Persian presented by Sultan Selim.'

I do my duty by the mosque, then go in search of the only other structure that attracted her attention: 'a fountain with 3 sarcoph[agi] for the water to run through, one with a carved lion on it'. An imposing fountain faces the entrance to the mosque but there's no lion. In the municipal planning department Yaşar Ali Selçuk studies Gertrude's photograph of a large dog of Kangalish appearance standing astride the fountain, then shakes his head sadly – he thinks it's buried beneath the highway. 'Turkey has so many old stones,' he says apologetically, 'and people didn't think much about history in the past.'

★ ★ ★

From Karapınar Gertrude intended to explore the Karaca Dağı, then ride across country to Hasan Dağı and western Cappadocia. Her plan had been to hire horses in Karapınar, where she was shown into the *han* to wait while negotiations were conducted. What ensued was a conversation that typified the problems faced by travellers of the time:

When I arrived I had asked if there were pack horses.

'As many as you like can be found' said the innkeeper. Presently he returned to say there were none.

Then said I 'I will take a cart to the village at the edge of the hills'.

'Most excellent' said the surrounding company. 'The cart will draw to the hills and there you will get camels.'

'Camels are to be found there?' said I.

'Many' said they.

Then arrived the Kaimakam and the Other and I explained that I was leaving at once for Salur with my luggage in a cart. They heartily approved this plan.

Over the coffee the Other let fall a remark to the effect that I should find no people at all at Salur as they had all gone up to yaila [*yayla*, the upland summer pastures].

'Then how shall I find camels?' said I.

'Effendim,' said he 'there will be no camels.'

Finally I resolved to take camels from here and after waiting for 4 hours the camels have appeared.

The Karaca Dağı is a remote mountainous area still barely mapped today. Even for Gertrude this was 'rather an adventure. No one has as yet explored the mountain. One man, a pupil of Sir W[illiam Ramsay']s once paid a flying visit … and gave a very flying account of it …I knew nothing about the whole mountain, neither where we could camp nor what we could find to eat nor nothing.' Despite its being July, a chill wind gusted along the rim of the volcanic crater at the summit. There were reports of local horse thieves, but she had 'no less than 6 men here, including the 2 camel drivers so I don't feel at all anxious'. Her tent looked out on a 'most barren plain flecked with white salt patches to salt flecked barren hills beyond. We are on the edge of the salt desert [Tuz Gölü].'

Over the next three days, with the help of a gypsy named Aziz, she tracked down the sites of several Byzantine churches as well as the fortresses at Mennek and Seg, all reduced to rubble. The churches, she estimated, were older than those of Binbirkilise, 'but it would be impossible to come to any definite conclusion without digging'. After a night passed inside the crater with a nightingale 'shouting' and a sweet scent of honeysuckle, she was starting to lose heart when she stumbled upon her reward in the village of Kurşuncu: 'a great cruciform church with monastic buildings and fortifications and all complete!' Of it she wrote: 'I do not doubt that this is the chief and central shrine of the Karajadagh [Karaca Dağı] … No one has been here before – it's a most curious sensation to step into these great ruined places and to be the first person of the same civilisation which they stand for since the last monks fell or fled before the Seljuks.'

16

Backwater Byzantium

KARAMAN–BİNBİRKİLİSE–İVRİZ–EREĞLİ

'Isn't it absurd (and suitable) that the only house of my own in which I have ever entertained guests of my own should be a tent.' Letter, 25 May 1907

On her way home from Syria in 1905 Gertrude had visited Binbirk-ilise (the Thousand and One Churches), a site consisting of twin clus-ters of Byzantine churches at Madenşehir and Değle on Kara Dağı (the Black Mountain). There she made an impression of an inscrip-tion that she thought would allow precise dating of one of them, showing it to Professor William Ramsay, then the greatest expert on Anatolia's ancient churches, when she bumped into him in Konya. In the time it took to drain a bowl of soup the two of them were hatching a plan to investigate the site more fully. That agreement provided the motivating force behind her gruelling trek across west-ern Anatolia in 1907.

Then, she was to spend the best part of six weeks at Binbirkilise. The 1905 visit, however, was just a brief side trip out of Konya facil-itated by a new train service to Arikören. From there she rode straight to Madenşehir, then up the hill to Değle, where the local sheikh furnished her with a room. 'As soon as I saw it,' she wrote, 'I knew that my best dreams were fulfilled. It was a little bare mud built room, with the name of God scratched up on the walls and be-fore the door a platform looking out over the great plain and the slopes of Kara Dagh. I turned out the felts and mats in it [and] put in my own furniture.' True to form, she still found the energy to measure up two of the ruined churches before dinner.

The next few days were spent happily pottering about on the hill-side, planning churches, photographing them, riding up to the crater on the summit of Kara Dağı and generally exulting in the spread of spring flowers – 'yellow fritillary, red tulips, crocus, wild pear and snowdrops'. Strangely, her diary was silent on the inscription that was to turn her into Ramsay's partner. Instead she focused on the purchase of one of the only four hens in Değle for her supper. Unreconciled to its fate, the hen 'took sanctuary in every ruined church in turn and was finally run to earth in a tomb where Fattuh shot it with my gun! It was full of shot in consequence – I might almost have been eating a pheasant.'

When the time came to leave she wrote to her father that it had 'been very amusing to be for 4 days a Turkish villager'. In conclusion, she described Değle as a 'fortress city of churches and monasteries' that might or might not have been the ancient Barata – 'but as even the learned know nothing of Barata but the name, it doesn't seem to me to matter much'. Her own introduction to the churches had been the Austrian art historian Josef Strzygowski's influential *Kleinasien, ein Neuland der Kunstgeschichte* (Asia Minor: A New Territory for Art History), but to her delight she discovered that although the churches of Madenşehir had been fully mapped, those of Değle had not – 'I have had the pleasure of doing it myself,' she wrote gleefully.

On her way to Binbirkilise in 1905 Gertrude passed the night in Karaman, a town with an impressive legacy of pre-Ottoman monuments. I arrive here on 29 May, when the country is celebrating the Ottoman conquest of Constantinople in 1453. A small booth in the town centre has been taken over by a group petitioning for the return of Jerusalem to the Palestinians, the return of Morsi to the Egyptian leadership and the reconversion of Istanbul's Ayasofya into a mosque. It's draped with black and white Islamic flags.

Two fez-wearing boys aged fifteen and sixteen rush over to press the Ayasofya cause. I glare at them. 'It was a church before it was a mosque. It brings in millions of tourists a year.'

'Religion is more important than tourism,' one of them fires back.

'But there are lots of mosques nearby where people can pray. There's the Sultanahmet Cami just across the park. There's even a *mescit* in the back of Ayasofya.'

The boys glower at me disbelievingly. Then the penny drops. 'Have you even been to Istanbul?' I ask them.

'No,' is the inevitable answer*.

* Ayasofya became a mosque again in 2020.

In Karaman Gertrude inspected the magnificent Hatuniye Medrese, commissioned towards the end of the fourteenth century by the wife of the local emir in the days when Karaman was the capital of the Karamanoğlu Beylik. She also visited the İbrahim Bey Cami and, perhaps, the Aktekke Cami, both of them in ruins. Finally, she made her way up to Karaman Castle, which surmounts a mound just west of the town centre. It offered, she wrote, a fine view of the town, although a modern visitor might be more struck by the walls, an elaborate patchwork of stones taken from the buildings destroyed by the Ottoman leader, Gedik Ahmed Paşa, when he rode in to expel the Karamanoğlus in 1471. Her photographs show the round towers of the castle rising like a jacket above a skirt of humble mud-brick dwellings, a vista completely unrecognizable today.

On a return visit to the Hatuniye Medrese Gertrude had a run-in with the local imam. Shocked to find that all the turquoise tiles she had seen there on her first visit were now missing, Gertrude nevertheless admitted that she herself possessed one of them. A tetchy exchange then ensued:

'You did very wrong', said he. 'You have stolen one of our tiles and carried it away.'

'I did not steal it,' I pleaded weakly. 'I found it at Konia.'

'It is all one,' he replied. 'You should give it back.'

But as we went out through the cloister I noticed that the columns which supported it were double columns of a type peculiar to Christian architecture. They had in all probability been removed from a church.

'Mullah Effendi,' said I, 'we are equal. I have taken a tile out of your Moslem tomb, and you the columns from our Christian church.'

The mullah's indignation vanished in a flash. 'Aferin!' he cried with a jolly laugh. 'Bravo!' and he clapped me on the back.

To get to Binbirkilise from Karaman Gertrude took the train to Ereğli, where she stayed at a 'wretched inn' run by a family of Austrian Jews. Ereğli was, she wrote, 'a hole', its only saving graces its gardens and the austere Ulu Cami, whose lofty minaret was decorated with bands of unpilfered tiles. But the main attraction that drew her back to Ereğli in 1907 was not the town itself so much as the opportunity it offered to visit a Hittite carving at nearby İvriz. This was, she wrote to her father, 'one of the great sights of Asia Minor … [set in] a wonderful valley with a rushing stream flowing through it', the water as 'clear as crystal'. Here on a rock she saw carved 'a God with curly hair and beard and pointed shoes and Phrygian cap adorned with a crown of horns; in his hands the fruits of the earth, corn and bunches of grapes, which he offers to a smaller figure, a king, standing before him with hands uplifted in prayer'. More almost than anything else she found in Turkey, that carving captivated Gertrude: 'If I had known the Hittite language I would have offered up a short thanksgiving in that tongue to the god with the curly hair and the tiara of horns who had brought such good things out of the naked earth.'

Carving of eighth-century BC Hittite King Warpalawas at İvriz near Ereğli; 2015

I come to view it with a taxi driver named Galip, a retiree from the local sugar factory with hair of a suspiciously ebony hue, and am delighted to find İvriz still a verdant little hideaway even though the opening of a dam in 1984 drove away most of the locals. It's a relief to find the carving still unscathed, despite its watery surroundings being a big hit with picnickers. A villager treated Gertrude to a snack of eggs, milk, honey and 'the biggest nuts in the world'. I make do with a boiled corncob. It's too early in the year for walnuts apparently.

In 1905 Ereğli was the last-but-one station on the expanding Berlin to Baghdad railway. The last station was at Bulgurluk, a pinprick of a place barely big enough to feature on a map, but the men responsible for the line had been contracted to lay two hundred kilometres of track, so two hundred kilometres of track they were going to lay. Gertrude was one of Bulgurluk's rare passengers, the station offering the speediest access to Binbirkilise by the time of her third visit in 1909.

'I'd like to go to the old Bulgurluk station,' I tell Metin, a startled Ereğli taxi driver.

'It's not there any more. It's been pulled down.'

'I know. But I'd still like to see where it used to be. Can you take me there?' And I reel off my spiel about Gertrude and the time before the First World War and how I'm trying to retrace the places she'd been to.

Metin leads me into the nearby teahouse, where a group of men sit playing *okey*. He leans over and speaks to Rasim, a grey fox of a man in a smart black business suit, who swivels round to examine this unexpected apparition. Yes, he does know where the station was and, yes, as it happens, he's quite happy to ditch the game and come with us to look for it.

Metin nudges me. 'He's a rich farmer. He has orchards and a cold-storage unit,' he says, as if I'd employed him to set me up with a husband rather than drive me to a lost station.

Off we set along the busy main road south to Adana. Rasim barks out orders with the confident air of a man used to being in charge, but it soon becomes apparent that his memory is not as exact as he'd suggested. We pull into a fuel station so he can phone a friend. On the forecourt a man is filling up with petrol. Yes, he remembers the station, he says in surprise.

'Get in, get in!' barks Rasim. 'You can show us the way.' Only by ferocious assertiveness can the petrol-buyer persuade him to settle for an alternative arrangement whereby we travel onwards in convoy.

Off we speed again, racing past the sugar factory, then beet fields as far as the eye can see. Finally our guide pulls over to the side of the road. Metin gets out to confer with him and I see an arm gesturing south towards a clump of trees stranded in a field. A track leads down to railway lines that nowadays terminate in Adana rather than Baghdad. We stroll towards the trees and on a rise in the ground beside them spot the foundation stones of the lost platform where Gertrude once waited with her luggage. Bizarrely, had she looked to the south she would have been staring at a line that, according to the contemporary Scottish journalist David Fraser, 'pursues its way into the lonely wilderness, to end with its pair of rails gauntly projecting … pointing in dumb amazement where the Taurus shares the horizon with the very skies' – terminating one kilometre beyond the station to comply precisely with the contract.

By the time Gertrude returned to Binbirkilise in 1907 she had finally found herself. After a twenties passed in a restless whirl of mountaineering, world travel and linguistic study, in her thirties she had settled into a rhythm in which archaeological research provided the backdrop and justification for more heavy-duty exploration. Better still, she had identified her own particular niche within archaeology, which, at least in the Turkish context, was Byzantium. But hers was not the glamorous Byzantium of Hagia Sophia and the Chora Church, of colourful frescoes and glittering mosaics. Rather, her sights had come to rest on the lower-key rediscovery of backwater Byzantium, on the minor monuments lying barely recognized in the countryside. Binbirkilise, and in particular the Değle part of it, perfectly fitted that bill.

On this second trip she settled in for the long haul, camping on the mountainside and walking or riding out to explore every last fallen stone. It was a place she came to love, a place of yellow roses and blue borage, a place where she could write that she 'had found

Mysterious exedra at Madenşehir (Binbirkilise); 2015

a Hittite inscription and [where] a Christian monastery stood guardian, as of old, over the green cup wherein had lain an ancient city', a place where, by the time she returned for a third brief visit in 1909, she could boast that she 'might have ridden up to the Kara Dagh without possessions, for there was no man in all the mountain who would not have been proud to offer us a lodging'.

Professor Ramsay arrived at Madenşehir a week after her, with his wife and digging companion Jane, and their son Louis, an expert on the local fauna. The fifty-six-year-old Ramsay was a renowned scholar who had done more than almost anyone else to identify the biblical sites of Asia Minor. On his first visit to Binbirkilise in 1882, Ramsay had been following the account given in 1836 by the British explorer William Hamilton, who had found the site deserted. By 1907, however, small villages were nestling inside both sets of remains. 'The process of ruin which formerly proceeded at the easy pace set by Nature, is now beginning to be accelerated by man,' Hamilton wrote in the introduction to *The Thousand and One Churches*. 'There is a melancholy difference between the facts of 1907 and the facts of 1909 ... We were just in time to save the memory of churches which can now never be studied except in our photographs.'

Despite the site's name, there were only ever twenty-eight churches divided between the two sites at Binbirkilise. They varied in date from the fifth to the eleventh century and their importance lay, as Ramsay explained in a letter to the *Athenaeum*, in the fact that 'nowhere else can one find Church development through so many centuries exhibited on one ruined site in such clear and well-preserved examples'.

'I believe this is the very first time anyone has set about to explore thoroughly a single district in central Asia Minor. See what we have got out of it! Two great Hittite sites and a vast amount of unexpected Byzantine remains,' Gertrude wrote of their work at Binbirkilise. But she and Ramsay were hampered not just by the restrictiveness of their permit – which only allowed for cleaning as opposed to excavation – but also by the remoteness of the location. Even drinking water was hard to come by: 'I have to send 2 hours up the hill for it daily and I find I can't supply the needs of the whole camp with one donkey load and the poor donkey can't go more than once a day,' she wrote. Food was also in short supply, the harsh preceding winter having killed most local livestock; to find a single lamb for sale, Fattuh was obliged to ride five hours by donkey, cheered only by thought of the much readier availability of hares and partridges. 'Housekeeping in the wilderness takes a great deal of thinking about!' she wrote to her mother.

A thoroughly hands-on member of her team, Gertrude recorded exhausting twelve-hour working days during which she directed the digging, took notes, planned and photographed churches, and made rubbings of inscriptions. Most of the men working with her were locals, although there were also a few Kurds, who went on strike for better pay in spite of her claim that 'I don't suppose so much money has passed hands in the Karadagh since the time of the Byzantines'. From time to time visitors came to see how they were getting on. Grateful for their company, Gertrude was at the same time glad to see the back of them because of the additional strain they put on their limited supplies.

In *The Thousand and One Churches* she wrote that 'except for the German excavations at Boghaz Keui* and some Russian diggings at

Ani**, I believe that Sir William Ramsay and I were the first to put spade into the ground in the interior of Asia Minor'. Her letters make plain that this was one of the happiest times in her life: working with a man she admired, making discoveries that she knew to be original, carrying out hard physical work that offered the perfect outlet for her boundless energy. Excitement oozes from her pen. Over and again she writes of the 'great, great fun' she was having, of the sense of achievement inspired by the discovery of the Hittite inscription ('I think I've never been so elated'). Even the routine problem of managing the workers excited her ('gorgeous fun – you should see me directing the labour of 20 Turks and 4 Kurds'). The weather – in particular the howling wind – was the main drawback, although she made light even of that, writing to her brother, 'if you find some earth in my letter it's the dust of Byzantines which flies round me'.

I venture up to Binbirkilise with a taxi driver named Cemal Koku on a day when the sky threatens a downpour then comes up triumphantly with something better. We drive first to Madenşehir, which resembles a single muddy farmyard with donkeys blinking flies from their eyes and dogs waiting to ambush us round every corner. I eye a chicken pecking at the ground beside a fallen lintel embossed with a cross and relish the casual intermingling of past and present. Alas, the authorities have other ideas. Like Geyre, this is a village that has outlived its purpose; its last residents are to be relocated so that it can be comprehensively excavated and developed as a tourist attraction.

In 1907 the ascent from Madenşehir to Değle had involved a major expedition: 'Today we have had the greatest known exodus since the days of the Jews. We have moved all our camp up to the yaila, the summer quarters. It took 11 camels and 4 donkeys to transport us,' Gertrude wrote. By car it's a matter of minutes to Değle, where we're greeted by site custodian Veysel Bey. Unlike Madenşehir, Değle was always thinly populated. Now only four families live here and one of them migrates downhill in winter to avoid the snow. There's no school, so Veysel's ten-year-old son must be bussed to the

*Boğazköy, site of the ancient Hittite capital of Hattuşa.
**The Bagratid Armenian capital from 961 to 1045.

nearest town every day. The mosque is in an abject state, tumble-down and as full of debris as the ruined churches. 'It stopped being used about twenty years ago,' Veysel tells me, his eyes misting as he recalls the *ezan* of his childhood.

Soon we're being quickmarched around the remains of the churches. One hundred years after Gertrude and Sir William dug out the rubble to plan and measure them, the same work is being re-peated; the churches are now as clean and clearly visible as they will have been at any time since the pair rode off down the mountain, the neat little apses accessible, the columns and flagstoned floors once again exposed. My face is in a Cheshire Cat grin until I spot the call-ing-card of one Hüseyin Tosun daubed in thick white paint on a wall. The same tag had disfigured one of the Madenşehir churches too.

'I'd like to give him a slap!' I snarl. 'I suppose he's some sixteen or seventeen-year-old kid!'

Veysel roars with laughter. 'No, he's not. I know him. He's thirty!' he says.

Our church-visiting works up an appetite and soon Veysel is lead-ing us into his home amid the ruins, where his wife, Döndü, has whipped up one of those simple yet utterly delectable lunches that are an essential feature of Turkish life. We sit on the floor around a low table, a cloth spread across our laps to catch the crumbs. Then out comes a chicken soup such as Fattuh could only have dreamt of, along with crispy roundels of village bread, crumbly village cheese, thick yoghurt and a green salad. We wash it down afterwards with copious glasses of *çay* as we loll on cushions against the walls. A rifle with bullets encircling it forms the centrepiece of the decor. 'For wolves,' says Veysel when I raise a questioning eyebrow.

We bid farewell on a veranda on which lies a mournful puppy, just a few months old. As I bend to stroke him, the reason for his distress becomes apparent: his ears have been cropped, a common precaution to prevent wolves from ripping them off. 'I did it myself,' says Veysel proudly. 'With my scissors. It didn't make much of a fuss.'

I try to cajole Cemal into driving me to the crater on the summit of Kara Dağı, where the remains of a temple have been uncovered. 'It's forbidden,' he says smartly, which I take to be his way of telling me he's done for the day.

17

Şalvar with Strawberries

SİLİFKE–UZUNCABURÇ–KIROBASI–KIZKALESİ

'I have fallen a hopeless victim to the Turk; he is the most charming of mortals and some day when I have a little more of his language, we shall be very intimate friends...'
Letter, 21 April 1905

I go to sleep in a north-of-Taurus, west-of-Turkey frame of mind and wake up the next morning in a south-of-Taurus, east-of-Turkey one. This is not especially logical since I've only come as far as Silifke, which according to the map is hardly in the east of Turkey at all. But the fact remains that as soon as I step off the hotel veranda I can feel a change in the atmosphere. No matter how much the plains around Karaman may have been brought under cultivation, there remains a sense that this is a travesty, an imposition, something that could come to an end with a single summer drought and an immediate return to the natural aridity. Here in Silifke though there's no mistaking the southern Mediterranean lushness. Suddenly every other balcony peeps out through puffs of pinky-purple bougainvillea. Suddenly lipstick-red hibiscuses are thrusting up from the pavement. Suddenly sugar-almond oleanders are rubbing shoulders with the hoary yellow blooms of the prickly pear.

I've crossed the Taurus Mountains not via the historic route through the pass known as the Cilician Gates but further west, along a road carved through the spectacular Göksu Canyon. It's brought me to Silifke, a dusty, rather woebegone little town that was once the ancient Seleucia ad Calycadnum, an identity it seems reluctant to advertize except half-heartedly via the neglected and fenced-off remains of a temple to Zeus. It's rather prouder of its castle, which looms on a hill above the town centre. Years ago, before health-and-safety concerns started to sneak their way into even the Turkish consciousness, I zoomed up to that castle in a sidecar attached to a motorcycle. The going up wasn't so bad, provided one didn't mind the bumpiness. The coming down again was something else. A chill northeasterly was blowing; even with my head retracted like a tortoise's into its shell I still felt as if I'd plunged headfirst into a freezer. 'The *poyraz*! The *poyraz*!' the driver chanted cheerfully. He'd come prepared in a hat with woolly earflaps. I hadn't. It wasn't a ride to forget in a hurry.

But now the sidecars have been banished and there's no alternative to the long slog up the hill. Arriving hot and breathless, I find the castle heaving with schoolchildren for whom a red-faced foreigner is far more entertaining than a history lesson. In 1905 Gertrude had come here to photograph the view. Far below me the Göksu river winds like a jade-green ribbon through the suburbs; the bridge that has crossed it since Roman times is concealed beneath the modern road. A deep cistern is just about visible. In these stinking-hot parts, hoarding water against a drought was always essential and the Seleucians had gone to town on the task with particular enthusiasm, hacking their cistern from the rock, then facing it carefully with decorative stone arcading.

Gertrude pitched camp on a stretch of grass near what is now the faded Hotel Göksu, with the river and its hungry mosquitoes beside her and the castle dominating the view. It's here that I team up with a taxi driver named Bora Gür, but only after fobbing off the man who's first in line for passengers. He's eighty-eight and totters towards me as if his legs wouldn't carry him to the nearest bench. I'm making my excuses when Bora comes striding over.

'Is there a problem?' he asks.

There's little point in trying to hide my kneejerk ageism. I gesture surreptitiously towards the would-be chauffeur. 'I want to go to Kırobası,' I say, 'and I don't think he's up to it.'

'Leave it to me,' says Bora firmly, and minutes later we're settling down together in his cab.

'What did you say to him?' I ask guiltily.

'I told you were foreign and had to have air conditioning!' he replies.

I've fallen on my feet with Bora, who is, by Turkish taxi-driver standards, a mere stripling of thirty. The son of a police officer, he comes from a family that was constantly in motion during his childhood, hence he's seen more of the country than most of its residents.

If he has a dream, it is to be an archaeologist himself. Best of all, his family came originally from Kırobası, the mountain village I am hoping to reach today.

Gertrude loved this part of Turkey, the old Roman province of Cilicia, where the hillsides are littered with shards of antiquity, scant reminders of settlements, once flourishing, whose names have all but vanished from memory. After breakfasting on chicken soup and rice pudding, she rode up to Uzuncaburç, the ancient Diocaesarea, along a road in shocking disrepair. Up it zig-

Bora Gür and *şalvar*-ed relative in Kırobası; 2015

zagged, as it still does today, passing the delicate temple-tombs of Imbriogon peeking out from the undergrowth. Passing *yörüks* paused to donate milk for her lunch. 'The fresh mountain coolness was indescribably pleasant after the stuffy heat of the coast,' she wrote.

In Uzuncaburç her tentpoles were erected beneath the shade of a Roman propylon. Then, while Fattuh rustled up dinner, she strode around the ruins of a settlement which stood in the same relationship to nearby Ura (Olba) as Didyma did to Miletus. That is to say, although the site had a theatre, pleasingly cut into the hillside near the monumental gateway, it was not a place of residence but a religious centre dominated by two temples, one to Zeus Olbios and the other to Tyche. Gertrude admired the temple to Tyche but was disparaging about the one to Zeus – 'hideous capitals such as no Greek wd ever have cut', she wrote.

Bora and I pop into the local *kahve*, the perversely named village teahouse, and find many of the elderly male *çay* drinkers sporting baggy black *şalvar* trousers. 'They're wonderfully comfortable,' Bora says. 'Great for sitting about in, although not so much for working. All that material flapping about between your legs …' His Kırobası grandfather would have walked around in şalvar apparently, although not his police-officer dad.

A natural-born lark, Gertrude was up at dawn to rush round the rock-cut necropolis. Then on she rode to nearby Ura to inspect the remains of a temple and church as well as an aqueduct dramatically straddling a steep-sided valley with tombs cut into its sides. On one facade she picked out carvings of a funerary meal: '4 figures, one seated on a couch, 2 on one side and one on the other'. Bora and I stroll through the valley admiring the tombs and lamenting the treasure-hunters for whom they provide fine sport. 'People used to store their cheeses in tombs like these,' he tells me apropos nothing at all.

But time is ticking on. If we're to reach Kırobası, once Mara, and be back in Silifke by nightfall we need to step on it, which makes it all the more unfortunate that just outside Ura the engine emits a groan and the taxi slithers to a halt. I glance around us. The landscape is still 'all rocks and sparse pine', hardly the ideal spot for a breakdown. A hoopoe traces a languid loop across the sky, cinnamon breast topped and tailed with stripes of black and white. It's hours since another vehicle has passed us, and neither Bora nor I has a physique designed for stiff uphill walks. Gloomily, he lifts the bonnet and fiddles about underneath it. Then, just as I'm wondering if this is payback for my unkind dismissal of the doddery taxi driver, the engine perks up again. It'll get us to Kırobası, Bora thinks, where he can find someone to take a proper look.

Kırobası, when we reach it, is the ultimate back of beyond, the sort of place whose youngsters no sooner turn eighteen than they're rushing south in search of a better life by the sea. Relishing the fresh mountain air after the muggy heat of the coast, Gertrude quickly set about recording the ruined churches in the vicinity of what she described as a largely Christian village, but the delay caused by the breakdown means that we're out of time. In a tiny shop so tightly packed with household necessities – rope, nails, buckets, şalvar – that it's hard to imagine anyone being able to lay their hands on anything, a Bora family member gifts me a chunk of tangy green cheese, matured, as I'd been warned, in an ancient tomb.

Bora struggles to find something to offer as consolation for the ruins rendered unvisitable by the motoring mishap. 'There was a church in the middle of the village when I was a child,' he says. 'Its bell was so loud that it could be heard three kilometres away. They used to ring it half an hour before school started to tell us when to set off.' It was an Armenian church, I learn later. Nothing now remains of it except some suggestive Cyclopean stonework flanking a flight of steps.

★ ★ ★

During the first weeks of my journey, Gertrude and I had been travelling companionably side by side in a steadily eastward direction. From now on, however, we will be travelling in contraflow. Waking in Kırobası to 'air like wine', Gertrude was soon cantering north towards Karaman. Of the onward road she wrote scathingly: 'Over this wild and barren country runs the road to Karaman ... surely the most useless road in Asia Minor. It seems a pity when they make so few that they should have wasted their energies on one by which no mortal travels but the Yuruks and me.'

Bora and I, however, are heading back south to Silifke, and I think rather wistfully that, of all the lovely taxi drivers who have shared my adventures, he has come closest to being my Fattuh. It's something to do with his enthusiasm, his readiness to join in, his ability to understand what I'm struggling to say even when my Turkish collapses into as much disarray as the ruins. It's something to do with an honesty that lets him confess to a fear of heights, a fear of snakes, a fear of insects. It's something, too, to do with his youthfulness that has brought a dynamic to our relationship like the one that must surely have existed between Gertrude and her manservant.

Perhaps most of all, we share a sense of humour. As we drive back into town, we pass a plethora of signs touting Silifke-grown strawberries. Are there more of them than there used to be, I ask, since I don't remember such signs from previous visits.

'Well, you know how it is here. Someone makes money growing strawberries. Then everyone thinks, great idea, and starts piling into strawberries, and now nobody can make a *kuruş* from them!'

I laugh. 'Yes, there'll probably be another Gertrude Bell wannabe coming along soon.'

'I won't take them! I'll tell them Uzuncaburç is in Cyprus, Ura is in Cyprus.'

'Kırobası?'

'Cyprus too!

★ ★ ★

It would be hard to imagine a sharper contrast than that between Kırobası and Kızkalesi, the ancient Corycos. One minute I'm up in the mountains amid crumbling stone houses held together with sheets of zinc, the next I'm down on the coast, where a wall of concrete high-rises screens the beach from the main road. Nor is it only the architecture that's changed. After weeks spent crossing the central Anatolian plain, where everybody, male and female, was comprehensively covered up, the paucity of clothing worn by the Kızkalesilis comes as almost as much of a shock to me as it would to a Konya grandmother. For the first time since leaving Bodrum I'm back in holiday country, which means that anything goes on the cultural front. Here, young women wearing shorts and tiny T-shirts walk arm in arm with their pierced and tattooed boyfriends. In Silifke bermudas had been battling it out with *şalvars* as the male trouser of choice; in Kızkalesi the bermudas have emerged the clear winner and even seniors nip up to the Migros supermarket to stock up on ciggies in little more than shorts.

Where Kırobası had felt like a sleeping dog that we had stirred to life with a gentle prod, Kızkalesi feels like a house in the anxious hour before a party is due to start. The season is yet to kick in and the people snapping up the beachballs and armbands wear the pasty look of those who've barely shrugged off their office personas. This is a town blessed with a splendid swath of sand that gazes out over the eponymous Maiden's Castle, a dream of a fairy-tale island fortress seemingly floating on the surface of the sea. Its misfortune is that the coast road is relatively new. Difficulty of access used to discourage people from settling here, which means no legacy of charming whitewashed houses to be converted into boutique hotels. A resort of sorts grew up here in the seventies by which time concrete was already king. Until recently it remained something of a backwater. Now it has become a bit too fashionable for its own good, with multi-coloured strobes lighting up the castle like a Lunapark at night and a clubbing scene that blasts away any fantasies that visitors might have about getting up early to explore the surrounding ruins.

A second castle, a mainly Armenian makeover of a much older original, dominates the eastern end of the beach, and Gertrude

Kız Kalesi (Maiden's Castle) at Kızkalesi near Mersin; 2015

camped beside it, 'in a heavenly place ... in a thicket of myrtle and oleander'. Facing her tent was 'a wall of rock cut tombs on one of which is a warrior cut in relief'; amazingly that same warrior still guards the Mersin road, still wearing a truncated tunic and wielding his sword, although his head has been plucked from his neck like a daisy from its stem. In 1905 labourers were slowly dismantling the castle to use its stones for new bazaars in Mersin. Today the seemingly undamaged walls look promising, although inside there's little but runaway gorse, cuckoopint and rubble. From the ramparts I gaze down on the beach where Gertrude bathed. Men are kicking a ball about on the sand. A young woman is edging into the waves in a burqini, which, once she's submerged, billows about her like a crash-landed parachute.

After much haggling over the price, Gertrude persuaded the owner of a boat used to transport manure to row her out to the island, and Fattuh took her gun along in the hope of bagging a few pigeons for the pot – 'they were there,' she wrote, 'till we came'. She was very taken with the castle, its courtyard bristling with irises as well as with 'the largest grey blue thistle balls I have ever seen'. More importantly, the walls were still largely in one piece – 'fortunately this castle they cannot carry away piecemeal'.

My own visit could have been scripted for a Kemal Sunal comedy*. The only transport available is a disco boat, and I arrive to find that the castle has been leased to Syrian filmmakers for whose benefit everything, from the coverlets on the double beds installed in the towers to the fake rocks littering the courtyard, has been painted gold. Heavy-handed restoration has imposed trailing wires and obtrusive lighting on the lovely old stonework. The main tower is closed and, when a guard unlocks it for me, I find the walls defaced with graffiti, the acronym 'PKK' sitting uncomfortably alongside my own name scrawled up in its Latinate long form, the 'Patricia' completely unknown to Turks.

The remains of ancient Corycos lurk unheeded on the inland side of the Mersin road. There were four huge churches there, Gertrude wrote, lined up along 'a sort of Via Sacra [Sacred Way]'. Following her there in the fading light of a May evening I struggle at first to pick out a path, then am astounded at where it leads me. From a distance the silhouettes had suggested further Armenian strongholds but close up the details of narthex and apse claim the buildings for Byzantium. The churches are barn-like in their simplicity, huge rectangular spaces with apologetic holes punched through the walls to form doors and windows. But, as with the mainland castle, seeming integrity turns out to be an illusion. The outer walls may be holding their own against the weather. Inside, however, the roofs and the columns that once supported them have subsided into mounds of inchoate dust and stone.

Miraculously, just metres from a major highway along which petrol tankers thunder, it's still possible to amble from one church to another along a stretch of Roman road, its dove-grey flagstones carving a path through a necropolis of giant sarcophagi. Of all the walks I take in Gertrude's footsteps, this evening stroll through the soaring, secretive remains of Corycos is perhaps the most magical. There are places such as Konya where even the recent past seems to have van-

*Kemal Sunal (1944-2000) was a Turkish comedian who starred in more than eighty films.

ished beyond the recollect of memory and then there are places such as this where there seems to be nothing but the distant past, as tangible now as it was more than a thousand years ago. In the cool of evening I feel very close to Gertrude, wrapped up in the silence of history, so near to modernity yet at the same time so utterly apart from it. I have only to narrow my eyes to see her struggling to straighten her tripod amid the ruins; to hear her instructing her servant, Mahmud, to lift his end of the tape measure to ensure a correct reading.

★ ★ ★

Tethering her horse to a pomegranate tree, Gertrude strode uphill from the coast at Narlıkuyu to explore the Corycean Cave. But in an era of snappy slogans such classical correctness weighs too heavily. 'The Chasm of Heaven', reads one arm of the signpost at the summit; 'The Pit of Hell', replies the other. In less fanciful reality, Cennet and Cehennem (Heaven and Hell) are outsize sinkholes, their walls humbug-striped in orange, cream and grey, their floors a wedge of impenetrable thicket. Perversely, it's into Heaven that one descends via an interminable staircase while Hell can only be admired from above.

At the bottom of the steps the ruins of a roofless chapel dedicated to the Virgin Mary stand Cerberus-like in the mouth of an actual cave that locals assured Gertrude ran all the way down to the sea. A row of arch-headed windows hint at the Romanesque yet to come, while frescoed saints with worn-away faces line up in the apse beneath a Pantocrator lost to time. The cave's gaping mouth looks more like the entrance to the underworld than to paradise. Once an oracle lurked inside its gloomy depths. Now a beard of leaves frames its mouth and the air vibrates with the clamour of nesting sparrows.

Back at the surface, I've barely recovered my breath when I bump into Deveci Ali (Camel-Driver Ali). The sinkholes lie in the middle of what used to be *yörük* country and, sure enough, Ali turns out to be of nomadic ancestry. A slight man in his early forties, he comes here every day to tout camel rides to the tourists. He has two of them for whom he paid sums that sound like kings' ransoms.

'That seems a lot.'

'Yes, but there are not many of them left now,' he says dreamily. According to Bora, it's not long since caravans of up to a thousand camels could have been seen plodding along the mountain road at any one time. 'That's true,' says Ali. 'They would have been carrying bread down to Silifke.'

Soon he's setting aside the newspapers that help him while away the long low-season hiatuses between customers, and we sit companionably beside the remains of a rock-cut wine press while he reminisces about his childhood. 'My family stopped travelling when I was about seventeen,' he says. 'As more and more families settled down on the coast it got harder for the rest of us to keep going. Our family was originally Alevi but became Sunni – you can tell it from our names, lots of Alis and Hasans. Life is better now, of course, but I still remember how it was in the black tents. It was wonderful after the rain. A cool mist of water would stroke our faces. When we travelled, we would put the babies into the *heybes* (donkey bags) to balance the kid goats on the other side.'

Ali takes me to meet his young wife, Arzu, who is also of nomadic descent. They have a relaxed, happy, surprisingly physical relationship for this part of the world. We sit in the sun munching strawberries and mulling over the rights and wrongs of Turkish politics. But what, I wonder, does his wife do with her time while her children are at school?

'Oh, we can always nip to Mersin,' she says. 'I go there regularly to get my legs waxed.' And she tips me a knowing wink.

Kızkalesi's role as a kitschy modern holiday resort is at odds with its geographical surroundings. For this is a part of the world where the Taurus Mountains press down on the coastline, leaving only thin strips of land for settlement in between dramatic defiles carved by mountain streams. From Corycos Gertrude rode into Şeytandere (Satan's Valley), a steep-sided gorge whose craggy walls exclude the outside world completely. In winter it's impassable, but in summer a track of sorts leads to the Adamkayalar, a set of funerary stelae carved high up in the rock. In 1905 it took her an hour just to get within sight of them and she could only examine them after a 'breakneck climb over rocks and through brushwood'. The stelae were 'very rude, but not without charm ... so we climbed down to our horses and having praised God who had delivered us from such perils, went to the Yuruk's tent and drank coffee,' she wrote.

In Kızkalesi taxi drivers quibble over a request to be taken to the Adamkayalar, but once we reach the canyon their reluctance makes sense. There is a putative path down to the carvings, but it's not one that would look inviting to anything marginally less nimble than a mountain goat. I glance at Mehmet, my driver. It's clear that he won't be volunteering to risk his neck on my behalf.

'Have you ever been down there?' I ask, trying to drum up some interest.

'In my youth,' he says cautiously, not wishing to encourage me.

'Has anyone fallen?'

'Of course!'

'And has anyone died?'

'Well, I wouldn't know about that.'

Thus concludes our conversation. I perch on a rock and look down on a 150-metre drop and out over an eagle's-eye panorama that sweeps round from the marine castle, serene on the surface of the sea, and all the way along the canyon floor. Gertrude never flunked a challenge, I think, but then again she approached the carvings from the valley floor rather than the rim. Nor was she alone. But the mystery still lingers. How was it that a society lady who, when at home, lavished as much attention on the latest fashions from Paris as on ancient monuments, could have become such a fearless explorer, hurling herself at enterprises that would defeat most men? I think of her standing in the station at Karaman, gazing into a mirror for the first time since arriving in Turkey, then scribbling a note to her father: 'I wonder what the Kaimakkam thinks of the hats of English travellers of distinction. I have worn mine for 4 months in all weathers – you can scarcely tell which is the crown of it and which the brim.' Yet just days earlier she had been clambering over terrifying terrain to reach these all but inaccessible carvings.

'The low hills are covered with the ruins of towns and villages with wine-presses and tombs, set in thickets of wild olive, carob and myrtle,' wrote Gertrude in 'Notes on a Journey through Cilicia and Lycaonia', the articles for the *Revue Archéologique* in which she described her journey from Antakya to Konya in 1905. How I wish that I too could have been travelling when all this part of the coast, notorious over the centuries as the lair of pirates, was still wild, uncultivated countryside. For kilometre after kilometre the monuments of Cilicia Trachea (Rough Cilicia) still await the attention of the explorer, but it's increasingly hard to spot them behind the wall of tourism development. Local hotels secure peerless sea views for their customers at the cost of blighting everybody else's outlook. Yet the names on the café fascias – Yörüklerin Yeri (Nomads' Place), Yörük Dedenin Yeri (Nomad Granddad's Place) – suggest a yearning for more innocent times among the urbanites who flock here to escape the stress of city living.

East of Kızkalesi at Ayaş, where Gertrude found 'the road white with enormous hail stones and … the green beans of the carob trees [scattered] upon the ground', I come across a uniquely Italian tile arrangement decorating the walls of a ruined *hamam* on a spit of land that was once an island, and smile at Roman mullets swimming in mosaic form beneath the remains of a later church in the hillside settlement of Elaiussa-Sebaste. Her 'immense columned building' on the beach has since been identified as the palace of the Byzantine military governor.

Shortly afterwards a road inland deposits me on the edge of a stupendous sinkhole. This is Kanlıdivane, a place so spectacular that lips automatically shape themselves into a silent 'O' of wonderment. It's not just 'the huge rocky gulf' that does it but the fact that the remains of five Byzantine churches circle the rim, testimony to the reverence such a setting has always inspired. I peer into the chasm and make out figures carved into the sides. Others adorn the tombs in the adjoining necropolis, children's-sketchbook figures in crudely rendered garments, hefting rough-cut weapons, their featureless faces balanced on necks as extended as those of the Padaung women of Myanmar.

Near the ticket office I run Gertrude's name past the local archaeologists.

'Ah, yes,' says one of them, 'she took black and white photos, didn't she? Rode around in a hat!'

I pat my bag smugly. Then I pull out a hat just as battered as hers to hoots of laughter all round.

18

Cardamon Coffee and Aleppo Number Plates

MERSİN–TARSUS–ADANA–ANAVARZA

'What it's like to travel in a roadless and bridgeless country after and during heavy, not to say torrential, rains you can't imagine.' Letter, 17 April 1905

For Bora in Silifke, Mersin is caffeine heaven, the nearest place to be sure of a decent cappuccino. For Arzu in Narlıkuyu, it's a paradise of pampering, the nearest place to be sure of a decent leg wax. From afar, then, Mersin represents Turkish modernity, the moated conference centre with its sub-Gehry pretensions making the point assertively. In reality the modernity is only skin-deep. Built on reclaimed land, the waterfront park may live up to the promise. One street back, though, and it's easy to see why, arriving by train from Tarsus in 1905, Gertrude, might have dismissed Mersin as a 'miserable little port'.

A thick canopy of magenta bougainvillea shades the restaurant of the İcel Sanat Kulübü (İcel Arts Club), where I sit down to lunch with a fine band of merry men. Amongst them is a retired judge who welcomes me with a belly laugh.

'Are you an *ajan* [secret agent]?' he asks, dribbling cheese sauce down his chin in his excitement.

Normally it's a question I brush aside with weary resignation, knowing that in Turkey the conviction that all foreigners are spies and/or missionaries rarely lies far beneath the surface. Today, though, he has reason on his side. For many Turks the words 'Gertrude Bell' and '*casus* [spy]' are as natural a collocation as bread and butter. We bat the topic back and forth over the spaghetti plates. Yes, I say, she certainly was a spy for the British once the First World War broke out and for some time afterwards. But, no, I continue, in her younger days when she was travelling around what is modern Turkey she was nothing of the kind, just a traveller who took a shine to Anatolian archaeology and went on to write about it.

It's through the Arts Club that I meet photographer Bülent Akbaş, a man with a mop of white hair and a bloodhound look about him. He's a Circassian whose family migrated from Sebastopol in the 1890s and whose expression darkens as he reminisces about the Crimea. At the same time he's a man with a passion for Gertrude second only to my own, having revisited most of the sites she saw in Cilicia and photographed them from the same spots to highlight the ravages of a century.

Of the hotel where she passed the night in Mersin, Gertrude commented only that it was near the sea. Bülent steers me up a side street to a parking lot shoehorned in between two banks, the site, he says, of the lost Imperial Hotel, whose terrace looked out over the water. His money, however, is on the equally absent Hotel d'Europe. The best show in town in 1905, it occupied a plaza behind the Ulu Cami on a spot now occupied by a jewellery shop. He brandishes a photograph of a neat two-storey building, its veranda overlooking a fountain in the square below. The contrast between the elegance of the past and the dreariness of the now is as painful as a stubbed toe.

On the bus into Mersin I'd come face to unsettling face with the individual tragedy that is the Syrian civil war.

I'd been gazing out of the window, fantasizing about the days when Cilicia had been as thoroughly Byzantine as distant Constantinople, its vintners cultivating grapes in sight of the sea at Akkale, when suddenly I became aware of movement, of the woman in the seat in front reaching across the aisle to a withered Kurd, her chin a swirl of indigo tattoos. She was passing over a small, passport-style photograph. I caught a glimpse of it. It showed a young man, in his mid-twenties probably, in his prime certainly, and from the sleeping gesture the woman made with her folded hands I had to conclude that he was her son and that he was dead.

As we'd boarded the bus she'd muttered, 'Syria, boom, boom,' to the same Kurdish woman, desperate for contact, desperate to communicate her story. The old woman had responded with a valiant attempt to establish their respective family trees that soon ran aground on their lack of a common language. Now I watched as in slow mo-

With Gertrude fan Bülent Akbaş in Mersin; 2016

tion her expression worked through the spectrum from uncertainty, to doubt, then finally to understanding. Then a look of horror filled her eyes. She threw her hands into the air and started to pray.

The refugees have been in evidence a long way west of Mersin. But now there is a ratcheting up of numbers; the border is close, the four-year-old war but a short flight away. The refugees are omnipresent here, their tragedies playing out on the roadside beside us while we go about our unaltered lives.

Mersin is all about the present and that present has been conspicuously shaped by a ferry service from Tripoli in Lebanon. Before it was suspended, that ferry helped many Syrians flee the civil war in their homeland, and now in the Mersin of today it's Arabic that tops the list of offerings in the translator's office, it's Arabic that follows Turkish on restaurant menus, and it's the number plates of Aleppo and Damascus that crowd the parking lots.

In the waterfront cafés they're used to serving coffee flavoured with cardamom as the Syrians like it. It's in one of these cafés that I meet Haldun and his wife Yalda. A resident of Homs, he had earned a good living as a guide at Krak des Chevaliers, where his father was custodian (and where Gertrude was lucky enough to pass the night in a guestroom in 1905). But then the war broke out and their son was arrested. When their boy arrived home with a broken leg, Haldun knew it was time to leave and they did so promptly via Tripoli, leaving Yalda in Homs, where their daughter was studying at university. But week by week the situation deteriorated. To attend classes their daughter had to pass through an ever-growing number of checkpoints manned by rapacious militiamen. Eventually she and Yalda moved in with friends closer to the university. Then a bomb hit their apartment block, reducing it to rubble. Yalda went to see the damage. 'Women were crying, fainting. It was unimaginable,' she tells me, wiping away a tear with a corner of her headscarf.

Now the family is reunited in Mersin, but life remains a struggle. Without work permits, the refugees are vulnerable to abusive employers who pay little, if anything, for their labour. Accommodation is hard to find and soaring demand is pushing up rents. They take me home to meet their son and daughters in an apartment in Little Latakia, where, Haldun tells me, there was already a strong Syrian presence before the war. The couple put a brave face on things, but behind the smiles lurks the shell-shocked horror of those who can't quite believe what has happened to them. Their apartment is austere, bereft of personal touches. In Homs they would have lived a comfortable middle-class life surrounded by family photos, souvenirs of holidays, the accumulated baggage of a lifetime. I leave wondering what will become of them. A year later, their eldest son risks the sea crossing to Greece. They hear from him in Holland, where a Dutch family is helping him start a new life. Soon afterwards, their eldest daughter joins her fiancé in Germany. 'Our family is scattered to the world,' Haldun says softly.

In the hairdresser's, Engin has a different take on things. A diminutive man with what looks like the British coronation crown tattooed on the back of his hand, he is himself a refugee from a bad marriage in Istanbul, which doesn't stop him from holding forth about the Syrians who come here fleeing war. Of course we have to help them, he says reflexively, but what about the Turks in need of cancer treatment, the Turks unable to afford bread for their families?

Aren't they equally deserving of assistance?

In his words I hear the echo of a UKIP voter complaining about Poles stealing British jobs, of a Republican voter whining about Mexicans snatching American jobs. But he has a point. Rents have soared, wages slumped. Why would an employer pay more when a desperate Syrian will do the work for less? How many Syrians are there in Mersin, I ask Engin? He says 500,000; Haldun counters with 250,000. Even splitting the difference, that's an awful lot of non-Turkish-speaking newcomers to be found homes and jobs in the space of a few years.

Gertrude lingered in Mersin just long enough to stock up for her onward journey. Toothbrushes and mosquito netting were easily found, she wrote, but otherwise it was slim pickings: 'Murray says that all the necessaries for a journey in the interior are to be found. I shld think from the look of the place that they were never to be found.'

'When she came here there were nineteen consulates,' Bülent tells me. Gertrude's first port of call in a new town was usually the consulate, where she could collect her mail and pick up the gossip from home, so he steers me towards the old British Consulate, a dejected house turned half-hearted nightclub, its garden sacrificed to a new-build.

It was as British consul in Mersin that Dick Doughty-Wylie, the man Gertrude had met in Konya and with whom she fell in love, revealed his courage and resolve. In 1908 the Committee of Union and Progress, otherwise known as the Young Turks, had succeeded in overthrowing Sultan Abdülhamid, but their triumph was short-lived. In April 1909 the ousted government rallied for the fightback and soon the sultan was once again the master of Yıldız Palace. The Armenians had supported the CUP government, seduced by its promise of equality for religious minorities. Inevitably, then, the about-turn left them caught in the crosshairs. The whole of the eastern Mediterranean and the Hatay, the tongue-shaped piece of land dangling into Syria, was soon convulsed by fighting, which took a particularly heavy toll on the area around Adana and Mersin; the mortality figures are disputed, but it seems likely that some thirty thousand people, most of them Armenian, lost their lives. Doughty-Wylie was active in trying to end the fighting, first in Mersin and then in Adana, taking a gunshot wound to the arm in the process.

While not a witness to these events, Gertrude began to hear of the massacres almost immediately, and for some time afterwards her diaries convulse with the contradictory accounts of those she spoke to. In Ereğli an English trader assured her that the Armenians were innocent of blame, but in Talas the Canadian missionary Herbert Irwin raved about incendiary preachers who had fanned the flames of a dream inspired by the burgeoning nationalism of the Balkans. Just as many Greeks cherished the idea of a Greater Greece to encompass the old territories of Asia Minor, so some Armenians came to believe that a new homeland, a *beylik* of Cilicia, could be carved out of the eastern Mediterranean. It was on the train from Arıkören that she met the Chambers, a British family who told her of Doughty-Wylie's heroism in preventing a rabble-rousing bishop from stirring up more trouble. Gertrude ended her recounting of these conversations with a devastating conclusion: 'It is believed that not one of the real leaders of the political agitation has been caught; the 6 who were executed were executed because somebody had to be.'

In a country of microclimates, the area around Adana and Mersin has drawn the humid short straw. At a juice stall in Tarsus I can hardly decipher the posted prices through the smudges on my glasses. My hair is flattened onto my forehead; rivulets of sweat course down my cheeks and drip from my chin.

'It's hot,' I say sheepishly to the juice-seller.

'Yes, very,' he says, dabbing a discreet bead of sweat from his own brow.

Tarsus. The birthplace of St Paul, but also the place where, in the aftermath of Julius Caesar's murder, Cleopatra came to meet Mark Antony, sailing up the Cydnus in 41 BC to greet him in a golden barge with silver oars and purple sails, or so Shakespeare would have us believe. A beautiful black-eyed woman of twenty-eight, Cleopatra quite possibly had more in mind than the need to reinforce Egypt's alliance with Rome. Certainly, she arrived for the assignation dressed as Aphrodite, the goddess of love. Antony fancied himself as the human embodiment of Dionysius, the god of partying. Theirs was soon a liaison as much about passion as politics, a story that surely merits a worthy monument, I think, instead of which it's commemorated, just barely, by Cleopatra's Gate, a clumsily restored last relic of the old city walls stranded in the middle of a busy traffic roundabout.

Gertrude arrived in Tarsus not in a glamorous purple-draped barge but more prosaically in a train from Adana, a train that had had to be delayed, what's more, when a cargo of horses, taking exception to their confinement, kicked their way through the walls of their carriage. Opened in 1886, the line from Adana to Mersin had been paid for by a French company based in London. But all the talk now was of the Berlin to Baghdad railway and the heroic endeavours of tunnel and viaduct that would be needed to carry it over the Taurus Mountains. The Tarsus stationmaster was keen to downplay any such expectations of his own more modest line. 'There are no works of art [and] only one bridge,' he informed her.

Her tents were pitched west of the town centre on Gözlükule Höyük, a tumulus dating back to Neolithic times, with 'traces of fortification about it and a good view'. After lunch she set off to explore the town guided by Darad, a member of the small Syrian Orthodox congregation exiled to Tarsus amid accusations of financial skulduggery. Modern travellers will have crossed swords with their own Darads, men with firmly fixed views on what should interest their charges, which, in his case, meant a Greek-owned cotton factory rather than heathen mosques. Only with difficulty was he persuaded to show Gertrude the Kilise Cami, a mosque conjured from what had been an Armenian church, and the great Ulu (Nur) Cami, where, admiring the round marble columns alternating with square stone piers, she leapt to the assumption that it too had started life as a church. In fact the columns had been reused in the creation of a structure which, despite having been built in the late sixteenth century, reflected in its design the eighth-century Umayyad mosque of Aleppo.

What Darad did show Gertrude that she might not have found for herself was the Donuktaş, literally the Frozen Stone. I track it down in a labyrinth of back streets and find the gate as firmly pad-locked against me as it had been against her. But today is my lucky day, and one of the boys playing football outside runs to fetch the key. Constructed from a Roman concrete of compressed pebbles, the Donuktaş looks from the outside like a single gargantuan stone. In-side, however, I find a weed-and-corn-filled hollow, crude, feature-less, easy to shrug off as another disused cistern. A sign quickly disabuses me of this notion. The Donuktaş was probably a temple to Jupiter built in the second century. Coins minted locally show just such a structure with ten columns running along its stepped facade. A single marble finger found in the early nineteenth century hints at the same sort of outsized cult statue as dominated the temple at Didyma.

Thwarted at the Donuktaş, Gertrude also struggled to track down the Tarsus waterfall. In the heat of a Tarsus summer this is a particu-larly popular hangout, the one place where the blue of a cloudless sky, the white of cascading water and the green of dense vegetation manage to vanquish the brown of dust and the ochre of the old stone buildings. Visitors lean over the railings to snap selfies. Youths in long shorts leap from the bridge into the water, then run back up to do it all over again. Locals linger in the teahouses, waiting for the evening to bring a release from the oppression. I feel the temperature drop, I relish the spray on my face, and I remember the young Deveci Ali smiling in the tent of childhood as the rain gently caressed his cheeks.

Gertrude took one last expedition from Tarsus, to Eshab-ı Keyf, the Shrine of the Seven Sleepers. I drive out there with Cengiz, an amiable taxi driver whose family hailed from Diyarbakır. In the fields along the way vineyards have replaced the cotton fields of the past. 'The factories all closed twenty years ago,' Cengiz explains. 'The price fell, the cost of the materials went up. They just couldn't survive.'

Cengiz is a man with five children, four daughters followed at last by the longed-for son. But he's no caricature of a conservative eastern paterfamilias. Instead, with the election almost upon us, he is a man focused on the importance of education and not at all happy about the growing number of *imam hatip* schools, originally intended to turn out imams and prayer leaders but increasingly a vehicle for the president's stated desire to create a 'pious generation'.

'There are too many *cahil* people already,' says Cengiz, using a word for ignorance that, in Turkish, comes freighted with a much heavier burden of meaning than its English equivalent, harking back as it does to the Jahiliyyah, the Age of Ignorance when darkness stalked the land before the advent of Islam.

We arrive at the shrine and immediately I want to turn tail and run. For this is a place of pilgrimage, reverent, respectful and very, very Turkish. The car park is overflowing, the steps are heaving with worshippers, women are kneeling on the ground grilling a local form of pancake. At the entrance to the female section of the tiny mosque, I hesitate, unsure whether I should venture inside. It's easier to make do with a look at the cave where, as the story has it, seven young men, fleeing persecution, fell into a deep sleep from which they didn't reawaken for three hundred years. Oddly, this story appears to relate to the reign of the emperor Decius, a great harrier of Christians. So, although it's recounted in the Koran, it clearly pre-dates Islam.

I spend the night in the Hotel Efsus, an atmospherically converted Ottoman house where ceiling fans swish the heavy air and wooden floorboards creak as I cross the hall. In the morning there's the very un-Turkish sound of a man pedalling past on a bicycle whistling. Twitching the curtain, I look out on an otherwise deserted street in a corner of Tarsus that reminds me so strongly of Tripoli in Lebanon that I almost have to pinch myself to remember that I'm still in Turkey. Tarsus's high street does it no favours, dishing up a down-at-heel string of retail outlets that only a shopkeeper in need of a low rent could love. Yet behind that unpromising front, the back streets still nurture the magnificent stone mansions of the cotton traders who made their fortunes here in the days when ships could still drop anchor in front of Cleopatra's Gate.

In the cool of morning before the humidity can lay its muggy paws on me, I wander down to a square beside a mundane courtyard well that has somehow managed to cloak itself in the sanctity of association with St Paul. There are mere days left until the election, but the only battlebus in sight is a little van belonging to the HDP (Halkların Demokratik Partisi or People's Democratic Party), a start-up body that stands in roughly the same relationship to the PKK as Sinn Fein did to the IRA. It's the latest in a string of parties aiming to represent the Kurds in the Turkish parliament. Throughout the 1990s the story was always the same: a new party had only to be named and assigned a set of initials than it would be closed by court order. The response was a changed strategy in which individuals would stand as independent election candidates, their political affiliations nonetheless clear to the electorate. Once elected, the independents would group together to form a Kurdish bloc in parliament. But in 2014, emboldened by peace talks that promised to bring an end to decades of fighting, a renewed attempt was made to campaign again as a legitimate and recognizable party that might be able to leap the hurdle requiring it to win ten per cent of the vote to enter parliament. To increase its chances of success the HDP had opened offices all over Turkey and tried to present itself as no longer just representative of the Kurds but of a new politics in general, leftish, greenish, liberal, promising co-mayorships shared between a man and a woman. Leading them into the election campaign is the young, charismatic, *saz*-playing Selahattin Demirtaş, a breath of fresh air when compared with the increasingly elderly men leading the other opposition parties. But it's a difficult balancing act to pull off and Demirtaş has sometimes struggled to present himself as a clean skin, a man non-Kurds can do business with. HDP offices have been firebombed, individual campaigners attacked. Yet in the number of Turks I've spoken to who've confessed to admiring Demirtaş I've sensed a yearning for something new, something better, something that they can believe in.

But now the gloves are off. While I had been hunting for the Donuktaş, two bombs had exploded at an election rally in Diyarbakır. Four people had been killed. Now there's something in the morning silence that speaks of embarrassment, of recognition that a pause is needed for reflection. Even the little van circling the square seems too chastened to throw itself wholeheartedly into campaigning.

'The only picturesque thing in Adana is the entrance with the bridge across the Seihan,' wrote Gertrude, before summing the place up as 'a squalid little town'. In Adana I book into the Bosnalı Hotel over-looking the Seyhan river and the stone bridge that has been carrying pedestrians across it since Roman times. Gertrude had also booked into a hotel near the bridge with 'a delightful big balcony hanging over the Jihan Chai* where I imagine her sitting after dinner looking out at the sweep of the river, her feet resting on a railing, a cigarette wafted in the air to ward off the hungry mosquitoes. Nothing re-mains of that hotel now, but the Bosnalı had been built as a home for a wheat merchant in 1889 and appears in the photograph she took from the bridge, its *cihannüma* (rooftop gazebo) rising up over lay-ered floors so cantilevered outwards that you could almost imagine them tipping over and depositing their occupants in the river.

After the wide openness of Mersin, Adana feels cramped and crowded. It's also chock-a-block with men striding around in *şalvars* as baggy as a rap artist's pants, teamed with eye-popping mauve scarves, the improbably unisex head covering of choice in uber-macho Urfa to the east. Adana was until recently, when Bursa leapfrogged over it, Turkey's fourth biggest city. That statistic might imply modernity, go-gettingness, a cosmopolitan outlook, especially given the booming industry in piping oil through the port at nearby Ceyhan and the big American air base at İncirlik. Instead a heat-in-duced lethargy hovers over Adana and belies the busy crush of peo-ple. Decades in the planning, the Metro seems as irrelevant to local transport needs as the Houston tramway. Pressed to find a compar-ison for the town, I'd be tempted to plump for Karachi.

These days you can barely slide a cigarette paper between Mersin and Adana, so far have the two once separate towns reached out to embrace each other. Of the two it's Adana that hangs onto the history, albeit with one hand waving half-heartedly at the future. Shorn of ten of its arches by road-widening, the Taş Köprü (Stone Bridge) was in Gertrude's day an even more magnificent Roman survivor, its twenty-four arches pushed up close to houses that lined a thin strip of foreshore. But now the view from the bridge is dominated by Adana's showstopper of a mosque, the Merkez Sabancı Cami, ten

*Apparent confusion of the Seyhan river with the Ceyhan.

years in the building and flourishing sextuplet minarets in a challenge to Istanbul's Sultanahmet Cami. The mosque attracts friends and foes in almost equal measure. The friends point to the proof it offers that there's life yet in the old dog of Ottoman mosque architecture. They trumpet its clean lines, the richness of its carvings, the sheer unabashed size of it. The foes slam it as faux, and hanker after something less Sinan-lite and more Zaha Hadid. But no one could fail to fall in love with the huge landscaped park that surrounds it, except perhaps a visiting Armenian muttering darkly about the cemetery that lies beneath it.

In the evening I treat myself to a real Adana kebab at a popular pavement café, where my presence attracts intrusive attention from the waiters ('Where are you from? No, really – where are you from?'). While I eat, I think of Gertrude bumping into a family friend in her hotel and of what a joy it must have been to be able to catch up on the news from home without the usual wait for mail. Then I reread the letter in which she offered a glimpse of her two worlds catching up and colliding with each other, the home-loving Gertrude looking over at the travelling Gertrude and seeing for herself the incongruity: 'The other inhabitants of the hotel are strange Greeks and Turks and parties in turbans and Circassians with rows of cartridges set in their brown frock coats – oh the oddest world! It doesn't surprise me when I'm in tents and part of it, but when I come into an hotel [and] put on civilised clothes, my surroundings astonish me at times.'

A sign on the gate of the Ala Cami in Kadirli (the old Kars Bazaar) apologizes for the suspension of services during restoration work on the mosque and directs worshippers to a porta-*mescit* to the rear. Inside, workmen are scraping the filth of centuries from a moulding adorning the sanctuary of what was once an early Byzantine church on the site of a Roman temple. Hard hats sit disregarded on shelves in front of them.

Suddenly a caretaker rushes up. 'What are you doing?' he demands.

'Looking at the church.'

'*Yasak* [Forbidden]!' he snaps.

I step outside. I start to walk around its exterior.

'What are you doing?' he yells.

'Walking round the church.'

'You must wear one of these!' And to my amazement he rushes into the church, snatches one of the helmets from the shelves then watches while I put it on.

In April 1905 a swollen river was blocking the most direct approach from Kadirli to Anavarza and the remains of ancient Caesarea ad Anazarbus. 'Girth deep in water, we splashed on through an aquatic world of frogs and water beetles, the broken piers of the aqueduct serving as signposts to the road. The air was heavy with the rank smell of the marsh, the very water seemed to rot under the sun,' Gertrude wrote. But trusting to 'Providence', she battled on, drawn by the 'great hog's back of Anazarbus [standing] up boldly like a long rocky island in the sea of the plain'. At last she passed through a ruinous gate leading into the walled enclosure of a lost town as the sun was setting. Her caravan having fallen behind, two soldiers swept out an empty room and brought curds and bread to pad out a sardine supper. 'I ate, saw to the comfort of my horses, spread my cloak upon the mud floor and slept as though the mosquitoes … were non-existent,' she wrote. In the morning the 'dense mass of verdure, waist high in places' was so initially discouraging that she decided to venture up the hog's back first. From there, she glimpsed her caravan finally nearing the gate and 'abandoned further researches for the joys of a bath and a reasonable luncheon'.

But over the next three days, she was able to record the remains of two fortresses and three churches at Anazarbus. The most intriguing turned out to be an Armenian church on the hog's back, although documenting it required nerves of steel – 'snakes dropped out of the vaulting and fell with a thud upon the floor as I measured and photographed'. Ultimately the great heat and the stench of the marshes drove her out, but not before she had written to her mother: 'I have fallen a hopeless victim to the Turk; he is the most charming of mortals and some day when I have a little more of his language, we shall be very intimate friends.'

Today the walled enclosure at the base of the escarpment has the feel of a Cotswold meadow fenced in by a drystone wall then blown up to ten times the usual size. Now cattle crop the grass here. Sheep too. The ruins seem like an afterthought except to the south, where archaeologists are striking out from the monumental gateway as single-mindedly as locusts, steadily lifting the turf to expose the flagstones of a Roman road buried just beneath the surface.

Anazarbus offers another of Anatolia's historical speed bumps, the evidence in this case taking the shape of the Armenian church. Empty now, it nonetheless once housed the tombs of members of the Rubenian dynasty that ruled over a part of the forgotten Armenian Kingdom of Cilicia. In the tortuous history of Turkey this is a complexity too far for most students. Still, the fact remains that at the time of the Selçuk invasion of Anatolia much of the east belonged to the Armenians. Driven south, they resettled in Cilicia, establishing their capital first here in Anazarbus (which they renamed Anarvaza), then at Tarsus and finally at Sis (modern Kozan). It was the Rubenians who repaired the ancient walls and commissioned the castles.

At the bottom of the steps running up the hog's back I find Adam Dede (Granddad Adam) waiting for visitors in a tea shack. It's as well I didn't pause to chat to him on the way up or I might have missed out on the splendid view from the summit. Because Adam Dede has a list almost as long as the escarpment of rock-based mishaps, few of them with happy endings.

'There was an American man,' he says. 'He fell off and died.'
'When?'

'Oh, ten years ago. Then there was an English woman. We told her not to go up there alone, but she went anyway and never came back. We waited and waited. Nothing.'

I rustle up a suitably shocked expression and off he goes again. 'Then there were the three people who climbed up in January about six years ago. They started out like you at ten o'clock but by four they still hadn't come back. I called up the rock. I phoned the headman. He went up with a cigarette lighter and shone it into all the holes. In the end he found them, huddled together and shivering.'

In the village proper I make the acquaintance of Hatun Teyze (Aunty Hatun), in whose garden are gathered many of the capitals, columns and sarcophagi rescued from the site over the years. Hatun Teyze has a face as wrinkled as a bedsheet after a sleepless night. Her claim to fame is that she was until she retired in 2005 Turkey's one and only female *bekci* (night-watchman) and the story of how this came about is delightful. When workmen digging in the family orchard stumbled upon a mosaic, the state agreed to build a house for the owners in return for giving up their rights to it. But when they started digging the foundations for the house, lo and behold, another mosaic appeared. By then Hatun Teyze's husband had died. Asked what recompense she wanted for this second mosaic, she asked to be appointed watchwoman, a post she clung to despite intermittent threats from would-be treasure-seekers.

With the late Hatun Teyze, Turkey's first female night watch (woman), at Anavarza; 2015

Like Adam Dede, Hatun Teyze launches into a recitation of lost-tourist horror stories. She's happy to reminisce about her *bekci* days over a thimble-sized cup of Turkish coffee, but mostly her energies are focused now on her vast family of eight children and sixteen grandchildren. Are you married, she asks me, and when I demur she looks bemused before collecting herself to offer words of reassurance. But the subject clearly bothers her and she returns to it again and again.

'Come and live with me,' she suggests. 'I'll find you a husband. It's not too late.'

Hatun Teyze's party piece used to be pouring a pitcher of water over the mosaic in her courtyard to bring out its jewel-like colours. Now it's a prize-in-waiting for the new Adana museum. A blanket covers the tesserae. Never again will a droplet sully them*.

*The museum opened in 2017; Hatun Teyze died in 2019.

19
The Room with Oxblood Walls
OSMANİYE–GÖZEN–PAYAS–İSKENDERUN

*'I feel out here more like the Heathen than ever, for the passion for
storks and stones becomes a positive worship.'* Letter, 6 May 1911

I go to sleep in Osmaniye and awake in the morning to find that a
political earthquake has taken place. Following the lost decade of the
1990s, during which one weak coalition government after another
tried and failed to cling to power, the AK Party has governed Turkey
unchallenged since 2002, its majority actually increasing in the 2007
and 2011 elections. The assumption had been that it would continue
on the same upward trajectory in this election too. But now I open
my eyes to find that the unthinkable has happened. The HDP has
not only breached the ten per cent barrier but landed twelve per cent
of the vote. Far from increasing its share of seats in parliament, the
government has lost its majority.

On the streets there is nothing to suggest that anything out of the
ordinary has happened. Osmaniye is the constituency of Devlet
Bahçeli, the leader of the MHP, the main nationalist party, in celebration of which it is flying a flag so outsized even in a country over-
stocked with outsized flags that on arrival I'd almost missed my
footing and fallen off the kerb at the sight of a blood-red sheet big
enough to cover fifteen beds flapping in the wind. The MHP has not
fared well in the polls, but no one here sees any need to disturb their
usual routine.

Just as doctors have their heartsink patients, the ones who return
time after time but for whom they can do little, so travel writers have
their heartsink destinations, the ones they profoundly hope never to
have to visit again. The reasons may vary. A dearth of attractions. A
paucity of decent places to stay. Even poorly designated infrastructure can do it. For me, Osmaniye is just such a place, its importance
predicated more on its crossroads position just north of the Hatay
than on anything peculiar to itself.

Camping on the outskirts, Gertrude had described it as 'a modern
Turkish village, beautifully situated at the foot of the Giour Dagh',

but today mist is obscuring the Gavur Dağı (Infidel Mountain), leaving little for me to admire except pavements laid with Astroturf. I pause to try a local dish of *bicibici*, a rosewater-flavoured iced delicacy with slithers of rose jelly for added bite. I down a *simit* the colour of fake suntan. Then I hasten to escape.

At Hierapolis, north of Osmaniye, cut straw weaves threads of gold through the fields while sunflowers turn radiant faces to the sky. The remains here are slight, overgrown and forgotten. Yet this was once the capital of a short-lived kingdom, another of those complicating speed bumps. Who now has heard of King Tarcondimotus? But for a century or so during the unsettled period when Rome was mutating from Republic to Empire, Tarcondimotus was a man on first-name terms with Julius Caesar and Mark Anthony. He and his family bestrode this busy part of Turkey like colossi, their writ extending at least as far as Anazarbus.

I amble along another stretch of exposed Roman road and poke about briefly in the remains of two Byzantine churches. Then I wander down to the scant ruins of the theatre. High up on yet another impossibly rocky pinnacle, sits the castle of Castabala, possibly built by the Crusaders, possibly by the Armenians. At its foot squats a row of solar panels, a casual slap to the face of history.

There's not much more to see at Geuzenne (modern Gözen), south of Osmaniye, although the walk to the ruins is considerably enlivened by a lengthy stretch of aqueduct, brooding basalt framing the ivy-dark foliage of an orange orchard. The track lurches left through a break in the arches. Beside it a curved hollow tinted blue by globe thistles marks the site of another buried and forgotten theatre. Arriving in a downpour, Gertrude was soon arguing with Mikhail, her sot of a cook. The baggage handlers showed up late and immediately fell to blaming each other for the trial of erecting sodden tents. This was a rare occasion when even she couldn't sugar-coat the hardships of early-twentieth-century travel in 'a roadless and bridgeless country ... I was tired and wet and hungry and bad weather travelling is exhausting to the mind and to the body.' It was also one of the rare occasions when she acknowledged the drawback of her sex: 'What my servants needed last night was a good beating and that's what they would have got if I had been a man ... but as it is I have to hold my tongue and get round them by wiles.' Forced to pitch in with putting up the tents, she went to bed on a cold supper of biscuits and Russian beer 'because no one would own that it was his duty to light the fire'.

Luckier with the weather, I press on to where stacked terracotta tiles indicate the hypocaust of a lost bathhouse. Little else is intelligible. In any case I'm starting to feel twitchy.

'Don't go down there. It's dangerous. There are thieves.' Such were the words of the man in the petrol station where I'd paused to ask for directions. Now I'm alarmed to see three young men on motorbikes cruising up and down the track along which I need to return. I walk purposefully. I look neither to left nor right. Yet still I can sense them, and it's hard to imagine that they've come here to admire the thistles.

In the nearby town of Erzin there had been much gossip about a golden crown. For somewhere in the vicinity lay the battlefield where Alexander the Great challenged, then put to flight, the great Persian leader Darius at the Battle of Issus in 33 BC. According to Plutarch, Darius had run away, scattering his belongings in his wake. Surely that must mean hidden treasure, whispered the locals. Rumours raged of trucks sneaking up to Gözen and driving away again piled high with gold. Could it be that these young men had hoped for a Sunday jaunt culminating in the discovery of riches greater than a lottery jackpot? Could it be that I was getting in the way of their plans?

At the break in the aqueduct they pull to a stop and turn to stare at me, a scene from a Hollywood heist movie of the type that rarely ends well for the heroine. I glance around. There's no one else in sight, no welcoming house to run to. If I retreat, they will know that I'm frightened. There's nothing for it but to press on. As I approach the gap, they move silently apart to let me through. Then as I pass, one of them leans over his handlebars.

'Want a ride to the main road?' he asks.

In the Sokollu Mehmet Paşa complex in Payas (modern Yakacık) they're celebrating the end of the school year. Behind the covered bazaar a teacher is showing her charges how to start a vegetable garden while a photographer for the local paper dances attendance. In

Gertrude Bell's campsite in front of Cin Kulesi (Djinn Tower) at Payas in 1905

the courtyard of the medrese a troupe of folk dancers go through their paces in front of an audience of proud parents. I've arrived at the perfect time apparently. After many years, restoration of the complex has just been completed. Now some of the sixteenth-century shops beneath the soaring vaults are once again welcoming customers.

In 1905 Gertrude could write that 'Payas is a most singular place; it consists of a ruined arched bazaar, a big ruined khan, a mosque half ruined … and a castle which is a prison. Nothing else.' As she rode towards it nothing could have been further from her mind than the industrial backdrop to her northern English upbringing. Her diary speaks of wild vines, of lemon trees, of lupins, blue in the sun. In their place I note down an unbroken line of fertilizer factories, iron and steelworks, slag heaps and power stations, the brief gaps in between filled with the concrete requirements of modern living – apartment blocks, mini strip-malls, the odd hotel. Nature is putting up a gallant last stand in the shape of candy-pink oleanders and the occasional defiant hollyhock. Otherwise it's an utterly degraded landscape where, on a misty day, rusty ships float like bath toys in a sky indistinguishable from the sea.

In Bodrum Gertrude had managed to talk her way into the castle-prison, but in Payas they were having none of it. 'Permission was refused on the ground that the prisoners were all on sentences of 100 and 200 years and very savage,' she wrote. The day before her arrival two prisoners had apparently died in a brawl. 'They are given no work and very little to eat ... they have absolutely nothing to do but to fight one another and to try and escape. Both these pursuits they follow freely,' she added.

A second small castle, the Cin Kulesi (Tower of the Djinns), stands alone on a lip of flat land above the sea. 'We camped by the sea under a small Arab fort,' wrote Gertrude, and a photograph shows her tent standing immediately beside it. This is one of those unforgettable moments when the past seems to catch up with the present and I can feel Gertrude breathing down my neck as clearly as if she were standing behind me. I want to rush up to the picnickers grilling their kebabs beneath scrubby trees and babble the story into their uncomprehending ears. Instead, I amble down to the shore and imagine her, sans boots and stockings, soaking her weary feet in the water and dreaming of a hot dinner. But the sea is surprisingly choppy. I look to my right. There's a foundry belching smoke from its chimneys on the horizon. I don't take off my sandals. I don't dip my toes in the water.

In 1905 Gertrude paid her second visit to İskenderun, the old Alexandretta. On a first fleeting visit in 1902 she had found the town enthusiastically celebrating Kurban Bayram, the Eid al-Adha. 'Everyone was walking here,' she wrote, 'the women in their best magenta gowns and the little girls with paper flowers stuck in their hair.' There was a 'tiny plaything of a railway line' that took the locals some way up the hill and she strolled along it to drink coffee in a pavilion amid streams and bridges 'with the nobility of the town who came riding out along the railway on Arab ponys'.

Despite her joy at being able to speak Arabic with the locals, she had not much cared for the town, 'a wretched little place built in a marsh; with splendid great mountains behind'. Today's İskenderun is assertively modern, yet midway along the waterfront a strikingly attractive old building has managed to dodge the developers. Painted the colour of wet sand, it has a loggia with Gothic arches whence residents would once have admired a fountain playing in the garden. Today, weeds have strangled the flowers, but when I

Hind Kuba, last honorary British vice-consul in İskenderun; 2015

walk round to the street-facing side of the building I'm thrilled to find a brass plate reading 'Catoni'. The Catonis were to İskenderun what the Whittalls were to Bornova: a Levantine family without whom little of the town's business could have been transacted. Accordingly, the office of the Catonis used to house the British Consulate and it was to this building that Gertrude headed as soon as she rode into town in 1905. It's here, too, that I make the acquaintance of eighty-eight-year-old Hind Kuba, the last person to have served as İskenderun's honorary British vice-consul. Small, slim and dressed in a nautically-striped top and black slacks, Hind was born in 1927, a year after Gertrude's death in Baghdad. But her great age makes her a living link to the Levantine past and she happily conjures up the cosmopolitan İskenderun of her childhood, a port town where, just as in Smyrna, a babel of languages echoed around the busy streets. The traders mainly spoke French, but most people were comfortably multilingual. 'I speak English, French, Arabic and Turkish, with a little Dutch and Italian too,' she laughs.

Now İskenderun turns a very Turkish face to the world, but Hind's is the story of a time when it was part of the Sanjak of Alexandretta, an autonomous entity that existed from 1921 to 1937 before being absorbed into the Turkish Republic. Her mother was from Aleppo, but her grandfather probably came from Cyprus. Her birth name was Hanvat Alexander, but 'having a Greek name wasn't a great idea in the new Republic. When Atatürk made everyone pick a surname in the 1930s my widowed mother didn't know what to choose. Some people came up with appropriate names such as Filipoğlu, but she was too busy caring for six children to be worrying about such things. So Kuba was the name we were given by the state.' The Hind part is Arabic.

When she was a girl there were only about fifteen thousand people in İskenderun, although the large Christian population could support nine separate churches. 'Everyone knew each other,' she sighs. 'My mother used to call it Little Paris.' That was a time, too, when even city dwellers practised a form of nomadism. Many families, especially the Armenian ones that had arrived in 1915, maintained summer homes with large gardens in *yayla* (upland) settlements, where mountain breezes moderated the sweltering summer heat. 'But in 1938 the Armenians went, leaving everything behind. The Turks took over the gardens but didn't know how to care for them. We had twelve acres of garden. It's all gone to seed now, but what can we do?'

As a young woman Hind worked for Catoni, the local agency for Lloyd's shipping insurance. At the same time, she served as an assistant to the vice-consul, before inheriting the role and continuing to hold it unofficially until she was seventy-two. Proudly she shows off pictures of a visit to Ankara to receive an MBE, a trip to London to visit Buckingham Palace. Hind's eyesight is failing and she rarely leaves her apartment. But 'impossible is not a word in my dictionary!' she laughs – a woman after Gertrude's own heart.

And so we sit side by side in a room with oxblood walls, two women who never married and built their lives around work brought together by the memory of another woman who never married and built a life around travel and politics; a woman who almost certainly sat in this self-same room more than a hundred years before us, gazing out at the sea and plotting the next stage of her journey.

20

A God Beneath a Mulberry Tree

ANTAKYA–HARBİYE–ÇEVLİK

'Antioch is like the pantaloon whose clothes have grown too wide for his lean shanks.' Letter, 7 April 1905

Straddling the rocky ravine behind the cave where St Peter is believed to have established the first Christian church outside Jerusalem stand a line of brick and tile arches with a stone wall balanced on top of them. No great beauty, this is nonetheless the Iron Gate (Demir Kapı), one of the last surviving fragments of the impregnable walls that used to protect Antakya in the days when, as Antioch-on-the-Orontes, it was the third biggest city in the Roman Empire, exceeded in size only by Rome itself and Alexandria.

In those days Antioch outranked Ephesus in the glamour stakes, its marble streets crowded with some 300,000 residents, the river chock-full of boats. Earthquakes sporadically battered the city*, shattering its great monuments. But Antioch was hemmed in between soaring mountains and the churning River Orontes (Asi). With nowhere obvious to relocate to, the decision to rebuild on the same site was made time and again. So while visitors can wander the abandoned streets of ancient Ephesus, sit down in its ancient theatre, even wander into houses preserved with Pompeii-like completeness, in Antioch they must be grateful for the occasional snatched glimpse of the past uncovered by builders' shovels as development rips through the modern town.

Until the middle of the nineteenth century the walls remained on life-support. Dating back to the founding of the city in the aftermath of the death of Alexander the Great, when this part of his kingdom fell to his general, Seleucus I Nicator, they had been strengthened in the fourth century during the reign of the Emperor Theodosius. 'Forty years ago the walls and towers of the Acropolis were still almost perfect,' wrote Gertrude in 1905, adding 'they are now almost destroyed'. Nor was there much mystery behind their loss. 'It is prosperity not

---

*In February 2023 two massive earthquakes destroyed much of the historic centre of modern Antakya.

earthquake that has wrought the havoc … To spare himself the trouble of quarrying, the Oriental will be deterred by no difficulty, and in spite of the labour of transporting the dressed stones of the fortress to the foot of the exceedingly steep hill on which it stands, all the modern houses have been built out of material taken from it.'

The Iron Gate was one of five entrances to the city. The Gate of St Paul opened onto the road from Aleppo, the Gate of St George onto the main road through town, and the Daphne Gate onto the road leading to what was then the wealthy suburb of Daphne and is now Harbiye. The Bridge Gate that stood on the Orontes itself survived into Gertrude's time but has since been demolished.

'Road-widening [the usual suspect]?' I ask local historian Mehmet Tekin.

'No. But times had changed. The city had grown. There were no security issues any more. The walls had gone. There was no longer any need for a gate.'

★   ★   ★

Gertrude arrived in Antakya in 1905 at the end of the journey through Palestine and Syria described in *The Desert and the Sown*. Her route brought her over the Orontes into Turkey from what is now Salqin in modern Syria and, on arrival, she was immediately struck by how completely the past had been erased. 'The Antioch of Seleucus Nicator is a city of the imagination only,' she wrote; '[it] is like the pantaloon whose clothes are far too wide for his lean shanks; the castle walls go climbing over rock and hill, enclosing an area from which the town has shrunk away'.

She set up camp near a cemetery in what she called the Nosairiyeh (Nusayri) neighbourhood, now the Affan Mahallesi. Mehmet Tekin tells me that the cemetery is buried beneath the state hospital, which helps me pin down the campsite's probable location to within sight of the only other significant reminder of the walls, an octagonal tower squatting like a toad between the houses. It's squeezed in between a hospital and a clinic, where an apology for a park now occupies a shelf of flat land, but Gertrude delighted in the view, with 'the whole town below us [and] the great castle rock above … I recognised that beauty is the inalienable heritage of Antioch.'

Her reference to the 'strange sect' called the Nusayri stirs up a sectarian hornet's nest. The Hatay is often said to be an Alevi stronghold, but in fact it's an Alawite, or Nusayri, stronghold, the similarity between the two names leading to glib conflation of two groups whose beliefs and traditions are quite different. The Alawites are the sect to which President Assad belongs and in Syria they are particularly numerous around the port city of Latakia. Latakia is a mere hundred kilometres south of Antakya, and the Alawite presence in Antakya speaks powerfully of the arbitrary line-in-the-sand nation-building that followed the end of the First World War. Indeed, at the time of the Sanjak of Alexandretta there was also an acknowledged Alawite State, the Sanjak of Latakia; it lasted barely twenty years before being absorbed into French-governed Syria in 1936. The Alawites were called Nusayri in memory of Ibn Nusayr, who founded the sect in the ninth century.

So far, so straightforward. But everything else about the Nusayri/Alawites is more complicated, not to say controversial. Like Turkish Alevis, the Alawites hold Ali, the fourth Muslim caliph, in particular esteem. However, the rest of their faith is cloaked in mystery. 'They have a secret religion of which rumour speaks very ill … The learned suppose them to be a remnant of original Canaanites … I believe the learned think the Canaanites were Cretans, or of the same stock,' Gertrude scribbled. Whereas the Alevis treat women as equals, she was told that Alawite men did not even confide their beliefs to their wives for fear that they might reveal them. What's more, she noted, they celebrated a festival around the same time as Christmas at which a visitor claimed to have witnessed a jug and a large bowl of wine placed in the centre of the gathering. 'The Sheikh Ud Din was conversing with the jug. He put questions to it … and it answered with a gurgling sound.' But, on spotting an outsider, the crowd grew agitated and swore him to silence over what he had seen.

That story may sound fanciful, but even modern researchers struggle to worm out the truth. In 2012, while investigating the dying religious traditions of the Middle East for his book *Heirs to Forgotten Kingdoms*, Gerard Russell succeeded in interviewing an Alawite sheikh and extracted from him the fact that members were not allowed to eat camel or rabbit meat, or indeed the meat of any animal that was not from the same sex as themselves. Another interviewee also mentioned the role played by consecrated wine in their rites, and Russell himself identified traits that seemed to derive from Zoroastrianism and the planet-revering beliefs of the ancient Harranians, such as facing towards the sun to pray.

Unfortunately, pinning down anything about the Alawites is like trying to catch a lizard only to find its tail dangling between your fingers. The term Nusayri is no longer in common use, indeed is actively disliked, adherents of the sect preferring to be called Arab Alevis, or so I have been told. But when I put this to the only overtly Arab Alevi I meet in Antakya she laughs it off. 'Of course I'm Nusayri,' she says. 'Why wouldn't I be?'

İskenderun has its back firmly turned on all reminders of its past. But Antakya is where the Occident finally dissolves into a maze of narrow streets, their cobbled pavements worn smooth by centuries of sandal-wearers. Nowhere is its allegiance to the East more obvious than in the bazaar, where merchants' stalls scented with thyme and cinnamon jostle minarets topped with witch's-hat roofs. The cheese stalls sell *sürk peyniri*, soft orange teardrop shapes laced with red pepper. The pastry stalls sell *külçe*, fried buns with a sprinkle of poppy seeds. Others sell *taş kadayıf*, which look like Scotch pancakes but turn out to be savoury. The locals pile walnuts on them, fold them into sandwiches and douse them in syrup. They're utterly delicious.

Behind the bazaar is busy Kurtuluş Caddesi (Liberation Street). Back in the glory days this was one of Antioch's main thoroughfares, paved in marble by Herod the Great and one of the first streets in the Roman Empire to boast permanent lighting. Today's Kurtuluş Caddesi is a traffic-congested rat-run, which makes it hard to appreciate the grandeur of its century-old stone mansions. Uncertain of its new identity, it's a place where a soap factory has been reborn as a boutique hotel and smart restaurants hang out flags to welcome foreign visitors but where a man in grubby *şalvar* can still struggle along the pavement clutching a full-grown sheep, its legs sticking out in front of it like a table.

In the Affan Kahvesi at the southern end of the street I find Harun
Cemal holding court in front of a black and white photograph of the
Antakya of fifty years ago, when the Orontes flowed wide and free
and the creaking of enormous waterwheels peppered the evening
air. Far from being an Arab Alevi, Harun is an even greater rarity,
one of the last sixteen Jews in a town that, at the time of Alexander
the Great, boasted a rollcall of twenty thousand. After Titus put
down the Great Revolt against Roman rule in Palestine in AD 70,
many Jews flocked north and resettled in Antakya. The congregation
dipped in the Middle Ages, after the introduction of laws that
favoured Christianity, but recovered after the Ottomans occupied
Palestine in the early sixteenth century. Now it has shrunk so much
that two men must fly from Istanbul every Saturday to guarantee
the minyan of ten required for prayers.

Harun leads me into a building that still flaunts a Star of David
above its door. In the courtyard what seems more like a chapel than
a full-blown synagogue* sits alongside an abandoned school. Inside,
he throws back the doors of the Ark to display a collection of Torah
scrolls dating back to the start of Ottoman rule. On the walls hang
memorials to his ancestors, originally from Mesopotamia, the land
between the Tigris and the Euphrates.

Most of the last Jews left not for Israel but for Istanbul in the
1980s, he tells me. 'Why didn't you go too?'

'I was born here. My relatives are buried in this soil. If I were to
leave, soon there would be no Jews left here at all.'

As he locks the door behind him and shuffles back towards the
café, it occurs to me that I have been observing him much as I would
an endangered species of animal: a northern white rhinoceros in
Kenya, for example. There is that same poignancy in learning of a
crumbling in numbers to below the level of sustainability. And the
fall has been precipitous. In Gertrude's day there were still five hundred Jews left in the city and as recently as 2001 around one hundred
were still keeping the faith alive. Now the end is in sight. Harun may
not be about to abandon his post, but soon there will be no one left
to unlock the doors on Saturdays. The imminent demise of Judaism
in Antakya is as certain as that of that last northern white rhino.

*The quakes of 2023 killed the head of the Jewish congregation and his wife, and
damaged the synagogue. The rest of the congregation left the city.

★ ★ ★

The first person Gertrude encountered in Antakya was a Jew named Mr Duwek, who held the post of British vice-consul in the city. I'm taken to visit Josef Naseh, a man with the town's history at his fingertips. Not so long ago the houses of old Antakya had been abandoned to their fate. Most are now being transformed into cafés and restaurants, but Josef still lives in his childhood home, a tiny place once shared with eight brothers and their parents, whose frozen mosaic images gaze down on his book-filled study. By extraordinary coincidence it turns out that Josef's late father had worked with a member of the Duwek family in the cotton trade. The Duweks were wealthy and cultured, he tells me, but to the best of his knowledge none of them still lives in the city.

I book into the Antik Beyazıt Hotel in the bohemian-but-not-quite French quarter, a place of tightly shuttered windows, curvy wrought-iron balconies and tiled hallways that wouldn't look out of place in a rundown arrondissement of Paris. It was probably near here that Gertrude met Mr Orr, a Scottish engineer who worked for the American Liquorice Trust. Thrilled to learn that he had visited the Bell family chemical works in Port Clarence, Gertrude let Mr Orr help her replace a troublesome bay mare with a livelier chestnut. Then together they rode out to the Mountain of the Cross, on whose slopes sat a cave-church said to have been preached in by saints Peter and Paul.

Given her passion for Byzantine churches, it's odd that this significant historic monument should have elicited no more effusive a summing-up than that it was a 'charming place'. Instead, it was a huge head carved into the nearby rockface that set her literary juices flowing. The head was said to have been placed there to fend off an outbreak of plague in the reign of Antiochus IV, and the locals thought it depicted Charon, the ferryman believed by the Ancient Greeks to row the dead across the River Styx to Hades. Gertrude, however, assumed it to be the Sphinx and waxed lyrical about its face, turned attentively eastwards. 'If she could speak she might tell us of great kings and gorgeous pageants, of battle and of siege, for she has seen them all from her rock on the hill side,' she wrote, and up she shinned to inspect the damage inflicted on its features by the centuries.

★ ★ ★

Mr Orr rode out with Gertrude to Harbiye, the old Defne, a leafy valley with a stream running through it that was associated with Daphne, the wood nymph beloved of Apollo who prayed to her father for protection from the sun god's advances and was turned into a laurel bush. Like most modern visitors, Gertrude was more taken with the site's natural beauty than with its mythology. 'The torrent … is born in a deep, still pool that lies, swathed in a robe of maidenhair

Gertrude Bell's 'Sphinx'
(more probably a carving of Charon)
in Antakya; 1905

fern … from the pool issues a translucent river, unbroken of surface, narrow and profound; it runs into swirls and eddies and then into foaming cataracts and waterfalls that toss their white spray into the branches of mulberry and plane,' she wrote, a description that might still be valid today were it not for the usual concrete spoliation and the souvenir stalls that race down the muddy access track then pass the baton to a scattering of restaurants.

Modern Harbiye wears its political allegiance on its sleeve. Alevis tend to be more left-wing than other Turks, a generalization that holds for their Alawite cousins too. This fact manifests itself in the produce on sale at the stalls, where, alongside images of the Caliph Ali and swords with distinctive forked blades, a veritable shooting gallery of leftist heroes is immortalized on factory-made rugs. There's Atatürk of course. There's the Communist poet Nazım Hikmet. There's Deniz Gezmiş, a student leader dubbed the 'Che Guevara of Turkish insurrectionary Marxism'. There's the imprisoned PKK leader Abdullah Öcalan. And, explicable only in the Alawite context, there is Bashar al-Assad, the leader whose refusal to accept the need for change precipitated the whole wretched Syrian catastrophe.

In 2013 Turkey was convulsed by the popular uprising that has come to be known simply as Gezi after the scruffy little Istanbul park whose planned replacement with a reconstructed Ottoman barracks proved the spark that ignited an inferno. During the ensuing mayhem eleven men lost their lives, including one who had been born in Hatay and another who was killed there. At that time Harbiye had felt like a frozen scream of pain and rage. In the cafés signs brandished a vocabulary of defiance and in-jokes that played to a sympathetic clientele. But time has passed and tempers cooled. It wasn't wise then to be so overt about one's politics. It's even less wise now.

A god beneath a mulberry tree. Cavefuls of silkworms. A sea-girt hall of columns fit for a triton's banquet. Gertrude's description of Çevlik has a lyrical quality which could hardly contrast more sharply with the grim reality of a modern seaside resort where concrete benches rough-cast to look like logs turn defiant faces to the sea. But then it was not of modern Çevlik that she was writing but of the ancient Seleucia Pieria, the last resting place, she seems to have believed, of Seleucus I Nicator, one of Alexander's greatest generals before he became a ruler in his own right. Seleucus is a monarch to whom history has not been kind, a wallflower forever overshadowed by his illustrious friend. Yet according to the Roman historian Appian he once ruled over an empire stretching all the way from Phrygia in central Anatolia to the banks of the Indus. It was second in size only to Alexander's own, and Gertrude had become an ardent fan while travelling through northern Syria.

Cantering in after a six-hour journey south from Antakya, she was anxious to explore the ruins of the town that once served as the port for ancient Antioch, built in the days when 'kings could create world-famous cities with a wave of the sceptre'. Finding 'sand and sea and hills, mulberry gardens filling all the enclosure of the ancient walls, and a little Armenian village scattered through the mulberry trees', she scratched plans to return to Antakya for the night. Pitching her tents on the spit of land that juts out into the sea in front of the modern military base, she was overcome by the sort of exhaustion that occasionally overwhelms even the hardiest of travellers and determined to permit herself a day of rest and recuperation. It was 'the first really idle day since I had left Jerusalem', she wrote, and that had been two months earlier.

It was April, peak season for silkworm breeders, and the rock at the back of the village was riddled with caves where Gertrude came upon villagers fattening up larvae behind curtains of greenery designed to shield the cocoons from the sun. Her 'bright-eyed and intelligent' guide İbrahim spoke Arabic and complained vociferously that this was a useless trade, barely providing work for two months, after which all were left unemployed. His heart was set on escape to Cyprus and thence to America, although the only way to do this, he told her, was to save enough of his paltry income to bribe the police.

The Çevlik Gertrude took such a shine to was predominantly Armenian and she makes it plain that even in 1905 the topic of the Armenians was one best avoided. She was helped in her determination to do just that by the fact that most of the villagers spoke only Armenian and Turkish, and 'the few words of Arabic that some of them possessed were not sufficient to enable them to enter into a detailed account of their wrongs'. But then, as now, it was not always easy to sidestep awkwardness completely. In the morning an English-speaking woman named Kymet came calling. Her father had converted to Islam in order to take a second wife, she told Gertrude, whereupon his first wife had left him, preferring to struggle alone with her children than endure such an indignity. Now Kymet herself lived in poverty and dreamed, like İbrahim, of a refuge in Cyprus. The next day she sent her husband to greet Gertrude with a chicken and a note that she reproduced in *The Desert and the Sown*:

Welcome, welcome, my dearest dear, we are happy by your coming!

For your coming welcome! Your arrival welcome!

Let us sing joyfully, joyfully,

Joyfully, my boys, joyfully!

İbrahim guided Gertrude through what the locals called the Gariz, a channel sliced through the rock, part railway cutting, part rabbit-eared curvaceous tunnel with helva-smooth walls, that prevented the silt carried downstream by the Orontes from clogging up the harbour. Its construction had taken so long that although Vespasian had been the emperor when it started, the imperial diadem had passed to Titus by the time it was finished*. Now it bears witness to Roman engineering skill, pitch dark inside except where cracks in the rock admit slithers of sunlight, silent except when cohorts of squawking schoolchildren are frogmarched through it by their teachers.

In the rock above the tunnel an irrigation channel ferries water to the fields. Following it, I come to the Beşikli Mağarası (Cradle Cave), a wall of rock-cut tombs where the movers and shakers of the Roman era were laid to rest. Inside, I balance precariously on the rims of bathtub-like graves, all empty. Once my eyes have adjusted to the darkness, decorations etched into the corners of the cave swim into view; for Gertrude they were 'lotus leaves and conches', for me the fanned tail feathers of miniature, monochrome peacocks.

A scramble through the back of another cave decants me onto a path meandering down behind the village. It's the perfect place for a country stroll, far from the fake logs of the waterfront, far from the crisp packets and chocolate wrappers dropped in the tunnel by the schoolchildren. The only people keeping me company are a trio of villagers bent double over hoes. Then what looks like the top of a temple buried architrave-deep in the soil appears and up jump Gertrude's words: 'I saw a long moulded cornice which was apparently in situ though the wall it covered was buried in a corn-field; so thickly does the earth cover the ruins of Seleucia'. Near it İbrahim showed Gertrude the statue of 'a god, bearded and robed, sitting under the mulberry trees'. He was not a very impressive god, she wrote, 'his attitude was stiff, his robe roughly fashioned, and the top of his head was gone, but the low sun gilded his marble shoulder and the mulberry boughs whispered his ancient titles'.

With the sun shining down on it, Gertrude saw in Çevlik the beauty of the Bay of Naples, the steep sides of Kel Dağı (the ancient

*Vespasian r. 69–79; Titus r. 79–81.

Mt Cassius) playing understudy to Vesuvius. From the beach she gazed out to sea and allowed herself to fantasize that she was camping near the spot where her hero, the great Seleucus, had been laid to rest. Ahead of her rose a hall of columns carved from rock. It was 'fragrant of the sea and fresh with the salt winds that blew through it: a very temple of nymphs and tritons'. Beneath the sultry sky of an overcast morning such thoughts seem almost wilfully whimsical. A military base now hogs the coastline, and, as I scan the horizon for that hall of columns, the hairs on the back of my neck

Vespasian and Titus Tunnel ('Gariz') at Çevlik; 1905

© GBPA

bristle as binoculars are trained on me. Then the clouds part, the sun comes out, and for an instant the perfect camping spot appears.

21
The Man in the Cummerbund
NİZİP–KARKAMIŞ–BİRECİK

'[Met] an interesting boy, he is going to make a traveller.' Letter, 21 May 1911

In the shade of an arch leading off Nizip's main square a group of elderly men are whiling away the morning over *çay*. They're sitting in front of the padlocked gate of what looks like a late-date *han*. Hoping for a closer look, I try to sneak past unobserved, but at once their heads pop up and swivel round like those of the ground squirrels that used to haunt the Anatolian plain. Momentary silence descends before curiosity gets the better of them. Because foreign visitors are almost as unlikely as those squirrels in Nizip, a backwater town midway between Gaziantep and Şanlıurfa.

We bat conversation gingerly back and forth as I try to interest them in the history of the *han* while they try in typically Turkish fashion to divert me onto the minutiae of my identity.

'Do you know what this building was?' I ask hopefully.

'A soap factory. Olive-oil soap. Everything belonged to the same family,' one of the men replies, waving a hand towards a bulkily corbeled building that forms one side of the square.

The man keenest to talk to me is neatly besuited – I half expect him to pull a fob watch out of a waistcoat pocket with a flourish. 'Are you Christian?' he asks.

'Sort of,' I reply, shuffling awkwardly.

'What?'

'Yes, I was born Christian,' I say, shamed into firming up my reply.

'We're Muslim,' he says, as if anything else was likely in this particular part of deepest Anatolia.

When I mention that I'm heading south for Karkamış, alarm sparks in his eyes. 'Don't go,' he pleads. 'It's dangerous. Go to Zeugma instead. It's much better. Very historic. The Romans were there. The Greeks too. Tourists love it,' he winds up desperately.

The *dolmuş* to Karkamış leaves from one of those curious quarters to be found in all of Turkey's eastern towns that seem unsure of the time zone they're inhabiting. The glossy new branch of the İstikbal furniture emporium, for example, suggests an enthusiasm for the future. On the other hand, the house with one side fallen away to leave the bedrooms exposed suggests that the past is still very much lingering into the present too.

Several men are waiting for the *dolmuş* to depart. 'Are you Italian?' one of them asks me, the only foreigners normally to be found lurking by the *dolmuş* stand being the Italian archaeologists who have been excavating the neo-Hittite site of Carchemish on the Turkish-Syrian border since 2011.

It is, of course, this archaeological site that has brought me to Nizip at precisely the moment when considered opinion would advise staying well away from the border. For it was at Carchemish in 1911 that Gertrude met Lawrence, in the days when he was not yet the Hollywood dreamboat Lawrence of Arabia but just plain Ned, a blue-eyed, wet-behind-the-ears archaeologist yet to make his mark on the world. Gertrude was forty-three, Lawrence just twenty-three, and it was hardly love at first sight. The man who walked towards her looked younger than his age and was often perceived as 'weird'. Even his clothing marked him out. He was still some years from jettisoning Western garb altogether in favour of a *thobe*, but already he was testing the sartorial waters with an idiosyncratic combination of college blazer, baggy shorts and cummerbund.

Never one to keep an opinion to herself, Gertrude was soon chiding Lawrence and his companion, Reginald Campbell Thompson, for what she dismissively called their 'prehistoric' methods of excavation. In a letter to David Hogarth who was in charge of the dig, Lawrence described having put her firmly in her place:

> She was taken (in 5 minutes) over Byzantine, Crusader, Roman, Hittite & French architecture (my part) and over Greek folklore, Assyrian architecture & Mesopotamian ethnology (by Thompson); prehistoric pottery & telephoto lenses, Bronze Age metal techniques, Meredith, Anatole France and the Octoberists (by me), the Young Turk movement, the construct state in Arabic, the price of riding camels, Assyrian burial-customs, and German methods of excavation with the Baghdad Railway (by

Thompson). This was a kind of hors d'oeuvre: and when it was over (she was getting more respectful) we settled down each to seven or eight subjects and questioned her upon them. She was quite glad to have tea after an hour and a half, & on going told Thompson that he had done wonders in his digging in the time, and that she thought we had got everything out of the place that could possibly have been got: she particularly admired the completeness of our note-books. So we did for her*.

I like to think that after these initial tetchy exchanges Gertrude and Lawrence sat down beneath the stars and found common ground in their shared alma mater (Oxford), in their mutual love of Arabic and Charles Doughty's *Travels in Arabia Deserta*, and in the remote outposts such as Krak des Chevaliers that they had both visited. Certainly they dined together, their meal rustled up by Lawrence's cook. At first light villagers were waiting to wave Gertrude off with sardonic grins. Only later did she learn that Lawrence had quashed their hopes that she might be a potential bride. Far too plain, he explained.

'[Met] an interesting boy, he is going to make a traveller,' she wrote to her mother, a patronizing put-down given that less than two years earlier Lawrence had trekked over a thousand miles through the exact same Middle East as she had, in search of Crusader castles for his thesis. Little can either of them have suspected that they would go on to become fast friends, Gerty and Ned against the establishment when it came to the fraught years of struggling to shape new countries from the embers of the Ottoman Empire.

This was not Gertrude's first viewing of the great *tell* (mound) at Karkamış. In 1909 she had paid it a brief visit at the start of the journey down the Euphrates that was to become *Amurath to Amurath*. 'One can't be within a few hours of the capital of an empire without visiting it,' she wrote, although the detour required a tricky crossing of the Euphrates from Tell Ahmar (now in Syria). At the crossing point she found the boat half-full of water, which the devoted Fattuh duly bailed out. But soon 'a little sharp west wind had got up and the boatmen began to shake their heads and eye the ruffled Euphrates gloomily'. Not to be thwarted, she led her horses into the

*Quoted in Anthony Sattin's *Young Lawrence: A Portrait of the Legend as a Young Man*.

river anyway and recorded that 'the wind drove us a quarter of a mile and more down stream … we made very slow progress … but with a good deal of labour and much invocation of God and the Prophet we were at length landed on the other side'.

Except that they were actually beached on an island mid-river! 'The stream had risen during the rain of the previous day and was racing angrily through the second channel, but we plunged in and, with the water swirling round the shoulders of our horses, succeeded in making the passage,' she wrote, before turning her thoughts to all the thousands of people who had made the same journey before her, 'going up and down to learn the news of the capital and bring back word of the movements of Assyrian armies and the market price of corn'.

The return crossing proved no less tricky, for word had leaked out that the foreigner would be returning and 'every one in the district who happened to have business on the opposite bank and recognized in our passage an unusually favourable opportunity for getting over for nothing' had assembled on the riverbank. No sooner had they boarded the boat than 'some twenty persons and four donkeys hustled in after us and were likely to swamp us'. But Fattuh was having none of this and 'ejected half of them, pitching the lean and slender Arab peasants over the gunwales and into the water at haphazard until we judged the boat to be sufficiently lightened'. As far as Gertrude was concerned, those who managed to stay onboard soon earned their crossing when the boat ran aground again and 'they leapt out and, wading waist high in the stream, pushed us off'.

Inside the *dolmuş*, three headscarf-wearing women with toddlers in their laps wait demurely, no doubt summing me up as a shameless hussy to be out on the pavement chatting with men. Then the engine starts up and we whisk through the outskirts of Nizip, before turning abruptly left and heading straight for the border. On either side of us fields of coffee-coloured soil sprout rows of pistachio trees. At Karanfil we hang a right and trundle through a village that is little more than a large turkey farm. Then we rattle into Karkamış and at once the halfway modern world of Nizip falls away, its place taken by a settlement that looks as if it can't quite make up its mind whether it's in Turkey or Syria.

The *dolmuş* pulls up in front of a wretched ticket office occupied by no ticket seller and kitted out with what looks like a cast-off office desk and a pair of blue plastic chairs. With an hour to wait before the archaeologists can collect me, I stroll up the road to drink *çay* in a men-only tea garden shaded by a pistachio tree and a vine-covered trellis. But this is a place where a sudden movement at the corner of one's eye that one takes at first for a passing pigeon turns out instead to be a plastic bag gently billowing in the breeze. Keeping me company beneath the pistachio tree are an assortment of discarded plastic water bottles resting on a carpet of cigarette butts. A commotion beside the rubbish bin comes from a cat and dog sparring over scraps.

If Nizip had had the rather jumpy air of a hostess caught on the hop by an unexpected dinner guest, Karkamış seems stupefied by the rapid change that has hit it. Not that long ago it had lived for the German-built railway line that still forms its perimeter.

'When did the trains stop running?' I ask a shopkeeper.

'Fifteen years ago,' he says. 'Then Karkamış was busy, busy. Now …' And, exhausted by that short exchange, he hastens back indoors.

'Can you speak Arabic?' his companion asks immediately.

I shake my head. 'Are you Syrian?'

'Yes.'

'When did you come here?' He struggles to explain, but his Turkish isn't up to it.

'Recently,' the shopkeeper says, popping out again to offer *çay*. 'He came recently. He has family here,' and he starts into one of the rambling sagas of family intricacy that are a staple of Turkish introductions: who is married to whom, who is brother or sister of whom, who is uncle or aunty twice removed.

'Are there many Syrians here?' I ask, to curtail the litany. A quick whip round the town had shown me the old border with Jarablus sealed up with breezeblocks. Across the road, the shops where visitors used to exchange Syrian money or hire cars to drive to Aleppo stood abandoned. 'Want go Syria?' a boy of about ten yelled at me.

It was enough to send me scurrying for the sanctuary of this shop.

'Up the road. A tent city. The population? Half as much again now with the Syrians,' the shopkeeper says.

I'm trying to imagine what this would mean for a small town with nothing going for it beyond the border crossing when a white van bringing the archaeologists back from work comes zooming up. The door opens and I step straight into another world, a world of excitement, and purpose, and discovery, and the sort of honest exhaustion that comes from physical toil. Here are young people in their twenties, bright-faced, cheerful, above all healthy, in a uniform of jeans, T-shirts and trainers. Some lean against the windows, snatching sleep. Others throw words around the bus like jugglers tossing balls in the air. On the floor baskets made from tyre re-treads hold the fruits of the morning's digging.

Off we race into the countryside again. When Gertrude had ridden to meet Lawrence there had been no border to impede her. Everything had been seamless Ottoman Empire; remote and quarrelsome, perhaps, but still a recognizable entity. Then, within the space of a few years, all the paraphernalia and basic hostility of a frontier sliced through the middle of Carchemish. Even before war broke out, relations between Turkey and Syria tended to be tense and access to the site was stymied by politics. Now, exploring the ruins is out of the question, I've been told, the proximity of fighting having forced the shelving of plans to evict the military base there in favour of an archaeopark. Instead, I've been invited to spend the night with the archaeologists, a very Gertrudey thing to do, I think, as I sit down at a long table and tuck into macaroni with tomato sauce and a green salad, an oh-so Italian lunch prepared, unsurprisingly, by refugees.

We're eating in a concrete barn of a building which picks up and magnifies every word so that it feels as if we're in an aviary full of twittering budgerigars. Inevitably conversation turns to the war.

'Aren't you worried about being so close to the border?' I ask.

'Well, yes, of course we are sometimes worried,' admits one of the archaeologists. 'The main trouble isn't here, but we have heard shooting in the night and once we had to duck down behind the walls to avoid the bullets. Lawrence started work here in 1911 but had to stop in 1914 because of the war. We started work in 2011 and now look – it's getting worse all the time.'

Digging resumes in mid-afternoon and I settle down in the court-yard with a bucket of water and a scrubbing brush. I may have come here in search of Gertrude and Lawrence, but really Carchem-ish is a site about prehistory, a site that is particularly famous be-cause its name crops up in the Bible and because it was here that the Babylonian king, Nebuchadnezzar II, defeated the combined forces of the Egyptians and Assyrians in 605 BC. The main news of the season as far as the archaeologists are concerned has been the discovery of the palace of the neo-Hittite king Sargon, and I'm keen to earn my keep by scrubbing mud off shards of Hittite pottery while awaiting their return.

Sitting beside me in the sun are a woman from Idlib and her son, members of a family of eleven, forced, like so many others, to flee their home in the face of civil war. She knows only Arabic, but her fourteen-year-old son is making strides with Turkish.

'What about school?' I ask him.

He pulls a face. 'In Syria school. Not now,' he answers.

In a room nearby, two brothers are bent over less mundane frag-ments of pot, carefully copying patterns onto paper with the aid of compasses and dividers. They are veterans of many digs, now hop-ing to find work in Turkey as Syria's lifeblood drains out into the rest of the Middle East, leaking not just the poor and desperate but also the talented and best.

In the evening the archaeologists flow back again, dirty, ex-hausted, hungry. Professor Nicolò Marchetti strides into the dining room as pudding is being served. Ahead of our introduction I've let myself imagine a latterday Lawrence, a fancy that has to be dropped as soon as I clap eyes on him. Lawrence was famously short, mop-haired and very English in appearance. Nicolò, on the other hand, is a beanpole of a man, tall, greying, distinguished, a man whose presence immediately dominates the room. He's spent the day battling bureaucracy in Antep and presumably would have loved to be able to retreat to his office now. Luckily for me, though, the Turkish tradition of hospitality has rubbed off on him and the plates have no sooner been cleared away than he is steering me into the room in which most of the finds are stored. There he picks up a particular stone, the front carved with a face in profile displaying the distinctive flipped-up hairdo and beaky nose of a Hittite. 'Gertrude was very scathing about the digging methods they were using here. She said they were old-fashioned. But everything was carefully recorded. Even after they found the big orthostats they still recorded these smaller pieces too,' he tells me. And, turning the piece over, he reveals the number painted on its smooth reverse. It's in Lawrence's hand. I hold it with reverence, fondly allowing myself to imagine him showing it to Gertrude more than a century earlier.

While washing the pottery I'd been piecing together the domestic arrangements for the pre-First World War dig at Carchemish. At first, David Hogarth, the brother of Gertrude's university pal Janet, rented an abandoned liquorice factory in Jalablus (now on the Syrian side of the border) where the archaeologists could live and store their finds. But once they knew that this was a dig with legs, Lawrence and Hogarth's successor as chief archaeologist, Leonard Woolley, had a more convenient house built right in the middle of the site.

Trained as a classical archaeologist, Sylvia di Christina has drawn what must have been regarded as the short straw – unearthing the remains of that house in the forlorn hope that the Lawrence name would attract visitors. Small and dark, she wears her hair tied to one side and falling to her waist. Multiple piercings top out her ears. Her English is brisk and competent. On her computer she shows me a photograph of Lawrence standing in front of the house. Above the lintel is a carving of a *faravahar*, a winged sun disc dating back to Assyrian times, that he had carved himself.

'I've looked and looked, but I can't find it,' says Sylvia sadly. 'It was made from soft limestone. It was probably taken away and reused for something else.'

Unlucky she may have been with that particular stone, but in every other way she has hit pay dirt. In 1920 the British archaeologists briefly returned to the site when it formed part of the French mandate, but after the area was taken over by the Turks the dig had to be abandoned. The locals who moved into the house later reused slabs of Hittite basalt to improvise divans around the walls, placing them directly on top of a Roman mosaic that had been used to floor it. 'The parts that were hidden by the divan survived,' explained Sylvia, 'but the area left exposed in the middle of the room was destroyed.'

In this house Lawrence and his colleague Leonard Woolley stored the smaller finds from the site, many of them re-emerging as the modern dig proceeds. 'Every time I uncover something I rush back here to see if I can find a photograph of it,' says Sylvia.

But it's another photo that particularly catches my eye. This one shows a cosy sitting room with vases of flowers on a wooden table in front of a fireplace framed by slabs of Hittite masonry. The ceiling consists of rough-hewn tree trunks, a style of rural architecture common throughout Anatolia until recently. The walls and floor are adorned with oriental carpets, Lawrence having been an avid collector. It could be a picture of a London sitting room belonging to a member of the Bloomsbury Set, I think, and I want to imagine Gertrude walking into it, unlacing her boots, bending to smell the flowers, then settling down at the table with a glass of wine, anticipating an evening of lively conversation in English after months of speaking Arabic. Alas for that fancy, though, her visit took place while the men were still muddling through in the liquorice factory.

Up beside us pops Dr Hasan Peker, a man as dark and jolly as Nicolò is fair and earnest. Hasan reminds me of a Labrador puppy, full of irrepressible bounce. He's that rare thing, a fully-fledged Hittiteologist. 'There can't be more than a hundred of us in the world,' he laughs. 'One bomb on a plane on the way to a conference and they'd be rid of us all!'

With night falling, we sit beneath the stars, indulging in the sort of archaeological chitchat that can't help but stray into the black humour of current affairs. This was a part of Turkey where many locals traditionally made a living by smuggling tea and cigarettes across the border. 'It used to be difficult to get labourers to work on the site because we paid less than they could earn from smuggling. But when ISIS started chopping hands off, all that stopped. This year they're keen to work for us,' chuckles Hasan.

Professor Nicolò Marchetti and Associate Professor Dr Hasan Peker at Karkamış

At the mention of ISIS my ears prick up. Before my visit I had assumed the jihadists were still much further east. Now reality is dawning. 'They're just one kilometre away,' says Nicolò.

'Can you see their flags?'

'See their flags? We can see their faces!'

During the night, planes roar overhead as the Americans fly east to drop bombs in defence of Kobani. I leave Karkamış on the morning *dolmuş*, my brain buzzing with the extraordinary disconnects along this border. In one place, Italians digging for Hittite remains, scrubbing pottery in the sun and tucking into tasty Italian food on the site where two famous people had once met in untroubled times; in the other, Kurds forcing their way through fences to go to the aid of their compatriots on the far side of a border whose very existence was in part dreamed up by those same two people. How they would have despaired to see their handiwork unravelling so spectacularly.

At Birecik the Euphrates is wide and dramatic. But Birecik is also hot

and dusty. Very hot and dusty. Stepping out of the *dolmuş* is like stepping up to a kiln, the heat so intense that it all but crushes me. Like so many carefully planned itineraries, mine has slowly slipped its moorings. A day here, a day there, and now it's early July and I've arrived in the southeast of the country just as the temperature has soared into the mid-forties.

Nor is that the only problem. I take as quick a turn around the town as the need to keep to the shade will permit, and then the boom of a cannon marks the end of a day of fasting with a puff of smoke and a flutter of frightened pigeons. For not only is this the start of the sizzling season, it is also the first day of Ramazan, the Muslim month of fasting. Since Ramazan follows the lunar calendar, every year it retreats by eleven days. This year it coincides not just with the hottest days but with some of the longest too. Now all those taking part in the fast – which, in the southeast, means virtually everyone – will have to go without food, drink or cigarettes for the more than seventeen hours that yawn between dawn and dusk.

Birecik has always been one of the main crossing points on the Euphrates and in *Amurath to Amurath* Gertrude noted that Seleucus I Nicator had built a bridge here. By the time she rode into town, however, it was long gone and instead both riverbanks were lined with the high-prowed wooden sailing boats used to ferry people, their produce and their livestock across the river. The sheer press of boats ensured that there would be no hanging about. 'Ferried over,' she recorded. Simple.

Between her visit and the 1950s not much changed in Birecik. It remained a pretty mini-Mardin of a place with the Euphrates lapping against the walls of the Ulu Cami and the upper storeys of the Ottoman houses leaning out over it. Then in 1956 a modern road bridge was thrown across the river, obliterating almost overnight the age-old ferry trade. Of the 'splendid' Birecik she had admired, its castle 'long and narrow like a sword', only hints now linger: the odd house, the odd stretch of town wall, the ruined castle, shadows more than substance.

Gertrude made camp at Karşıyaka on the opposite side of the river, ready to head on to Carchemish at first light. With no boats to

Boats waiting to ferry passengers across the Euphrates (Fırat) in 1911

ferry me over, I force myself to walk across the bridge in defiance of the pounding traffic and then stumble down rusty stairs that look as if they might give way at any moment. In what should theoretically be a sublime setting, a few sad cows have been put out to pasture amid scattered rubbish. At the spot where I conclude from her photographs that she probably pitched her tents, trailing electricity wires prevent a closer look. A Kangal dog is snoozing in the sun in front of an abandoned tea shack, its legs as neatly crossed as a missionary's. It doesn't bother to lift its head as I pass. It's that hot.

22

City of Prophets

ŞANLIURFA–HARRAN–SUAYİP ŞEHRİ–SÜRÜÇ

'The pool itself with its mosques and cypress trees is one of the loveliest places I have seen in Turkey.' Letter, 14 May 1911

In the grounds of Şanlıurfa's Ulu Cami four great capitals hark back to the days when the church of St Stephen was erected over the remnants of an earlier synagogue. This is an extraordinary place, hallowed by time, where ghostly curves and huge stone uprights in the graveyard wall silently evoke the past, while an understated mosque ensures contemporary relevance. At the same time it's a humdrum, homely sort of place, its walls left to crumble, not yet subjected to sharp new pointing. Locals use the grounds as a shortcut from the bazaar to their homes in the medina-like back streets. Municipal refuse collectors in smart green and yellow jumpsuits gather here at the end of their shifts for a quick communal smoke. Boys kick footballs through an arched gateway that must be at least 1,800 years old. Another bends to wash an armful of aubergines in the *şadırvan*. And those plagued by a superfluity of cats sneak down here under cover of darkness to abandon them.

Those enormous capitals serve as handy perches on which men can sit and wait for the call to prayer and exhausted women can rest their shopping bags. One of the capitals is streaked with blood and for a brief moment I think of sacrifice, of the goats whose necks are still slit to celebrate good fortune. But reality is far kinder. Every evening a man stops by on his way home for dinner to toss the liver scrounged from a butcher onto the stone. The cats come running. The bloody scraps are gone in five minutes.

It's here that I settle down to wait for the call to prayer that will end the day's fast. In the corner of the enclosure an octagonal minaret that started life as the church tower now supports a lofty clock with Arabic numerals, a visual and aural landmark for the neighbourhood. With seconds to spare I see the muezzin dash to unlock a door neatly framed by Byzantine mouldings. A brief struggle with the key and then the familiar words ring out, *Allahu akbar*, and I envisage thousands of glasses of water being drained, thousands of cigarettes being lit, thousands of spoons being raised to hungry lips; the general heaving of a sigh of relief that a second never-ending day of religiously-sanctioned deprivation has drawn to its close.

© GBPA

Sacred Gölbaşı area of Şanlıurfa (Urfa) in 1911

Of all Turkey's cities, Urfa – as Şanlıurfa is generally known – is the one that most oozes Middle Eastern atmosphere, and its pulsating heart is Gölbaşı at the base of the rocky escarpment that is its most conspicuous feature. On one level Gölbaşı is a carefully tended municipal park, resplendent with roses in spring, on another it's a large and pleasingly understated evocation in physical form of the story of the Prophet İbrahim, the biblical Abraham. At one end sits Balıklıgöl, a picture-perfect pool of water framed on three sides by honey-coloured medieval buildings. It takes its name, meaning 'Lake with Fish', from the fat and sleepy carp that swim around in it. Those carp lead a particularly charmed existence even in a country where fish and birds take precedence as pets over dogs and cats. The reason is not hard to understand. Urfa is believed to have been the birthplace of İbrahim. Here, in a cave at the foot of the escarpment, İbrahim's mother was said to have hidden her new-born son from the murderous King Nimrod, who, in a copycat rendition of the story of Herod, ordered that all boy babies should be slaughtered lest one prove a threat to his supremacy. By her quick-wittedness İbrahim's mother saved her son, who grew up to be a monotheistic thorn in the polytheistic king's side. In desperation, Nimrod decreed that he should be burnt to death. A pyre was prepared but at the last moment Allah intervened, turning the flames into water and the coals into fish. Bingo, the Balıklıgöl.

Few places in Turkey can match the beauty of the setting: the turquoise water beneath the blazing sun; the rippling reflections of the mosques and medreses; the Kurdish and Arab women in their sequin-splattered robes pausing to toss pellets of food to the carp. Gertrude was mesmerised:

> The pool itself with its mosques and cypress trees is one of the loveliest places I have seen in Turkey. I spent a long time there under pretence of feeding the fish but really because after weary days of desert it was impossible to drag oneself away from the beauty of clear water and trees and graceful towers.

Of course she was more aware than the other fish-feeders of ancient antecedents for the reverence with which the carp were treated:

> it goes back into the dimmest mists of Oriental history, of which it preserves the memory in sacred pools stocked with unmolested fish which may not be caught … (though the pious Mohammedan who says his prayers by the Pool of Abraham and feeds the fish with corn is unaware of the reason) – because they were once consecrated to the goddess Atergatis [a fertility deity lustily worshipped at Lake Chalys in Hierapolis (modern Manbij) in northern Syria].

I pay my lira, toss sustenance to the carp and watch as they transform into ravening monsters. Bodies clump together, yellow mouths gaping wide to expose shiny white throats like those of baby swallows awaiting the return to the nest of their mother. But no sooner does the last pellet vanish than they separate out again and swim away, fins briefly jutting from the water like those of mini sharks, as nonchalant as cats simulating insouciance after a fall.

For a city as theoretically parched as Urfa there's actually a surprising amount of water about. The Balıklıgöl is fed from inside the Halilurrahman Cami, where tin cups chained to stone basins let visitors quench their thirst on the very spot where İbrahim so narrowly avoided sacrificing his son, İsmail (the biblical Isaac). But Gölbaşı floats on a network of water, one channel striking out across the park and pooling to a lucrative halt in front of the cafés of Ayn Zeliha, where Gertrude took tea in something resembling an eco-warrior's

Late afternoon at Hasan Paşa Cami in Şanlıurfa (Urfa) during Ramazan in 2015

bender. Water gurgles beneath the labyrinthine bazaar, popping up from time to time in drinking fountains that keep the shopkeepers hydrated. And, delightfully, it flows through the courtyard of the Hasan Paşa Cami. Here, where Gertrude photographed only seren-ity, a summer Ramazan licences small boys to strip to their under-wear and cavort in the stream. There, as the long day drags on, they're joined by their fathers, who roll up their trouser-legs to dunk heat-swollen ankles, then sit gossiping with friends as they await the *iftar* call to prayer.

At the end of the high street the now bone-dry Karakoyun river used to cascade prettily downhill beneath a series of bridges. Calling into the governor's palace on her way back from Syria in 1911, Gertrude was directed to a terrace overlooking it with space enough to pitch tents. They rode up, she wrote, to the grounds of an abandoned casino. There was 'a little kiosk with water running though it. Exquisite camp'. ·

My preferred candidate for that campsite is a piece of empty ground in front of the Mahmud Nedim Konaği, now a museum. Inside, I am introduced to Yusuf Sabri Dişli, who thinks there was once a *gazino* near the mansion, *gazino* being the Turkish name for a drinking-hole. We toss up whether an imperfect grasp of Turkish might have led Gertrude to confuse a *gazino* with a casino before moving on to more general matters.

'She was an imperialist. All the British were,' Yusuf guffaws.

'Well, I'm not an imperialist,' I retort, and the laughter turns quickly to stuttering apology, to reassurance of a joke.

We scroll through more pictures of Urfa on his computer. Then I knock against a glass ornament on his desk, a souvenir of participation in a conference. It falls to the floor and shatters. Blood snakes down my ankle, but I'm too embarrassed to mention it.

'British imperialism!' I say sheepishly.

'*Boş ver!*' says Yusuf. 'I have hundreds of those things. It's nothing.' And he pulls down a box that is indeed full of commendations and from it plucks a replacement, to much relieved chuckling all round.

The cave in which İbrahim was supposedly born seems barely big enough to bear the weight of the significance attached to it. The fact that the neighbouring Mevlidi Halil Cami is successor to a temple, synagogue and church on the same spot highlights its consistent numinosity. But even the mosque is modest, given an unexpected air of domesticity by a collection of crockery – rose-painted tea plates, Turkish *çay* saucers, even willow-pattern platters – embedded in its walls. In the way of modern Turkey, the modest mosque is now outstripped in importance by the pompous new Dergah Cami right beside it. The cave hunkers down on the other side. I duck my head under a low stone lintel and enter the women's side. The grotesque heat means that only the most ardent believers have ventured out to pray, so there is plenty of room to spare. I sit down for a few quiet moments but feel strangely uncomfortable. My head is covered, my shoes outside the door; I'm not doing anything obviously irreverent. But the deep piety of the other women humbles me. In this dank, confined space, generation after generation of their ancestors have gathered to worship. Their spirit pervades the atmosphere like autumn mist and my *gavur* status weighs as heavily as a superfluous overcoat. Outside, Koranic verses are being relayed from the minarets. They drift like the humming of bees over the bodies of the men dozing in the rose garden, the timeless Arabic words of faith melting into the heat, as soothing as a lullaby.

On the escarpment above Gölbaşı Gertrude took photographs of columns left over from the days when this was Osroene, the short-lived Nabataean Arab kingdom of Edessa. Even now the view is jaw-dropping, sweeping from the apparent flying saucer recently built to shelter a priceless collection of mosaics over a landscape of almost uniformly *balkaymak* (honey and cream) tones, with Gölbaşı a rare dollop of greenery. But if nature has conspired to rob their city of colour, the locals are having none of it, injecting reds, blues, yellows and oranges into their lives at every turn. Tubs outside shops are loaded with the deep purple flakes of the fiery *isot* pepper, a local delicacy. Every meal table is laid with a plate of scarlet peppers to be bitten into as casually as the bread. The clothes are the icing on the cake. Stepping out to feed the carp, young women glitter like birds of paradise. Elsewhere one might assume from their floating robes, their glittering gold jewellery, their delicate veils that they were en route to a fancy-dress party. Here, though, it's perfectly normal for a matron to pop to the mall in a lace-embroidered gown of purple velvet, not at all outré for a grizzled patriarch to cover his head with a lilac scarf that would normally be shelved on the female side of the store.

Urfa is full of such contradictions. This, the most conservatively Muslim of cities, maintained a large Christian population right through until the First World War, and the architectural evidence is still plain to see, albeit disguised beneath later Islamic trappings. It's there in the clocktower-minaret of the Ulu Cami, and it's there in the campanile of the Halilurrahman Cami beside the Balıklıgöl. It's there in the Selahaddin Eyyubi Cami, once the enormous Armenian Apostolic cathedral of St John the Baptist. And it's there, most of all, in the Fırfırlı Cami, hidden behind high walls, its frilly name commemorating an early wind turbine.

Originally the Armenian Protestant Church of the Twelve Apostles, the Fırfırlı Cami is a unique piece of Gothic architecture with an interior patterned on Norwich and an exterior that wouldn't look out of place in Nicosia. At the turn of the twentieth century the church was part of an American missionary complex incorporating a school for the blind. The prime mover was Corinna Shattuck, a woman from Kentucky whose death in 1910 after fifteen years of devoted service Gertrude recorded in her diary alongside the sad fact that many of the boys being taught to turn wood and make shoes at the school had been orphaned during the Adana massacre.

Old Urfa is blessed with some of Turkey's most distinctive architecture, a reminder that nineteenth-century Anatolia was still a hotchpotch of local building styles before twenty-first-century architects achieved what Atatürk had tried and failed to do and unified Turkey through the medium of concrete high-rises. Across the road from the Ulu Cami a doglegged corridor designed to guarantee family privacy leads from a windowless exterior into the courtyard of the Hacıbanlar Evi, a stunning mansion adorned with amber-coloured carvings as delicate as embroidery. Its inward-looking nature may be utterly Urfan, yet at the same time the architecture gives off a faint hint of medieval Europe: Romanesque in the thick-set corbels supporting the pigeon-houses along one wall, Gothic in the quadripartite vaulting converging on a central boss in a living room. In common parlance the Turkish word *avlu*, meaning courtyard, is often replaced by *hayat*, meaning 'life'. Seated in one of the *liwans* (open-fronted halls) framing the courtyard, Ahmet Polat explains: 'We called the courtyard the *hayat* because it really was the centre of our lives. When the *poyraz* was blowing, we would sit in the *liwan* facing the sun for shelter. In the morning, when we were shivering, we would move to the other side to make the most of the sun.'

I note his use of the past tense and remember from a year ago a gateway in the back streets, the door ajar; remember walking into a courtyard bigger and even more breathtakingly beautiful; remember a woman about my own age perched on the rim of the central fountain. A sign on the gate read '*Satılık* [For Sale]'.

'It's so beautiful. Why would you want to sell?' I asked.

But would-be hoteliers were circling like vultures. She cast a sad look around her. 'My family has grown up. They've left. There's just me now. What do I need with all this space?'

In the carefully restored Narlı Evi, Müzaffer Bey, the snowy-haired caretaker, shows me the public lounge where *sıra gecesis* used to be held. Men-only gatherings hosted in rotation in neighbourhood homes, traditional *sıra gecesi* offered a chance to catch up on news and devise ways to help those fallen on hard times. A loudly trumpeted component of the local tourism industry, their latterday namesakes are standard Turkish entertainment nights dressed up with an alluringly local name. Music and alcohol feature heavily.

For Müzaffer, the tourist *sıra gecesis* are noise pollution, good for the organizers, a nightly irritation for everyone else. 'Bang, bang, bang,' he says, mimicking the beating of a drum then sticking his fingers in his ears.

'Are there still any genuine *sıra gecesis*?'

'Yes,' he replies, before backtracking. 'At least there were before the Syrian war. Now there are just too many people in need. No one can cope. So they've had to stop.'

In the dusty wastes of old Harran, south of Urfa, a solitary minaret thrusts twenty-four metres into the sky. Commissioned by the last Umayyad caliph, Marwan II, during the brief period in the mid-eighth century when Harran was the capital of a kingdom reaching from Spain to Central Asia, this Ulu Cami was Turkey's oldest purpose-designed mosque. In its heyday it may have been able to accommodate twelve thousand worshippers, which is rather strange given that in the not so distant past the people of Harran had not been Muslims at all but ostensibly Sabians, a planet-worshipping people whose temple to the moon god Sin had once been one of the most revered in Mesopotamia. As the story goes, the newly arrived Marwan approached some of the locals and asked to which of the religious groups acknowledged by the Koran they belonged. When they replied only that they were Harranians, he pressed them to specify whether they were Christian, Jewish or Zoroastrian Harranians. Panicked, the men sought advice from a Muslim lawyer, who advised them to claim that they were Sabians since they were also accorded protection in the Koran.

Did Marwan show up with an army large enough to fill such a supersized mosque? Did he build big to make a statement? Or did the locals see the writing on the wall and convert en masse to fill the space? Whatever the reason, the new mosque was built with stones reused from the ancient temple. Later, the Mongols rampaged through town and levelled it to the ground, leaving little more than the minaret standing. By the time Gertrude arrived to camp amid the ruins she could write: 'There is no town now, only a collection of mudbuilt huts inhabited by half-settled Arabs, and the mound with an immense ruin field around it, all inclosed by the remains of a fine stone wall.'

That reference to the wall suggests that the defences were holding up better in her day than they are now. As so often, it wasn't so much the Mongols as stone quarriers who were the guilty party. Now the walls have been 'restored' with little regard for their great antiquity and wooden kiosks have been positioned to let tourists admire the end result. Except that the work was completed just as tourism to the southeast was about to collapse, so now the kiosks are acting as makeshift homes for refugees whose clothes and blankets are heaped up on the benches as in a rummage sale.

Harran is home to curious adobe houses with domed roofs designed to keep them cool even in summer. Their shape means that they're commonly called beehive houses, which makes perfect sense to fans of *Winnie-the-Pooh* and absolutely none to Turks, whose bees build their combs in flat-topped wooden boxes. Once upon a time, the beehives provided homes for families of Iraqi descent. Nowa-

Beehive houses in Harran in 1911

days, however, most are just temperature-controlled storage units attached to living quarters in modern concrete annexes. Wise to the expectations of their visitors, a few families have converted their old homes into cafés offering basic accommodation, and, while planning my trip, I'd fondly imagined bedding down for the night in one of them. But now security is uppermost in my mind. The Syrian border is only twenty-five kilometres away and I'm the only Westerner for miles around. Harran is crawling with desperate incomers who have lost everything. Fear of kidnapping eclipses desire to sleep as close to Gertrude's campsite as possible.

In one of the cafés I meet two young Syrians who come to work as much to escape the cramped conditions of the refugee camps as to scrape together some semblance of a wage. Twenty-two-year-old Mohammed was studying agricultural engineering at Aleppo University when his family was forced to flee. He still clings to hope of completing his studies, unlike sixteen-year-old Hasan, for whom education is no longer even a dream. Mohammed's family is living in a tented camp, Hasan's in one created out of shipping containers.

'Which is better?' I ask awkwardly.

They glance at each other. They shrug. The containers have it by a whisker, apparently.

★ ★ ★

Gertrude arrived in Harran at the end of a long day's ride from Ras al-Ain, across the border from the modern Ceylanpınar. By 1911 she was road-hardened, experienced, a woman with the culture and languages of the Middle East at her fingertips, a woman who would make less fuss about a twelve-hour ride through semi-desert than most people make about a bus ride half as long. Her route had brought her through the Tektek Dağları (Tektek Mountains), which she described as 'very arid desert … it isn't really a mountain, not to notice it at least, but rolling barren ground lifted a little above the level of the Mesopotamian plain'. One of the first Western travellers to leave an account of it she was, like those who had gone before her, mainly interested in transiting such inhospitable terrain as quickly as possible. Having found no fodder for their horses in Ras al-Ain, her party scoured the surrounding desolation anxiously for grass. They did, however, pause in Şuayip Şehri, a semi-subterranean settlement where a handful of villagers still eke out a living amid the ruins of what must once have been a sizeable town grown up around the cave-shrine of the Prophet Jethro.

I come here with Mustafa, a cheery taxi driver in his mid-thirties who grew up in the Arabic-speaking border town of Akçakale. He plays me big-band Kurdish music of a rousing nature. 'I can't understand the words,' he laughs, 'but I love the music.'

We breeze along a brand-new road, a jet-black slash across the yellow landscape. 'It's not very nice to look at,' I grumble. 'Not very romantic.'

'Boş ver, romantik! It's quick, that's the main thing.'

Tarmacked in the hope of offering touristic access to a string of previously remote historic sites, the new road tracks the old one to Baghdad and takes us past the Han El Ba'rur, an Ayyubid-era caravanserai, where I wriggle with difficulty out of buying a coin that looks to have been minted yesterday then 'aged' by rubbing it in the goat manure from which the *han* took its name. The landscape of this part of Turkey was completely transformed in the 1980s by GAP (Güneydoğu Anadolu Projesi), a vast dam-building project designed to bring water to semi-desert. 'Before GAP our grandfathers grew wheat, barley and lentils here,' Mustafa tells me. Now cotton fields stretch for miles in every direction and columns of smoke rise from burning chaff, peaceful counterpoints to the lethal versions thrown up by fighting on the other side of the border.

At Şuayip I leave Mustafa to snooze in the shade of a rare tree and strike off uphill, past mysterious stone structures half-buried in the hillside that remind me of the dromos tombs in Northern Cyprus where the skeletons of sacrificial horses were uncovered on ramps sloping down to the entrances. But there are no horses here and these rocky hollows are much smaller. Were they tombs long since ransacked, or were they perhaps, like the underground 'cities' of Cappadocia, places where the locals could take refuge from their enemies? Whatever their past, there's no mistaking their present purpose: each and every one of them has been turned into a rubbish bin. No municipal refuse collectors in green and yellow jumpsuits make it out here. The villagers are alone with their garbage.

I manage perhaps ten minutes of undisturbed exploration before two children pop up beside me, glad of a distraction to help them while away the interminable three-month summer break from school. Soon I've acquired an entourage of fifteen children, including one bully of a boy who asserts his leadership by thumping one of the girls. A woman pops her head out of a window and orders them to scarper, but I'm far too good a prize to let go; they simply regroup out of sight, then re-emerge to ambush me again by the shrine. I take a quick look at a dank cave room laid with prayer mats and rosaries, then return to rouse Mustafa from his slumbers.

'Did you see any snakes?' he demands.

'No. Should I have done?'

'*Yılan yok, akrep çok* [No snakes, but many scorpions],' he chortles, before flooring the accelerator and twiddling the radio. Off we roar, back to Harran, big-band music blaring.

In Urfa it's a grey day, misty, the sky heavy with what the breakfast waiter assures me is desert dust. In the street outside, the word Kobani is being bandied about. A car bomb has just exploded in that godforsaken border town and my erstwhile empty hotel has filled with journalists, tapping at keyboards, bellowing into mobile phones and lounging all over the lobby. War talk hangs as heavy as the dust in the air. The next day they all rush back to Istanbul again.

Turkey's border with Syria is an ethnic mishmash, dotted with towns that are alternately Arabic and Kurdish in language and culture. Most are adjacent to or within sight of towns on the other side of the border with which they shared a common history that was abruptly severed in the 1920s. Thus it was with the largely Kurdish towns of Suruç and Kobani. So when Kobani fell to ISIS in October 2014, Suruç shared in the disaster, terrified people pouring over the border and coming to an immediate stop once they were beyond the reach of the guns.

Despite the heat, I'm determined to revisit Suruç, southwest of Urfa, where, less than a year earlier, I'd arrived during the chaos following Kobani's fall. Gertrude had ridden towards the town, although not right into it. But nowhere could there have been a sharper contrast than between the Suruç of 1911 and the one of 2014. The Suruç of Gertrude's day was a dot of a place, a handful of beehive houses marooned in the desert. My Suruç, however, was a place of nightmares. Always dirt-poor, deprived and forgotten by the rest of the country, it had been transformed beyond recognition in the space of a few weeks. By the time I reached it, it was crammed to overflowing with desperate refugees, the main square so full of men that one might have assumed, but for their grim expressions, that some forgotten festival was in progress.

Away from the square, Suruç dissolved into a world of women and frighteningly young children. Every mosque courtyard was full of them, as were the grounds of the local wedding hall, and every open space right down to the building sites. On the railings surrounding the Ulu Cami children's clothing hung in a parody of festive bunting; five families were squashed into the portico. Another fifteen were camping in a mosque, whose courtyard resembled a school playground. When I tried to hand out sweets to the children a fight broke out between two fathers. Everything and everyone was under intolerable strain.

In the grounds of what had been until a few weeks previously the cheerful Suruç Cultural Centre, a drama teacher named Mehmet explained that the ground floor had been converted into living quarters, while a small hospital had been installed upstairs. But: 'It's not a usual situation,' he told me. 'Most of the refugees are women and children. They've left their men to fight. Now they need so much from us. We have to be their fathers and mothers. We can't just hand them a bar of soap and walk away. We have to stop and chat. It's hard.'

Amid the desolation, the parallel worlds that characterize disaster zones perpetuated their separate existences. Here were people whose lives had imploded living in utter degradation while for the average Suruçlu life continued much as before. Women were shopping for gold to pin to bridal sashes. They were buying pastries for tea. In the sweetshop men swapped black jokes about ISIS decapitations. Yet around the corner the pharmacy still sported adverts for the latest haemorrhoid treatment.

The fighting was invisible from the centre of Suruç but a short taxi ride past crumbling mud-brick settlements led to a vantage point from which it was possible to view the action. There was a surreality about it that seemed to epitomize an age that makes it impossible to shake off the shackles of the videogame, an age when everyone can watch everything in real time without being able to do a thing about it. Men had gathered to observe what was happening on the far side of the border. Some stood on the roof of the local mosque and trained their binoculars towards plumes of smoke rising up from Kobani. Others sat companionably amid ploughed furrows reading newspapers as if on a carefree Sunday outing. Car upon car pulled up to disgorge more onlookers. It felt disconcertingly like a gathering of twitchers come to eyeball some rare species of warbler. Meanwhile ambulances, sirens wailing, raced towards Suruç with the injured, barely navigating the obstacle course created by the carloads of spectators.

As we drove back to town, Galip, my taxi driver, reflected on the dilemmas thrown up by all this human misery. 'I saw a woman crying. She was heavily pregnant, just crying and crying. I felt so sorry for her. I wanted to take her into my house,' he said. But this was Kurdish Suruç, where honour still trumped everything else. 'I'm single,' he wound up sadly. 'What would people have said?'

A year later and I'm relieved to find Suruç back to normal, at least on the surface. The refugees have been resettled in camps; the mosque courtyards are back to hosting worshippers; the tents in the grounds of the Cultural Centre have been folded away and Mehmet is back to coaching would-be thespians. I return to Urfa in the *dolmuş* confident that Suruç is on the mend.

★ ★ ★

In the City of Prophets* *iftar* is a serious matter, the hour before the all-important *ezan* filled with preparations for the blowout meal that will conclude the day's fasting. Every evening I navigate a parade of pavement-blocking tables, places already set with spoons and forks in mid-afternoon. In the back streets people rush towards the outsized ovens of the *pide* shops carrying trays of family favourites – mince-filled aubergines, stuffed peppers and tomatoes, juicy chicken wings – for communal baking. In the bazaar wheelbarrows are loaded with plastic bags containing fruit squashes in lurid yellow and liquorice black. The mouth-watering aroma of grilling kebabs fills the air.

During Ramazan charitable giving tops the agenda, as does solidarity with others. Hosting free *iftar* dinners for those too poor or too chronically disorganized to arrange their own by the appointed time is regarded as particularly virtuous. Municipal authorities host them, as do civil society organizations, and the menu tends to be much of a muchness: lentil soup, slithers of lamb on a bed of rice, perhaps a slice of watermelon, certainly a bottle of water.

In the Topçu Meydanı (Square) Belediye bods are doling out food to an assembled throng swelling to the hundreds. They're wearing hairnets, surgical gloves, plastic elbow guards and hi-vis orange T-shirts, and they're going at it with the steady rhythm of robots, ladling food into polystyrene trays while their colleagues organize the lines and chase down the queue-jumpers. On big screens to one side of the square, the *Vali* (local governor) broadcasts a message of solidarity; on another, preparations are being made for the post-*iftar* entertainment, which, in Urfa, is guaranteed to be of a religious nature. On a plinth in the corner the inevitable statue of Atatürk looks on in barely-concealed exasperation.

*Urfa and the surrounding area have associations with the prophets İbrahim, Job, Jethro, Jacob and Moses, hence the nickname 'City of Prophets'.

It's a privilege to be able to spend time in Urfa during Ramazan, but at the same time it's also a curse. The privilege lies in seeing the curtain lifted briefly on the city's private life, the inner workings of its pious soul. The curse lies in the sizzling, stifling, life-defying heat. The sun is a relentless companion from whose laser-like persistence the only escape is the meagre patch of shade thrown out by minaret or plane tree. By ten in the morning it has sucked every hint of moisture from the ground. It beats down on heads. It bounces off brass plates. It rages up from paving stones. *Sahur* drummers wake the Ramazan fasters for a binge breakfast at one in the morning; by 10 a.m. they already have seven hours of parched throats behind them, and still have another ten to endure.

The only way to survive is to turn life upside down. Day becomes night for the work-free. By noon men sprawl gracelessly on the lawns of Gölbaşı. They snooze, heads on arms, on shop counters. And they treat the mosques as dormitories so that wandering in to admire a mihrab feels as transgressive as popping into the men's room to examine the tiling.

I stick it out for ten days, before the combination of Ramazan privations and July heat defeats me. My journey judders to a halt. It's time for a break.

23
The Sultan's Man in Viranşehir
VİRANŞEHİR–CİMDİN KALESİ

'I meet with nothing but friendly assistance wherever I go in this country.'
Letter, 7 May 1911

In mid-July 2015 a bomb goes off in Suruç. It does so in the grounds of the Cultural Centre, the one place of almost-beauty in that whole benighted town. Thirty-five people, most of them youthful idealists on their way to help rebuild Kobani, have been blown to pieces, probably by ISIS. A few days later the PKK retaliates by killing two off-duty policemen in Ceylanpınar. These events mark the start of a descent into darkness, the reasons for which cannot be entirely separated from the result of the June election that had robbed the government of its majority. Three opposition parties with wholly different agendas have spent the summer making little effort to find common cause in the national interest. By the time I resume my journey after a six-week break, a repeat election is in the offing. Foreign governments have stepped up warnings to travellers. In July Urfa's hotels had been empty because only the most hardened of travellers braves the southeast in high summer. They're empty now because the tourists have been frightened away.

In the early twentieth-century Viranşehir, east of Urfa, was the fiefdom of a rogue named İbrahim Paşa, chief of the Milli tribe and the leader of one of the feared Hamidiye militias, the largely Kurdish cavalry groups that had been established in eastern Turkey by Sultan Abdülhamid II. In cahoots with the faraway sultan, İbrahim lorded it over the surrounding countryside, robbing and raiding and generally terrorizing into submission those who didn't immediately bend to his will. He was said to have twenty thousand men at his beck and call and, according to the Scottish journalist David Fraser, who was travelling in the region in 1908 and lost a finger to one of them, they were mostly 'truants from justice, cattle-lifters, ravishers, murderers, deserters from the army and individuals who were wanted for the satisfaction of blood feuds'. İbrahim's father had been summoned to Aleppo to account for his own misdeeds. Suspecting the outcome of the meeting, he had entrusted his valuables to a friend from Urfa. His fears turned out to have been justified since not long after arriving in Aleppo he was almost certainly poisoned. His son succeeded him as leader of the tribe, but when he sought the return of his father's valuables, he found that the friend to whom they had been entrusted was also dead. His son, Nedim Efendi, refused to return them, leading to the sort of feud that, in this part of the world, tends to rumble on for generations.

By the time Gertrude arrived in Viranşehir in 1911, she was two years too late to meet İbrahim, who had been removed, she noted, as the 'first act of the Constitutional Govt' that overthrew Sultan Abdülhamid, and then assassinated. In northern Syria complaints about İbrahim's cattle-rustlers had been frequent, although her personal belief was that he had been 'a great protector of the Christians' in troubled times. In his place she met his widow ('or one of his widows'), Hanza Hatun, leaving a portrait of her that stands out not least because few of the women she met on her travels inspired either praise or curiosity:

> She was renowned for her beauty and though she is now old you can see the traces of it in the fine shape of the face and in the splendid carriage of the head ... We sat together on a carpet outside the house by the edge of a spring, among willow trees: it was early morning, the women were churning the sour curds in skins hung from the willow branches. The men of her household stood back while we discussed her position and the possibility of the sons' return. She manages all the estates, which are still very large, during their absence. She wore a long European man's coat over her dress, and an Arab cloak over that; on her head the male keffiyeh, silk kerchief, bound over the brow with a thick roll of black silk. I looked back after I had bidden her farewell and mounted; she stood under the willow trees with shrouded head and gazed after me with her deep set eyes – a very striking figure.

Some time in the fourth or fifth century a spectacular church was built in what are now the outskirts of Viranşehir. Its centrepiece was a huge octagonal tower beneath which, perhaps, the bones of some long-forgotten saint were venerated. The tower was topped with a dome supported on lofty arches and round it paced an ambulatory. Running off on one side was a short nave, on the other a chancel with a gallery and crypt. Hundreds of tesserae collected in the vicinity imply the rich mosaics that once adorned it. The church must have loomed like a desert mirage, signalling to travellers cantering between the walled enclaves of Urfa, Harran and Viranşehir their imminent return to civilization.

Careless of its history, İbrahim Paşa turned what remained of the church into a military base. By the time Gertrude set up her tripod amid the ruins of what she called simply 'the octagon', only the great supporting pillars of the arches were standing, although the shape of the structure was still just about discernible. Now just one battered pillar and a few marble columns sprawled on the grass where she pitched her tents live on, and even their survival must be in doubt. I can almost hear the arguments raging in local council meetings: why bother to safeguard such inconsequential relics when the ground they stand on could be rendered profitable by the erection of an apartment block or shopping mall?

In the town centre stretches of basalt wall dating back to the reign of Justinian attest to the far reach of Byzantine power. Converted into a barracks in İbrahim's day, the İckale (Inner Castle) still serves as an off-limits military base. The local library is housed in a more accessible reminder of his rule, a small stone pavilion of Mardin-like gracefulness. I want to believe it's where Hanza Hatun bemoaned the fate of her sons to Gertrude, although since it was commissioned for the military top brass it almost certainly isn't.

At a snack stand in Viranşehir I team up with Mehmet Tüfek, a sixty-three-year-old father of nine children, all grown up, who agrees to drive me back into the Tektek Dağları. Weathered and grizzled, he's a kindly soul with an un-Turkish readiness to stop and seek directions. We're in largely empty countryside stretching south to the border. Sporadic hamlets pop up amid the rocks and from time to time we have to wind up the windows as shelter against sprinklers set to

irrigate small fields of maize. But it's a part of the country where outsiders are rare; those we ask for help waffle through a catalogue of
forks in the road, storehouses, farm outhouses and a myriad other
landmarks, none of which could be known to us, so that it seems a
near miracle when at last we see rising up ahead the walls of a castle
whose name seems to have dropped out of history.

Unable to find a guide in Ras al-Ain, Gertrude had picked her
way through the desert with only a compass and an unreliable map
to help her. Given its size and magnificence it's hard to believe that
she wouldn't have stopped to take a picture of Çimdin Kalesi (Es-
kikale) if her route had taken her round it. On the other hand, she
does mention rushing past 'a very interesting fortress – I expect it
was a part of Justinian's line of fortifications against the Persians'.
Could it have been Çimdin? I certainly want to think so.

Çimdin village is tiny, a speck in the desert down to its last 350 inhabitants. It's the sort of place whose children must arrive at high
school in Viranşehir and determine within the day never to return
to their birthplace except for holidays. Its primary school hangs on
by a teacher's prayer. Once it closes – as close it surely will – it will
sound the death knell for the village.

In the Köy Odası (Village Meeting Hall) we pick up Mustafa ('my
father was Mustafa, I'm Mustafa and my son is Mustafa too!'), a
young man in black *şalvar*, who volunteers to show us round the castle. It's extraordinary, huge and forbidding, sited on a mound to provide a clear view of anyone approaching from north, south, east or
west. On one side soars a lofty arch reminiscent of those in the cisterns of Syria. But hard facts about its history are there none. It was
built. It endured. It crumbled. And now its ruins stand here awaiting
the day when a pen pusher in Ankara will decide that it should be
restored, whereupon wires will appear and light fittings and sharp-
cut paving stones and all its romance will be destroyed.

From the ramparts of the castle I gaze down on the plain. Scattered about it are the standard components of life in these parts: the
blue-painted rooftop *tahts* (metal platforms) which can be curtained
off at night to let families sleep in the relative cool of outdoors; and

the piled-up pats of *tezek* (dried dung) that will see them through a winter of free fuel. It's a very Gertrudey landscape, I think. Dusty. Sandy. Infinitely empty. It's easy to imagine her riding across it, cantering ahead of the baggage animals with Fattuh beside her, regaling her with stories full of cultural glitches and non-sequiturs which she would laugh at, then commit to her diary once the tents were up and the campfire lit.

On the veranda of the Köy Odası we stop for *çay* and a catch-up on local gossip. What I know for sure is that Gertrude had visited a site she called Kasr'ül Benat, where she had photographed a building that looks unlike a church. Ah, the Kızlar Sarayı (Maidens' Palace), Mustafa replies. My ears prick up. But there's nothing left there, he continues, just a few carved crosses in caves. I glance at Mehmet. I check my watch. The *çay* has been a long time brewing and by now it's four o'clock. To see it we would still have to drive quite a long way south, straight towards the border. Which at this time, in this place, hardly seems the wisest of ideas. I drop the subject. It seems only fair.

24
How Light Mesopotamia Became
MARDİN–DARA–SAVUR–DEREİÇİ

'It rained like the devil on Saturday night and like ten thousand devils on Sunday.'
Letter, 17 April 1911

In the low light of a stone-vaulted church young men approach the altar as the priest recites a prayer over the bread and wine. They hold aloft fans that look from a distance like egg poachers ringed with bells but when they rattle them a tremolo fills the air. Like the dying 'hoo' of the dervishes, it makes the hairs on my neck stand on end. It reminds me of bee-eaters twittering in the late summer sky. It's intended to suggest the beating of angels' wings in the heavens.

On a Sunday morning in September the church of Mor Shmuni boasts a congregation a London vicar would give his eyeteeth for. I've arrived late, having struggled to find it in the Mardin back streets, but a steady stream of even later worshippers follows me down the steps and through the door, the women dragging lacy scarves from handbags to cover their heads. As in a London church, the front pews feature a line-up of white thatch and male pattern baldness. Here though there are plenty of younger women, some of them clad, rather jarringly after overdressed Urfa, in knee-skimming skirts and long shorts.

This is a service to gladden a Catholic's heart with plentiful incense and regular ringing of bells. But those fans give the game away. Along with the painted altar curtains they proclaim this a shrine to Syrian Orthodoxy, a relic of the time when this distant corner of Turkey boasted a large Syriac population.

Resplendent in a gold cassock trimmed in scarlet, Father Gabriel Akyüz leads the congregation through the responses from in front of a soaring stone reredos reminiscent in its carvings of the portal of a Selçuk caravanserai. Congregants mix and match rituals, crossing themselves as they enter the church and shaking hands with their neighbours in good Catholic fashion, then running their hands down their faces after praying in a quintessentially Islamic gesture. But what is most striking about the service is that much of it is conducted in Aramaic, a close relative of the language spoken by Jesus and a living linguistic link to the Palestine of the first century.

Outside, it's still the early hours and municipal refuse collectors are parading the alleyways stepped back into the hillside, leading large white donkeys. Beautiful Mardin may be, but its architects didn't factor in the need for rubbish disposal. Even now the streets are too narrow for cars let alone bulky refuse trucks. So in Mardin it's donkeys that carry out the rubbish, their knees and manes hennaed orange in a salute to the importance of their role.

'Mardin stands more splendidly than any place I have ever seen. The town lies on the steep hillside below a great crown of rock which is girdled with towers and broken walls. You cannot imagine a town more boldly seated among the hills,' Gertrude wrote after trotting in and heading straight for the American Mission. At first I conclude that this has been demolished; it takes some very strong pulling of teeth to extract any sense from the occupants of the teahouse near the Diyarbakır Gate, who do their best to redirect me to the Deyrulzafaran Monastery, destination of choice for all sensible tourists. Finally, though, memory stirs and someone points me down a side street. There, sure enough, a complex of buildings erected in a burst of Protestant missionary fervour in the 1850s persists, albeit in abject condition. A man drinking *çay* in the shade of a tree jumps up to unlock a so-called Kültür Evi (Cultural House) even more dejected than the mission. There's a drawing of imprisoned PKK leader Abdullah Öcalan on one wall, a signed photograph of satin-voiced Kurdish singer Şivan Perwer on another. Anything that could fall over has fallen over. Anything that could peel at the corners has peeled at the corners. Anything that could be covered in dust is covered in dust.

I scurry out again and take a turn around the complex, peering through windows and rattling doorknobs but there's nothing to see. The American past is as long dead as the missionaries.

I've arrived in Mardin at a difficult time. In the early 2010s this was a boomtown, with Istanbullus and Ankaralıs pouring in to enjoy up-market mini-breaks in a choice of boutique hotels overlooking the Mesopotamian Plain. But now the bottom has dropped out of the market. The Suruç bomb and the Ceylanpınar killings have sparked a revival of the decades-old conflict between the PKK and the state. The ceasefire that had allowed Mardin to flaunt its touristic wealth has evaporated like summer rain. This was a market made up mainly of foreign tour groups and Turks. The foreign tour companies can no longer buy insurance, so they've cancelled. The Turks are afraid of the reception they will receive, so they've cancelled. Suddenly I can have my pick of beds in any hotel in any price bracket. It's a ter-rifying situation.

Of course there were no boutique places to stay in Gertrude's day. Instead, she was 'lodged in the house of Dr and Mrs Thom and fed by Mr and Mrs Emrich', stalwarts of the Mission who introduced her to Dr Alpheus Andrus, 'the man who knows the Tur Abdin better than any other person … to him is due most of the mapping of the country'. Over dinner the Thoms entertained her with tales of a Mardin snowed in by drifts so deep that they could barely be swept from the alleys. But this was 1911 and inevitably the conversation darkened as they confessed to their fear that the Adana killings might be replicated in Mardin and their relief when the sultan's fall put an end to the threat. But the reprieve was to be short-lived. In 1915 they could only watch in horror as hundreds of Armenians were forced out onto the road south to Mosul and Deir ez-Zor. Desperate mothers abandoned babies at their door and the missionaries strug-gled to treat the wounds of the few who managed to escape. For their pains, the two men were themselves marched to imprisonment in Sivas, where Dr Thom expired from typhus. Left alone in the mis-sion, Dr Andrus's wife died without seeing her husband again.

Presiding over the rocky plateau against which Mardin reclines is what Gertrude described as an 'inconceivably splendid fortress', where she recorded carved lions and leopards guarding the gate while writing snippily that she saw 'nothing old', by which she meant nothing Byzantine. Throughout the 1990s the castle was dominated by two giant golf balls, the monitoring devices of a state at odds with its own citizens. There had been no question then of going anywhere near it; nor does there seem much more hope now. But the trudge up the rock on the off-chance offers as a consolation prize the opportunity to gaze out across the Mesopotamian Plain towards Syria. It's a spellbinding vista, a patchwork quilt in shades of ochre spread over the landscape as far as the eye can see. Of that view, Gertrude wrote that it was 'the most glorious thing I ever beheld, more beautiful than the sea, and, when I saw it, perpetually varied by the storms that came sweeping over it'.

Even now that comparison with the sea lingers on. Hunkered down at the back of Mardin's busy bazaar I meet Tacettin Toparlı, a hipster of a man whose beard makes a mystery of his age. Tacettin is a *şahmarancı*, one of an elite band of craftsmen who spend their days layering tinsel paper over tinsel paper to create multi-coloured evocations of the Şahmaran, a Mesopotamian fertility god with the head of a woman and the body of a snake. The Şahmaran is a fashionably gender-fluid being. In Mardin the locals insist that it was a female who governed the snakes. In Tarsus, however, they're equally convinced that she was a he, and a bit of a dodgy he at that, who clambered onto the roof of a *hamam* to eye up a beautiful woman, leading the locals to lynch him. Near the scene of the crime a statue depicts him much like a cobra-entangled Indian deity.

Şahmarans are big business in Mardin and there are *şahmarancıs* aplenty to choose from. But what draws me to Tacettin's shop is not so much the artwork as the fact that the portico in front of it is pasted with little slips of paper, each offering a nutshell encapsulation in words of the town as a local sees it. Locks and keys feature prominently, as do pigeons, monasteries, mosques, cockfights, the extreme heat and extreme cold, the stones that built Mardin, and the family feuds that have sometimes threatened to tear it apart. There are references to a more innocent past when storytellers kept tea-drinkers on the edge of their seats in the *kahves*, when schoolboys thumped footballs against the walls of the castle, and when charms to ward off snake and scorpion dangled from the arches of the Ulu Cami. There are rueful references to pell-mell change ('nobody was expect-

Şahmarancı Tacettin Toparlı in Mardin; 2015

ing the new town'). And through everything runs a dark undercurrent that suggests why it took outsiders so long to relax here ('The Kasimiye cinema. It was before the 80s. Animals used to live there. At night we would go there to practise making molotov cocktails. It was a place for guerrilla experiments.').

The Mardin of these snippets is mystical, elusive, a place where Şahmarans would surely have roamed. At the same time, it's clearly a town facing change on a transformative scale. It's among these slips of papers that I read an anonymous description of how it has altered the 'sea' that brings tears to my eyes:

> How light Mesopotamia became
> How crowded with colourful lights
> The ships sailing in the desert gone
> The sky disappeared by lights
> Is light that destructive?
> It has destroyed the desert of sea in which it swam.
> Although the west will never destroy its wheat
> The sand sea seems to be destroyed
> How quickly we adapted to the end.

★ ★ ★

'The houses are all cut back into the rock, the roof of one on a level with the threshold of the next ... The rock [is] very porous and damp and [the people] sleep with closed windows and doors,' wrote Gertrude, whose conversations with the missionaries had alerted her to a big local problem with consumption. Roll on a century and those same damp rock-cut houses have blossomed into the cornerstone of Mardin tourism. Architectural beauty is the town's essence. Windows are zigzagged with chevrons, doorways triple-moulded in stone. If Urfa is the discreetly covered woman who reveals her hair only to her husband, Mardin is the harlot who struts the streets brazenly without a scarf, her beauty plain for all the world to see.

In the bazaar I stumble upon the Ulu Cami, its proximity signposted by an eruption of tourist tat. Running my eye up the trunk of its minaret, I see stone teardrops and sharp-edged Kufic inscriptions, an exuberance of carving dating back to the days of the medieval Artukid dynasty, picked up and played with later by the architects who created the tier upon tier of golden houses. Foremost amongst these architects was Sarkis Elyas Lole, who designed the much younger but even more dressed-up minaret of the Şehidiye Cami. By rights Lole should be the nineteenth-century equivalent of Sinan in the fame stakes. Instead he's a shadowy genius, little more than a name and a rollcall of masterpieces, the minutiae of his private life – even the details of his birth and death – lost to us. The fact that he was working so far away from Constantinople probably explains why he has been so little acknowledged. But the fact that he was also in possession of an Armenian name at a time when such a thing was a liability can hardly have helped. Although he managed to hang onto his life, his name would have rendered him immediately suspect to those who came to power after the First World War.

Alas, poor Lole, I'm thinking, as I walk up the steps leading to what used to be, until recent conversion into a guesthouse, one of the most beautiful post offices in the world. I'm thinking of him, too, as I mount more steps to the museum in the main square and as I peer through the padlocked gates of the old primary school. I'm thinking of him again as a stroll along Birinci Caddesi and glance up at the Italianate loggia of the Şahkulu Bey Evi and as I drop in to eat at the trendy Cercis Murat Restaurant. But I'm thinking of him most of all as I stand by the roadside leading down to the new town and gaze back up at the exquisite house he designed for his own family, carefully slotted into the hillside and designed to scoop an unimpeded view of the 'sea'. Lole was prolific, with an unerring eye for how to draw beauty from limestone. But his many buildings, which time has so mellowed that it's hard to believe that they weren't always adorning the hillside, were mostly built between 1895 and 1910. They were works in progress, then, when Gertrude came to town and it's easy to imagine the sniffy nouveau-riche, what-does-he-think-he's-up-to putdowns that she would have heard as she ambled from building site to building site.

Gertrude's Mardin photographs favour the monumental over the vernacular. One of her favourite subjects was the Zinciriye Medrese, a seminary whose twin domes, ribbed like lemon squeezers, preside over a flight of steps off Birinci Caddesi. But her endeavours could hardly have failed to pass unnoticed. 'A huge crowd gathered as I photographed the inscrips,' she wrote, with the irritation of one most at ease in her own company.

As ever, it was the ancient churches that were her primary concern. In the early twentieth century Mardin's population was roughly half Muslim and half Christian, although the Christians were as fissiparous as a group of twenty-first-century left-wingers. Around twelve thousand Syriacs, some of them Orthodox, some of them Catholic, faced off against 7,500 Armenians subdivided similarly. Then there were the Protestants converted by the American missionaries, not to mention the Chaldean Catholics, in front of whose church on the high street now sits what looks like a giant ostrich egg. A young man named Mehmet unlocks the door and ushers me into a Pantheon-like space with a high brick dome. A plaque claims a late-fourth-century foundation date for the church, but it's so newly restored that the smell of paint lingers in the air.

It's unlikely that this was one of the churches that Gertrude visited. However, the names she uses for them render certainty an illusion. The 'Old Syrian church', for example. Was that what is now the most active of the Syriac churches, the Church of the Forty Martyrs? In the garden of the house nuzzling up beside it, Father Gabriel helps solve some local place-name conundrums, a tough task not just because of the intrinsic complications in a part of the world where even the tiniest village may recognize at least four monikers but because he is simultaneously trying to offer advice to a Christian refugee newly arrived from Syria. Where to stay. Who can help with food. Bus times. The list of requirements is long and the young man frequently tearful.

The one church about whose identity there can be no doubt is the venerable Mor Mihael, which clings to a slope on the outskirts of the old town. Surrounded by a sturdy wall, it reminds me of a cutdown version of the great monastery of St Catherine's in the Sinai and it's irresistibly alluring, not least because the Austrian priest-historian of the Tur Abdin, Hans Hollerweger, recorded in the grounds the stub of a column that might have offered a platform for a stylite monk, one of those unfathomable individuals who believed they could achieve salvation by spending their life alone on top of a pillar. Probably the first church built in Mardin, Mor Mihael has been much knocked about over the centuries; Gertrude wrote dismissively that 'nothing but the plan seemed to be old'.

The magnet for visitors to this part of the world has always been Deyrulzafaran, where a monastery has existed since the fifth century. Gertrude trotted out there on an April day when the almond trees were in blossom and found it 'very interesting, 8th century I should think and full of exciting decoration'. She was welcomed by an elderly bishop, who gave her permission to photograph at will. I, however, must pay to enter via an EU-funded visitor centre built in a flourish of mid-2000s' confidence that the flow of visitors would from now on be unstoppable. The guide is young, beefy and far more interested in Facebook than his guests. Reluctantly he conducts us into the crypt where, long before the Christians, Shemsis congregated to pray to the sun as it blazed through a slit in the wall. The Shemsis shared many beliefs with the Yezidis and Sabians, but, like the Alawites, they preferred to keep the details to themselves. By the mid-eighteenth century only about a hundred Shemsis remained in Mardin; long before that, most converted to Syrian Orthodoxy, at least superficially.

The monastic church has an achingly ancient quality, the intricate Byzantine conches and acanthus leaves that decorate it slowly blurring back into the amorphousness from which they were carved. Pressing the guide, I manage to extract the information that five priests and fifteen students still live here and that crowds flock in from the neighbouring Tur Abdin for the feast-day of the Dormition of St Mary celebrated on 28 August according to the old Julian calendar. But that's the most he's giving me. The rest of the group is already halfway to the next must-see attraction. He can't wait to show me the door.

Thirty kilometres east of Mardin, the old stone quarry at Dara is a place of unexpected beauty whose ziggurat-like walls once reverberated with the thudding of picks and the voices of weary workmen raised in protest against the merciless heat. Dara was the old Anastasiopolis, a town uncomfortably caught between the mighty Byzantine and Sassanian empires. Throughout the sixth century rival armies fought a furious game of military ping-pong, taking and retaking the town for themselves, destroying it, then rebuilding it in their preferred image. Then in 639 the Arabs seized Anastasiopolis. They were to hang onto it for the next three hundred years.

In 1911 Gertrude struggled through a storm to reach Dara from Nisibin (Nusaybin). After pitching camp near the bridge, she explored the 'huge vaulted cisterns which were planned and built by a Greek architect from Alexandria' before calling on the priest of the small Armenian Catholic community. Her reward for braving the 'streaming rain' was an 'amazing sunset with … great rainbow. All the world aflame.'

The following morning it was the turn of Sheikh Muhammad Said, who claimed descent from the Prophet, to receive her. Then, with her caravan marching ahead, she rode into the great quarry.

Part of it had been hollowed out to form a vast rock-cut necropolis where I find a couple of noisily enthusiastic Kurds inspecting the most elaborately carved tombs. By the gate a young man rocks back and forth, crooning for money. 'Put a sock in it,' the custodian snarls.

I've come here with Rifat, a young taxi driver once employed as a chef at the Conrad Hotel in Istanbul. It was a good job, with decent pay and working conditions, but then his family decided to move back to Mardin. 'Here chefs have no rights,' he sniffs, hence this abrupt career change. A man of few words, Rifat does nonetheless stir himself to assure me that Dara is a Kurdish village now, the vanished Armenians a memory best left undisturbed.

On a stinking hot day, it's as much as I can do to force myself to examine the remains of the bridge and a tower left over from 'one of the strongest of Justinian's frontier fortresses'. The word '*zindan* [dungeon]' is scrawled across a wall to seduce visitors, but Gertrude immediately recognized the 'so called prison' beneath it for what it really is – a cavernous, barrel-vaulted cistern, reminder of the water supply that had made Dara a prize so worth fighting over. A church once bestrode the cistern, its place now taken by a newish house belonging to Hamza Kaya, who runs the local café. In the middle of it an outsized Corinthian capital does more to evoke the size and splendour of old Anastasiopolis than the rest of the ruins put together. Resting my elbows on it, I start on my explanatory spiel – 'Before the First World War there was an Englishwoman who was travelling around Turkey on horseback taking photographs. I'm following her journeys …' – when to my surprise Hamza's face lights up. 'My grandfather Yusuf guided her,' he says.

It's an extraordinary moment. Already I've met several Turks who know of Gertrude, but this is the first time I've encountered someone with an actual connection to her. Suddenly time slips into reverse and I sense her standing between us, a soft smile playing on her lips. Hamza heads into the house and comes back with a newly minted guidebook illustrated with her photographs.

'My grandfather had three wives and many children, but he died before I was born so I never met him,' he says. I do a quick back-of-a-matchbox calculation and conclude that when he says grandfather,

he probably means great-grandfather, but it makes no difference.
I leave Dara wearing a grin as
wide as the cistern.

The stairwell leading up to the
Hacı Abdullah Bey Konağı in
Savur, northeast of Mardin,
could be that of an apartment
block in Istanbul. Nor does the
all-too-ordinary front door at the
top of the stairs suggest that it
conceals anything unusual. But
behind that door lurks a home so
exquisite that it's often described
as a museum-house. When the
door swings open to reveal
Niven Öztürk's smiling face I
know I'm in for a treat.

Hamza Kaya, whose great-grandfather
guided Gertrude Bell, at Dara,
near Mardin; 2015

Gertrude camped near Savur rather than in the town itself, but
I'm unable to pass up the chance to bed down for the night in one of
the oldest – if not *the* oldest – houses in the area, a dream of a *konak*,
its huge rooms still furnished in Ottoman style, its rooftop overlooking a panorama of the 'Little Mardin' to the north of its much more
familiar namesake. The story of how the house became Turkey's
finest homestay is telling of times past and present. The eponymous
Hacı Abdullah's ancestors were traders who arrived here from Baghdad in the fifteenth century, but it was an eighteenth-century Abdullah who commissioned this fine stone mansion. Over the gate he had
inscribed the words 'May my children continue to live here in happiness', and, sure enough, the house is still inhabited by his descendants, who carefully maintained its period appearance even as their
neighbours were whipping the original features out of their homes
in the rush to modernity. In the early 2000s Niven noticed a trickle
of tourists straying out of Mardin and into Savur, but lack of a hotel
ensured that their visits were brief. Why don't we open the house to

paying guests, she suggested to her brother, Abidin, and the rest was tourism history, especially after the house featured as the set for several popular soap operas.

As we share a simple village supper of *dolma* (stuffed vines leaves), *labneh* (strained yoghurt) and *ayran* (salted yoghurt drink), Niven tells me her story. Exceptionally for a woman of the southeast, she had been an unenthusiastic bride ('I was afraid. I didn't know what it would be like'). Then, during the filming of the television series *Sıla*, her now husband, Şahin, arrived in town. Before the wrap was complete, he was asking her to marry him, to no avail. Five years later he returned to Savur, popped the same question and received the same reply. Then her brother cued up a meeting in Istanbul. On the third time of asking, Şahin finally got his way. They married on Valentine's Day in 2007. A year later their son completed the family.

We're joined at the table by Niven's elderly mother, Nezihe, who, despite being in her late seventies, still welcomes guests to her home with unreserved delight. Side by side they epitomize a dramatic generational difference. Mum is wearing an ankle-length gown of imprecisely floral pattern that completely conceals the shape of her body; a gauzy white headscarf hangs down beneath her chin like a breastplate. Niven's dress also reaches to her ankles but favours strong maritime stripes of blue and white and clings wherever it wants to. Her hair is long and loose. No one expects her to cover it.

I'm soon lost in the twists and turns of their vast extended family, so after dinner we stand in the flagstoned hallway and inspect a family tree said to trace their ancestry back to the Prophet Mohammed. Niven's name is there. Not so Nezihe's. 'Our family is too big to squeeze us all in,' she laughs.

In the morning the three of us assemble for photographs in a sitting room that, with its wood and glass ceiling and exquisitely carved *mihrab*, is the *konak*'s glory. I am the first guest they've hosted in three months. It's hard to believe another will be along any time soon.

In 1909 Gertrude rode into Dereiçi (once Killit) and pitched camp in the leafiest of villages. That she left no description of it is a particular shame, given that she would have seen, still thriving, a village in its prime, once dubbed the 'Paradise of the Tur Abdin', that I can witness only in its death throes. I'm driven there by Niven's nephews, Ahmet and Mert, cheerful, chatty lads whose first language is Arabic. When asked if they think the renewed fighting will affect Savur, they shake their heads vehemently. 'We're Arabs. We wouldn't put up with it.'

Years earlier I'd met İlyas, the elderly *muhtar* of Dereiçi. Then in robust health, he'd been happy to fling open the door of the church of Mor Yuhanon to unexpected visitors. Now I find him much frailer, his eyes rheumy, his hearing on its way out. In old age his Turkish is also fading as he reverts to childhood Arabic to converse with the handful of villagers still living here. There are no more than a hundred of us, he tells me. Fifteen hundred ex-Dereiçilis have made new lives in Sweden and the United States.

Pausing in the nave, İlyas looks as if he'd like to cry as he recalls the 1970s when Sunday mornings could still guarantee full pews. Now there's not even a priest in a village that once boasted both Syrian Orthodox and Syrian Catholic churches as well as a Protestant interloper sneaked in by nineteenth-century missionaries. Of İlyas's nine children only one has stayed to farm the land here; the others are far away. We part at the church gate and I wander off to explore the silent back streets of a village that could almost have cut adrift from Cappadocia. Except that here the recipe that brought touristic wealth to Göreme – the honey-coloured houses, the unspoiled rural surroundings – has fallen as flat as an undercooked soufflé. Here there are no cave hotels or hot-air balloons filling the skies at dawn. İlyas is a dab hand at winemaking, but no one other than Mert comes to sample the end product. And, in truth, beneath the beauty there lurks the usual southeastern story of killing and despair. In 1998, İlyas's predecessor as *muhtar* was gunned down. It was the signal for most of those who had stuck out the troubles to pack up and join their families in exile.

25

The Twelve Wise Men

MİDYAT–MOR GABRİEL–TUR ABDİN VILLAGES

*'Here you have the earliest hermit ideal of monasticism
going on uninterrupted and unchanged until today.'* Letter, 20 May 1909

In an age when successful food bloggers bask in celebrity status, it can seem surprising how little Gertrude had to say about food, which she seemed to regard as nothing more than fuel to get her through each day. From time to time she mentions gifts of *ayran* (drinking yoghurt) and *kaymak* (cream) in the villages, and there are passing references to Fattuh's gallant struggles to conjure edibility from stringy chickens, to the perking up of their monotonous diet with a helping of lamb, hare or partridge, but that's about it. I, on the other hand, can get quite excited about the quirkier rewards of Turkish cuisine, amongst which I count *perde pilav*, a risotto of almonds, raisins and shredded chicken baked inside a crispy pastry crust that is a staple of Midyat's Cihan Lokantası.

The waiter bears a plate to my table. There's plenty of rice but precious little piecrust. 'More pastry, please,' I plead, and back he troops with a dish piled high.

I'm still licking flakes of pastry off my lips when I amble out to explore old Midyat, a town that looks much as Mardin would if someone squashed it flat then pulled its streets apart to expose the filigree flourishes of the old houses. Gertrude came here twice, the first time in the spring of 1909, then again in 1911 to fine-tune observations made on the first trip. Despite there being rooms available in an impressive *han*, she still opted to camp, nights under canvas by then second nature to her.

Paid for by a Baghdad gold merchant, the Gelüşke Han was a stopping place straddling one of the great trade routes across Anatolia, and it too became a big hit with the makers of Turkish soap operas, before the imploding security situation put paid to all that. Kicking his heels at a table overlooking the fountain I find Veli Güneş, a man of patriarchal mien from a Kurdish farming family who bought the *han*, shovelled out decades of accumulated garbage and turned it into a restaurant. Now he's dreaming of a boutique hotel, which, in the current circumstances, seems like wishful thinking of the most extravagant kind. While he outlines his plans, a waiter scurries back and forth with glasses of lemon tea. He's a refugee from Qamishli, near Nusaybin, and, as refugees go, he's one of the lucky ones, his family having escaped the Syrian horror with the wherewithal to rent a new home.

★ ★ ★

I've arrived in Midyat on the eve of Kurban Bayram, the holiday that commemorates İbrahim's near-sacrifice of his son, İsmail, and the day on which every Turkish family aspires to slaughter a sheep or cow, then share the meat out between friends, family and the poor. There's a mosque behind my hotel in the modern Estel district and on the eve of the *bayram* a relentless polyphonic chanting thunders from the minaret. It has a melancholy but also mildly disturbing quality. It's a relief when it finally stops.

Midyat is a town that prides itself on its multicultural heritage. On the clocktower a peacock displays its stone tail in between a minaret and a church tower representing the Muslim and Syrian Orthodox communities. It's a quiet reminder that before the First World War this part of Anatolia was home to a large community of Yezidis, for whom the Melektavus, or Peacock Angel, is sacred. Until 2014 the world had more or less forgotten the Yezidis. Then television screens filled with horrific scenes as ISIS drove men, women and children out of northern Iraq. Thousands fled onto bleak, waterless Mt Sinjar. How many died there may never be known.

But the clocktower's signalling of religious harmony is largely PR puff. It's true that in Gertrude's day the courtyard of the Gelüşke Han would have resounded with the voices of Arabic speakers swapping gossip from Baghdad and Constantinople. It's true that the back streets would have thronged with people for whom Kurdish was the first language, some of them Sunni, some of them Yezidi. It's true that the myriad jewellery shops would have been filled with Christians conversing in Turoyo, the local dialect of Aramaic; indeed, before the First World War Midyat was the only non-metropolitan town in Anatolia to boast a majority Christian population. But the Sayfo did for most of the Christians and Yezidis. Midyat was merged with nearby Estel to create a Muslim-majority town. Now only a handful of Syriac families still live in Midyat. As for the Yezidis, until some fled here to escape the Syrian conflict, theirs was a vanishingly rare presence.

★ ★ ★

Midyat still has five churches, whose identikit bell towers poke their heads up above the old houses. Gertrude was most interested in the ruinous church of St Philoxenos, although her attempts to sketch its ground plan were hampered by the attentions of the locals:

> The population of Midyad, men, women and children, stationed themselves upon the ruined walls, and for them it was no doubt the most entertaining afternoon which they had spent for many a long week, but for me and for the patient bearers of the measuring tape the hours were charged with exasperation… The Kaimmakam, when he appeared upon this agitated scene, succeeded in clearing the ruins for a few moments, but as soon as he had turned his back, the hordes reassembled with a greater zest than before.

A photograph shows the townspeople lined up on the walls clad in long white skirts and candy-striped jackets. 'The task of planning [the church] was a labour of hatred,' she concluded.

She has my heartfelt sympathy, not least because as I wander the back streets, I too am mobbed, if only by children. They chase after me, yelling '*Tu-rist, tu-rist!*', putting a spin on the 's' that makes them sound like Hissing Sid. With no *kaymakam* to rescue me, I'm all but reduced to tears by their attentions. Eventually I take refuge in Mor Barsawmo, which, like almost all the Syriac Orthodox churches of the Tur Abdin, has been meticulously restored over the last few years. It's not an old church and the teardrop-shaped windows and frilly inner arches echo nineteenth-century vernacular architecture, but its walls are radiant with brightly coloured painted cloths depicting Bible stories rendered with child-like reductiveness. Haloed in egg-yolk, St George spears a dragon about as fearsome as a cuddly toy. A Christ with a bad case of sunburn dances on coffins shaped like gold bars. Angels with blue wings and red cummerbunds float on a sky of black. They bear the signature of Nasra Şimmeshindi. As

Gertrude Bell sometimes struggled to complete her work because of the crowds that assembled to watch, as here in Midyat in 1909

I admire them, ninety-two-year-old Nasra is still wielding her paintbrushes in Mardin. Just months later she dies, bringing to an end a folk-art tradition passed down through her family for generations.

Midyat is the gateway to the Tur Abdin (see map overleaf), a slice of rural Turkey whose curious name makes it sound like a tour company. Its meaning in Syriac – 'the Mountain of the Servants of God' – is more promising, although the 'mountain' part is a tad misleading. The Tur Abdin is actually a high, waterless plateau that was traditionally home to a large population of Syrian Orthodox Christians known as Syriacs or Suryanis. Here, myriad biscuit-coloured villages straddle ridges and slither down hillsides with three obligatory signifiers jutting above their roofs: the minaret of the modern mosque, the bell tower of a church dating back to Byzantine times, and the water tank raised on concrete stilts that makes life possible amid the aridity. Hunkered down on the outskirts of the villages or isolated in the countryside are forgotten monasteries slowly returning to faltering life. Nowhere else in the country has Christianity left such a solid physical legacy.

'It was almost by chance that I took my way from Mosul to Diar-bekr through the Djebel Tur Abdin,' Gertrude wrote of her 1909 visit in the preface to the ensuing *The Churches and Monasteries of the Tur Abdin*. 'Into this country I came, entirely ignorant of its architectural wealth, because it was entirely unrecorded,' she wrote in *Amurath to Amurath*. Mistakenly believing that the French consul and archaeol-ogist Henri Pognon had already studied the area, she was so struck by her own discoveries that she rushed out the unfinished research, arguing that 'half a loaf, in matters archaeological, is very much bet-ter than no bread'. 'Nowhere in the world,' she declared, 'does there exist a group of early Christian shrines more remarkable than that which lies about Midyat, and few monastic establishments can rival in interest the great houses of Mar Augen and Mar Gabriel.' She would have been amazed to learn that almost a century after her vis-its the priest Hans Hollerweger could still write in the preface to his study of the Tur Abdin: 'It is astounding how little is known in the western world about the Syriac Christian tradition in the Middle East. To a still greater extent, this applies to this out-of-the-way plateau which has been the formative spiritual power in the region for centuries.'

Today the monastery of Mor Gabriel is the seat of the archdiocese of the Tur Abdin, presided over by Archbishop Timotheos Samuel Aktaş and peopled by many determined – one might even say hard-ened – monks and priests who live in virtual solitude between Midyat and Cizre. The monastery dates back to 397, but its venerable 1,600-year-old history has not been enough to protect it from frac-tious land-ownership disputes. The quarrels rage both with local Kurds who covet the grazing and with a government greedy for tax, entangling the residents in a plethora of costly lawsuits. In 2014 the government dropped some of its claims, but others have found their way to the European Court of Human Rights, where they languish unresolved. The ever more fortress-like external walls are a reminder in stone of the disputatiousness.

In the early days, however, Mor Gabriel (then the Abbey of Mor Shem'un of Kartmin) was such a hit in Constantinople that the em-peror Anastasius forwarded on the workmen sent to reinforce Dara to build a new prayer hall for it. By the late eighth century its popu-

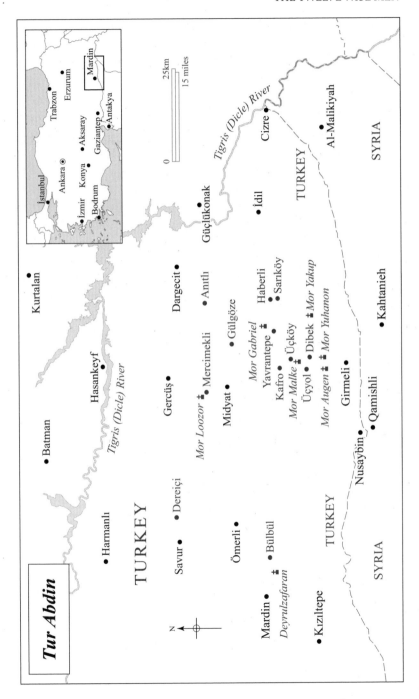

lation was large enough for it to lose ninety-four monks to the plague; a gruesome tale related how the body of the seventh-century Bishop Gabriel was exhumed and placed upright in the church to ward off the sickness, the success of this venture explaining the re-naming of the monastery in his honour.

Of course the Mor Gabriel visited by Gertrude had neither plague nor legal hassles to worry about. In her book she described it as 'perhaps the most famous Jacobite [Syriac] establishment in Asia', before going on to comment that 'it almost passes belief that this exceptionally important site should never have been carefully studied'. But the obstacles to such study were many. Most of the complex stood in ruins, apart from substructures converted into stables. Even the redoubtable Gertrude baulked at entering some of them. 'Though they are of little architectural importance, I would have tried to get some more accurate plan of them but for the horrible state of filth in which I found them. I leave it to a braver explorer to face the legions of fleas.' Inside the church she improvised a torch from magnesium wire. The flare lasted just long enough for her to make out a soot-blackened cross set in a field of glittering gold tesserae, the most easterly of Byzantine mosaics to survive in Turkey.

I'm shown that same cross, now scrubbed clean of soot to reveal its jewelled arms and the vine scrolls surrounding it, by the Mor Gabriel guide Şabo Alkan, who also points out a multicoloured opus sectile pavement believed to date back to 512. Then he leads me into a high-ceilinged chamber, nicknamed the Dome of Theodora to give it a spurious connection with the famous wife of Justinian. The dome – it 'looks as if the builder had just put his finishing touches upon it' – is completely invisible from the outside.

I've come to Mor Gabriel with an obliging Midyat taxi driver named Feyzi and am hoping to continue to the village of Sarıköy except that he doesn't know where it is. On the slopes below the monastery we spot a burly shepherd watching his goats.

'Do you know the way to Sarıköy?' Feyzi yells.

The man looks blank. I consult the alternative names listed by Hollerweger.

'Sare?'

Nothing.

'İstir?'

Nothing.

'Gawayto?'

Nothing.

Then: 'What's it called in Kurdish?' he yells back at us.

Gertrude had camped at Sarıköy in 1909 despite its being 'no easy matter on account of the interminable vines'. Recent restoration of the church has given it a smart new kitchen, where I meet Seyde, a trim seventysomething with ink-black hair who spends half the year here and half in Berlin. Had I visited a year earlier I would have found about forty returnees from Europe, she tells me. 'But this year they didn't come. They're afraid.' Understandably, given the proximity of ISIS and the renewed fighting between the government and the Kurds.

Inside the church she unveils a prize: a Parthian stele carved with a cloaked figure that was upside down in the courtyard in Gertrude's day. Today, the nave is spotless. Poor Gertrude wrote, however, that 'I had not stood for more than a minute inside the building than I happened to look down on to the floor and perceived it to be black with fleas. I made a hasty exit, tore off my stockings and plunged them into a tank of water.'

'They are all swept out on Sunday morning,' the priest said apologetically.

Cleansed of fleas, Gertrude fell to chatting with the local *ağa*, who was entertaining friends nearby, 'tricked out in all the finery which their birth warranted ... their short jackets were covered with embroidery, silver-mounted daggers were stuck into their girdles, and upon their heads they wore immense erections of white felt, wrapped round with a silken handkerchief of which the ends stuck out like wings over their foreheads'.

The *ağa* pressed on her a gift of partridges. Lacking any such bounty to offer, Seyde and her companions duck into the kitchen and rustle up a Nescafé. Then we sit in the sun oohing and aahing over toddler Tiberia, born in a time of optimism, when it had briefly seemed as if those who had left the Tur Abdin in the 1970s could return and restart their lives here.

But soon I detect a twitchiness. I've mistaken Seyde's black get-

up and calf-length skirt for the sort of clothing once worn by widowed Greeks when it is actually mourning dress for one of the summer returnees who has just died in neighbouring Haberli. The
Sarıköy women are anxious not to miss the funeral. Despite their
thickened ankles, they had been planning to walk, so the arrival of
our taxi is a lifesaver. Soon we're bumping up the road to Haberli,
where, in a timeless, quasi-Old Testament scene, we glimpse black-
clad Syriac men and women pouring down the treeless hillsides and
streaming into the chapel.

After his exhumation, Bishop Gabriel's right arm was sent north to
Anıtlı (Hah) to ward off the plague there too. Of all the Tur Abdin
churches, Hah's Church of the Mother of God is the most spectacular,
its roof topped with a unique superstructure squared off with blind
arcading. How a church in such an out-of-the-way location could
put on such airs is explained by a history that included two stints as
the seat of a bishopric. But beyond that lies Hah's own twist on the
Nativity narrative, in which it was twelve rather than the customary
three wise men who followed the star to greet the new-born Messiah.
Reaching Hah, they agreed that only three of them need complete
the long journey. In Bethlehem the chosen three were gifted a souvenir swaddling-band, but, reluctant to divide it up, they determined
to burn it and share out the ashes, whereupon the fire smelted the
smouldering cloth into twelve gold medallions. Suitably impressed,
King Hanna of Hah determined to build a church resilient enough
to commemorate the miracle forever.

Riding into Hah in 1909, Gertrude was greeted by the rays of the
setting sun illuminating the great dome that then surmounted the
church. She pitched camp behind it, settling down for the night beside a pond close to where the division of the ashes had been agreed.
Delirious with pleasure, she wrote: 'It seemed to me that I had ended
the most wonderful day since that which had brought me to Ukhei-
dir* by dropping into a village of the fifth century, complete and
prosperous in every part.'

---

*Abbasid-era fortress of Al-Ukhaidir in Iraq. In 1914 Bell wrote a detailed des-
cription of it and was disappointed when a French archaeologist published his
account before hers.

Church of the Mother of God at Anıtlı (Hah) in 1909 when it still had a dome

In the light of day things looked rather different: 'the houses were mere hovels, and except for the church of the Virgin, not one of the ancient buildings but had fallen into the extremity of decay'. In the church the one resident nun begged Gertrude for a revolver. 'We are afraid … We are all afraid of massacre.'

That fear sprang from the depredations of bands of Kurds who roamed the countryside in search of booty. Over her travelling years Gertrude herself had many close calls, the worst being the eleven days yet to come when she would be held prisoner in the Arabian desert stronghold of Hayyil. But it was here in Hah that she experienced the sort of commonplace mishap with which all off-the-beaten-track travellers will empathize. In the middle of the night a rustling awoke her and in the darkness she glimpsed 'a shadowy figure outlined against the sky'. By the time she'd struggled out of her mosquito net, he'd fled. Alas, his companions had already snatched whatever they wanted. All her money was gone. More distressingly, so were the notebooks containing the records of four months of desert exploration. 'In a moment there was a clean sweep, photographs, plans, notes all had vanished – Rakka, Sammara, half Khethar*, all the churches at which I had toiled, all the odds and ends

*Alternative name for Al-Ukhaidir.

along the road: I might just as well not have travelled at all,' she wrote to her mother in despair.

The notebooks being far too valuable to let go without a fight, Gertrude duly raised a stink, despatching Fattuh to fetch the *Çelebi*, 'the feudal chief of the Kurdish tribes in the Tur Abdin' and a 'man with far more authority than the government possesses'. Having poured out her woes, she told him that she 'wd ruin the world if my things did not appear', her threats reinforced by the priest, who assured him that all the governments of Europe would descend on the village if he did not act swiftly. Off rode the *Çelebi* towards neighbouring Zakhuran. 'It chanced that the thieves had carried off a parcel of my gloves, and these they shed along the path as they ran. Gloves lying upon the rocky ways of the Tur Abdin are exceptional objects, and the path by which they were found was that which led to Za'khuran,' she wrote.

In the morning he returned with a 'picturesque following robed in white and armed with rifles' and sent a request for reinforcements to Midyat. On day three he was back again, this time with '5 prisoners selected I fancy at haphazard'. By the time that a troop of fifty infantry rode in from Midyat, most of the villagers had taken fright and fled with their flocks, so the soldiers simply rode straight home again, taking with them some prisoners and Hah's innocent *muhtar*.

By then, while still distraught over her loss, Gertrude was starting to regret having caused such a commotion. 'The nature of evidence is not clearly grasped in the East, and by the third day after the robbery there was no person in the country-side, except, I believe, myself, against whom a charge of complicity had not been raised,' she wrote. 'My servants were plunged in grief; their honour was gone.' She had also started to blame herself for what had happened. 'We had grown careless with months of safe journeying in dangerous places,' she wrote; as a result, neither she nor Fattuh had checked that a guard had been posted before they slept.

On the morning of the fifth day it must have come as a quite a relief to hear excited yells – 'Your goods have come back! Your goods have come back!' – from across the valley. There, 'on a big stone', were all the items taken except the money, 'which was after all the least important'. She rode over to Zakhuran and found it 'completely

The Çelebi – 'a splendid, handsome Kurd he is, the six feet of him robed in white and cloaked in a gold embroidered abbayah' – who arrived to help find Bell's missing notebooks after they were stolen in Anıtlı (Hah) in 1909

deserted except for cocks and hens'. While the *Çelebi* went in search of the lost flocks, Gertrude napped, then awoke to find a bishop robed in purple and clasping a bejewelled cross watching over her. Later she wrote to Midyat requesting that the *muhtar* be freed and Hah's sheep returned. 'Revenge,' she found, 'is not so sweet as it is said to be, nor is it so easy when wrong is afoot to determine who is the more wronged.'

★ ★ ★

For Gertrude, Hah's Church of the Mother of God was the 'jewel of the Tur Abdin'. It is a building that exults in playing games with perspective. From the outside the superstructure suggests something large and cathedral-like. Inside, however, reality shrinks back down into a little Byzantine church with a rather odd north-south axis. Gertrude doubted it could have been built any later than the fifth century and wrote in raptures of the 'splendid' mouldings and capitals hung with what looked like stone cords and tassels.

In the courtyard a trio of stumpy columns serve as lecterns for al fresco sermons. Here I chat to the caretaker, Hanna, shy mother to three young children. We line up on either side of one of the lecterns just as Gertrude had done with the youthful resident nun. 'The church used to be crowded on the Feast of the Assumption,' she says, 'but not for the last two years. Now people are too frightened to come here.'

We are exchanging looks of commiseration when suddenly the courtyard explodes into a pantomime of multicoloured clothing, ill-fitting hats and bare pink kneecaps. I've hardly seen another Westerner since restarting my journey, so nothing could have been more startling than this invasion of well-meaning Slovenians who squeeze their way into the church, snapping selfies and exchanging jokes as if all were normal when clearly it's not. The night before, the thump of an explosion had echoed round their Mardin hotel bedrooms, the tour leader says. The news carried no comment. Just another flash bang, we conclude; all noise and no knickers.

Leaving the tourists to their picture-snapping, I head off towards the ruins of Mor Sobo, a sixth-century basilica that was probably the village's main church, and bump into Hanem, who's on her way to grape-pick but happily stops for a chat instead. She's strikingly beautiful, fortyish, her jet-black hair and eyebrows bestowing on her a look more Semitic than Anatolian. From the shade of the *beth slotho*, a free-standing exedra once used for weekday prayers, Hanem points out a clump of olive trees in the courtyard. 'On 16 August we celebrated the Zeytin Pazarı (Olive Market). We would parade round the courtyard and toss olives at the priest as a symbol of peace,' she says.

There was a darker side to this story of peasant merrymaking though. 'Of course we were always *gavurs*. People wouldn't share their *pekmez* with us. And when one of our relatives was sick and went to a doctor in Midyat, he sent her away empty-handed because she spoke to him in Turoyo.'

'Is it any better now?'

'Not really. Since the AK Party came to power there has been even more emphasis on religion.'

We look at each other sadly. Then I turn to Gertrude's diary to read out her entry for Hah and once again time freezes.

'My grandfather Şi'mün guided her!' Hanem says with a grin. 'When I was growing up, he told us all about the strange English lady who came to look at the churches.'

As we walk back together towards my taxi, Hanem recites a by now familiar story of families tossed around the globe, some gone to Sweden, some to Germany, some to Australia.

'But you've stayed?'

'Yes. We wanted our children to grow up in our own culture, speaking our own language. So we stayed.'

★ ★ ★

In the village of Mercimekli (Habsus), Feyzi and I settle down to drink çay with Abdullah and Nisani Kurt. I'd met Nisani in 2011 and will forever treasure my first glimpse of her striding towards me along the cobbled street, a tiny woman in her early seventies wearing an ankle-length baby-blue robe and violet flipflops, a white scarf anchored to her head by a band like an Arab *agal*. In her hand she held a key almost as big as she was. On her face she wore a beaming smile. At that time, she and her husband made up two thirds of Mercimekli's surviving Syriac population.

Nisani had shown me around the church of Mor Shemun, of all the Tur Abdin churches the one that felt the most lived in. Red and white cassocks hung from hooks, as if their owners might be passing them over their heads again at any moment. A photograph commemorated the patriarchs of the Syriac church, earnest men in black with pincushion hats and bushy beards to shame a Salafi. Coloured lightbulbs framed the altar, a jarring dollop of Hollywood glamour in such an out-of-the-way place.

Roll on five years and Abdullah and a considerably frailer Nisani are now Mercimekli's last Syriacs. As we sit on floor cushions with our backs against the wall, Abdullah speaks to Feyzi in Arabic, Nisani speaks to me in Turkish and they speak to each other in Turoyo, never skipping a beat. The house is spacious and full of light. 'I worked as a market gardener in Beirut for three years to save the money to build it,' explains Abdullah.

The daughter of an Armenian mother, Nisani was born on 23 April, hence the decision to call her 'the April one'. Of course most of the villagers baulked at such a neologism. 'They call me Hayrün-nisa!' she laughs. Their children are long gone to Belgium. 'Twice we've applied for visas to visit, but we've never got them.'

As I scan a line-up of family photographs my eye snags on the image of a bearded Muslim sheikh. Abdullah smiles. 'That's Şeyh Fethullah Hamdi from Batman,' he says. 'At the time of the *ferman* he tried to protect people from the massacres.'

I note that word *ferman*. In Turkish it means 'decree' or 'edict'. Silence descends. I'm not ready to address its particular meaning to the Tur Abdin yet.

'Can I take your picture?' I ask, to break the silence. And in a moment of heart-breaking poignancy, Nisani slips her hand into that of her equally elderly husband as they pose in front of the images of their scattered family.

In the walled courtyard of an abandoned monastery on the outskirts of Mercimekli Gertrude noted the cylindrical base of what she thought was a belfry but was more probably the bottom of another stylite pillar. In 2011 Nisani and I had walked there together, arriving to find the gate locked. With a snort of disgust, she'd picked out a crumbled section of the wall, then, hitching up her skirt, she'd been up and over, leaving me whimpering on the other side. Now, sadly, such gymnastics are beyond her and it's with Abdullah that I return to Mor Loozor (St Lazarus). This time we find the gate open and stroll around the courtyard together.

'That was the kitchen, that was for animals, this was the oven, this was the well – we stored our yoghurt in there before there were refrigerators.' As Abdullah talks, his wife's reminiscences come back to me: 'On feast days there were long tables set up and we all ate together. It was wonderful.'

The question has to be asked. 'What happened to the monks?'

'There were twelve of them. They died at the time of the *ferman*.'

'You say the *ferman*. I thought it was called the Sayfo?'

'That's what people overseas call it. We prefer *ferman*.'

With that we go our separate ways. Abdullah rejects the offer of a lift back to the village. I watch him walk away, a tall, straight-backed man, flat cap on his head, wearing the trousers and waistcoat of a suit, the very picture of a village Atatürkist.

The *ferman*. The Sayfo. Like it or not, this is ground zero for understanding the Tur Abdin. Whichever term one prefers to use, sooner or later one has to get to grips with what happened here in 1915, otherwise there is no way to comprehend the multiplicity of churches without congregations, the proliferation of monasteries without monks. Uproar in Turkey over the use of the term 'genocide' has at least ensured that the wholesale slaughter of the Armenians in 1915 crops up regularly in world news. But 1915 is a matryoshka doll of a date. Unscrew the visible head and all sorts of much less familiar things come to light in the innards. Foremost amongst them is the Sayfo, the Syriac word meaning 'sword'.

The *ferman* to which the locals refer was the edict issued by the Young Turk Talat Paşa towards the end of 1914 in which he called for the Assyrians (Syriacs) to be deported. Although the order was rescinded three days later, local officialdom seemingly lumped many of the Syriacs in with the Armenians and treated them accordingly. An estimated 100,000 Syriacs living within the territory of what is now Turkey lost their lives, some of them summarily massacred, others driven out of their villages and herded towards Syria in a weeks-long desert trudge that spelt almost certain death from hunger, thirst or exhaustion. Half the Syriac population of the Tur Abdin is believed to have perished. There's barely a surviving family that was unaffected.

In the village of Gülgöze, the old Inwardo, Mor Had Bshabo, with its keep-out towers and arrow-slit windows, is the most fortress-like of the Tur Abdin churches. That, combined with its central location, ensured that in times of trouble Syriacs tended to flock to it for refuge; even today, bullet holes preserved in the re-rendered walls make the bloody past unforgettable. Johanno tells me that the 1,500 Syriac families in the village were once served by several churches, each with its own priest. Now only four families remain – 'and only two of them have any young people'. Four family members from his grandfather's generation perished in the Sayfo, but he has chosen to stay and maintain their jewellery business in Midyat. Otherwise, 'most of us are scattered to the world, to the US, to Germany, to Switzerland …' he chants in the familiar southeastern refrain.

It was at Inwardo that Şeyh Fethullah Hamdi showed his mettle. Fearing the worst after the Ottoman Empire picked its side in the war, villagers from all over the Tur Abdin fled to Inwardo, constructing walls between the houses and turning it into a fortified encampment. The Ottoman army, reinforced by Kurdish irregulars, then laid siege to it, a siege that endured for three years, with the villagers growing hungrier and hungrier. Finally, cholera ripped through the army, weakening the besieging troops to such an extent that men from Inwardo felt emboldened to sneak out and attack the barracks in Midyat. It was at this point that Şeyh Fethullah presented himself as a mediator, offering his son as hostage to the army's good faith. Eventually he persuaded the troops to retreat, guaranteeing his place in Syriac memories.

Gertrude doesn't seem to have visited Inwardo and, had she done so, it would have been in a time of peace when, no matter how ugly the stories dribbling out of Cilicia, she could hardly have imagined that she was observing the last days of Syrian Orthodoxy in the Tur Abdin. I, however, am burdened by knowledge of the afterwards. Because not even the Sayfo can entirely explain the empty villages, the abandoned houses. At the end of the Turkish War of Independence the Treaty of Lausanne promised some protection to Turkey's Greek, Armenian and Jewish minorities but, carelessly, not to the Syriacs. Like the Kurds, they found their right to maintain a separate culture and language coming under pressure as waves of Turkification policies saw even their villages renamed. In the 1960s, when Germany was crying out for immigrant labour, many of them abandoned the struggle to secure their land against Kurdish nomads and the niggling fear of attacks such as those that followed the Cyprus crisis of 1964, and emigrated. Others followed in the 1980s and 90s as the whole southeast collapsed into unrest. As priests departed, whole villages followed them to Europe. As late as the mid-1990s, the British travel writer William Dalrymple met many Syriacs still living in the Tur Abdin. Now Mercimekli is typical. Recent optimistic returnees aside, hardly any now remain.

★ ★ ★

On the third day of the *bayram* Feyzi and I head for the remote monasteries south of Midyat. We haven't gone far before we stumble upon a settlement that stands out like a last rose flowering in a winter garden. Almost all the other villages we've visited have fitted a pattern, their narrow streets lined with abandoned stone houses, the odd smart new-build hunkered down behind high walls and razor wire. The roads have gloried in a rustic shambolickness, designed as much for cattle as for people. Now suddenly we're driving through what could be a modern housing estate in the Cotswolds. All the houses are of sharp-edged stone, the upper storeys stepped back to provide terraces and shady verandas that never obscure a neighbour's view. Neat gardens face onto a high street without a single discarded cigarette butt. It's a Turkish village, but at the same time it's totally un-Turkish. It is Kafro Tachtayto (Lower Kafro).

In front of a vine-shaded café we're greeted by Nial, a man in his forties who came here from Stuttgart in 2008 and opened the only eatery for miles around. But the picture he paints of life in the twenty-first-century Tur Abdin is not particularly encouraging.

In one of his last acts as prime minister in 2001, Bülent Ecevit announced that those Syriacs who wanted to return to Turkey should feel safe to do so. While hardly couched in gushing terms, his invitation sparked hope in the hearts of homesick European émigrés and soon the most enthusiastic were packing their suitcases. In most instances the pioneers headed back to their ancestral villages and attempted either to reclaim their family homes or build new ones. But all too soon they were up against the gulf between words and reality. For in the years since their families had left, local Kurds had moved into many of their houses and they had no intention of giving them up again without a fight.

Here in Kafro an enterprising group of families attempted something more ambitious. A hamlet of thirty families in 1900, Kafro had been completely abandoned in 1995, its houses and church ransacked and destroyed. Rather than trying to fight a costly battle for compensation, its returnees resolved to rebuild from scratch, anticipating not just a few summer months of retirement here but a whole new life. But then they too ran aground on reality.

'Young people are not interested,' says Nial sadly as he shows off the unused pizza oven installed in the early days of hopefulness. 'And now look – there are no visitors either.'

Because of course all their plans turned on the one common requirement for all development in the southeast: namely, continued peace, and progress towards democracy. Now, with peace exiting the stage faster than the proverbial bear, the returnees are losing heart and reimagining a European future.

'A few weeks ago there was a shootout here between the PKK and the army,' Nial adds. So even in this ostensibly tranquil setting all is not quite as it seems.

I'm thinking about this as we press on south. At the same time I'm thinking about the start-up hotels of Mardin and Midyat. I fear for the future of Kafro as I fear for these towns whose future had looked so rosy just one short year ago. If people who were encouraged to invest here lose their savings to renewed fighting, how will they be persuaded to risk the gamble again? A one-off opportunity for a fresh start in the southeast is melting as swiftly as an ice cube in the sun.

In 1909 Gertrude passed through Üçköy, the old Harabale, on her way north from Nusaybin to Mor Gabriel. 'There we went wrong,' she confided to her diary. Feyzi and I don't go wrong. However, we do arrive to find the newly restored church of Mor Efrem locked, its keyholder absent. On the village outskirts we pass one of the fortified military posts nicknamed *kalekols* in a conflation of the words for castle (*kale*) and police station (*karakol*). So far on my trip I have been pleasantly surprised by the absence of security checks. Throughout the 1990s it was impossible to travel from one southeastern village to the next without having to produce your paperwork. But this year I've travelled to most of the Syrian border towns without requests for ID. I view the *kalekol* with alarm, but Feyzi beams up at the approaching soldier. 'She wants to visit Mor Malke,' he says, rolling his eyes in a 'you know these crazy foreigners' kind of way. It does the trick. We're waved on, no papers sought.

Approaching from the opposite direction in 1909, Gertrude noted that the monastery of Mor Malke 'stands up square on its hill and has a very fortress-like air' and 'the b[isho]p has 3 monks here'. Now there are two monks and two nuns and while we wait for them to conclude their prayers, Feyzi and I wander onto the terrace and exclaim at the vista unrolling in front of us: nothing but wild, empty countryside threaded with scrub oak in a palette of unvariegated yellow and green. Feyzi snaps away enthusiastically, as much a first-time visitor as I am. Then a boy comes running to fetch us.

Aziz, the middle-aged priest, is a dour man, short on small talk, so it comes as a surprise as I prepare to embark on my usual explanatory spiel when he beats me to it. 'A long time ago there was an Englishwoman like you. Gertrude Bell. She took the earliest photos of this monastery …' It's the first time that anyone has pipped me to the post with Gertrude's name, but the words are no sooner uttered than Aziz lapses back into silence again.

Unable 'to hazard any conjecture as to the date of the building', not least because most signs of great age had been plastered over, Gertrude was, however, shown the tomb of the eponymous Mor Malke, who had brought with him to Üçköy the rites of the Persian-influenced East Syrian rather than the Byzantine-influenced West Syrian church. In a part of the country where great fables are the stuff of life, a particularly good story attaches itself to the name of this saint. Summoned to Constantinople by the emperor, he successfully exorcised the demons troubling his daughter, in return for which the grateful father was willing to grant him his heart's desire. A man of simple needs, Malke asked for a stone with a hole in the middle of it, which he draped round the neck of the exorcised demon before attaching a chain and forcing him to carry it all the way back to the monastery.

'There it is,' says Aziz, pointing to a chunky doughnut of stone covering the well. In the church itself he shows me a collar and chain with reputed powers to put an end to fits and madness. Beside the altar an icon depicts the emperor's daughter vomiting out what looks like a long pink tapeworm.

Feyzi and I press on south towards the newly rebuilt monastery of Mor Yakup at Badibe, the modern Dibek. Most of the Tur Abdin monasteries exist in a haze of historic vagueness. Unusually, a precise date can be assigned to Mor Yakup and it's a late date – 1172 – which would no doubt have had Gertrude turning up her nose in disappointment had she reached it. Her route had taken her across country from Sarıköy to Usudere (the modern Sedere), passing Hatem Tai, a hilltop castle with the usual chequered history stretching back to Byzantine times. Even with the help of a guide from Sarıköy she struggled to navigate this remote part of the Tur Abdin. 'There was no road', she wrote, and 'we struggled down through the woods, dragging our horses over rocks and fallen trees'. Nor was the way ahead any easier. From the village of Geliyeh – where she was offered and refused a bed in a cave, and a banquet of mutton – she pressed on with a Yezidi guide 'through oak woods where the bees had hived in every hollow trunk'. Finally they emerged in the village of Kınık, where an attempt to have one of the horses re-shoed failed because the local farrier had died and the village was unable to 'produce a single nail'. At that point their guide abandoned them to the mercies of their inadequate map. A few hard hours of travelling later, they arrived 'tired and hungry' at the foot of the hill leading up to Kal'at Jedid*. Tempting as it looked, Gertrude had to throw up the chance to explore the castle for fear of not making their campsite before nightfall. 'It remains in my memory as a vision of wall and tower and precipitous rock rising into the ruddy sunset light above a shadowy gorge, a citadel as bold and menacing as any that I have seen,' she wrote.

How those words eat away at me! How I long to beat Gertrude to the ruins of this forgotten castle. But there are bears in the woods, besides which we're close to the border in a military-designated 'Forbidden Zone' where to be on the road after 5 p.m. is to attract suspicion. I'm feeling a tad downhearted, then, as we stroll down the newly laid path to the monastery of Mor Yakup, St Jacob the Teacher. But disappointment soon gives way to relief as we're welcomed into the complex, home now to just one monk, the redoubtable and un-

*Kal'at Jedid, the 'New Castle', probably a medieval Kurdish powerbase.

expectedly youthful Father Aho. Soon Feyzi, Aho and I are sitting in the cool of a stone-arched *liwan*. As if by magic, bowls of grapes, melon, cucumber and figs appear, along with coffee. A man of impish demeanour, Aho describes an apprenticeship for his calling that had taken him to Chichester University, then to Deyrulzafaran and finally to Damascus. Now a priest-monk, he officiates at services attended by local villagers. 'My parents didn't want me to do this,' he admits. 'But they've come round to the idea. Now my father is here to help me start a garden.'

In the library of Mor Yakup Monastery Father Aho shows off his copy of *The Churches and Monasteries of the Tur Abdin* in 2015

I can quite understand his parents' apprehension; it's hard for an outsider to imagine what motivates men to embrace such an ancient and lonely calling in the modern age, especially when it means living with tangible risk. We stand on the terrace and scan the empty landscape. Off to the right we can just make out Mor Malke. The great monastery of Mor Augen, Aho's home before Mor Yakup reopened in 2013, is tucked out of sight beyond the ridge in front of us. 'I could walk back there, 'he says. 'It takes an hour and a half, but that was in different times …'

Aho is a great fan of Gertrude, whose books have pride of place in his library. Together we chew over why she didn't visit this particular monastery. It seems a strange omission until we remember the daunting journey she had just undertaken: the scrubland, the lack of water, the uncertainty over how much further they must travel before darkness fell.

But Aho has tougher questions for me. Why was Gertrude interested in the Tur Abdin in the first place? Was she a Roman Catholic? It's painful to have to tell him that his heroine was an atheist and that it was buildings, not belief, that drew her here. Then he poses the hardest question of all: why did I think that she had killed herself? It's a question I've asked myself over and again and I struggle to articulate my conclusions: that she probably felt that she had fulfilled her destiny; that there was nothing more attractive for her to return to in England than the role of eccentric maiden aunt; that a lifetime of smoking had left her in poor health; that an unreciprocated crush on a friend must have robbed her of any last lingering hope of a husband; that she was probably menopausal (although this is a thought I don't voice); that lack of religious faith might have made it easier to swallow a lethal dose of sleeping pills. But all must be speculation and we stand sadly side by side thinking about that lonely Baghdad grave.

'She was so important to us,' Aho whispers as we say our farewells.

Back in Midyat, I open my computer. Up pops a message. The army had swooped on a PKK encampment just down the road from Mor Yakup, it warns. What's more, the PKK had strafed an army munitions truck near the turnoff to Savur. I snap it shut and pull the sheet over my head. I feel like a mouse skulking behind the skirting board, acutely conscious of a hungry cat on the other side. But tomorrow is another day and come what may my sights are set on reaching the Mor Augen monastery. A previous attempt had ended in failure after a local was killed by a landmine forgotten on the hillside. This time I'm not going to be defeated.

26

In Search of Noah's Ark

NUSAYBİN–MOR AUGEN–CİZRE

'I wasn't just taking the air in the mountains, I went up to look at – the Ark.'
Letter, 14 May 1909

It's the last day of the *bayram* and Midyat is emptying of holiday-makers. It's also the day on which eight-year-old Elif Şimşek is killed during a curfew in the forgotten backwater of Bismil. Over breakfast I gaze at her photograph in the newspaper. She looks like any other innocent child who should have been playing with her doll and bugging her mother about what they were having for lunch. The government is blaming the PKK. The PKK is blaming the government. In the middle of their quarrel lie a dead eight-year-old child and her grieving family.

After several days of driving around the Tur Abdin with Feyzi I've decided to strike out on my own again. I'm heading for Nusaybin, the old Nisibis, on the Syrian border. The news may be increasingly alarming, but the fact of having been there before buoys me with misplaced confidence.

The *dolmuş* from Midyat speeds south down the highway and bumps to a halt in wasteland on the edge of Nusaybin. I start off into the centre. All the shops are closed, their shutters rolled down. That I'm back in Kurdish territory is made plain by the exposed graffiti: over and again in silent rhythm, 'PKK' and 'Apo', the deceptively innocent nickname used for the organization's imprisoned leader, Abdullah Öcalan. Those closed shutters bother me. It's the end of *bayram*, I tell myself; the shopkeepers are away visiting their families. But still they remind me of a day in Hakkari when the PKK ordered a rolling strike and the entire town snapped shut as comprehensively as a car with central locking.

But soon I'm passing the cultural centre, a sandstone beauty, its facade embossed with a showily Mesopotamian *faravahar* sun symbol. A banner hangs from the roof. It depicts the local MP, a woman, and spouts words of defiance – in Turkish, rather surprisingly. I cross a small bridge and gaze gloomily down on turtles swimming in fetid water, but my confidence picks up as people begin to crowd the pavements. Then I pass a pet shop. A caged kitten howls piteously; the shopkeeper has cleaned up by hosing down cat and cage simultaneously. Furious, I turn away and spot something unexpected: the technicolour facade of a trendy café.

It goes without saying that trendy cafés are not what I was expecting to find in distant Nusaybin but I've stumbled on the hangout of the local chattering class. The bookshelves groan with works of politics and philosophy. Lefty magazines hang like pillowcases from washing lines. Photographs of Kobani decorate the walls. I sink into a sofa. I order a coffee. I let out a sigh of relief.

Too soon. Up ahead, police barriers bookend the road. Beyond them lies the Syrian border. I hang a right towards the ancient monastery of Mor Yakup. An unfeasible number of young men are loitering in the street, which appears to be hemmed in with barricades, unless my jittery imagination is conjuring monsters from everyday fencing. In the middle of the road a man waves me back. I gesture towards the church. His expression softens. His hand drops to his side. He marches over to the gate and rings the bell.

The door is opened by Daniel, a member of the last Christian family living in Nusaybin, a disheartening fact considering that there have been Christians here from at least the second century. Daniel leads me into the church's soot-blackened interior, where much of the original Byzantine decoration still survives; restorers have yet to reach Nusaybin, leaving intact the patina of the church's 1,700-year existence. Capitals carved with acanthus leaves still support the sanctuary arch while separate flights of stairs to the undercroft, one for down, the other for up, recall the days when Canterbury Cathedral-sized crowds flocked to pay their respects to the remains of Mor Yakup, the local man who became bishop of the Nisibis see and is known to have attended the Council of Nicaea in 325.

Gertrude arrived in Nusaybin in 1911, trotting across a many-arched stone bridge (now lost) at the tail end of a ride from Syria that had degenerated into a nightmare of torrential rain, bedraggled tents and paperwork barely saved from gusting wind. Nisibis was, she wrote, 'a tiny village lying in the midst of the ruin heaps which were once the greatest fortified city of the Roman frontier'. What she didn't mention was that its foundation owed much to the same King Seleucus whose work she had so admired in Çevlik and who had re-founded the originally Aramaean city as Antiochia Mygdonia. In 363, after the Persian king Sapur defeated the emperor Julian in Mesopotamia, the occupants of Nisibis were exiled to Amida (Diyarbakır), their place taken by Persians from as far afield as Isfahan.

Nusaybin is the quintessential Turkish border town, divided from Qamishli on the Syrian side by little more than the ownership-asserting paraphernalia of modern statehood. Gertrude pitched her tents beside a row of storks'-nest-supporting columns and took a cursory look at the solid block of a church that she found 'deep in masses of earth and ruin'; it must once have been much larger, she concluded. Recent excavations have uncovered the remains not just of the monastic complex but also of a famous school that used to be attached to it. Founded in 326 and so even more ancient than the better known one at Harran, this school was apparently able to accommodate a thousand students who were taught philosophy and science in Aramaic. Its most famous teacher was a poet-monk named Ephrem the Syrian, who taught here until the school was forced to relocate to Urfa after Sapur seized the city. Revived in the late fifth century, the school became a hotbed of Nestorianism, a theology that emphasized the divide between Christ's divine and human natures (in contrast to the Syriac tradition which believed his two natures to be indivisible). After church councils of the fifth century classified Nestorianism as a heresy, most of its adherents moved to Sassanian Persia, where they merged with the Chaldean Church of the East.

'The school was enormous,' Daniel tells me as he leads me back towards the barriers, where we swivel right and head for the border. On the far side he points out the row of stocky columns with neat Corinthian capitals that had backed onto Gertrude's campsite, now inaccessible in Syria. They were, he says, part of the complex. Like a naughty schoolgirl lurking behind the bike shed with a cigarette, I hide behind a tree to snatch a photo.

But the real reason for coming to Nusaybin at such an unsettled time is to visit the monastery of Mor Augen, which slumbers on Mt Izla some way east of town. To get there I'm going to need transport. Daniel makes some calls but finds no takers. Then he leads me into a tiny office beside a grocery. Reclining on a sofa is a young man.

'This is Şeyhmus,' says Daniel. 'He'll take you to Mor Augen.'

I eye Şeyhmus without enthusiasm. He is not my ideal 'taxi' driver. In the first place he looks about twenty. In the second he has what looks like a scar running down from his forehead and into his cheek. My ideal driver is a man in his forties or fifties, mature enough to want to drive at a sensible speed, old enough to know something about where we're going. Gut instinct screams that this is a bad idea. At the same time every ounce of my British upbringing is telling me that I can't reject a driver on the basis of a scar.

'Maybe I'll see if there's an official taxi,' I venture, playing for time.

Daniel fixes me with a stare. 'Right now, the important thing is to go with someone you can trust, someone known to us. This man is my neighbour.'

There's an undertow to this conversation, a great deal that is going unsaid. Such as that we're right on the border, where it would be easy for someone to sell me to ISIS or the PKK; where it would be rewarding to trade me to the army as a spy, financial incentives having just been announced for tip-offs. Usually I assume that being female is a plus in situations like this, since few men get their kicks out of sizing up against women. But these are different times, and ISIS hardly a beast to mess with.

Some of this must be apparent from my expression because Daniel pulls out his phone again. 'I'll call my son,' he says. 'He will go with you.' Which is how it happens that half an hour later I'm bouncing east along the road that parallels the border with not one but two small boys in the back of the van as hostages for my safe return.

Şeyhmus is a slight man who looks as if the wind might blow him over. His first language is Kurdish, but we muddle through in Turkish. His primary concern turns out to have nothing to do with politics and everything to do with women. 'It's hard to get married here if you don't own a car,' he tells me, and when I mention the floods that have just swept through Bodrum he grins. 'Girls in shorts!' he says gleefully. 'Green-eyed girls in shorts!' Not for anything will he be-

lieve me when I tell him that un-
married Syrian Orthodox priests
are bound to celibacy. 'It's impossible,' he states flatly.

A newly tarmacked road
whisks us up to the monastery,
where we're greeted by a man in
civvies demanding to know if we
have an appointment. Behind
him I spot Father Joachim, the
resident priest, hurrying across
the courtyard, modesty vest-
ments draped over his arm, as he
rushes to prepare for an unexpected guest.

Like Father Aho, Father
Joachim is young and steely
nerved. In 2010 Mor Augen
stood in ruins, its last occupant

With Father Dale Johnson at Mor
Augen Monastery in 2015

having died in 1974. A returnee from Amsterdam, Joachim was determined to bring the monastery back to life, and the local government was happy to help, at least in terms of improving access to it.
Now as I sit on the terrace sipping coffee, I notice incongruous whiffs
of domesticity rubbing shoulders with monumental history. Sheets
flap on the washing line. An air-conditioning unit hums on a wall. A
vegetable garden is going great guns on a plateau overlooking the
Mesopotamian Plain.

★ ★ ★

'Look up there. See that cave – that's where the bishop was living
when Gertrude came here,' says Father Dale Johnson.

I'm in luck. Not only is Father Joachim at home but I've arrived
during a visit by Dale, a native of the Skagit Valley and one of only
two ordained Syrian Orthodox priests in the USA. A brave and re-
sourceful man at the tipping point between middle and old age, Dale
has devoted much of his life to helping refugees, paying for his ventures in benighted parts by being taken hostage twice. Now, like
Joachim, he's conscious that the hands stand at a minute to midnight

for Christianity in the Tur Abdin. He's also another big Gertrude fan. By now, word of a strange Englishwoman who is retracing her travels is doing the rounds of the Tur Abdin monasteries and he has been waiting to greet me.

Mor Augen was a little busier in Gertrude's day. 'Ten monks [were] ... lodged in the rock-cut cells of their remote forerunners,' she wrote, and she was greeted by the prior, a man of about thirty 'with melancholy eyes ... [and a face] marked with the lines drawn by solitude and hunger'. Soon he was explaining their way of life to her. 'They spend their days in meditation; their diet is bread and oil and lentils; no meat, and neither milk nor eggs may pass their lips; they may see no woman ...'

At that last remark Gertrude let out a squeak. '"But may you see me?" I asked.'

The prior replied that they had made an exception for her since they had so few visitors. Still: 'Some of the monks have shut themselves into their cells until you go.' As for the bishop, when Gertrude asked to see him, she was told that he had left the world, a statement that turned out to be code for his having retreated to the cave once occupied by Mor Augen himself that Dale is now pointing out to me some fifty feet above the ground.

'He is the father of eighty years ... and it is now a year since he took a vow of silence and renounced the world. Once a day, at sunset, he lets down a basket on a rope and we place therein a small portion of bread ... When he is sick to death he will send down a written word telling us to come up ... and fetch his body,' the prior explained.

I peer up at that cave, its mouth partially stopped-up with stone. It's hard to believe that men were ever content to subject themselves to such privations, but the prior made plain to Gertrude that he anticipated the same future for himself. 'The idea has some romantic appeal to me too,' admits Dale.

'Is it okay to talk to women now?' I ask Joachim, suddenly self-conscious.

A gentle smile lifts the corners of his lips. 'After the *ferman* everything changed,' he says quietly.

Together we wander around what Gertrude called 'the most striking monastery' in the Tur Abdin, 'a kind of citadel in the heart of a system of monastic fortifications'. Mor Augen has a complicated history liturgically speaking because in 363 when the new boundary was drawn between the Byzantine and Persian spheres of interest it fell on the Persian side of the fence, gradually becoming a stronghold of Nestorianism. In 1505 the Nestorian monks were driven out, and Henri Pognon, the French explorer who paid a visit before Gertrude, believed that it was then abandoned until the eighteenth century, when Syriacs rebuilt the complex. She was less convinced, carefully noting every suggestion of an earlier date in the capitals and brickwork and concluding that 'a considerable part of the masonry may well belong to the earliest period'.

Joachim and Dale show me the tomb of Mor Augen, a Red Sea pearl fisherman and purported disciple of St Anthony of Egypt, who is believed to have arrived here with a large following and established the monastery. I'm also shown a sealed niche containing the bones of Gertrude's unseen bishop. Joachim snaps a picture of Dale and me standing in exactly the same spot as Gertrude had herself been photographed. Then we progress into the dimly lit church. In a moment of sheer poetry, I light a candle for Gertrude while behind me Dale and Joachim quietly recite the Lord's Prayer in Aramaic.

Gertrude reported that it was 'the habit of the monks to let no traveller depart without food', a habit much exploited by the local Kurds. A meal of 'eggs and bread, raisins and sour curds' was quickly rustled up for her party, and once it was consumed she set off to walk around the side of the mountain to the even more remote monastery of Mor Yuhanon, which she described as 'neither so finely placed nor so interesting architecturally as Mar Augen, though the rough walls of church and monastic building, which cling to the rocky slopes, are not without a certain wild beauty'.

Here she was greeted by an elderly prior and reported that 'the bishop who rules over the house of Mar Yuhanna is less exclusive than the prelate at Mar Augen, for he shares a tower with his four monks, but he was still too exclusive to receive my visit'. Here, too, she committed the sort of faux pas all travellers dread. Offered a second omelette, she turned it down, whereupon the prior became 'so deeply hurt' that he refused to bid her farewell. 'We left under the cloud of his displeasure,' she reported.

Dale points out the path she would have taken to reach Mor Yuhanon, although we both know that no such walk is possible in these troubled times. As we drive away from Mor Augen, I glance back up at the monastery as it dissolves like a desert mirage into the parched ochre landscape. But Gertrude had visited in wildflower season and when she turned to look back what met her eyes was a sea of grey. 'Perhaps you wonder why a monk from Egypt should have come so far,' she wrote. 'I know why: it was because Iris Susiana grows wild among the rocks … gleaming silver in the strong sun, so perfect in form and so exquisitely delicate in texture that you hold your breath in wonder.'

'I do not doubt that this is the real primitive monasticism,' she concluded of her visit to Mor Augen. As I reflect on what motivates these brave and isolated men, Father Aho and Father Joachim, true successors to the Desert Fathers in their caves and up their pillars, bearing witness to Christianity against all the odds, living with loneliness and occasional fear, I want to think that there will be more of them. But in my heart of hearts, I fear that they are the last of their kind.

Back in Midyat, I treat myself to a night of luxury in the Shmayaa, a hotel of stone-traceried exuberance that once housed the Iraqi owner of the Gelüşke Han. Spread-eagled in front of the air conditioning unit, I wrestle with what to do next. In 1909 Gertrude had ridden into Turkey from Iraq, crossing the border near Cizre. The account she left of her wanderings in its hinterland makes me yearn to retrace them. The trouble is that much of her route lies in what are – and always have been – deeply troubled places.

With no sign of a ferry, her party had been forced to wade across the Hezil Suyu, a tributary of the Habur river – 'in mid-stream its waters touched the top of my riding boots and buffeted my mare,' she wrote; it was only saved from drowning by locals who rolled up their robes and waded in to hold its head above the water. She pitched camp that night in the part-Nestorian, part-Protestant village of Hasana (modern Kösreli), which 'nestles under rocky peaks' in

Sefinet Nebi Nuh (Ark of the Prophet Noah) on the summit of Cudi Dağı (Mt Cudi) in 1911. The Kurds and Syriacs believed the Ark had come to rest here.

the shadow of Mt Cudi. There, Kas Mattai, a 'Protestant Nestorian' priest, came to greet her, his arms as full of pink garden roses as a suitor at Rounton Grange (the Bell family home in Yorkshire). Together they clambered up a rocky gorge to inspect the carving of an Assyrian king, then explored the remains of what she took to be a monastery at its foot.

To read this now is to be seduced by a dream of innocence and beauty. Unfortunately it was only half the story, as she quickly learned. The villagers often fell prey to marauding Kurds who extorted hospitality at gunpoint. Nor did the sorrows of Hasana end there. Unless Gertrude had got her religions in a twist, at some point the Nestorians and Protestants were joined by Syriacs, and it was Syriacs that British journalist Tim Kelsey talked to in Hasana when he visited in the early 1990s. He too was struck by the beauty of the village with its solid stone houses, its canal, its fruit trees and vines. The priest was living in a partially rock-cut 'cottage from mythology'. But already the beauty was illusory. The schoolhouse had been destroyed and the villagers were struggling to walk the tightrope strung between the government and the PKK. Ultimately it was to no avail. In *Dervish*, his account of his Turkish travels, Kelsey reported that at the end of 1993 the last villagers were driven from their homes. Most now live in Mechelen in Flanders.

There was never much likelihood of my being allowed to visit Hasana, even without the renewed troubles. Nor do I hold out hope for Mt Cudi, last resting place in Kurdish and Syriac tradition of

Noah's Ark. Gertrude had been as keen to get up to that Ark as I am, if for rather different reasons. 'The heavy air was like an enveloping garment which it was impossible to cast off … I was overmastered by a desire for the snow patches that lay upon the peaks.' With nothing standing in her way, she set off in the morning, and the botanist in her was soon rewarded by the sight of a rich blue and yellow spread of globe daisies, ranunculi and squills. The 'Ark' itself 'had run aground in a bed of scarlet tulips'.

What Gertrude found on the summit of the 2,089-metre-high Mt Cudi was a structure known locally as the Sefinet Nebi Nuh (Ark of the Prophet Noah). Once upon a time a Nestorian monastery had also stood here and she was convinced that she had identified some of its stonework, despite Kas Mattai's insistence that it came from a later Muslim shrine. All that remained were unremarkable stone walls that could be roofed with drapes during a multi-faith pilgrimage held every summer*. 'The prospect … was as wild, as rugged and as splendid as the heart could desire,' she wrote.

So happy was she to be up in the snow that she sent back the stragglers in her party and continued along a ridge with Kas Mattai. Before long they came across shepherds who had brought their flocks up here to evade taxmen intent on levying a double charge on them. The first shepherds reeled off the tale of an elderly holy man who had spent a month trying to find the Ark only to bump into the Devil, who swore that he still had a month's walking ahead of him; demoralized, he gave up and built a hut right there, where he lived out his last days within sight of an Ark he was by then too blind to see. Suspecting Mattai of being a soldier, a second group opened fire on him. Later, the ever-imperturbable Gertrude was to write: 'I was standing, when the shots began, in the middle of a neve, and thinking that I must offer a fine mark, I stepped off the snow and sat down upon a grey rock to await developments.'

In Hasana, Kelsey was assured that members of the PKK had taken up residence in the Ark. Even if there are no longer Ark-dwelling guerrillas on the mountain, Hasana sits directly between Cizre and

*Gertrude Bell's is the oldest surviving photograph of this structure.

Silopi, and I know that any attempt to head there now is bound to end unhappily. Which leaves Cizre (Jazirat ibn Umar), a town I'd always assumed I'd be able to visit but which has only just emerged from a curfew bearing all the hallmarks of a medieval siege: water and electricity severed; ditto all forms of communication with the outside world. In 2014 a Kurdish group calling itself the Patriotic Revolutionary Youth Movement had declared autonomy in parts of Cizre, throwing up barricades and digging trenches to create no-go areas. That rebellion had been swiftly crushed, but in August of this year they had repeated the same tactics. This time the government was in no mood for compromise. The response was swift and heavy-handed. For eight days the town was cut off from its utilities. As journalists were kept at bay, it was hard to learn much more. With a heavy heart, I had crossed Cizre from my itinerary.

But now, reassured by the Nusaybin adventure, I'm starting to have second thoughts. The siege has been lifted. Traffic is flowing eastwards again. Life must surely be returning to some semblance of normality. Over dinner I weigh up the options. On a previous visit I had changed buses in İdil (old Azakh), a brooding town where unfriendly eyes had glowered at me from darkened shop interiors. Feyzi has offered to ferry me directly to Cizre. Normally I reject all such driverly offers intended to parlay cheap bus journeys into expensive taxi runs. But second only to Bora in Silifke, Feyzi has been my Fattuh. I trust him. I like him. For the most part he understands me. And were the military to stop us, he would be able to laugh off my unlikely presence with tales of crazy church-going in the Tur Abdin.

Dinner over, I pull out my phone. 'It's a date,' I tell him.

Enraptured by the mountains, Gertrude sent her caravan ahead of her to Cizre while she and Kas Mattai's brother Shim'un rode through oak woods to a village called Evler, 'buried in a profusion of pomegranate and walnut, fig, almond and mulberry trees', then onto Shakh (Şah), where she explored a castle high up on the rocks and was shown three life-sized Assyrian reliefs with cuneiform inscriptions.

In Cizre her tents were pitched on the far side of the Tigris facing a castle on a bluff above the water. In the morning she made a hasty visit to what she called a 'horrid squalid little town', a visit that took her nonetheless to the Ulu Cami, where she admired the 'fine bronze door with lovely knockers made each one of a dragon'. They were the handiwork of İsmail al-Jazari, a twelfth-century inventor believed to have worked in the palace of the Artukids in Diyarbakır, and their existence suggests that the talented al-Jazari may have been from Cizre. Alas, in 1969 thieves made off with one of the knockers, which now languishes in the David Collection in Copenhagen. The other is in the Museum of Turkish and Islamic Arts in Istanbul.

Feyzi and I arrive in Cizre in a battered taxi with a cracked windscreen and no seatbelts. We've taken the new road that bypasses İdil and from a distance I make out only an uncomfortable mash-up of elderly black basalt and modern pastel-painted concrete. But in 1909 Gertrude camped nearby and recorded that the population was largely Syriac with a smattering of Protestant converts. Her description made it sound like an early-twentieth-century Turkish take on the Scottish island of Lewis – 'the Xtians are very fanatical here. They won't sell us as much as an egg because it is Sunday.' The Protestant priest came rushing to greet her, relaying alarums emanating from Adana. 'It was impossible to make out whether the events which were related to us were past or present, how serious the massacre had been or whether it were now at an end,' she wrote. I don't know it as we whizz past, but already peace is starting to break down in İdil. Within weeks it too will be under curfew; within six months ten per cent of its population will have fled.

After all that's happened, I'm fully expecting to be stopped at the approach to Cizre, so it's a pleasant surprise to sail straight into town unchecked. We plough down the high street, past hawkers selling a random selection of knives and watermelons. Above, the traffic banners tout beauty treatments; in the *lokantas* people queue to heap up plates of ribs; and smuggled cigarettes are still being retailed for knockdown prices in a curious continuity of normal life in abnormal circumstances.

'It looks all right. It looks just the same,' Feyzi mutters, and I feel him letting out a sigh of relief, the first sign that he might have been a little less gung-ho about this expedition than he had been prepared to admit. But I'm surprised by how quickly the anxiety falls away from us. We start down the road towards the Ulu Cami as if life were just as it always had been. Women robed in black stroll past, the lower halves of their faces veiled in white. Feyzi chuckles. 'The women here are so beautiful,' he says. 'Underneath – so beautiful.'

'How can you possibly know that?'

'I grew up in Silopi [a border town east of Cizre].'

We park outside the Ulu Cami and find it mercifully undamaged – a relief, given that it's a singular mosque, its detached twelfth-century minaret telescoping up from square base to columnar tower. Gertrude having rued her failure to venture inside, I take a quick look round on her behalf. Then while Feyzi kneels to pray, I wander round the courtyard, puzzling over how terrible things could have happened here so recently without there being any obvious signs of them.

Worshippers are arriving for Friday prayers. Inevitably they are surprised, even shocked, to find a foreigner lurking in the courtyard, and on their way out again a couple stop to speak to me. One is an avuncular elderly man with a bushy beard and baggy *şalvar*. Initially jovial, he soon changes once he discovers that I understand Turkish. His expression becomes almost tearful. 'It was awful, awful,' he mumbles before stumbling away. A younger friend nods along, then adds, 'Islam is the best of all religions,' before bestowing a blessing on me*.

Gertrude took the castle, overlooking the Tigris with its 'alternate bands of black basalt and white limestone', to be 'Seljuk or something of the kind'. Surprisingly, restoration work is pushing ahead despite the recent turmoil and no one seems at all bothered by my camera. But the 'blazon of lions' mentioned in her diary eludes me. A cultural centre now occupies what was once an office of the local authority. Inside, *sazes* are racked on the wall and women are signing up to learn how to sketch tulips using the *ebru* (paper marbling) technique. 'I'm looking for a carving of lions,' I say rather apologetically to the three men taking enrolments. One of them jumps up immediately and leads me round to the side of the building, where we clamber over the scaffolding pole blocking an arch, then turn and look

---

*In December 2015 Cizre was once again besieged. It is thought that more than 150 people died in the two months the second siege lasted.

upwards. And there, sure enough, are the lions, a little more weathered perhaps, but with manes still abundantly shaggy.

Back indoors, I feel obliged to offer an explanation for my presence at such a difficult time. Osman's face lights up. 'Ah yes,' he says. 'Gertrude!'

We sit down at the desk and I start to translate what she had written about their town, in particular her comments about a bridge 'with some curious reliefs representing the signs of the zodiac'. The men shake their heads. Demolished, they assure me*. From Cizre Gertrude had ridden to Finik, where, at Kasr Ghelli, she viewed 'the ancient guardian of the pass', a stele of a Parthian warrior on horseback. Already its twin had fallen away and now this carving too was threatened. 'The winter rains have worn thin his armour, the spring floods have undermined the rock on which he stands,' she wrote, before adding that, unlike the carvings at Hasana, this one echoed a Western tradition, 'its prototypes … to be sought not among the bearded divinities and winged monsters of Assyria, but in the work of Western sculptors'.

The men eye me blankly as I read this out, but they perk up considerably when I get to the bit about Finik itself, poised at the mouth of a dramatic gorge where 'the river bursts … through the last barrier of mountain which divides it from the Mesopotamian plain'.

'There's a castle at Finik,' one of them ventures.

'And a picnic place,' adds another.

'Should I go there?' I ask brightly.

They stare at me as if I'd enquired about access to the local mortuary.

'Oh no, *abla*,' they intone. 'Not until after the election.'

For this is the situation we have arrived at. The election in June having produced the 'wrong' result and the three opposition parties having proved unable to form a coalition, we are now facing a second election in November. Hopes are pinned on this poll bringing a speedy return to the relative peace and stability of May. I share that hope. We are to be bitterly disappointed.

*In fact, the bridge survives just over the Syrian border.

27

The Shadow of the Dam

HASANKEYF–BATMAN–SİLVAN

*'No one knew, any more than I did when I arrived, what a wealth of material
there was at Mayafarkin...I felt as if I were receiving the dying
will and testament as I worked at it...'* Letter, 3 April 1911

'I like this list. It's succinct, but at the same time it's representative,'
says John Crofoot. 'Gertrude was only here for three days, but I'd been
here a year before I got to the Haçlı Kilise [Church with Crosses].'

I've arrived in the 'rock-cut bazaar' of Hasankeyf and am reading
out to John all the monuments that Gertrude saw there. An American
from Arkansas, John is a member of a small-to-vanishing group of
Westerners who've made new homes for themselves not in sun-
soaked Bodrum or Marmaris but in the remote and troubled southeast. A writer and financial analyst, John cut his Turkish teeth in
Istanbul. Then in 2010 he discovered Hasankeyf, the small town on
the Tigris whose timeline stretches back to at least the fourteenth century BC. 'It opened up a whole new period of history for me,' he
says. 'Istanbul introduces you to the world of Rome, Byzantium and
the Ottomans. Hasankeyf offers the opportunity to look east towards
Persia and the Arab lands, and to the Selçuks. It's the mixing of four
currents – Persian, Arab, Kurdish and Turkish.'

We're sitting in a café whose terrace looks straight down onto the
Tigris and across to the soaring struts of the broken bridge that once
spanned it. It seems impossible that glorious Hasankeyf should not
be as thoroughly protected as Ephesus or Aphrodisias, but instead a
dam-shaped cloud hangs over it. In Turkey, as elsewhere, dams have
long since shed their innocence, particularly the big versions that
alter the local ecology, and the Ilısu Dam that threatens Hasankeyf
has become a cause célèbre in environmental circles. First mooted in
1975 as part of the overall GAP project, the proposed dam seemed
to have been quietly shelved until the late 1990s when suddenly it

was back on the drawing-board. At first the international community was enthusiastic, wheeling out guarantees for the funding at a time when Turkey's currency was floundering. But once a slew of articles screamed that the new dam would drown Hasankeyf's rich heritage of Ayyubid and Artukid monuments bank CEOs began to eye their balance sheets nervously.

The foundation stone was finally laid in 2006, triggering demands for a proper environmental audit, but by then the political situation had been transformed. The 1990s were Turkey's lost decade, with a succession of weak coalition governments unable to push through their pet projects. But by 2006 there was a new government, the first for eleven years with a strong enough mandate to govern alone. The economy was booming, the currency had stabilized. Prime Minister Erdoğan was the blue-eyed boy not just of Turkey but also of the international community, which saw in him an Islamic leader with whom it could do business. Even then he was not a man inclined to take no for an answer. So when the international guarantors withdrew their backing it made no difference – the Turkish government simply announced that it would finance the project itself.

Now the dam is almost finished, the access road completed, and on the horizon sits Yeni Hasankeyf (New Hasankeyf), to which those villagers who have not already moved elsewhere will be relocated. Done deal, this says to me, but John is a born optimist. 'There's still a chance that the decision-makers might come to see Hasankeyf's value,' he says in the tone of someone trying to persuade himself as much as anyone else.

★ ★ ★

Hasankeyf is acclaimed for its rare intermingling of natural and man-made beauty. Here a great wall of rock topped off with a medieval castle and a village of beautiful Tur Abdin-style housing looms up beside the Tigris. Piercing the rock are simple cave houses. Deep in the back streets stand a trio of mosques, sweeps and curls of delicate stucco framing their mihrabs like ringlets. The majority of Hasankeyf's most striking buildings were the handiwork of either the Selçuk sub-dynasty, the Artukids; the Ayyubids, the Kurdish dynasty founded by Saladin; or the Akkoyunlus (White Sheep), a Turcoman dynasty whose greatest leader, in a part of the world well known for its short-arses, gloried in the name of Uzun Hasan (Tall Hasan). Their combined legacy is writ large in the decorative minarets, the stalactite adornment of the mosques and the blue tiles adorning the tomb of Zeynel Bey, warrior son of Uzun Hasan. I will never forget arriving in Hasankeyf in 2000 as the international campaign against the dam was hotting up, and lunching on grilled trout at a table set in the river with icy water lapping my ankles. Above me reared reminders of all-but-forgotten Middle Eastern dynasties. Sun. Water. History. It was paradise incarnate.

Tourism was a late starter in this part of the world, more than fifteen years of PKK and government fighting having ensured that the treasures of the southeast were largely inaccessible throughout the 1990s. Then came the dam project to stymie upstart thoughts of hotels and restaurants. Hasankeyf was reduced to one of those sad little places that must make do with the scraps of day-trippery, its visitors bussed in to do a quick whip round the sights and snap up a cheap souvenir ashtray before heading on to overnight in Mardin or Diyarbakır. The result was a street bazaar full of tacky souvenirs funnelling visitors towards the castle. Now the risk of rockfalls has barred access to it. With the tourists frightened away again, the souvenir stalls look as deflated as the balloons shredded with airguns on the shores of the Bosphorus.

John and I wander into the grounds of the Er Rızk Cami, whose minaret has come to symbolize Hasankeyf. From there we view the shattered piers of the early-twelfth-century bridge standing like a crazed art installation in the river. Once it boasted one of the largest central-arch spans in the country, so lofty that a three-hundred-ton galleon could pass beneath it without lowering its sails. We're on the lookout for Gertrude's 'two figures, apparently of warriors carved on SW side of the first pier ... the water washing up to them'.

'There they are,' John says, directing my eyes towards the base of the pier.

And there, sure enough, lurk two small carvings, their features rubbed out, their clothing mere triangles, reminders that in the early days of Islam the ban on depicting living things was not as absolute as it was to become.

★ ★ ★

A Hasankeyf tour guide, Süleyman Ağalday was caring for an in-jured eagle when he and I first met. The eagle has long since flown away, but Süleyman is hanging on, casting around for custom in harsh times. Over *çay* I ask if he will move to Yeni Hasankeyf, a ques-tion that elicits a short answer. 'No. I'll go to Istanbul or Antalya.'

It's what I expect to hear, although the picture is not completely black and white, this being a very modern story of men versus women, of nostalgia versus yearning for a better future. 'No true Hasankeyfli will want to go to that place,' Süleyman continues, be-fore admitting that his own wife looks with more favour on the prospect of a brand-new home, free of dust and damp. Three women are drinking *çay* with us. Two are Hasankeyf born and bred and nod along with Süleyman. The third is from Batman. 'I'll be going there,' she says firmly.

The years of uncertainty have cut a swathe through Hasankeyf's population, but in the Middle Ages it was a large and important town and Süleyman has volunteered to guide me round the less ob-vious reminders of its past. A rustic path between drystone walls winds past a soaring *liwan* cut into the rock. Then we're scrambling up to a cave-church whose soot-blackened walls are etched with crosses in all shapes and sizes, a miraculous survival considering the pits in the ground attesting to the efforts of nighthawkers.

I catch up with Süleyman on what feels like the top of the world. A panoramic view across the gorge reveals the wrecks of houses on the plateau above the castle. 'Of course they once had windows and doors. But people have removed them, or kids damaged them – I did it myself when I was young,' he confesses.

Hasankeyf is in flux, the soft rock relentlessly claiming back man's handiwork via the ceaseless pitter-patter of erosion. The soft-ness of that rock gave rise to a very site-specific way of life that has now passed its sell-by date. Hasankeyf was sometimes called the Mağaralar Şehri (City of Caves) and, sure enough, those seemingly fine stone houses that now turn blind eyes towards us once con-cealed a darker reality of rough-hewn cave rooms behind the facade. The gorge below is riddled with even simpler cave dwellings, their fronts bricked up, then pierced with doors and windows to provide homes for the poorest. Passing through in 1966, Prime Minister Sü-

Crossing the Tigris on a *kelek* (raft) at Hasankeyf in 1911

leyman Demirel took one horrified look and decreed that all must be rehoused immediately in new-builds.

Years ago, an erstwhile pen pusher in Adana retired to his hometown to live out his days as one of Hasankeyf's last true troglodytes. Mehmet had reoccupied a cluster of caves and settled down to a bare-bones existence without his wife, who preferred (wise woman) to stick near the Mersin shopping malls. When I met him in 2014 he was stirring a stew over a gas burner in the most basic of cave kitchens while a covey of caged partridges chuckled in front of the television. Now Süleyman and I gaze up towards those caves. The windows are dark. It looks as if even the last diehard has called time on the caveman lifestyle.

Gertrude arrived in Hasankeyf from the south and camped beside the bridge with a small dervish lodge as a backdrop. For two days the water swirled and roared, making it impossible for a caravan to cross safely. In any case this was no Birecik with sturdy boats waiting to ferry travellers to the other side. The loss of the bridge meant that the only way to cross was in a *kelek*, one of the primitive rafts buoyed on inflated goatskins that were the main mode of transport on the Tigris. In a letter to her mother she left a vivid description of the crossing:

> The landing place on the opposite side was nearly a quarter of a mile below the bridge – it looked a very long way off and the rush of water

against the piers of the bridge was anything but encouraging. So the horses thought, for when we drove them into the water they struggled about in the deep backwater by the bridge and continually returned to us. Then we devised another scheme. We tied two of them to the raft, which was loaded with the pack saddles and drove the rest in again. They, seeing the raft swirling down the stream, and two of their companions with it, swam after it, all but 2 who again were swept back to our bank. These 2 we tied to the raft on its final journey, when I also crossed, and so we all got over in safety – but I shall long remember the rather too exhilarating sensations of that ferrying, the raft darting down the flood and the two horses panting and groaning in the water beside it.

The tile-domed tomb of Zeynel Bey is already fenced off, pending removal to an archaeological park.* With the death of Hasankeyf seemingly imminent, I start walking towards the Yeni (New) version to see if it's as bad as people claim. A passing farmer stops to offer me a lift in the way of the old Turkey when cars were luxuries and those who had them felt sorry for those who didn't. He drops me off near the new mosque (concrete, no stucco), to which men are heading for Friday prayers. I peep round the door. The windows are lined up so that worshippers will be able to look across at where they used to live as they pray.

But as new settlements go Yeni Hasankeyf could be worse, I conclude. This is not to be a town of soul-sapping high-rises but of apartment blocks the height that used to be taken for granted before greed conquered everything. The small shopping mall reminds me of an old-fashioned *pasaj* (arcade). There's a hospital. And there's a school that is already going great guns, students leaning out of the windows to chant '*Tu-rist! Tu-rist!*' at me with gusto.**

Next stop is Batman, a city whose moniker – a disappointing contraction of the name of the Batı Raman mountains – can hardly help but bring a smile to the lips, a smile which rapidly fades once the eyes come to rest on the reality of a modern concrete oil town. In

---

*The İmam Abdullah lodge has since been moved to the new Hasankeyf Cultural Park along with the Zeynel Bey tomb and the Er Rızk Cami.

**Old Hasankeyf was drowned in April 2020.

Gertrude's day Batman would have been little more than a cluster of rural homesteads, and not so very long ago it was still a much smaller place, dark, unsettled, subject to nightly curfews for much of the 1990s. Now it's something of a boomtown, full of ritzy modern hotels and with frappucinos on tap in the shopping centre. As darkness falls, I stretch out on my bed and listen to sirens screeching as what sounds as if it might be a protest march gets into its stride. I twitch the curtains and eye the high street. Nothing. Then comes the explosive crack of gunfire followed by ululation. Just a wedding, I comfort myself, thinking how strange it is to be bedding down in a town where gunfire can as easily indicate happiness and celebration as misery and death.

In the morning I head for the grungy little bus terminal that services local *dolmuşes*. I'm after the one north to Silvan and am surprised to find that none is waiting when every other parking bay is busy. There's a palpable tension in the air. The word '*terörism*' ripples alarmingly through conversations.

Eventually a *dolmuş* arrives. The delay means that it's packed to overflowing, which in these parts means that the aisle gets filled with low plastic stools on which excess bottoms must perch uncomfortably. Off we go. No one is speaking and I comfort myself that I was probably imagining the tension. Then out of the corner of my eye I spot white vans parked by the roadside, helmeted soldiers in camouflage gear striding towards us. The *dolmuş* slows and I dig into my bag for my identity card, preparing to justify my presence. Then it speeds up again. We don't stop. I lean over to the man on the stool beside me.

'Is something wrong?' I ask.

'Yes,' he says. 'A bomb.'

'When?'

'Last night.'

'Was anyone killed?'

'Yes, a soldier.'

The delay and the tension make perfect sense then. I glance out of the window at tomatoes squashed into the tarmac. I sneak a look at my phone. Together with the soldier, a truck driver from Kula had been killed. Three other police officers and five civilians were wounded. Collateral damage, that ugliest of modern euphemisms, in an unwinnable war.

There had always been a question mark over whether I should go to Silvan. Snared by a poster coyly enquiring if I'd seen the wonders of medieval Silvan, I'd once taken a turn round the walls of the Zembilfroş Castle. Immediately, a swarm of schoolchildren had descended like locusts on a field. 'Go into the cemetery,' advised a passer-by. 'You can look at the walls from there and no one will be able to see you.' But almost instantly a pebble had pinged against my back. Spinning round, I saw a youth of sixteen or so perched on a gravestone with a smirk plastered across his face.

'*Yapma* [Don't do that]!' I shouted. The smirk froze. I turned my back and continued walking. Then a full bottle of water struck my calf, bowled at it with the force of a cricket ball. When I turned round, the youth wore a different smile, a smile that challenged me to do anything about it.

It was not a memory to fill me with desire for a speedy return. What's more, some of Silvan's fierier youths, like their Cizre cousins, had recently staked a claim to autonomy with the exact same consequences. Silvan, too, had had a curfew slapped on it, which had only just been lifted. But Gertrude had passed through it, ipso facto so must I.

The *dolmuş* scoots past the elegant arch of the Malabadi Bridge, a cutdown copy, it's thought, of the lost bridge at Hasankeyf. Then it comes to a stop just shy of the town centre and I walk on, arriving once more in front of the walls. 'The splendid broken towers gave me some idea of what must lie within,' wrote Gertrude, who pitched her tent nearby 'above cornfields. Very lovely.'

Most Turks would be hard pressed to mark Silvan on a map and there is nothing new about this anonymity, Gertrude having confided to her diary that 'the outside of the domed church struck me by surprise, which reached bewilderment when I came to the splendid mosque, and culminated in the basilica'. Yet once upon a time this was another Roman frontier town and the walls must date back at least in essence to those years. In these troubled parts they have been rebuilt/destroyed/rebuilt/destroyed, not least by the Kurdish Marwanids who for some time made this their capital. It was the

© GBPA

Ruins of Selahaddin-i Eyubbi Cami in Silvan in 1911

Mongols who finally put paid to Zembilfroş, leaving just the shattered walls, the surviving inscriptions, in graceful curvilinear, testifying to an earlier interlude of stability.

I press on into town, pausing to pass the time of day with a fishmonger who's keen to pose with a glittering, golden, it-was-*this*-big *sazan* (carp) newly dredged from the Tigris. Lest I need to make a quick departure, I head straight for the mosque that Gertrude saw in 1911 'at a fortunate moment for it was cleared out and not yet restored'. Named after the great Kurdish leader Saladin, the Selahaddin-i Eyyubi Cami dates back to 1185. On the steps leading up to it stands Mehmet Şerif Coşuk, a gentle-eyed man in his mid-fifties with a face as weatherbeaten as a sailor's. In his youth he used to be a singer of the *dengbej* sagas that were passed down from father to son. Now he ekes out a living selling religious paraphernalia. Slap in the middle of his wares lies a copy of the local newspaper,

Retired *dengbej* singer Mehmet Şerif Coşuk in Silvan in 2015

289

Mezopotamya, dating from the summer just passed. '*Silvan savaş alanı gibi* [Silvan like a war zone],' screams the headline.

'But it's not like that now, is it?' I ask, glancing at the shoppers thronging the high street, at the worshippers milling about in front of the mosque.

He shrugs, smiles and changes the subject, reeling off instead a litany of Silvan's previous incarnations – Martyropolis, Mayafarqin, Farkin … In Mehmet's take on history, the mosque was once a large church, although it probably stands beside the site of the church rather than over it. The Martyropolis moniker is a reminder that it was the last resting place of Christians martyred in Sassanian Persia whose remains had been retrieved by a bishop canonized for the endeavour. Gertrude concluded that some of the church columns had been incorporated into the mosque, which suggests that it was already in ruins by the start of the twelfth century.

Mehmet speaks impeccable Turkish even though his first language is the Kurmanci dialect of Kurdish. 'I've had three wives,' he tells me proudly, although it's unclear whether this was simultaneously or consecutively. 'We all want peace,' he adds before I leave him to inspect the mosque, a strung-out, Selçuk-style barn of a place with a central dome resting on stalactite squinches. Elsewhere in Turkey, long, thin mosques like this tend to look out on a courtyard enclosed by living and studying quarters, but if ever there were enclosing walls here, they've vanished now. Its closest cousin may be the Artukid-era Ulu Cami in Kızıltepe, built roughly fifty years afterwards.

Back on the high street I'm hoping for a taxi to run me back to the Malabadi Bridge but instead find myself ambling round a crater of wasteland. Inside it, cows crop the grass amid broken brick uprights that look like Byzantine leftovers. Could this be the site of the Church of the Virgin Mary that Gertrude found still substantially intact in 1911, I wonder?

The urgent gaze of under-occupied male eyes monitors my circumnavigation of the crater from a teahouse on its rim. That teahouse, then, is the obvious starting point for further enquiries. But the men pooh-pooh my church suggestion. 'The ground was being cleared for a new building,' they tell me. 'Work stopped when the ruins came to light. It was probably a *hamam*.'

Their theory is as good as mine, Ottoman architecture often sharing common traits with its Byzantine forebears and the precise location of Silvan's other two churches being unknown. I sit down to share a *çay* with the men, who are as eager to chat to me as I am to them.

'When did you come here?' one of them enquires.

'Today.'

'Today? Not yesterday?'

And I remember the bomb, the dead soldier, the dead truck driver. I shuffle on my stool and give my *çay* a vigorous stir. I rattle off my justificatory spiel about the Gertrude project. They nod sagely, no doubt chalking up my madness to my foreign nationality. I run through with them the buildings Gertrude mentioned. 'She walked along the walls. She had coffee with an *ağa* who had set up a tent in one of the towers,' I tell them, 'and she saw houses opening out onto the top of the walls.'

More nods. An arm waved vaguely in a direction I have not so far traversed. 'There are fantastic *konaks* down that road,' one of them says. There's a slight pause. 'But don't go there ...'

'Why not?'

'*Gerillalar* [Guerrillas],' he says, and then, just in case I might have misunderstood, 'PKK.'

In the Tur Abdin I'd been advised to avoid all political conversation and, above all, never to take sides, but already I can feel myself being sucked into a quagmire of controversy. The men are insistent. They want to get their opinion across and they want me to agree with them. To a man they are supporters of the pro-Kurdish HDP.

'We're not allowed to speak our own language,' they say, which was certainly true once but isn't any longer. 'How can that be right?'

I try to look sympathetic, attempting to contextualize their grievance by telling them about the campaign, complete with second-home burnings and protracted governmental foot-dragging, to have Welsh elevated into an official language of the UK. They stare at me blankly.

'Are there any taxis?' I ask quickly.

'Perhaps at the bus station,' they reply in tones that suggest what a disappointment I have been to them. So back up the high street I trek, bypassing a chair standing on the pavement with its back laced up like a Victorian corset. Then off to the left I glimpse another stretch of wall. I pause, uncertain. The men had warned me against one side street, but this is a different one. Surely it can't do any harm to walk along it.

I start down the street and come almost immediately to a pile of sand running across it. It looks as if it could be one of the barricades erected to keep officialdom at bay. Then again, this being Turkey, it could just as easily be surplus building material casually dumped without thought for pedestrians.

I walk round it. I continue up the street and, sure enough, on the left-hand side of the road another fine length of wall rises up with, built right into it, a magnificent stone *konak* overlooking an orchard. I stop to take pictures and almost at once a woman in a *pardesü* approaches me. Conscious that I must look as out of place as a stray pygmy, I try to chat as if nothing's wrong and it's the most normal thing in the world to be taking pictures. She smiles, she has a stab at small talk, but in her eyes I see apprehension, a desire to whisper the Kurdish equivalent of 'get the hell out of here, you fool' warring with the instinct honed since childhood to extend a welcome to a stranger.

'Are things any better now?' I ask quietly.

I can see her struggling to come up with a judicious answer. 'Not really,' she says. 'It's very *karışık* [troubled] at the moment.'

A middle-aged man strides up behind us. He too pauses and his voice is less friendly as he enquires after my business. Then a second woman also stops. The three of them stand staring at me, frozen like participants in a game of musical statues. Anxiety drips from them like rain. It's obvious that I shouldn't be here. It's obvious that I shouldn't venture any further round the walls. I turn back, mourning the orphaned Ayyubid minaret seen by Gertrude in the suburbs. Then, as I near the sandbar blocking the road again, a young man emerges from a nearby house. My pulse speeds up immediately. Am I about to pay the price of my curiosity with kidnap?

He turns towards me with a smile.

'Welcome to Silvan!' he says.

28

The Zebra-Striped City

DİYARBAKIR

'I have never before lived for 2 days in a mosque, so to speak, watched the court fill and empty with the calls to prayer all the day through...' Letter, 9 May 1911

'Black are the dogs and black the walls and black the hearts of black Amid.' Thus did a local proverb describe Diyarbakır, and as Gertrude trotted across the Ten-Eyed Bridge over the Tigris and up towards the mighty Mardin Gate she would indeed have seen its walls looming black ahead of her, a coronet of jet above the shawl of dazzling green formed by the 'gardens of mulberry and vine' tripping down to the water.

On her first visit in 1909 she had written that Diyarbakır 'stands upon the high crest of the Tigris bank, a great fenced city built of basalt'. Trotting beside her had been Thomas Efendi, an Armenian *dragoman*, who led her straight to the British Consulate, where she was invited to stay with the consul, Mr Rawlins, and his German wife. Soon they were firm friends, promenading around town with their by now illustrious visitor.

I must make do with arriving in a remote bus terminal in a prosaic *dolmuş*, before heading for the Dağkapı (Mountain Gate) on the built-up northern side of town, where a series of modern hotels still wait half-heartedly for the tourists who have scratched Diyarbakır from their itineraries. I had planned to stay in the Büyük Kervansaray Hotel inside the old Deliller Hanı, which Gertrude must have trotted past en route to the consulate. But most of the recent uproar in Diyarbakır has been focused on the southern side of the walled city where the *han* stands. In the event of renewed trouble there would be no escape from eye-scalding teargas, so I must content myself with something more workaday outside the walls.

'How are things?' I ask the receptionist, injecting what I hope is a note of optimism into my voice.

He puts down his phone and pins the normal tourist-friendly smile into place.

'*Karışık*. But it's okay here,' he answers.

In front of the hotel a large and very protest-friendly square has taken the place of the old local bus terminal. I ask for a room at the back. That way, should things kick off again, I'll be safely out of range of stray bullets.

Fretful spring was segueing into the anxious summer of 1909 when Gertrude arrived in Diyarbakır to find the bazaar running hot with rumours. For momentous events had been taking place in faraway Constantinople. In the July of 1908, Sultan Abdülhamid II had been forced to cede power to a group formally called the Committee of Union and Progress but better known to the world as the Young Turks. Nine months later the sultan had fought back and the CUP was briefly ousted. When they regained the upper hand, it was the end for Abdülhamid. The man whom Gertrude had watched processing across the Galata Bridge in 1889 was removed from office and sent into exile, his place on the throne taken by his brother. Gertrude viewed these developments with broad approval. 'I saw the latest Amurath succeed to Amurath [sultan to sultan] and rejoiced with all those who love justice and freedom to hear him proclaimed. For Abdülhamid … was the symbol for retrogression,' she wrote to Lord Cromer, the former British consul-general in Egypt.

News of the Cilician massacres had also reached Diyarbakır, stirring up fear of a similar assault. The population of Diyarbakır was, at that time, around 500,000, ten per cent of it Armenian but with sizeable minorities of Syriacs, Greeks and Jews too. In 1895 a killing spree that had broken out in Constantinople had rapidly rippled southeastwards. 'The heavy air, lying stagnant between the high walls, is charged with memories of the massacres of 1895, and when I was in Diyarbekr the news from Cilicia had rekindled animosity and fear,' Gertrude wrote. 'Tales of fresh outbreaks in different parts of the empire were constantly circulated in the bazaars, and the men who listened went home and fingered at their rifles.'

In mid-April a telegram from Constantinople 'ordering disturbances' had been intercepted. 'For a few hours the town was in a panic. Mr R[awlins] walked through the streets quieting the people,'

Gertrude wrote, adding that half the bazaar had been burnt down. She also recorded the downfall of Abdülhamid's favourite, the villainous İbrahim Paşa of Viranşehir. 'All the Kurdish tribes turned against him as soon as he fell,' she noted.

I've arrived in Diyarbakır in no less unhappy times. Throughout the 1980s and 90s this was a city associated with the PKK insurgency, a place deprived of investment, with a shantytown sprawling in the shadow of the walls to which villagers driven from their homes fled in search of safety. It had always been at the heart of the troubles, so if Cizre and Silvan had made a bid for autonomy, it went without saying that Diyarbakır would do the same. The crucial difference is that Diyarbakır is a city that, just months beforehand, had had a glittering touristic future in its sights.

As I sit in the zebra-striped Hasanpaşa Han, where Gertrude stabled her horses, memories trail me like a ragged bridal train. This is a place whose recent history encapsulates that of the old walled town as a whole. In 1992 two sleepy carpet shops had been competing for business across the courtyard. By 1996 they were gone, the owners having shot each other over a feud, or so I was told. Years later and blowout-breakfast cafés started to recolonize the void. Hasanpaşa became hip, the voices of students reverberating round the gallery even as their elders sipped *çay* and completed crosswords around the fountain below.

In the 1990s it was hard to move in the poverty-stricken warren of back streets without being mobbed by the offspring of the vast families that were still the local norm. In *Amurath to Amurath* Gertrude had commented that the street layout followed the traditional Roman grid plan, with two main thoroughfares cutting across the old city from north to south and east to west. Throughout the 1990s a tank brooded at their intersection like a watchful tarantula. Dog-eared posters on hotel walls tried hard with pictures of chubby babies cradled in the town's famously fat watermelons, but that tank cast a long shadow. It was usual to have the monuments to oneself.

Then in the mid-2000s change began to stir. The pavements were repaired. The street lighting was improved. Work began on restoring the Ulu Cami. The reopening of the ruined Armenian church of Surp Giragos (St Kyriakos) in 2011 served as a potent symbol of that change. Then, the streets had been buzzing with new energy. Then, the wonderful old houses 'adorned with patterns and stripes of white' were being converted into cafés and restaurants as fast as credit could be raised. Then, the tank had finally been retired to barracks. I thought it was a breakthrough moment. I thought that Diyarbakır's day in the sun had finally arrived.

Except that it hadn't. In the blink of a 'wrong' election result, all that hope and energy has been jettisoned. Like Cizre and Silvan, the old walled district of Diyarbakır has been subjected to a siege that has only just been lifted. I turn into Gazi Caddesi, the main north-south axis. Superficially things look much as they did a year earlier. Near the Dağkapı an elderly man is still bringing pet partridges to keep him company while he sells fruit from the shade of a tree. The clang of metal cups still echoes along the street as liquorice-root sherbet-sellers tout for trade. But all too soon I'm passing a Toma, one of the armoured water cannons that have become a conspicuous addition to modern Turkish streetlife. It's sitting mere metres from one of the glitzy new hotels opened to cash in on the anticipated tourism boom. A few steps more and I'm up against the police station, whose defences now spill across both sides of the street. Inching nervously through the gap between armed officers, I think how easy it would be for something to go wrong, how a shot fired in panic could rip its way through the shoppers. It's a relief to arrive at the junction and find it still tank-free. But as soon as I turn down the side street that leads to Surp Giragos I pass out of normality and into Looking-Glass Land. Nothing is any longer as it was such a short time ago.

Skirting the Dört Ayaklı minaret perched on its four unfeasibly short legs, I come to another junction. A curtain hangs down across the street like the ones swept across the rear of mosques lest the sight of female worshippers put the men off their prayers. Beyond it I glimpse what looks like one of the Che Guevara posters with which lefty students of the 1970s delighted in decorating their bedrooms. I turn left into the street where the church stands. Not long after its restoration I had attended a service there with a party of visiting Armenians. In the cavernous nave the priest had offered prayers for their lost relatives. Some quietly wept. Some intoned the responses defiantly. Afterwards one of the group whispered: 'We are a forgiving people. We don't want compensation. All we want is recognition.' It had been an intensely moving experience full of promise of a brighter, more tolerant future.

Now I find the gate firmly locked. Ditto at the Chaldean Church and at the Esma Ocak Evi that used to be open to visitors. Up ahead, another sheet obscures the rest of the street from view.

I walk back to the junction and eye the Che Guevara-ish poster. A man is sitting on the kerb in front of a sad selection of bruised carrots and wilted lettuces. His demeanour doesn't suggest that much is wrong.

'What's happening down there?' I ask, gesturing towards the sheet.

'*Savaş* [War],' he says simply. Then, in case I might have misunderstood, he holds two fingers to his forehead and squeezes an imaginary trigger.

In 1909, wisdom dictated that Gertrude keep her head down and busy herself with ancient monuments. In particular she was keen to document the Ulu Cami, which dated back to the seventh century, making it one of Anatolia's oldest mosques.

> Next to the walls, the mosque is the great feature of Diarbekr...it stands to one side of a huge court that must have belonged to a palace (or possibly a church?) of the 5th-6th centuries ...perhaps even late 4th. One side of this court has been pulled down when the mosque was built, the other three are occupied by gorgeous colonnades, two storeys high to the east, the west, and every inch covered with an incredible wealth of decoration.

But, she added sadly:

> the buildings need a more exhaustive study than the fanaticism of the Mohammadan population will at present admit ... this hasty survey of Diyarbekr was sufficient to convince me that the treasures which it contains are still unexplored.

Two years later, frustrated by how little she had been able to record on that first visit, she rushed round to the *Vali* to seek his approval for photography. His intervention worked like magic. Men who had been standoffish now fell over themselves to be helpful. 'The Sayyids [men descended from the Prophet Mohammed] helped to read the inscrips and the sheikhs invited me into their rooms to measure. It was a delightful experience to be living in a mosque for 2 days,' she wrote.

The Ulu Cami. The Great Mosque. The hauntingly ancient place of worship with its elderly *sayyids* still casting a watchful eye over intruders as they rest arthriticky spines against its severe grey walls; and with its extravaganza of a marble screen angled towards the *şadırvan*, a more fitting backdrop for a Donizetti opera, one might think, than religious devotions. As I pass beneath the low Artukid arch that opens into its courtyard, my heart is pounding. Centimetre by meticulous centimetre, restoration has been progressing for years, and fear that it might have halted – worse, that new damage might have been inflicted on the building – is almost too much to bear. It's a relief, then, to find the scaffolding still in place, to hear the tap-tapping of hammers, the buzz of workmanly banter.

In the medina-like back streets behind the mosque very different sounds drift from the Dengbej Evi, whose opening in 2007 had been one of the most promising signs of change apace in Diyarbakır. Housed in one of the many magnificent stone mansions overtaken by hard times, it was set up to promote the rap music of southeastern Turkey. Or rather to bring it back to life again, because *dengbej*, an unaccompanied saga-singing tradition, was effectively killed off in the 1980s, when merely speaking Kurdish became an offence for which people could be jailed. Only after the ban was lifted in 1991 could the old men whose heads still ring with the old songs raise their voices once again, albeit warily with an eye to the sort of topics – ill-starred love affairs rather than village burnings – that met with government approval.

In the courtyard, grey-bearded Mehemede Periki and walrus-moustached Emere Entaxe are taking it in turns to sing, cupping their hands to their ears to hold the tune. Their audience is, without exception, middle-aged and male. In a memorial volume I find a picture of Mehmet Şerif Coşuk, the retired *dengbej* singer I'd met in

© GBPA

Courtyard of Ulu Cami in Diyarbakır in 1909

Silvan. On a table nearby, the headline of a local newspaper spits fury over a photograph showing the body of a young man killed in recent clashes in Şırnak. It's being dragged behind a police vehicle.

Shaken, I wander out into the street and pause to contemplate the shattered remains of another magnificent mansion now reduced to ignominious service as a parking lot. At once a boy rushes up and demands to know where I'm from. Then an older man marches over. I address him quietly in Turkish.

'I Kurdish people,' he snarls. 'I no speak Turkish.'

On both her visits to Diyarbakır Gertrude strolled along the tops of the walls*, sometimes with Mr Rawlins, sometimes with the French consul, Louis Charles Talansier, a regular dining companion. 'The lie of the ground makes it certain that the oldest fortifications of the city must have occupied much the same position as those which still surround it, and though the latter are proved by numerous inscriptions to be Mohammadan work of different periods, I should judge them to be built mainly upon ancient foundations,' she concluded.

* Parts of the walls were damaged in the 2023 earthquakes.

In planning my own trip, I had fondly imagined strolling along those walls with a friend and long-time Diyarbakır resident. But in another indication of how fast things are unravelling in the southeast, she has been deported. Thrown back on my own company, I'm unsure what to do. The most architecturally interesting stretch of the walls overlooks the shantytown. It's not somewhere I'm keen to visit alone.

Inside a nearby tower I find Mehmet scratching a living from the sale of soft drinks.

'Is it dangerous?' I ask him.

'Not for you,' he replies. 'You are our guest. The only problem will be the children. Calling out "Hello, mello," that sort of thing. But the police can't go in there,' he adds, and, before I can stop him, he's launching into exactly the sort of tirade against the state from which I've been warned to stay away. 'They killed the Armenians. There were massacres of Alevis in Maraş and Sivas. We are powerless. We have nothing. A child throws a stone or makes a V-sign and he gets sent to prison for twenty years. The prison is full of them. Maybe he saw his father killed and now he's in prison. What else will he do with no money?' Then, just in case I might still be in doubt as to where his sympathies lie, 'There is no PKK. They harm no one. There are just the Kurds.'

Backing hastily out before a passer-by can overhear us, I press on in search of safer subject matter; namely, the delicate lion carvings and rich calligraphy emblazoned on the Artukid-era Yedi Kardeş (Seven Brothers) tower. But it's hard to stay focused on the distant past when the present staring me in the face is so relentlessly grim. In an effort to keep up their spirits, the inhabitants of the flimsy concrete cottages have painted them in uplifting shades of pink and blue, which can hardly disguise the fact that one and all deserve to be condemned. They reek of poverty, of flight, of the desperate struggle to eke out a life on the margins of society. From the doorways, young mothers in dresses as ostentatiously perky as the walls of their homes call out cheery greetings. I pass a couple of simple *bakkals* (corner shops). I pass the odd soot-blackened communal oven. Otherwise there is no infrastructure of any kind.

Near the Mardin Gate I pause for refreshment inside a 'great hall [whose] vault is borne on columns', the Keçi Burçu (Goat Tower). Further east sprawls another neighbourhood of *gecekondus*. Wary of venturing into it unaccompanied, I turn back. It was a lost last chance. In less than nine months the entire neighbourhood will have been levelled to the ground.

On her second visit, Gertrude was so determined to penetrate the ancient Greek Orthodox church of St George that she despatched a message to the grand vizier, Mahmud Şevket, in Constantinople, enclosing a testimonial from Halil Edhem Eldem, who had succeeded his brother Hamdi Bey as director of the Imperial Museum. Such shameless string-pulling did the trick, enabling her to stride under another loftier Artukid arch and set up her tripod inside what was then a functioning arsenal. Surprisingly, she found the church with its elliptical brick ceiling and stocky white columns 'not very interesting'. She hazarded that it dated back no further than the ninth century, although most judge it to be a good six centuries older than that.

The church is hidden inside the İçkale (Inner Castle), which was created inside the walls right beside the mound 'whereon stood the castle of the first Mohammadan princes'. Its modern history offers little to be proud of; it came as no surprise to the locals when excavations in 2012 exposed the remains of men almost certainly murdered by agents of JİTEM, a shadowy branch of the deep state that operated here in the 1980s. Now the military have been given their marching orders and the fine buildings they occupied have been opened to the public as part of an innovative heritage development. The old courthouse now houses the Archaeology Museum. Conservationists are repairing ancient artefacts in the prison. The barracks hosts a stylish café looking over the Tigris.

But there are no other visitors to share the view. I sit down in the café and sip lemonade through a straw from the sort of fashionable jamjar drinking glass one would not hitherto have expected to encounter in the southeast. The waitress is a young woman whose assertively bottle-blonde hair defies preconceptions of what it means to be a Diyarbakırlı woman.

'There's no one here,' I say, unable to stop myself from stating the obvious.

She screws up her face. 'We're Syria now.'

'Well, not exactly,' I reply, thinking of the refugee camps, the women begging at the roadside.

'No, but we're afraid we soon will be,' she retorts, and hurries away to find something more exciting than serving her one customer to fill the working day.

I'm seized with a mixture of misery and rage. Misery at the thought of the years of dreaming and planning that had finally brought such an imaginative project to fruition; rage at the senseless squandering of opportunity, at the pitiless men on both sides who think any price worth paying as long as they get their own way. Less than four months earlier UNESCO had added the walls of Diyarbakır and the Hevsel Gardens on the banks of the Tigris to the World Heritage List. Their timing could hardly have been less opportune.

★ ★ ★

Still fuming, I hail a taxi to take me to the Ten-Eyed Bridge, an elegant Artukid work of the tenth century. Riding across it in 1909, Gertrude would have seen ahead of her not just the minarets rising above the basalt walls but also the fields of giant lettuces that formed the Hevsel Gardens. Then she would have cantered past striking black and white *köşks*, garden houses that offered refuge from the blistering heat of summer. Not so long ago, the Gazi Köşkü housed a flourishing out-of-town restaurant, so it's disappointing to find weeds pushing up through the paving stones, to detect the despondent air of a business that is watching its working model drain away as swiftly as a flushing toilet.

Further down the road, the Erdebil Köşkü is faring no better. 'Business was good until Ramazan,' says Mehmet, who is still trying to keep his café open. 'But now people are afraid to come down here.'

'That's why I took a taxi. Usually I'd have walked.'

'Well, it probably wouldn't have been a problem, but with you being a foreigner ...' And he trails off, unwilling to put a name to the risk I might have been running.

From the middle of the bridge, it's easy to fool myself that the view is little changed since Gertrude's day. But I only have to turn round for any such illusion to be shattered. On the ridge facing it, a row of high-rises strides defiantly across the skyline.

'They're illegal,' Mehmet assures me. 'It's in court. They'll have to be pulled down again.'

But a behemoth of an earthmover is making its ponderous way along the ridge, signalling more work in the offing. The chance of those towers ever seeing a demolition charge is about as likely as Gertrude popping up beside me, Murray's guidebook in hand.

Inside the walls of Diyarbakır, the narrow streets are so tightly interwoven that it can be hard for an outsider to penetrate them. Tiny doors on either side open onto houses as big as those of Urfa and Mardin, and set round similarly inviting courtyards, although here the atmosphere could hardly be more different. In Urfa and Mardin the honey-coloured stone makes for a sunny, upbeat mood. Here the houses are formed from charcoal-grey basalt rendered only marginally less forbidding by the floral patterns in white limestone inlaid in the walls.

On a day when the sky is as sullenly leaden as the houses, I set off in search of the Syrian Orthodox Church of St Mary, circling the walls as far as the Urfa Gate, where lettuces the size of cartwheels are for sale. Just inside the gate is a warehouse full of woolsacks round which a pure white Van cat with one yellow and one blue eye is chasing another pure white non-Van cat with two yellow eyes. A burly man is watching them from the doorway. Asked for directions, he waves vaguely down the street. Ahead I see a barricade of breezeblocks and sandbags. A small girl in a candyfloss dress is skipping over it as if it were a climbing frame. Pressing my back against the wall, I slither through the gap at one end. Beyond lies a second barrier with an armchair inverted on top of it, its legs kicking the air like a horse fallen at a jump. Squeezing round it, I can't help but smile at how speedily humans adapt to even the most bizarre of changes. Just a week ago I would no more have expected to be hopping over a street barricade than taking up trainspotting as a hobby. But already the necessary mental rearranging of the deckchairs has taken place. This is Diyarbakır's new normal: matrons with shopping bags sidling around obstacles in the middle of the road; little girls leapfrogging over barricades; and nervous foreigners joining in with the best of them, feigning nonchalance.

Thankfully there are no more obstructions and soon I'm standing in the nave beneath another soaring brick dome, chatting to Father Yusuf Akbulut, a stocky, middle-aged native of Inwardo, whose flock is down to its last forty members. They've gone through tough times, he concedes, but now an admission fee and a turnstile keep unwelcome guests at bay. Like the one at Inwardo, his church, believed to date back to the sixth century, has been painstakingly restored. Its portico of stocky white columns mirrors those of St George's; its capitals hung with stone garlands reflect those of Hah. As we bid friendly farewells, it's impossible to imagine that the next time I see Father Yusuf it will be less than four months later, when grainy video footage will show him shepherding his wife and children along the pavement behind the hastily improvised protection of a white flag.

Before leaving town, I decide to give Surp Giragos another try. My path takes me back past the Dört Ayaklı minaret, in front of which the human rights lawyer Tahir Elçi will be shot dead a mere seven weeks later, his last words an appeal to the fighters to respect the city's irreplaceable monuments. At the church my knocks still go unanswered. Ditto at its Chaldean counterpart. The door of the Esma Ocak Evi creaks open to reveal two unsmiling men taking tea in the courtyard. No, the house is not closed because it's dangerous, they insist, but because too few tourists venture down here now to justify paying a caretaker.

I wander back to the street junction. The vegetable seller is still sitting on the kerb retailing his handful of dejected vegetables. A sheet still hangs above a line of sandbags, obscuring whatever's going on behind it. But women in long macs and headscarves are walking towards us with their shopping bags. How dangerous can it be?

'Is this road open?' I ask the vegetable seller.

'Yes,' he says, then adds as an afterthought, 'during the day.'

I slide gingerly round the sheet to find some half-dozen young men in their late teens and early twenties reclining on floor cushions as if in a rural tea garden. One of them strides over to greet me. I glance at the sheet. Onto its back the words '*Şehit Gelahat Cephesi* [Martyr Galahad Front]' are inked in thick black lettering.

'Who was he?'

'He died a couple of weeks ago.'

'A friend?'

'Yes.'

'I'm sorry. Are you the leader of this front?'

A shrug.

'Here there are no leaders. We're all leaders,' a voice pipes up from the floor cushions.

I gaze at the Che Guevara-ish poster. Close up I can see that it actually portrays a woman.

'And who is that?'

'Rehana, the Angel of Kobani*.'

Reports suggest that the nearby Kurtuluş Cami has been damaged in a shootout and I long to take a look. But the situation feels simultaneously surreal and knife-edged. No government could allow a no-go area such as this to endure. The young men are playing with fire. Retreat is the only sensible option.

*Purportedly a Kurdish fighter against ISIS in Kobani who killed more than one hundred people before herself being killed. Details of her story are sketchy and unauthenticated.

29

Copper Mines and Opium Poppies

ERGANİ-MADEN-HARPUT-MALATYA-DARENDE

'I didn't go up to the mines…I have to climb so many hills after monasteries.'
Letter, 6 June 1909

At the Ergani Cultural Centre manager Mehmet Ali is so excited by the arrival of a foreigner that he does his utmost to throw a spanner in the works of a Nigella Lawson lookalike waitress just itching to arrange for her uncle to drive me up Makam Dağı. Over çay after çay he insists that we watch every second of a video clip featuring a man riding his motorbike up to the summit with a GoPro camera clipped to his helmet. Only then does he reluctantly permit me to approach the mountain myself.

A 'precipitous pointed hill', Makem Dağı was once topped with an outsized Armenian monastery dedicated to Surp Asdvadzadzin (Holy Mother of God). 'We were rewarded by a magnificent view and by a pleasant talk with the prior who informed me, as I drank his excellent coffee, that the monastery was founded in the first century of the Christian era,' wrote Gertrude, whose own judgement assigned it to the fourteenth. Now all that remains of the church is a scant shell blending so perfectly into the sepia landscape that it's easy to overlook.

My latest taxi driver is Abbas Yılmaz, who wields the weight of his thirty-five years as if they were twice as many. A man of soft fleshiness, he's smartly dressed and courteous, a man for whom taxi driving is a profession to be treated seriously. As we zigzag up a road newly asphalted to encourage tourism, Abbas tells me that his two children have just started school. 'My wife and I spoke Kurdish to them until they were about three, then switched to Turkish. That way they would know their *ana dil* [mother tongue] but wouldn't get the same shock as we did when we went to school and couldn't understand the teachers,' he explains.

Far from eavesdropping ears, I feel emboldened to ask his opinion on an independent Kurdistan. Does he like the idea? 'Not really.

It's not necessary or useful. But there should be greater respect for our culture. For our elders, for example, who only speak Kurdish.'

Abbas may have frolicked on the mountainside as a child, but he's in the dark as regards the lost monastery. He shows me a cistern that must surely have formed part of the complex but reacts with as much surprise as I do when, from a newly laid boardwalk, we glimpse the shattered walls. But, oh, the view! On and on it rolls, a flat plain of ochre with just the occasional hillock pushing up from it like a pebble disrupting a picnic rug. Only the town of Ergani (old Arghana) obtrudes, along with the turquoise waters corralled behind yet another dam.

From Ergani, Gertrude and her caravan trotted north along the banks of the Tigris as far as Maden, surely one of the most unexpected sights of her Anatolian travels. For Maden was – and is – an industrial settlement in the middle of nowhere, a place vaguely reminiscent of a hillside mill town in northern England (Gertrude compared it to Loftus in Yorkshire), its houses side-stepping down an incline beside a river in layer after picturesque layer. 'On a shelf of the opposite hill-side the smoke drifted perpetually from the smelting furnaces of the richest copper mines in Turkey. The metal, smelted on the site, is cast into disks, two of which go to a camel load, and [are] sent across the hills to Diyarbekr and Caesarea, Sivas and Tokat,' she wrote of one of the few places in Turkey – camels aside – that must have reminded her of a childhood passed in the midst of heavy industry. The hills rose so steeply on either side of the river that there was nowhere to pitch her tents. Instead, she lodged in a 'charming khan above the village by the water's edge – but for the fact that it was innocent of furniture I could have fancied myself in an English country inn by the side of a rushing trout stream'.

Alighting from the *dolmuş* by a minimal bridge, I look down at the Tigris tumbling like Shakespeare's babbling brook over the rocks. But high above it a rusty gash in the hillside, the crumbling brick chimneys of a disused factory and the boxy sides of its successor shout of something far less bucolic. As I wander into the town, distant beauty dissolves into close-up squalor. Even the mosque is a youngster; it would have been barely twenty years old when Gertrude passed through.

It's not only the buildings that shed their beauty on closer acquaintance. For Maden has a dark history it prefers to gloss over. It was in Maden that the lawyer and human rights activist Fethiye Çetin was born in 1950 and her memoir, *My Grandmother*, provides a vivid description of the small town where her father managed the copper works. In later life Fethiye discovered that the family history with which she had grown up had been a deceit. Instead, she confronted the typically grim tale of individual suffering that lurks behind stale arguments over the statistics and semantics of 1915. For her maternal grandmother, whom she had always known as a Turkish Muslim called Seher, turned out to have been born an Armenian Christian, baptized Heranuş, who owed her life to a Turkish gendarme who had grabbed her from her mother's arms. Only towards the end of her life could her grandmother bring herself to reveal the story. What she told Fethiye of her own grandmother's fate permanently transformed that 'babbling brook' from a thing of beauty into the stuff of nightmares:

> After crossing the bridge at Maden – at Havler – my grandmother threw two of her grandchildren into the water. These were my uncle's daughters. They'd lost both their mother and their father, and they couldn't walk. One of the children sank right away but the other child's head bobbed up in the water. My grandmother – my father's mother – pushed her head back underwater. The child's head popped out of the water again, and this was the last he saw of the world, for my grandmother pushed him back under again ... Then she threw herself into the madly rushing water and disappeared from sight.

From Maden, Gertrude's party pressed on towards Harput and Elazığ in a downpour that brought welcome relief after Diyarbakır's stifling heat. Their track meandered through corn-growing countryside that put her in mind of Europe 'with the tiny Tigris flowing peacefully through it from willow clump to willow clump'. It skirted the lake at Gölcük (now Hazar Gölü), which was 'encircled by peaks, of which the northern slopes were white with snow patches' as late as early June. As my *dolmuş* sweeps past it the afternoon sun is casting a silvery sheen over the water. Thick white cloud lines the top of the southern hills like icing squeezed from a piping bag. It's a land-

scape from the Scottish Highlands. But just as their picturesque valleys sometimes harbour ugly secrets, this is a part of the world in
which it rarely does to wax too lyrical too quickly. For in 1915 the
shores of Gölcük became the backdrop for apocalyptic scenes of
human suffering. Dead bodies lay everywhere, wrote the American
consul for Elazığ, Leslie Davis, in *The Slaughterhouse Province*. A doctor and photographer were co-opted to record the awful scene.

İshak Tanoğlu kneels on the ground and reaches a meaty paw
through a space the size and shape of a cat flap. Stretching his arm
as far as possible, he reaches up behind the door and eventually, after
much awkward jiggling about, slides a bolt that allows him to open
it so that we can pass through. For me this is a third-time-lucky success story. Despite signs around Harput touting the Syriac church of
St Mary as a tourist attraction, its entrance has hitherto remained a
closely guarded secret.

Now, however, all is plain. By bending double to squeeze through
a small opening, we have been able to enter a shallow porch tacked
onto the side of the church. Then poor burly İshak Bey, a dentist by
profession and besuited accordingly, has had to perform this complicated manoeuvre to open an outer door concealing a grille over
the main entrance. It's easy to understand why the key has hitherto
been unforthcoming.

Fortunately, the palaver proves to have been worth it. Gertrude
had written that the west end of the church was 'rock-cut', but the
north and south walls actually look as if they were edged up against
the bare rock like a lorry backing into a parking bay. The foundation
stone is said to have been laid in 179, which would make this one of
the very oldest – if not *the* oldest – surviving church in Anatolia.
Gertrude wrote that 'its plan [repeated] the old scheme of the
parochial church of the Tur Abdin', although it's as plain to me, as it
was to her, that it must have been repeatedly rebuilt.

İshak cheers up considerably once he can stand up straight again.
'Our most important festival is the Feast of St Mary [15 August],' he
tells me. 'The church is full then. You should come and join us next
year.'

I eye the white plastic chairs filling the nave. They are sprinkled with a crumble of fallen rock. It doesn't look as if anyone has been in here since then.

'There are only five Syriac families left locally,' İshak explains. 'We use a house in Elazığ for normal Sunday services.'

İshak leaves me beside the barn-like Ulu Cami, from whose roof a stumpy minaret sticks up like a hitchhiker's thumb. But Harput is a strange place. Looming over it is a castle which 'for all its frowning walls and bastions [has] … but a heap of ruins within'. The streets had enchanted Gertrude, reminding her of 'a hill built Italian town' with 'roofs of red tiles':

> The castle, standing upon the highest crag, guards a shallow ravine wherein is stretched the greater part of the town, but the houses climb up on to the rocky headlands overhanging the plain and, from below, the mountain seems to be crowned with a series of fortresses. The streets are so narrow that a cart can hardly pass along the cobbled ways; very silent and peaceful they seemed, the shops heaped with cherries, the cool breezes stirring the vine tendrils that wreathed together overhead.

But the disjuncture between her words and the present reality is staggering. Now the centre is eerily empty, as if some crazed urban gardener has swept through with giant secateurs, deadheading the houses, leaving just the mosques and *hamams* to bloom. The demography of the past reveals the ugly truth. In 1909 almost half the population of Harput had been Armenian, another sizeable chunk Syriac. While camping in the outskirts of Elazığ, Gertrude had been visited by the American consul, William Wesley Masterson, from whom she learned that the villages on the plain beneath Harput 'had felt yet more sharply than Diyarbekr and the Tur Abdin the wave of panic that had emanated from Cilicia'. Three days after the massacres in Adana, Kurdish peasants had descended on the Armenian villages and threatened to kill everyone, while the Elazığ *Vali* had come under pressure to give the signal for an attack; in a letter to his mother, Masterson wrote that he had been readying the consulate to shelter up to one thousand Armenians. Luckily the *Vali* had held out against orders and when word came that Sultan Abdülhamid had been deposed, 'the agitation went out like a candle in the wind'.

By the time Gertrude reached Harput the surrounding country-side was in the grips of a drought. Days earlier, Elazığ's most prominent imam had summoned the locals to a shrine where 'Christian and Moslem, who but five weeks before had with difficulty been restrained from leaping at each other's throats, stood side by side and listened to the sermon ... [The imam's] eloquence reduced the assembled audience to tears, and for three days their united orisons rose to heaven'. Their prayers were answered and 'rain fell abundantly'.

But the restoration of harmonious relations was to be short-lived. In 1895 Harput's enormous American Euphrates College had already been attacked; around one hundred townspeople were killed and almost four thousand more slaughtered in the surrounding area. But far worse was to come. Photographs from 1915 show Armenian men being herded to their deaths in the Elazığ prison. Others were marched towards Malatya. It is thought that some fifty-one thousand Armenians were driven from Harput to Syria. At least ten thousand are believed to have died.

As autumn fades to winter, the crinkled leaves of an ancient plane tree litter the garden of the Dilek Çınarı café. Inside, framed photographs recall the Harput of Gertrude's day when elegant houses, each fitted with a wooden oriel, tripped down the slope beneath the castle. Outside, a young man is struggling to control a boisterous young Kangal sheepdog with distinctive yellow-brown fur. 'That's Garbis,' says the waiter. 'He's Armenian. A few Armenians still live in Elazığ, although they keep their heads down.'

I quiz Garbis about the lost Euphrates College. Founded in 1852 to train Armenian priests, this had ballooned to incorporate a hospital, an orphanage and separate schools for boys and girls until it became almost as domineering a presence on the horizon as the castle. He pulls aside a wooden hoarding leaning against a wall behind the café. Behind it a line of blocked arches imply the foundations of a huge stone structure. 'The last part burnt down about twenty years ago,' he tells me, covering it up again.

A silence falls. It's a silence weighted with the knowledge of death. Garbis returns to playing with his dog. I board the *dolmuş* for Elazığ.

★ ★ ★

Harput is a place that thrusts thoughtfulness upon its visitors, so it's hardly surprising that Gertrude reported an evening spent gazing upon nature's beauty – 'the shattered crags of Kharput and the hollow plain, clothed in abundance of fruits, and sheltered by its ring of noble hills' – while simultaneously fretting over what it was about humanity that resulted in the routine slaughter of its fellows. 'Like a tornado it bursts over the peaceful earth, blots out the daily life of town and village, destroys, uproots and slays – and passes,' she wrote.

In the morning her caravan forged west on the same road towards Malatya along which many residents of Harput and Elazığ would be driven to their deaths in 1915. Eventually she asked one of her muleteers whether 'in the day of slaughter' he would kill her or others of their party. He reassured her that he would spare her since they had eaten bread together, and Fattuh and his fellow muleteers because they were 'brothers', although he would be ready to kill all other Christians. Even Fattuh, himself an Armenian Catholic, offered little comfort. They had not been travelling long before they passed a caravan train heading south to Belen. Fattuh enquired after the fate of the Christians of Kırıkkale (then Kırk Khan) and was informed that all the *gavurs* had been killed and their houses burnt. 'Praise be to God,' he responded, only to be chided by Gertrude. 'Those men were all happy, they were all rejoicing,' he replied.

The caravan was unable to reach Malatya that day. Instead, after an exhausting twelve-hour ride, they pitched camp just past Kömürhan, with the ancient mound of İzollu (now underwater) rising up in front of her. In the morning they pressed on 'over hill and dale', passing fields waist-high in corn and poplar-fringed meadows. Finally, Malatya appeared 'lying in gardens at our feet'.

Through the *dolmuş* window the landscape stretches ochre upon ochre until Kömürhan, where a reservoir injects an abrupt splash of David Hockney azure. But I'm barely conscious of it. Because this is the day on which a bomb, almost certainly planted by ISIS, explodes in front of Ankara Station, killing 103 people*, many of them

*By 2021 the number of fatalities had increased to 109.

young peaceniks calling for an end to the renewed fighting between the government and the PKK. It's hard to think about Gertrude on a day so harrowing. Yet at the same time her story is a reminder that it's perhaps peace that is the exception and fighting the norm. As I check into my hotel overlooking the Ulu Cami* in Malatya town centre, I'm as pensive and critical of humanity as was Gertrude a hundred years earlier.

After overtly cosmopolitan Diyarbakır and Harput, Gertrude found Malatya 'quite a Turkish town [with] veiled women [and] latticed windows'. She pitched camp on the road to Eski (Old) Malatya, noting that there were purple and white 'opium poppies everywhere … they are just gathering the opium'. Through the open flaps of her tent she gazed out at the Dersim Mountains (Munzur Dağları), still snow-capped in mid-June.

It's hard now to recognize the garden city of her writings, for Malatya has swollen from a population of some thirty thousand before the First World War to one of almost 500,000 today. As the *dolmuş* approaches, it's not opium poppies that greet my eyes but a boastful new football stadium and a flashy private hospital, all glistening glass and steel. This is another modern town on the up with little time for sentimentality.

Just a handful of Ottoman houses still cling to uncertain life in the centre. Gertrude quoted the German field marshal Helmuth von Moltke, who, in his *Letters on Conditions and Events in Turkey in the Years 1835 to 1839*, described the local adobe homes as having being made from 'exactly the same material as that with which the swallows make their nests', a traditional take on sustainable living now as despised as the beehive roofs of Harran. The assertive Turkishness is, however, still alive and kicking. In a side street near the Ulu Cami diners feast alfresco in patriotic pride beneath a canopy of inverted umbrellas emblazoned with the colours of the Turkish flag.

---

* The dome of the Ulu Cami collapsed in the 2023 earthquakes.

In 1909 Eski Malatya was largely deserted, which is just as well, since passers-by would have been astonished to see a fair-skinned woman in a long skirt peering in through the windows of their Ulu Cami's dome. Gertrude had arrived to find the mosque locked. But this was the woman who had risked her neck scrambling up to the Adamkayalar, who had waded waist-deep in Lake Eğirdir and who had forded rivers even the locals viewed with trepidation. 'I climbed by its carved and half-ruined gateway on to the roof,' she wrote, 'and peering through the windows of the dome, saw that the interior was beautifully decorated with tiles and inscriptions.'

The emptiness she found in Eski Malatya was partly the product of a decision taken in 1838 when the town was chosen as a base from which to repel the Egyptian invader, Mohammed Ali. Fearing for the honour of their womenfolk, families fled down the road to the tiny settlement of Aspuzi, now Malatya. That was the story doing the rounds anyway, although Gertrude noted that Eski Malatya had been 'the Roman Melitene, a great frontier fort, and since their day it has been taken and retaken so often that finally it has dropped into complete decay'. The ban on growing *haşhaş* (opium poppies) in 1972 would have been one of the last nails in what was by then a very small coffin. Now, however, an urban adventurer setting their sights on that same rooftop would soon be given their marching orders. New life is flooding back to Eski Malatya as those who can afford to abandon the congested modern town for the fresh air and greater space of the ancestral one rush to do so.

Now the doors of the Ulu Cami stand open, inviting visitors to wander in and admire a slice of Central Asia strayed into deepest Anatolia. Navy and turquoise tiles that wouldn't look out of place in an Isfahan suburb emblazon the walls enclosing a small interior courtyard. A brick dome rests on stalactite squinches. The delicate *mimber* sprouts wooden flowers with gossamer stems. The contributions of modernity amount to air-conditioning units, fire extinguishers and glass panels, necessities, I reluctantly concede, for year-round comfort and safety.

Gertrude found 'the walls and bastions' that once enclosed Old Malatya 'dropping piecemeal into the poppy-fields that fill the moat'. I find them under reconstruction, the workers shouting cheery salu-

New restaurant in Levent Vadisi, near Darende, in 2015

tations as I hurry past, trying not to let my eyes linger on the brash new stones with which they're encasing the ancient infill.

At Elemendik, west of Malatya, carved stallions rampant guard the gateway of the Sultansuyu Harası, a stud farm for Arab horses which belonged to Abdülhamid until his downfall in 1909. A modern highway speeds directly to Darende, but Gertrude's route took her down into the Levent Valley, which lies a little to the east. Until recently this was a rarely visited part of the Turkish interior, the high quality of the main road ensuring that almost no one deviated from it. Then permission was given for a restaurant overlooking the valley. Cantilevered out from the rocks, it looks like a carelessly driven car poised precariously between catastrophe and salvation; it's hard not to imagine the intrusion of a single diner spelling the end. But the view is enough to overcome such worries. From the windows I gaze down on a scale model of the Grand Canyon for those who'll never see it.

Gertrude camped the night in Levent, a village buried amid oak trees with 'beautiful hills and cliffs all around' and a population of '*Kizilbash* [Redheads]', or Alevis. On a finger-freezingly cold morning, they struggled over a mountain into the adjoining Tohma Valley, carved out by a tributary of the Euphrates, where they passed a second night. 'Our path would have done credit to the most sensational of journeys. It led us over wild and rocky hills and down into gorges incredibly deep and narrow, and when we stopped to draw breath at the bottom of one of these breakneck descents we saw the track in front of us climbing mercilessly up the opposite precipice,' she wrote, adding that they were frequently forced to dismount and lead their horses. When they finally reached it, Darende turned out to be a settlement so 'immensely long and narrow' that her caravan took three-quarters of an hour to traverse it.

Now Darende is famous for its shrine to Somuncu Baba, a 15th-century holy man who spent many years roaming Iran and Syria before settling down to study theology in Bursa where he eked out a meagre living – and earned a nickname – by selling loaves of bread (*somun*). When his celebrity threatened to destroy the peace needed for his studies, he retreated to the seclusion of Darende where the Tohma had carved a 'very narrow, rocky gorge'.

Gertrude had nothing to say of the bread-selling hermit or the cult around him which has in any case exploded in recent years so that what was once a small mosque with a squat minaret sitting at the mouth of the gorge has mushroomed into a huge complex fronted by a pavement so highly polished that it could easily double as a skating rink. Instead, she scrambled up the rock to inspect the forlorn remnants of Zengibar Castle 'upon a bold promontory of rock overhanging the stream', then slithered back down again to find the police commissioner waiting to meet her, 'the hills through which I passed [being] reputed dangerous and full of robbers'.

I had hoped to explore the canyon's narrowest point, where the Tohma river hops and skips across ledges, throwing out pools then snatching them back again. But a child has tumbled into the water and drowned, and a barrier now bars access. Disappointed, I hook up with Mehmet, a taxi driver whose suit is as neatly pressed as that of a politician up for re-election and who tries to interest me in the shrine of Hasan Gazi high above the town.

I'm not exactly sold on the idea. 'Turks love tombs,' I moan. 'But we *yabancıs* have never heard of the people buried in them.'

But Mehmet is insistent and the closure of the canyon has reduced Darende to a thumb-twiddler of a stopover. So off we go, winding uphill through the back streets along the dusty road that leads to a shrine said to be the last resting place of the uncle and father-in-law of Seyyid Battalgazi, an Islamic hero believed to have taken part in the siege of Constantinople in 718. I give the tomb an obligatory five-minute whirl to satisfy Mehmet before turning my attention to the landscape. To the west there's a stunning vista of smooth golden hills scrubbed clean of vegetation. Then I look east towards Malatya and my eyes snag on a wall of TOKİ towers* dumped on the hillside in a wholly perverse location, sans shops, sans school, sans everything.

Deep in the valleys, Gertrude photographed a magnificent Roman tomb at Ozan and Hamit Ataş, an amateur historian-turned-taxi driver, agrees to show it to me. Down we plunge to the valley floor, where he's soon outlining the changes to a seemingly timeless vista. 'The road used to be much narrower,' he tells me. 'And the river came up much higher. Fifty years ago there weren't any apricot trees here either, just forest.'

Then comes the tricky topic. 'Many Armenians used to live in the villages down here,' he tells me. We ease past the contentious word *soykırım* (genocide), but Hamit readily concedes that most of them died in 1915. 'Three Armenians still live in Darende,' he winds up. 'They're shopkeepers.'

'Are they hidden?'

'No, not really. But they're Muslims now anyway.'

Hamit points out the Dileklitaş, a clifftop rock pierced with a Polo hole, through which snipers would line up their sights during the First World War. Away from the road we glimpse Gertrude's 'charming big village' of Ilıca. Then we arrive in rather less charming Esenbey, where a snooze of seniors are sunning themselves on footstools

---

*TOKİ (Toplu Konut İdaresi) is the government body responsible for social housing projects. It's notorious for building concrete tower blocks countrywide.

in front of the solitary shop. They cluster round the car window and are soon matching up old and new place-names as if this were the most exciting of party games.

'Palanka?'

'That was Ilıca.'

'Tozeli?'

'That's here – Esenbey.'

'Samah?'

'That's Çatalbahçe.'

'Mollaasağı?'

'That's the same. They didn't change it.'

Hamit points out Develi Deresi, the break in the hills through which Gertrude rode down into the Ozan Valley. Then finally we reach Ozan itself, where the tomb sits alone in the middle of a pumpkin field, a miniature temple of fawn-coloured stone buttressed with Ionic columns and wreathed with stone garlands, as forgotten today as it was a hundred years ago. Gertrude described it as 'charming … a little tomb that might have graced the Appian Way'. Charming, too, was the village *muhtar*, who handed her a dish of ripe mulberries as a reward for her measuring and photographing. 'There are no inscriptions upon it, nor anything to tell whose bones were laid within the vaulted chamber; I sent a greeting across the ages to the shade of him who had brought into this remote and inaccessible valley the arts of the West, and journeyed on,' she wrote.

'It was used as a church,' Hamit says. 'Then they turned it into a *mescit*. But no one comes here any more.' In lieu of facts, the locals have fallen back on fable, attributing its conversion into a *mescit* to the same Battalgazi whose relative is buried above Darende. Hamit and I step carefully around the lumpy green pumpkins. We duck our heads beneath the lintel and go inside. Above the mihrab taggers have been at work with their spraycans. Hamit stutters with embarrassment. I rush to console him, but it's hard to disagree that the tomb deserves much better.

★ ★ ★

Hamit and I are nearing Darende again when a wave of melancholy washes over me. My trip is not yet at an end, but it's certainly nearing it. For seven months I've lived and breathed Gertrude, waking

Roman tomb at Ozan in Levent Vadisi in 1909

each morning to do not what I might have chosen to do but what I need to do to follow in her footsteps. The ghost of Gertrude has been my constant companion, beside me always, urging me on, the best travelling companion ever. But now I sense it starting to fade. Approaching is the morning when the alarm will go off and I will have to make up my own mind what to do with the day.

Hamit has been a fantastic companion, one of the rare taxi drivers to have thrown himself into my project rather than paying lip service to a fare. So it's to him, unexpectedly, that I voice my sudden sadness. He nods. A wan smile makes hamster pouches of his cheeks. Then he drops me off in the high street and I board the bus to Kayseri.

30

The Devil versus the Kayserilis

PINARBAŞI–ŞAR–TOMARZA–TALAS–KAYSERİ

'Stories of Caesarea. If a serpent bites a Caesarean the serpent dies..'
Diary, 22 June 1909

From Darende Gertrude pressed on over the hills to Yazıköy, where she camped for the night 'upon the grassy margin of the stream ... under willows by the water'. From the *dolmuş* I can see the old village slumbering at the foot of the hills, its old adobe houses the colour of fading magnolias. In place of the willows, poplars guard the riverbanks. A huge stone quarry has erupted on the outskirts.

In the morning she was, as ever, up at first light, riding into the hills in search of rock-cut tombs. Then she made camp above the village of Osmandede, 'in a flowery meadow, through which hurried the Tokhma Su, a tiny flashing brook'.

Given the steely determination it had required to force her way through the Levent and Tohma valleys, Gertrude made a remarkable assertion about the next stretch of her Turkish travels: 'We had now before us the roughest part of our journey, for we had reached the hills that part the waters tributary to the Euphrates, from those that are tributary to the Saihun [Seyhan] – the Persian Gulf from the Mediterranean.' And it was now that this woman so commonly associated with the desert broke into one of her most lyrical descriptions of landscape, rhapsodizing about the flowers she had loved since childhood:

> We found ourselves on a wide upland, swept by cold airs and ringed about with mountains. The wheat was scarcely up, the grass sodden with newly melted snow, the peaks all white ... upon the slopes that closed the western end of the plateau was the village of Bey Punar [modern Beypınar]. Having passed the latter, we climbed into the hills by a shallow gorge down which flowed the head-waters of the Tokhma Su ... daphne and androsace, veronica and dianthus grew among the rocks, and purple primulas edged the channel of the stream. The gullies were still full of snow. So we came to the water parting, 2,040 to 2,070 metres above sea-level according to Kiepert, and bidding farewell to the last source of the Mesopotamian rivers, rode down into the basin of the Mediterranean. The

Afşar nomadic woman outside her tent near Borandere; 1909

long gently-sloping meadows were rich in grass, but no flocks grazed
there, and no summer villages were to be seen among the juniper-bushes.
The lonely beauty of these alpine pastures … fell upon us like a benison

That night her caravan reached a village called Borandere in the
Zamantı Valley where they pitched their tents within sight of snow-
capped Erciyes Dağı (Mt Argaeus). Borandere had 'quite the air of a
European village', she decided, with 'hedges made of pine branches
surrounding fields and vegetable gardens, poplars and willows,
houses with glass windows'. It had been settled by Circassian immigrants, whose bullock wagons, piled high with wood, somehow
managed to negotiate paths she had thought almost too much for
her baggage animals. They had been settled around Borandere in the
1860s and had rapidly displaced the native Afşar nomads who
brought their animals to pasture here in summer but baulked at cultivating the land. 'Now it is all under the plough,' wrote Gertrude,
adding that 'nomad life dies out in a cultivated country, and the
Avshars are settling into villages, though their houses are not so well
built, nor their gardens so well kept as those of the Circassians'.

Muslims like their Turkish neighbours but speaking their own
language, the Circassians had been expelled from the Caucasus at

the end of the Russo-Circassian War in 1864. Gertrude commented that they were 'not liked by the indigenous population [although] their coming has raised very sensibly the level of civilization'. As for the Afşars, they were descendants of the Oğuz Turks from Central Asia, their origins indicated by their *yurts* (tents). 'Entirely different from that of the Arabs … [their tents] are round, with a domed roof of felt supported on bent withes, and the sides are of plaited rushes over which a woollen curtain is hung when the nights are cold,' she wrote. Her photograph shows tents that would have looked perfectly at home in the Gobi Desert.

★ ★ ★

Strolling into Pınarbaşı (old Aziziye), I'm chatting to a friend on the phone. 'I need to find a taxi,' I'm telling her, and the ears of a passer-by prick up.

'You want a taxi? Where do you want to go? Şar? Let me take you to my father-in-law. He will be happy to help,' twitters Ahmet, and he whips me off to a nearby apartment block.

Fifteen minutes later I'm cruising with İbo down the smart new road that connects Pınarbaşı to Adana. A man on the downward slope to old age, İbo is white-haired and courteous, with a tic of parroting my words back to me. We're heading for Şar, the ancient Komana, which we find clinging to a riverbank amid scenes of heart-stopping autumnal beauty. Gertrude herself had approached from the west, coming upon it from on high and pausing for lunch in front of a unique temple-mausoleum. With burial niches lining the barrel-vaulted lower chamber and space for family to gather in an upper chamber, the mausoleum is thought to date back to the mid-fourth century, and Gertrude was much taken with it, seeing in it 'the true forerunner of the memorial churches of the Anatolian plateau'. Until 2014 it languished in obscurity. Then distant bureaucrats decided that the addition of lampposts would be an improvement. The light comes courtesy of eco-friendly solar panels, which makes it no less annoyingly intrusive.

Continuing into the village, Gertrude came to the slight remains of a 'beautifully decorated temple' which, in its prime, boasted some six thousand priests and priestesses, devotees of the obscure Anatolian goddess Ma, who was 'worshipped with orgiastic rites after the

Semitic fashion' twice a year along with her shepherd-boy companion, Men. Şar may be a forgotten backwater now, but in pre-Roman times Komana was one of the most important towns of the then province of Katpaduca (Cappadocia), and in the village proper, a jewel of an assemblage of whitewashed houses with corrugated-iron roofs, every gatepost incorporates a piece of masonry quietly pilfered from the ruins. In a place of such rare unspoilt beauty I'm not inclined to dwell on the horrors of the past, but Gertrude's diary makes clear how the post-Adana terror of 1909 rippled out even into settlements as remote as this. 'The hot breath of massacre had passed down the smiling vale and left Shahr a heap of ashes,' she wrote, and the inhabitants told a frightening story:

> The Kurds, Turks and Circassians from 60 villages came on Ap[ril] 20 and announced that they did not intend to leave a single living soul. The Armenians all took refuge in the houses on top of the bluff and there defended themselves for 9 days till help was sent from Azizieh [Pınarbaşı]. All the houses on the low ground, left bank of the river, were looted and burnt, including the bazaar, and some of the houses on the low ground on the right bank. The bridge partly burnt. When they asked the attackers to give them back some of their goods and not burn them all, they replied why shd they? what they did was by order of the govt. The gardens and cornfields untouched – the invaders looked to appropriating them. Sheep and cattle driven off and only 1/10 have been returned. When the soldiers came they did not punish the looters but a few of the ringleaders were afterwards put into prison. They have now been released. This tale was told me by the school teacher, Harechem Boyajan, who spoke English … we stood in the charred fragments of his house as he talked.

It went without saying that the village guestroom had been incinerated. Instead, she was offered 'a little wooden room over the water wheel' so full of bugs that she and Fattuh opted to return to a campsite near the Karabel Pass instead. As supper was stewing, a cuckoo called across the valley and a fork-tailed kite soared on a thermal. It was the 'loveliest camp we have had, close under the snows,' she noted. Back in England, she would write that 'the ruins of Shahr were the sole evidence which I saw with my own eyes of the far-reaching havoc wrought by the outbreak at Adana.'

★ ★ ★

Gertrude made her way to Şar from Tomarza, at that time an almost entirely Armenian settlement in the lee of Erciyes Dağı, which she described as a 'curious lava village, all of stone, the roads and fields edged with the lava slabs set upright'. Her caravan got there ahead of her and she arrived to find that, instead of pitching the tents, the men had sneaked up to the monastery of Surp Asdvadzadzin (Holy Mother of God). Tired and perhaps dreading the thought of obligatory small talk, she flew off the handle and was only talked round by Fattuh gently pointing out what uncomfortable mattresses the lava slabs would have made. Mollified by being given 'a splendid great room with many windows facing Mt Argaeus', she sat down to tea with the priest, a worrywart of a man who complained vociferously about the taxes imposed on Christians and claimed that Muslims seized Christian children for their own. 'He regarded my interest in antiquities as a mere cloak wherewith to cover a political purpose,' she wrote. 'By all Tomarza I was regarded as an itinerant missionary collecting evidence with regard to the massacre.'

The back streets of Tomarza hug their secrets tightly. Gertrude's photographs make plain that the monastic complex was enormous, with three entirely separate churches, in spite of which not a trace of it appears to survive. When the last houses trickle out beside a shelf of sheet-sized volcanic slabs, I turn back, thwarted. Then I see on the left-hand side of the road a deep hollow and, standing beside it, a young man whom I had previously sent away with a flea in his ear. I'm lucky that he didn't hold this against me since he turns out to know what I want better than I do myself. For he is pointing downwards and when I follow the trajectory of his finger I realize that this hollow with just a few sad stones clinging to its sides was once the site of the monastery, a last whispering reminder of an Armenian population that had lived here since the tenth century. But I can make out little more than the curve of an apse, the foundation of a wall. It would take a stupendous leap of the imagination to repopulate these scraps with the flourishing community that could once summon pilgrims by the thousand to the annual Feast of the Assumption.

At one time Tomarza was home to an elaborately carved Byzantine church of the Panagia (the Virgin Mary), which archaeologist Stephen Hill described as 'the most perfect specimen of a group of churches found in Western Cappadocia'. Probably dating back to the early sixth century, its decoration suggested strong Syrian influence, intriguing Gertrude, who wrote that it was of 'the Anatolian type of

Lost Armenian monastery of Surp Asdvadzadzin (Holy Mother of God)
at Tomarza;1909

the domed cruciform … but the decorative details, the engaged pilasters upon the outer walls, the elaborate mouldings, the string-
courses carved over doors and windows, are not to be found in the
churches that lie further west'. Snug in her monastery bed that night,
she pondered 'the artistic tradition which these things revealed, and
the mingling of occidental with oriental themes which they implied'.
In all she took forty photographs of it, which is just as well since it
was lost to fire in 1921.

Hoping for better news of a second, more toned down Panagia
in the vicinity, I wander into the town hall. 'Ah, Gertrude,' sighs
Gürhan, the local planning supremo, who welcomes me with chocolate and a sprinkle of cologne before pulling her pictures up onto his
computer and shaking his head. The church used to stand in the
fields beyond Köpeklı, now the village of Turanlı, 'but there's nothing left. Just a few stones. It was demolished in the 1950s.'

Gürhan offers the Armenian church of Surp Poghos-Petros (Sts
Paul and Peter) as a consolation prize, despatching an underling for
the key. Minutes later I'm standing in front of a battered apology for
a nineteenth-century church, its narthex demolished, its windows
bricked -up, old gravestones embedded willy-nilly in the walls. In a
hollowed-out interior spattered with pigeon droppings, I stare at
fast-peeling frescoes curtaining the sanctuary and at Gospel symbols
decorating the vault where a dome might have been expected. Erol
the keyholder babbles enthusiastically about imminent restoration
so that 'people like you' will be able to worship here again. I smile.
I shake his hand. I don't enquire about the people who actually did
worship here.

In the cobbled back streets of Talas the only sound to ruffle the silence is a great tit calling insistently for a mate. On the one hand this is rather odd given Talas's history as a greenly desirable hillside village within easy reach of Kayseri. On the other, a glimpse at its history immediately explains the quiet. For Talas was once a predominantly minority settlement, a place much loved by Greeks and Armenians, who counted amongst their number the ancestors of Greek shipping magnate Aristotle Onassis, and Armenian oil baron Calouste Gulbenkian. Two dates defined the Talas of the early twentieth century. In 1915 its Armenian inhabitants were either expelled or killed. Then in 1923, under the terms of the Treaty of Lausanne that concluded the Turkish War of Independence, its Greek residents were forced to leave for the Greek 'homeland' most would never have seen.

By the late 1920s the curtain had fallen on Talas, once home, too, to a thriving American college whose students were predominantly Armenian. Nonetheless it remains leafily lovely, with vines rampaging along trellises and berries cascading down walls. Talas houses once lined up on terraces, but many have been demolished, their hillside foundations playacting a quarry. Now the village has been absorbed into Greater Kayseri and life is starting to return as the university colonizes abandoned college buildings while those seeking a slower lifestyle snap up the ruinous homes.

Potent symbol of this new life is the Yamaç Dede Cami. Originally the Greek Orthodox church of the Panagia, it was built in 1886 at a time when no one could have foreseen that its entire congregation would have vanished in less than forty years. Now it's newly restored, its stonework sparkling, and if the Arabic for Allah does sit rather oddly with the un-Islamic swags of stone roses framing the entrance, this only reflects the familiar pattern in which places of worship cling to their significance no matter what the about-faces in the prevailing culture. Inside, the altar has gone and a mihrab has been punched into the wall. In what was once the nave a man sits reading the Koran while in the curtained-off north aisle a woman quietly prays, then checks for status updates on her phone. I wonder vaguely if Gertrude poked her head around the door. But the church would have been less than twenty-five years old then, the frescoed saints garishly new on the walls. 'Not interesting,' I hear her say.

Gertrude rode into Talas from Tomarza in 1909, bypassing the shattered ruins of the thirteenth-century Sarı Hanı on the outskirts of modern Kefes, then circling the flanks of Ali Dağı (Mt Ali), which, her police escort informed her, was a 'stray boulder dropped by Ali ibn abi Talib when he was engaged in helping the Prophet to pile up the huge mass of Argaeus'. Her intention had been to camp on the outskirts of Kayseri, but, hardened traveller as she was by then, she was as happy as the next person to be seduced into a change of plan when a better offer came along. Pausing to lunch with the American missionaries who ran Talas College and its small hospital, she needed little persuasion to extend that meal break into an overnight stay. 'The hospital stands on the hillside above the village, and above the hospital its charming gardens run up the hill in terraces,' she wrote, adding that 'the American colony is large' and that she 'passed many hours in the hospital garden at the feet of men and women whose words were instinct with a wise tolerance and weighted by a profound experience of every aspect of Oriental life'.

But even in such a seemingly peaceful setting there was no escaping from recent trauma. Amongst the men and women of Talas was Herbert Moffat Irwin, a Canadian priest in his early fifties who, with his wife Genevieve, ran clubs for young men in Talas and Kayseri. He had just returned from Adana bearing details of recent events there. Gertrude reproduced much of what he told her in her diary:

> The beginning of the troubles there was the state of political agitation created by the Armenians ever since last July [1908]. They had all been buying arms and the Hemchag [Hunchak] Society had loudly been saying that the Armenians demanded a Beylik, but not in Armenia, nothing short of Cilicia itself. They wanted to be independent but if they cd not manage that they would probably have put up with a semi independence under European guarantee like the Lebanon. The Metropolitan of the vilayet went about loudly preaching this doctrine from the pulpit.

The people of Kayseri (old Caesarea Mazaca) gloried in a reputation for rapaciousness and sharp practice, and as Gertrude rode towards the town, her muleteers entertained her with stories to illustrate this. A devil came to Kayseri, they told her, and was welcomed by the locals, who showed him round and plied him with food and drink. But when the time came for him to depart, his cloak and belt had vanished. 'The devil is not safe from the thieves of Kaisariyehi!' ended her escort triumphantly. It was with such words ringing in her ears that Gertrude arrived in Talas. 'I do not know whether it was the effect produced by these tales which prevented me from lodging in Kaisariyeh, or whether the prospect of two days spent in the society of people of my own speech and civilisation would not have proved too strong a temptation, even if the Caesareans had shone with every virtue,' she wrote.

But with her great journey along the Euphrates now nearing its end she was obliged to head into town to sell her horses. Like Diyarbakır, the Kayseri she ventured into was a town hemmed in by heavy basalt walls dating back to Byzantine times. Inside them she found 'narrow streets, the houses being built partly of ancient materials' that she assumed had come either from the original Byzantine town or from its satellite on the slopes of Erciyes Dağı (Mt Argaeus). But, unlike in Diyarbakır, the Selçuk town had overflowed the walls, with mosques, medreses and *hamams* spilling out like books from an overstuffed satchel. 'The memory of the Seljuk conquerors, who gave it a fresh glory during the Middle Ages, is still preserved in many a decaying mosque and school,' she wrote.

For many weeks Gertrude had been travelling through parts of Anatolia where Christianity was largely represented by the Armenian and Syriac congregations. But in Kayseri she was back in the heartland of Greek Orthodoxy. Above the town loomed Erciyes Dağı, where legend insisted that St George had wrestled his dragon. More importantly, Caesarea Mazaca had been home to St Basil, one of the influential early Christian theologians known as the Cappadocian Fathers and the man credited with introducing communal monasticism to the region. In the latter half of the fourth century Basil had founded a monastery together with a hospital and poorhouse that went on to become the 'greatest ecclesiastical centre of the Anatolian plateau'. It must have come as a terrible disappointment to find only a few foundation stones lying neglected beyond the city boundaries. Today not even as much as that remains of a complex which was in its time as big and imposing as the American College in Talas.

31
The Funniest Mountaineering
NİGDE–AKSARAY–GÜZELYURT–HASAN DAĞI–ESKİŞEHİR

'Everything comes to an end, even the road from Akserai to Konia.'
Letter, 16 July 1907

'The mighty buttresses of Argaeus, rising out of the immense flats of the Anatolian plateau, are as imposing as the flanks of Etna rising from the sea, and its height, over 13,000 feet, is scarcely less from base to summit than that of the Sicilian volcano.' So wrote Gertrude of Erciyes Dağı, adding that it 'dominates all Cappadocia ... very splendid, his two peaks wrapped in snow' even in mid-June.

As I start down the road south from Kayseri to Niğde, Erciyes is still just as assertive, no matter how much the sprawl of the big city is creeping up on it. Like most Turkish towns, Kayseri resembles a cushion stuffed beneath hefty buttocks, its old buildings huddling together in the centre, pleasantly low-rise and human-scale, the newer ones squashed out into the suburbs, where they're free to soar skywards, multi-coloured excrescences, comfortable for the families that live in them but eyesores for everyone else. It's early in the day and the peaks of Erciyes are embraced not by snow but by cloud that tucks itself in like a blanket around its base. The *dolmuş* is carrying me over the *yufka*-flat Develi Plain, a quilt of alternating green and brown squares stitched with stands of poplar. For weeks I've been travelling in shades of ochre. Now the landscape is mutating slowly through the khaki of autumn into the umber of winter. As we rumble on to the Konaklı Plain the fields fill up with families making a weekend of picking potatoes and stuffing them into big red sacks. From time to time new-look farms spread out from the road, generating energy from rows of solar panels.

Having sold her horses in Kayseri, Gertrude travelled on towards Niğde in a horse-drawn cart. Unable to complete the journey in a single day, she could nevertheless take her pick of stopping places; in Selçuk times this had been one of the great arterial trade routes along which the camel trains plodded, with caravanserais conveniently placed along it, each one an easy day's ride from the next. Finally, after a three-day journey, she reached the village of Eski Andaval (near modern Aktaş), opting to sleep outdoors again so she could take a last look at Erciyes before fastening her tent flaps for the night.

Daybreak revealed the remains of the Byzantine church of St Constantine, a favourite with pilgrims since it was believed to occupy the site of a much older edifice founded by the emperor's mother, Helena, as she travelled from Constantinople to Jerusalem in the fourth century. In Gertrude's day the ruins stood alone in the landscape. Now an airport hangar of a shelter looms over them to protect twelfth-century frescoes in a particularly tragic case of locking the stable door after the horse has bolted. For by the 1970s villagers had commandeered the abandoned church as a storehouse; rather than surrender it to the authorities, a farmer dynamited it, capsizing the roof.

On market day in Niğde retailers tout tomatoes and onions in front of the early-fourteenth-century Sungurbey Cami, where the sandstone arabesques adorning the porch are shedding patterned particles like flakes of dandruff. Gertrude was more interested in the Alaadin Cami, commissioned by the Selçuk leader Alaadin Keykubad in 1223, where her imagination dutifully conjured the 'female heads with long plaits hanging down (the faces are obliterated) on either side of the door' pointed out by her guide. But what most tickled her Niğde fancy was the tomb of Hüdavend Hatun, daughter of the Selçuk ruler Rukeddin Kılıçarslan IV. 'The spandrils above the windows are decorated with pairs of sphinxes,' she wrote, 'and the door is framed in a delicate tracery of lace-like patterns.' It was enough to confirm her ardent advocacy for the Selçuks: '[they] stand in the front rank of [builders], together with the Moguls and the Mameluks'.

Two years earlier she had trotted into Aksaray, pitched her tents 'below the town by poplars and willows near the stream [with] Hassan D [Hasan Dağı] watching over all', then treated herself to a cold bath, reward for days of dusty bumping across the plain from Konya. In the morning a stork was 'walking through the hay field next to my tent' and a kite screeching overhead; her photos show villagers in comically conical hats at work in the fields. But it was 'bitter hot' and, with the heat dulling her appetite, she spent the morning fine-tuning plans of churches already visited before setting off to call on the *Kaymakam* and explore the local attractions.

In 1907 foreign female visitors to Aksaray were as rare as swallows in winter, so she was soon attracting attention of the unwanted kind. '[I] defeated the curious eyes of the town by taking refuge in the minaret [of the Ulu

Selçuk tomb of Hüdavend Hatun in Niğde; 2015

Cami] while the key was being brought,' she wrote. The mosque was 'splendid with groves of columns and great arches, rows and rows of them. A very fine mimber I shd think of the time*.' There followed a quick turn round the İbrahim Bey Medrese (now the Zinciriye Medrese), whose 'plain outer walls' she praised as 'magnificent pieces of building, showing even more than the decoration [of the portal] the hand of the great builder'.

It was a relief that evening when a little summer rain cooled the atmosphere. It was also a relief to receive a return visit from the *Kaymakam*, who had succeeded, where Fattuh had not, in securing transport for her onward journey.

An otherwise familiar expanse of bleak concrete, Aksaray's main square is framed with a triptych of handsome fin-de-siècle government offices. Near them I hunt for a taxi driver to run me to the Çanlı Kilise (Church with a Bell) at Çeltek, a quest that doesn't get off to a promising start.

*Karamanoğlu Beylik (c. mid-1200s to 1487).

'Çanlı Kilise? Never heard of it!' booms the man staffing the booth, before phoning a better-informed friend, who relays directions to the younger colleague selected to accompany me. Along the road we make frequent checking stops. 'What do you want to go there for?' comes one particularly suspicious reaction. But such folly can always be blamed on the pesky foreigner (me) and off we go again.

Mehmet has never been to Çeltek and sees this as such a great adventure that I almost regret my failure to have packed a picnic hamper. But actually I'm feeling pretty excited too, since the discovery that Gertrude had visited this remote church had been one of the spurs to my own journey. The Çanlı Kilise lies just beyond Akhisar, a small village where modern duplexes lord it over the shells of the older houses. But if it was already quiet in Akhisar, the silence becomes deafening once we start up the track that leads to the church. We might as well be skirting the outer reaches of the Sahara for all there is anyone about, and I find myself fretting for our tyres and weighing up the likelihood of there being a spare in the boot.

With no idea what we're looking for, Mehmet perks up as soon as we round a bend and see, to the side of the road, traces of the abandoned troglodytic settlement of Çeltek. Up we scramble to a collection of rock-cut rooms with the occasional blind-arcaded facade and lots of roosting holes for pigeons, the remains of an ancient cave monastery, one might assume, except that the Byzantine scholar Robert Ousterhout believes them to have been the homes of a forgotten community who carved out residences adorned with private chapels, enigmatically large halls and million-dollar mountain views.

We've barely settled back into the car when the Byzantine church rears up ahead of us, magnificent not only for its proud solitude and lack of restoration but also because the windows still stare across to Mt Hasan from under thick eyebrows of rust-red tile. 'My heart sank when I saw it for I knew I could do nothing at it in under 3 hours,' wrote Gertrude, who dated it to the tenth century and photographed it before its dome came crashing down, exposing the frescoes. Even here, though, she has the better of me. The ruins may have been impressive enough to compensate for the likely damage to his tyres, but three-quarters of an hour is all I'm allowed before Mehmet's enthusiasm is exhausted and he's revving the engine for the return.

Çanlı Kilise at Çeltek, near Aksaray, in 2015; when Bell visited in 1907 its dome was still intact.

Gertrude arrived in the Aksaray area from Binbirkilise, travelling via Karapınar, where she had been obliged to hire camels instead of horses. A circuitous route to Güzelyurt took her through Gaziemir, which used to call itself Emirgazi before some bright spark cottoned on to the fact that by flipping the two halves of its name they could go from commemorating some long forgotten medieval hero to celebrating the greatest *gazi* (war hero) of all time: Mustafa Kemal Atatürk. Then it skirted what may be the site of ancient Arianzus, birthplace in the early fourth century of St Gregory of Nazianzus, one of the influential early Christian theologians known as the Cappadocian Fathers. There, to her delight, she found 'a great church [the Kızıl Kilise/Red Church] standing all by itself with heaps of featureless ruins round it ... the finest church I have yet seen ... a building like this is worth 7 days' journey. It pulls all one's other work straight and having thoroughly understood this one ... I can correct several other plans from it.'

In nearby Sivrihisar Gertrude called on a priest from whose chin a beard radiated like the petals of a sunflower and caught her first glimpse of Cappadocia's now famously troglodytic lifestyle. He lived, she wrote, 'in a rock cut house of one room opening into a narthex with 3 arches', and he must have offered refreshment, since she mentioned the 'most excellent sort of dry kaimah [cream]'.

I arrive in Sivrihisar, now a village of ruinous honey-coloured houses built against a pointed rock, with a pint-sized individual named Serkan. Following the population exchange, the village was resettled in 1924 by Turks from Thessaloniki, who knew nothing about farming. Most took one look at their new homes and moved hastily on; the few villagers who remained were recently rehoused into a Yeni Sivrihisar (New Sivrihisar) of concrete bungalows. As we park, a man named Ahmet sidles up to us. 'There are only three of us living here now,' he tells us. 'Me – poor – and two other rich people.' I'm not sure how rich anyone still living in this place of abandonment could be, but at least Ahmet points us towards the rock-cut churches seen by Gertrude, which have collapsed so completely that we would never have found them unaided. Dusting ourselves off after a scramble over loose scree, Serkan and I sit down to admire the view, the deserted houses melting slowly back into the earth, the landscape a natural colour chart running from palest lemon to deepest gold.

'Tell me about the crosses,' demands Serkan, and I launch into what I assume to be a helpful recitation of the Christian take on the story of the Prophet İsa (Jesus), which involves a crucifixion unknown in the Muslim version.

'Yes, yes,' says Serkan impatiently. 'But if there's a cross on a stone, does it mean that there will be buried gold?'

My heart sinks. 'No! Why would there be?'

'People buried their gold before they left. That's what I've heard.'

'But why would they do that? They would have needed it for their new life. They would have wanted to give it to their children.'

'The Egyptians buried gold with the dead. So did the Hittites.'

'Yes, but they believed that bodies were resurrected, not just souls.'

Serkan glares at me. 'People come here with maps,' he says. 'Not the ones who had to leave, but their children. They're looking for treasure.'

'And does anyone ever find any?'

'Yes,' he mumbles unconvincingly.

On the outskirts of Gelveri (modern Güzelyurt), the Yüksek Kilise (High Church) perches on a rock overlooking a small lake. Gertrude remarked that it had been entirely rebuilt and that the 'very monosyllabic Greek who showed us round said no one remembered the original dome of the church', whose prior existence she accordingly doubted. The rebuilders had been homesick Gelverilis living in Odessa who had paid for it to be erected in 1895 on the site of a much older Byzantine church, and the priest shared the lofty location and its splendid views with a couple of other monks. She camped nearby in 'a delightful poplar grove' with a fine view of Hasan Dağı and there endured a 'preposterous conversation' with Fattuh:

> G.B. Oh Fattuh, to whom does this poplar garden belong?
>
> F. To a priest my lady.
>
> G.B. Doesn't he mind our camping in it?
>
> F. He didn't say anything.
>
> G.B. Did you ask him?
>
> F. No my lady.
>
> G.B. We must give him some backshish.
>
> F. At your Excellency's command.
>
> A pause.
>
> F. My lady –
>
> G.B. Yes?
>
> F. That priest is dead.
>
> G.B. !!! Then I don't think we need bother about the backshish.
>
> F. No my lady.

★ ★ ★

On the western flank of Cappadocia, Güzelyurt wears the baffled look of a village that has never really recovered from the summer day in 1924 when, under the terms of the Treaty of Lausanne, the Greeks, who made up the overwhelming majority of the population, were driven in oxcarts to Aksaray and thence to Mersin, where they took ship for Greece, huddling in tents until the new settlement of Nea Karvali was ready to accommodate them.

Looming over the main square is a solid two-storey building with a serrated roofline. Built as a monastery in 1856, it came to house a school for both boys and girls, its functions typifying the promise of the nineteenth and early twentieth centuries when new government edicts made it possible for the minority communities to restore their places of worship and build new properties at the same time as émigré businessmen who had made good in Constantinople started to remit money to help their relatives back home. When deciding how that money should be allocated, schools tended to top the list of priorities. But some of it also went to endow the village with fine stone mansions that were an aristocratic cut above the old rock homes clustered around the valley church of St Gregory of Nazianzus (now the Kilise Cami/Church Mosque).

A tree-shaded path winds down from the main square to the church-mosque inside a walled garden that contains an *ayazma*, or sacred spring. The original church was commissioned by the Emperor Theodosius in 385 and named after a local-boy-made-good who had risen to hold the prestigious post of Archbishop of Constantinople. Almost as soon as the law permitted in 1835, it was modernized, but once the Greeks had been expelled, it was converted into a mosque with a minaret erected over the gate in a finishing flourish. Happily, although the walls were whitewashed to conceal distracting frescoes, the wood from the old iconostasis was refashioned into a frame for the new mihrab. The matching pulpit, donated by Tsar Nicholas II, still adheres to a pillar above a rug-strewn floor.

Gertrude described Gelveri as 'one of the queer places you see in this country where all the rocks are honeycombed with houses and churches'. Concluding that the church-mosque had been too much hacked about to be worth her while planning it, she did nonetheless take an endearing photo of a Greek father and son standing beside the apse in matching fezzes. Inside the church she was shown the bones of St Gregory – 'done up in silk cloths and laid in a box, and a cross sent from Mount Athos laid upon them' – as well as his house, 'a large cave of 3 chambers ... the roof decorated with panels and crosses and the walls with panel niches'. The well that provided drinking water had already dried up by 1907, as had the respect shown to the occupant – 'in the fourth century when [Gregory] lived there, Gelvere was an important place in the Christian world. Rome and Constantinople listened to St Gregory's voice – they don't pay so much attention to the remarks of the present dweller in the cave house'.

Later, she wandered into the Manastır (Monastery) Valley and found 'lots of rock cut rooms with steps leading up into upper rooms high up in the rocks'. It was late afternoon and 'the sun was low and touched the rocks and the grass with level yellow rays, the tinkling bells of a flock of sheep filled the valley and the shepherd was the only person there besides ourselves ... I felt inclined to thank someone for making the world so delightful'.

More than a century later, the valley is just as delightful and just as silent, a line of black poplars wandering down its spine. I amble through it without even the shepherd and his flock for company, scrambling up to churches so tiny that had more than four people gathered for a baptism they would have struggled to squeeze past each other. But despite the pleasure of the walk it was in the Manastır Vadisi that Gertrude's normally unflagging energy finally deserted her. 'I really can't begin on rock cut churches now,' she wrote home wearily, 'or I should be another two months out here.' She planned just the late-seventh-century Church of Agios Efthimios 'on account of the close relation it bore to the built churches'. Boulders block its entrance now so I must make do with the cute little Çömlekçi Kilise (Potters' Church) next door, where a fat frescoed Judas embraces Jesus while a miniature ox pops its head over the side of the crib.

Gelveri is usually described as having been a Greek town before the population exchange, but the locals were more accurately known as Karamanlıs, Central Anatolians of Greek origin who had over the centuries spoken Turkish while using the Greek alphabet to write it. Gertrude's diary homes in on this linguistic peculiarity. 'The Greek women were an awful nuisance. All these people speak Turkish; scarcely any of them know Greek at all.' Yet a mere sixteen years later, a politicians' edict would force them to 'return' to Greece, their Gelveri homes bestowed on Greek-speaking Turks 'returning' from Thrace.

Low down on the western wall of the small Yılan Kilise (Snake Church) in the Ihlara Gorge the twisting coils of a serpent form the centrepiece of a Last Judgement nightmare. Time and questing fingers have not been kind to the fresco, but to one side it's still just about possible to make out four naked women under assault from snakes. Greek inscriptions explain that the first is being bitten all over for adultery; the next is having her breasts nibbled for child abandonment; the third is being stung on the lips for slander; while the fourth's ears are being chewed for disobedience.

The gorge was carved out by the Melendiz river, whose waters provide a cooling accompaniment to a hot summer stroll. Once, though, it must have been much mightier, capable of chiselling out a canyon with walls that exclude the outside world. In a letter* to his friend St Basil, St Gregory of Nazianzus wrote that: 'Down below roars a river … teeming less with fish than rocks … It is huge, this river, and terrible and its reverberations drown out the psalmody of the brethren who live above it.' Nowadays, holidaying Turks lounge in wooden *köşks* anchored in the river and lunch on trout while ducks swim around them. It's a river tamed, a tool of the tourism industry, but none the less enchanting for all that.

In the summer of 1907 Gertrude left Güzelyurt at six in the morning, descending into what she called the Irkhala Dere via the village of Belisirma with a Gelveri butcher named Nicoli. With time only for a quick look at a couple of the churches dug into the valley walls, she signed up 'an agreeable old man' to offer a taster. Her diary records that they visited a church that 'they call Ilankisle', which she describes as a built church 'standing under the cliff', ruling out the obvious but rock-cut Yılan Kilise. Instead, the church of her photographs turns out to be the late-tenth-century Karagedik Kilise (Black Pass Church), perched in 'a very lovely place' on a valley shoulder midway between the village and the Snake Church. Then it must have been immensely striking, even though 'a great boulder had [already] destroyed the S wall and the W end'. Her description suggests that the three apses and the 'very high dome' that have since subsided were still intact. Of the many frescoes, 'which are almost perfect', only hints still shadow the window splays. 'I think no one has seen it before,' she wrote home enthusiastically. Alas, the German scholar Hans Rott pipped her to publication.

*Quoted in John Ash's *A Byzantine Journey.*

The path back along the valley to Ihlara village winds its way in, out and occasionally over the great boulders that have tumbled from the canyon walls. Blackbirds shrill. Donkeys hee-haw gustily. Willow fronds trail in the water. And ahead of me I can see Gertrude bending to pluck wildflowers whose names eluded her in this Cappadocian manifestation of the Garden of Eden.

★ ★ ★

Contemplating an assault on Hasan Dağı in 1907, Gertrude camped in the village of Helvadere, 'deliciously situated in a sort of cup and all trees and gardens'. Her tents were pitched amid willows and poplars – it was a 'heavenly place but midgy'. In the afternoon she rode up to the ruins of Viranşehir*, where she found an 'enormous quantity of ruins built of large undressed stones laid loosely together. I suppose there must have been mud between.' Eventually she came across a place 'like a great amphitheatre, Hassan Dagh overlooking it to the S', where she measured the remains of two forgotten Byzantine monuments, the Kara (Black) and Kemerli (Arched) churches. Despite its being high summer a sudden downpour forced her to take refuge in a vault half-buried in the hillside. Consolation came from a radiancy that backlit the ruins when the rain stopped. It was 'divinely lovely', she wrote. Yet almost nothing is known of this Viranşehir. Was it the ancient city of Nora? No one is certain.

I take a taxi to Helvadere from Aksaray, passing through Karaören and Karkın, whose residents, my driver informs me, all now live in northern Europe. Above us the first teardrops of snow are appearing on the summit of Hasan Dağı; in the fields women are parcelling peat to see them through the winter. But the driver is a young man intent on completing his assignment without breaking a sweat. He rallies slightly as we reach the foot of the track leading to the ruins. 'It's about three degrees cooler up here,' he says. 'It makes all the difference.' Then he slumps down for a nap, leaving me to the legwork.

A short, scree-covered path cuts up beside the track, emerging on a plateau over which loom the peaks of Hasan Dağı. The ground is so densely strewn with chunks of basalt that it's not always easy to

---

*Not to be confused with the town of Viranşehir, east of Urfa, or Viranşehir Antik Kenti (Soli-Pompeiopolis) in Mersin which Bell also visited. Viranşehir means "ruined city" in Turkish.

be sure which are ruins, which modern cattle pens and which the detritus of volcanic activity. Cows amble in and out of sketchy buildings. There's nobody here, no evidence that any humans have lived here since the day the population migrated down the mountain to Helvadere many centuries earlier. 'It was one of the most beautiful sites I have ever seen,' wrote Gertrude.

Almost at once she determined to make the ascent. Hasan Dağı 'was so splendid from this side that I felt I should not have done him justice if I did not go to the top of him. One should not pass by such a lovely a mountain without spending a day on it.' But the result was not quite what she had anticipated. 'No sooner had I reached this great determination than everyone who had said there were no ruins on it began to say of course there were any quantity.' In 1907 the population of Helvadere was half Turkish Muslim and half Greek Christian, and a certain confusion appears to have existed as to what had become of its Byzantine heritage:

An aged man appeared this morning ... and professed to know all the ruins round about, so Fattuh engaged him as guide-in-chief for the day. His name was Ali as I had presently cause to know ... I questioned the aged man as to what I should ride out and see. He said: 'Many churches there are, a very great many.'

'Where?' said I.

'Over there,' said he 'that side,' waving his hand vaguely round the mountains, 'there is one.'

'What is his name? said I (there's no neuter in Turkish).

'Ali,' said he.

'Not your name, the church's name.'

'Chanderlik,' said he.

'Aren't there any in the other direction?' said I, for the way he seemed to be pointing was my route for tomorrow.

'Not any at all,' said he.

A bystander, 'Many, a great many; over there there is one.'

'What is his name?' said I.

The bystander, 'Ali.'

'Not his name, the church's name!'

'Uleuren there is, and Kareuren, and Yazlikisle and ...' so on and so on. (Euren means ruin and kisle means church.)

Ali indignantly, 'No churches. Ruins muins (you repeat the word changing the first letter to 'm' when you want to say 'and so forth'). 'Euren meuren,' said he louder and louder, 'all destroyed mestroyed, pulled down, broken, all ruins.'

'It's ruins I want to see,' said I.

'All ruins,' he said, 'all broken moken, no marble churches, all marble and so forth, not any at all.'

In the evening an elderly priest came calling. While nightingales serenaded them, he sat in front of her tent and outlined the locations of five churches. No doubt she would have been sleeping soundly in anticipation of seeking them out the next day when the crack of gunfire jerked her awake again to find the guards in pursuit of another would-be thief.

Her decision to climb the mountain was hardly surprising. This was, after all, the same woman who had ascended the Finsteraarhorn in the Swiss Alps just five years earlier. That exploit had taken her to more than four thousand metres in treacherous weather, an adventure from which she had been lucky to return alive. In comparison, Hasan Dağı, at a mere 3,268 metres, was small fry and the ascent 'the funniest mountaineering I have ever done'. At three in the morning she started up it with two Turkmen called Umar Ali and Elyas, 'merry fellows who went briskly all day'. In early July, buttercups, forget-me-nots and anemones were in flower. 'We were in the shade nearly to the top but it was really never hot all day,' she wrote. Boosting her energy with chocolate, she scrambled over boulders and loose scree, eventually reaching the crater at the top, inside which she found the tombstone of the eponymous Has(s)an – 'what Hassan is not related' – although there was 'a good deal of blowing cloud which hid the view at times'. The crater itself was 'scarcely recognizable as a crater it is so much filled up; moreover one of the summit peaks rises almost in it'. On the summit there were also traces of a chapel and, in accordance with what she had already concluded at Binbirkilise, she wrote that 'I suspect the great mountain was an ancient holy place long before Christian or Moslem came to it, but of the old religions no trace remains for the summit is itself all a huge ruin, the rocks splintering away and falling down the steep sides.'

At midday they started back down the mountain, braving a short-cut proposed by a local, only to wind up in a 'stone couloir down which rocks might fall at any moment'. She insisted on backtracking to the summit and starting again, eventually descending via a route that took them 'across endless gullies till we got to the oak scrub again'. As they stumbled towards their tents, even the doughty Gertrude had to admit to being 'very tired, too tired for real enjoyment. Every muscle ached – I had not walked for so long.'

At four in the morning I arrive on the mountain with Osman Diler, a graduate of German literature turned local travel agent, and Mevlüt Demir, former hotel manager, former traffic cop and former shepherd boy from Sivas. We drive to the end of the road in pitch darkness and crack our breakfast eggshells beneath a night sky familiar only to those living in the middle of nowhere. Above us the stars sparkle like sequins on a black velvet ballgown, the constellations familiar to all of us – Orion's Belt, the Great Bear – exposed as a front for a hidden galaxy of blurry, mysterious stars to which only dedicated astronomers could attach names, the glittering firmament stretching to infinity.

As we start up the slope, we sense the mountain rather than see it. Then, slowly, dawn breaks and the peak rears up above us. Or rather several peaks rear up, because 'Hasan Dağı' is really a mountain in quintuplicate. There's Büyük Hasan (Big Hasan, the peak which we are hoping to climb). There's Küçük Hasan (Little Hasan). And then there are a string of baby Hasans, trailing in the wake of their parents. Mesmerized by the sight of them, I spin round as a salmon-pink glow ignites the sky. In the grass behind us partridges cackle morning greetings to each other. Far below, sheep stream out to pasture, bells tinkling.

With not so much as a goat track to follow, we must pick our way step by step across the boulders tossed from the crater many thousands of years ago*. The slope rises fairly gently, scattered with boulders and scrub grass, with just the occasional tiny yellow flower and Gertrude's 'little clustering white alpine things' to distract us. An odd wisp of cloud wafts across the sky like a floating chiffon scarf. From time to time we pause to graze on fruit and nuts. Below us, the

---

*A mural found in a Çatalhöyük homestead and dated to about 6,600 BC is believed to show the last cataclysmic eruption.

Near the summit of Hasan Dağı (Mt Hasan), near Aksaray, in 2016

view sprawls endlessly, pink-tinged volcanic craters lined up like a rack of snazzy egg poachers in an upmarket kitchen.

But the climb that starts out so seductively soon takes a more aggressive turn. As I start to flag, Mevlüt serenades us with a love song featuring a local beauty. We're nearing three thousand metres when he shakes his head and gently suggests turning back. I gaze up at the craggy, shattered rocks above us. Rumour has it that a chocolate company has erected a cow-shaped advertising hoarding on the summit. I want to rage and stamp my foot and insist on pressing on to see if it's true, but really there's nothing for it but to bow to his experience. Stumbling over one boulder after the next at the end of a gruelling ten-hour haul, I'm even more exhausted than Gertrude was, although too exhilarated by the experience to care.

The great road that strikes west across the Anatolian plain from Aksaray to Konya boasts a venerable history stretching back to the fifth century BC when the Persians held sway over much of Anatolia. To link their capital at Sardis, near the Aegean coast, with Susa in Persia, where they maintained a summer palace, they created the Kral Yolu (King's Road), which originally passed to the north of the great Anatolian Salt Lake but was eventually rerouted south more or less along what was to become the busiest section of the Silk Road network. The discovery of faster sea routes from West to East in the sixteenth century spelt the end for the fabled road. Slowly but surely the grand old caravanserais disintegrated into stone quarries. Now they're being done up again hurriedly with a tourist clientele in mind.

In 1907 Gertrude set off along the road towards Konya in a *tatar arabası*, which she described as a 'springless wooden cart with a hood of plaited straw with a cloth thrown over it. I should think less luxurious carriages do not exist.' After spreading rugs along its bottom, she decided that even if it was still 'uncommonly jolty ... it really wasn't so bad. At any rate we were out of the glare and much less hot than we should have been riding.' But they 'scarcely ever went beyond a foot's pace'; it took a full three and a half hours just to reach Aksaray from her campsite. As she and Fattuh bumped uncomfortably along the road, she noted with surprise that it was her birthday: 'for the first time in my life I forgot'.

After many hours they finally paused in front of the Sultan Han, 'a most magnificent place, the prince of khans'. But her photographs reveal that even this, the greatest of all the caravanserais, was at the start of the twentieth century teetering on its last legs, its outer walls crumbling, the *mescit* in the courtyard on the verge of collapse.

Completed in 1278, the Sultan Han took the standard blueprint for an Anatolian caravanserai then blew it up big, its grand entrance portal staring across the courtyard at a second only marginally less grand entrance to the stables. Windowless bedrooms traipsed along one side of the courtyard while on the other a portico provided alfresco sleeping arrangements for breezeless summer nights. Gertrude was enraptured by one of the most magnificent stable blocks ever designed. 'The great vaulted inner chamber is superb,' she wrote of a hall that, despite its seemingly lowly status, boasts the proportions of a small cathedral, Gothic in the pointed arches of its aisles yet Romanesque in the slit windows through which, today, sunlight filters down onto a carpet of pigeon dung. To complete the impression of a secular cathedral there's even a dome over the crossing, the soot-blackened squinches that support it adorned with stone stalactites. Once this would have been a noisy place, resounding with the snorting of camels and the braying of donkeys. Now, however, the silence is broken only by the cooing of pigeons and the flapping of wings as they swoop under the lintel, then up again to their roosts above the arches.

Gertrude was dismissive of the Anatolian plateau. 'From Akserai we have 3 days of absolutely uninteresting travel across the great plains to Konia,' she wrote. 'The road was absolutely flat all day, the plain is scarcely inhabited – scarcely cultivated.' Eventually she reached Obruk, where a thirteenth-century caravanserai with a crenellated gateway perches on the lip of a sinkhole. Pea-green water fills a lake that the carriage driver assured her was so deep 'that if a boy fell in and sank you could see the bubbles and circles for half an hour rising while he sank to the bottom'.

But, 'everything comes to an end, even the road from Akserai to Konia,' she eventually wrote.

It had been a punishing journey, rising before dawn to avoid the worst of the heat, then pressing on for up to ten hours a day to make decent headway. Not surprisingly, on finally trundling into Konya she was only too happy to pay off the cart drivers and take up an invitation from the Doughty-Wylies, friends of two months standing, to stay in the consulate. Lingering for a week, she was there to celebrate Dick's birthday. Then she headed for the station to board the train to Constantinople.

Obliged to change in Eskişehir, Gertrude spent the night at the Hotel Tadia, whose hostess, Austrian-born Frau Tadia, could be relied upon to rustle up an excellent meal. I'm ambling along the road to the station, glancing anxiously to left and right just in case, when suddenly my eyes alight on a sign down a side street. 'Madame Tadia Otel', it reads. To be fair, this is a mundane modern building with none of the panache of the one that hosted Gertrude. Still, I can feel my pulse starting to speed up as I stride towards the reception and it positively races as I flip the pages of a book on the counter and spot a reference to Madame Tadia. Of course no twenty-first-century equivalent of the divine Madame T is going to be rustling up Scotch broth and café au lait for me. Still, it's the decision of a moment to check in, thrilling to be spending the night so close to where Gertrude laid her head at the end of a very long journey from the east.

32

Constantinople Swansong

ISTANBUL

*'There are troops of professors and people of that kind here who have all been
to see me. I find it vastly entertaining!'* Letter, 30 July 1907

In Pera House, the grand mansion in the heart of Beyoğlu that was
home first to the British Embassy, then to the Consulate after the advent of the Republic, a watercolour depicts a top-heavy wooden
building looming over the Bosphorus at Tarabya (then Therapia).
This was the summer embassy, to which, in pre-war days, the diplomatic community would transfer as soon as the mercury began its
ascent. *Sweet Waters*, Harold Nicolson's story of pre-First World War
Constantinople, offers a lively portrayal of an urban nomadism that
pirouetted the well-heeled from their winter homes in Pera to their
summer boltholes in Tarabya. The Hotel d'Angleterre presided over
the waterfront. It was there that Gertrude stayed on her first stopover
in 1899, relishing the magical Bosphorus views now commandeered
by the Grand Tarabya Hotel.

Later she was to pass many a happy night as a guest in the summer embassy before fire wrote it off in 1911. At the abandoned site
I'm greeted by Kemal, a minaret of a man with prematurely grey hair
scraped back in a ponytail. Kemal shows me an arch marking the
spot where caiques bringing visitors to the embassy would have
moored. Then we pop our heads inside a cottage where a sketch from
The Graphic shows it as it was in 1877, a mongrel of a building, its
wooden framework evoking the guesthouse at Yıldız Palace, the
small domes of its roof the onion cupolas of Moscow.

From the lawn in front, Kemal and I gaze towards the struts of
the third Bosphorus bridge soon to straddle the entrance to the Black
Sea. Not long ago we would have been looking at emptiness, at a
horizon stretching unimpeded between the last landfalls of Europe
and Asia. It was a vista much praised in literature. 'It would be almost a sacrilege – at any rate an unjustifiable intrusion on nature's
rights – were a bridge, no matter how light and graceful of design,

to unite these shores for utilitarian purposes,' wrote Istanbul resident Mary Poynter, the wife of a Bell family friend. Now we're looking at a game-changer of a project. By the summer of 2016 the void will be filled, the silence overtaken by clangourous activity as lorries pour across the bridge to bypass inner-city snarl-ups.

Kemal is no fan of the bridge. 'So many trees will have to be cut down,' he sighs. 'And Istanbul will swell to thirty million people.' A few months previously a young wild boar, driven from its home in the Belgrade Forest by the construction work, had swum up to the promenade in front of the embassy. 'We called an animal welfare organisation. They took it away,' he tells me.

As we stroll around the grounds, I sense Gertrude in front of me, auburn hair finally unhatted, cigarette holder between her fingers. Her presence grows even stronger on a lawn sprinkled with tables and chairs. There I imagine her swaying in a hammock, book face down in her lap, inkpot open beside her. Perhaps she was reliving her adventures, perhaps brooding over the disappointing news that she had been beaten in the race to publish the first details of the ruined fortress at Ukhaidir in Iraq, the very details that had so nearly been lost to thieves in Hah. And all the time, just ahead of her, she would have had that peerless, unfettered view towards the Black Sea.

From Tarabya a road shaded by plane trees carves its way inland, ducking under the eighteenth-century aqueduct of Sultan Mahmud I as it reaches the village of Bahçeköy on the edge of the Belgrade Forest. I'm particularly keen to explore the forest because in 1899 Gertrude deviated from the standard tourist itinerary to look for the site of the old Belgrade Village, home for a few days in the June of 1717 to Lady Mary Wortley Montagu, wife of then British ambassador Edward Montagu, who had travelled overland with him to Constantinople. In *The Turkish Embassy Letters*, published in 1763, she left a vivid behind-the-scenes portrait of the life of Ottoman women that remains a counterblast to frequently fantastical male accounts. My own visit will add a third link to a chain of British female writers extending back over three centuries.

After Sultan Süleyman the Magnificent captured the Serbian city of Belgrade in 1521, some of its inhabitants were relocated to a village inside the forest (which was renamed accordingly) and tasked with maintaining Constantinople's water supply. Within two centuries the village had evolved into a refuge from the heat, humidity and sporadic plague outbreaks for the city's foreign inhabitants, most particularly the British. Lady Mary waxed lyrical about what she found there to her friend, the poet Alexander Pope:

> The heats of Constantinople have driven me to this place which perfectly answers the description of the Elysian fields. I am in the middle of a wood, consisting chiefly of fruit trees, watered by a vast number of fountains famous for the excellency of their water, and divided into many shady walks upon short grass, that seems to me artificial but that I am assured is the pure work of nature, within view of the Black Sea, from whence we perpetually enjoy the refreshment of cool breezes that makes us insensible of the heat of the summer. The village is wholly inhabited by the richest amongst the Christians, who meet here every night at the fountain forty paces from my house to sing and dance, the beauty and dress of the women exactly resembling the ideas of the ancient nymphs as they are given us by the representations of the poets and painters.

Capitalizing on the forest's popularity, the first summer embassies of the foreign powers were planted here. But the singing and dancing ended abruptly in 1826, when Sultan Mahmud II disbanded his powerful janissary corps and ordered the burning of the forest to smoke out fleeing soldiers, an event that resulted in thousands of deaths and came to be known as the 'Auspicious Incident'. After the flames died down, new embassies were constructed on the waterfront and trees recolonized the village.

Gertrude found the revived forest 'most heavenly green and hot' and admired the array of aqueducts and *bends* (reservoirs) designed to bring Thracian water into the city since Byzantine times. But when it came to the village, both she and I are chasing a chimera. 'The village is destroyed and Lady Mary W. M.'s house,' she concluded.

Local guide Gencer Emiroğlu is as familiar with the lost village as with his own terrace. 'It was at its most popular during the Tulip Era*, when Lady Mary came here,' he says. 'While the Turks were

---

*The Tulip Era from 1718 to 1730 was named after the mania for tulips that seized the Ottoman court during the reign of Sultan Ahmed III.

picnicking at the Sweet Waters, the Europeans were doing the same thing here, partly because women could feel freer.'

Now the forest is the picnic spot of choice for contemporary Istanbullus and, as we wander amid the oaks, a mouth-watering aroma of grilling *köfte* perfumes the air. 'The site of the village has never been excavated,' Gencer explains, but he's a man with the sharp eyes of a mushroom-forager-cum-orienteer and is soon pointing out the evidence for its existence in the corrugations of the soil. 'The trees have grown back, but where the village stood, the undergrowth is still to recover. Look,' he says, 'you can work out the extent of the village from where it stops.'

At the end of a sandy track he unveils his clinching argument: the remains of the substantial church of St George, all but asphyxiated by a thick wrap of ivy. 'It was Anglican,' he tells me. 'Probably built in the mid-seventeenth century. After the British left, this became a Greek village and the Greeks took over the church too.'

On a second visit to Tarabya in the May of 1905, Gertrude dined with Mark Sykes and his wife Edith, whose acquaintance she had made just months earlier in Haifa. An initially promising friendship based on a shared love of the Middle East soon ended in a spectacular falling-out, in which he accused her of deliberately trying to beat him to the Jebel Druze; in one of the great putdowns of history he blasted her to his wife as a 'silly, chattering windbag of conceited, gushing, flat-chested, man-woman, globe-trotting, rump-wagging, blethering ass!'. Sykes was one half of the Anglo-French duo of border-designators who stand charged with being behind so much of the misery in the modern Middle East. But, whatever their differences, he and Gertrude had to learn to put them aside when, as Major Bell, she joined him as a paid-up member of the British-run Arab Bureau in Cairo after the outbreak of the First World War.

In 1907, on her way home from her marathon expedition along the Euphrates, she returned to Tarabya to dine with Sir Nicholas O'-Conor, the then British ambassador. Soon she was a regular at the embassy, leaving a description of the foreign community, with its cricket matches, polo and bridge nights, that varied little from that of the Levantines in Smyrna. The big difference was that by now she was the Person with a capital 'P' she had always wanted to be, a woman completely at home among the cream of Constantinople society. Over and again she crisscrossed the city, soaking up its history, revisiting its monuments, then settling down to the life of if not an expat then at least of a semi-pat, with a ready-made social circle to slot back into as if she'd never been away.

In contrast with the immigrant Levantine world of Smyrna, the Tarabya community was truly expatriate, with a regular churn of old and new faces coming and going as postings kicked in and then expired again. The guest lists for the gatherings Gertrude attended read like a rollcall of the city's great and good: foreign diplomats, bankers and administrators sitting down to dine alongside archaeologists, historians and journalists. Her determined socializing in Constantinople sits at odds with the usual image of her as a loner, wandering those parts of the globe few others would ever get to see, but her letters home suggest that she relished the change of pace, describing as 'vastly entertaining' the 'troops of professors and people of that kind' who came to lap up tales of her latest exploits. But one account written from the perspective of a fellow guest suggests that she sometimes chafed at the social niceties. For twenty-eight years Dorina Clifton and her family lived in the Clifton Yalı across the water at Kandilli and, as a child, Dorina was so much a feature of the life of the waterway that Russian seamen dubbed her the 'Queen of the Bosphorus'. Decades later, in *Romance of the Bosphorus*, she described meeting Gertrude at a lunch party where Sir Nicholas O'Conor introduced her as 'a traveller of great repute and a most wonderful woman. Much against my wish she has travelled alone, visiting inland towns in Arabia where foreigners have seldom penetrated … she has succeeded in winning the respect and admiration not only of the Sheiks of all Arabian tribes but also of their Chief'. Dorina was 'thrilled to meet Miss Bell, of whom I had heard so much', but the pleasure appears to have been entirely one-sided. When not speaking to the ambassador, Gertrude sat in 'deep silence' and 'made no attempt to join in the general conversation'.

Dorina tried to put a positive spin on the encounter, writing that it seemed 'amazing that so fearless and courageous a character could be so unassuming'. But she also summarized the exchange that eventually took place between Gertrude and the ambassador, in which Gertrude alerted him to her fears of an imminent Arab uprising against the sultan. Her report is interesting for the light it throws on the habitual Turkish categorization of Gertrude as a *casus* (spy). In 1907 she may not have been being paid to feed information to the British government as she would be after the outbreak of war, but it certainly illustrates the fine line she was treading. Her diary entries for later visits to Constantinople are full of Wikileaks-style diplomatic gossip, the unredacted thoughts of the high and mighty scribbled down in the evening alongside thumbnail sketches of the monuments.

Most remarkable is her apparent lack of interest in a fellow countrywoman. Dorina's mother was a Cumberbatch, her uncle the Bell family friend Sir Adam Block, with whose help the younger Gertrude had infiltrated the Bursa *hamam*. But the fact that the two women had acquaintances in common made no difference. Gertrude is often accused of having been a man's woman, casually putting down the wives of colleagues as 'little' women; and it has always seemed particularly odd that someone whose adventures cast her as the perfect feminist icon should at the same time have thrown her energy into campaigning for the Anti-Suffrage League. Despite losing her mother when she was only three, Gertrude had always enjoyed a close relationship with her stepmother, Florence. She doted on her sisters and maintained several lifelong female friendships. Yet the fact remains that she was disinclined to generosity towards other women. Does that explain her snubbing of Dorina or was she just worn out from her travels? Was she desperate to confide in the ambassador privately? Or is it possible that she was just the teensiest bit jealous of a fellow Englishwoman – and a younger one to boot – whom others might have regarded as more of an insider than herself?

The Bosphorus villages may have been a popular summer retreat for the foreign community, but many city residents preferred to head to the Princes' Islands in the Sea of Marmara. Safely distanced from the mainland, they had served not just as a spiritual retreat for a myriad of medieval monks but also as a handy Alcatraz-style holding-pen for enemies of the Byzantine emperors. By the end of the nineteenth century, however, new ferries promoted the islands into super-desirable real estate and soon wealthy city residents, many of them Greeks, Armenians and Jews, were building lavish second homes there. In their wake flowed a steady trickle of tourists for whom the largest of the Princes' Islands, Büyükada (the old Prinkipo), became a must-see attraction.

On her fourth visit to Constantinople in 1899 Gertrude squeezed in a voyage to Prinkipo, choosing a hot spring day in May when the cistus and heath were in flower. I choose an even hotter day in July, when the island is awash with hibiscus and oleander but a noisome stench hangs like rotting garbage over the streets. For over a hundred years Büyükada's horse-drawn phaetons have been the only vehicles allowed on the island, the inevitable consequence being a faint whiff of manure that greets ferry arrivals then swells into a nose-assailing pong in the main square*. Like Gertrude, I queue to rent a phaeton. Unlike Gertrude, I stand in line to do so with what appears to be half the population of Abu Dhabi, Dubai and Kuwait, the women shrouded, despite the suffocating heat, in full, face-concealing hijab, their men dressed in the shorts, T-shirts and sandals of a summer outing.

The route followed by visitors has hardly changed since 1899. Gertrude recorded being conveyed round the island, then strolling uphill to the Monastery of St George, where a shepherd boy, hearing the sound of bells tolling underground, was reputed to have dug down and retrieved an ancient icon of St George. There she was served Turkish coffee with rose jam by friendly Greeks. Alas, the rose jam and coffee are no more. Ditto the rustic café where a glorious city panorama used to accompany *köfte* lunches. But today's Arab guests give the monastery a wide berth and the *köfte* trade has expired from lack of custom. Miffed, I traipse back downhill to re-join my grumpy coachman. Gertrude dined on the terrace of the lost Hotel Calypso. I make do with cheesecake at the local branch of Kahve Dünyası.

---

*In 2020 the phaetons were banned, their place taken by electric vehicles.

★ ★ ★

The Sweet Waters of Nicolson's novel were, in the late nineteenth and early twentieth centuries, a renowned beauty spot at the point where the Kağıthane and Alibey streams flowed into the Golden Horn. Here, from the Tulip Era onwards, the sultans had built elaborate summer-houses from which they could feast their eyes on marble fountains and rose-filled flowerbeds; at the height of its glory more than 170 mansions – most notably the Sadabad Palace – lined the marble quays, although none survived the fury of the mob when Sultan Ahmed III was overthrown and his grand vizier, Nevşehirli Damad Ibrahim Paşa, lynched in 1730. Later, the sultan's subjects would come here to picnic, listen to music and serenade the moonlight reflected in the water. In due course the tourists followed, as did Gertrude, who was rowed up the Golden Horn in a caique when the Sweet Waters were 'crowded with people for it was the 1st day of summer'.

The caiques are beautiful museum pieces now, but one sunny afternoon I board the Golden Horn ferry in Eminönü, enjoying a grandstand view from the deck as we cruise up to Sütlüce. There I disembark beside a mustard-coloured building that is now an all-mod-cons conference centre but was, until the 1980s, the reeking hell-hole of the city's abattoir. Beside it, motorized *sandals* (rowing boats) tout for trade. 'I want to go to Kağıthane,' I tell the man in charge.

'It'll cost you,' he says with a shake of his head.

'How much?' I ask, anticipating from his expression a fare of at least a hundred lira.

'Twenty-five lira.'

'Done!' I say and follow him to the quay, where I'm introduced to Yılmaz, a man of a certain age wearing a fez-coloured beret at a debonair angle.

We continue up the inlet, the *sandal* offering an intimate look at life at water level. Soon we're nearing the bridge that carries the road over the Kağıthane stream. Yılmaz plans to ram the boat into the soft mudbank so that I can jump ashore, but a quick poke with a paddle puts paid to that idea. Back we track to a concrete jetty built for much bigger vessels, where I jump-roll inelegantly onto the landing stage then stride off without a backward glance.

To be honest, I'm not expecting much of this excursion having seen enough of the area through bus windows to know that it's a sprawling mess of high-rises and concrete-box housing intermingled with ferociously busy highways and unsightly flyovers. Whichever stream I end up following, I assume that it will be a polluted trickle. There is, to the best of my knowledge, nothing left of the eighteenth-century splendour.

But almost immediately my spirits start to lift. The Kağıthane river flows along one side of a park, where some wag has decorated an electricity box with a picture of the Sweet Waters in their heyday, a befezzed boatman leaning on the oars as he rows two women in headscarves and face veils, parasols open to shade them from the sun. The rest of the afternoon is delightful. While hardly pristine, the river is less filthy than many village streams, and although busy roads and ugly flyovers do occasionally block the path, for much of the time I stroll in step with gold-leaved poplars until eventually the Sadabad Cami looms up, its single minaret perfectly reflected in the water.

Beside the mosque an imposing gate is punched through a stone wall. It leads into the grounds of the Kağıthane town hall and I'm just about to backtrack when something persuades me to keep walking. Which is just as well because eventually I find myself staring down on the last unexpected traces of the fabled Sadabad. A shallow dam inset with marble basins over which water would once have cascaded straddles a moat in front of the town hall. An eighteenth-century fountain needs only new taps to recommence refreshing passers-by. Finally, a small 'open-air museum' preserves the last remnants of the palaces, bridges and pools, some of which clung to life into the 1950s before being euthanized in the rush to modernization. The third incarnation of the Sadabad Palace was demolished in 1943 to make way for the town hall.

★　★　★

The Newest Hotel in Town. Splendid View of the Golden Horn, Stamboul and the Bosphorus. The Healthiest Quarter of the City. Near the Embassies and the Churches. Baths. Hydraulic Lift. Telephone and Post at the Hotel. English and French Cooking. Electric Light. Steam Heated. Private Tea Rooms. Dancing Hall.

Thus did the Pera Palace Hotel advertise its up-to-the-minute credentials to customers when it opened its doors in 1892. In 1888 the first Orient Express train had steamed into Constantinople. Spotting a gap in the market for a modern hotel to suit the new service's well-heeled passengers, the Belgian railway entrepreneur, Georges Nagelmackers, ploughed some of his profits into building the most famous of all Constantinople hotels. His was an all-inclusive offering with sedan chairs provided to carry guests up from Sirkeci station to the hotel.

Pera Palace Hotel as it was in 2015 - the only Turkish hotel still in the same business on the same site and using the same name as when Bell stayed there

On summer visits to the city Gertrude may have enjoyed the cool of Tarabya but sometimes Pera's proximity to the historic monuments still won out and by 1907 the Pera Palace had become her second home. 'I like this hotel better than any other that I've been to here,' she wrote to her father. 'The rooms are so much less stuffy.' Of its other famous residents, she noted: 'There is always a spy or two living at the Pera Palace – once she was a woman [Mata Hari, presumably], now it is a Syrian with a most unhappy face, a Xian from Baalbek.'

The Pera Palace is not just the only one of the five Constantinople hotels in which Gertrude stayed to remain in business as a hotel, it's also the only one whose historic interior can still be savoured in photographic form. As I sashay down the staircase to take tea beneath the glass-studded domes of Alexandre Vallaury's salon, I pause to admire the pictures taken by Abdullah Frères, the trio of Turkish Armenian brothers who maintained a photographic studio nearby. They show a drawing room designated for female guests, the smoking and billiard rooms, the café in which Gertrude might perhaps have paused to sample a macaroon, and the restaurant where she sat down to dinner with a glittering cast of contemporaries.

But it must have been a relief sometimes to forsake hotel dining rooms for the more relaxing lounges of acquaintances, one of whom was the novelist Vita Sackville-West. Vita had moved to Cihangir in Beyoğlu in the October of 1913 after marrying Harold Nicolson, who worked at the British Embassy. It was a short stay since she returned to England ten months later for the birth of her son. Still, I'm keen to know where Gertrude would have visited them.

In the Pera Palace's Orient Bar I share a glass of wine with Lucy Wood, a British expatriate who once played a most un-lookalike Gertrude in a television drama, and Hüseyin Karagöz, a cheery individual on the cusp of middle age who organizes what he describes as 'gossiping tours' focused on the private lives of the city's past residents. While studying in England, Hüseyin visited Sissinghurst Castle and stumbled across the complicated love story and sexual shenanigans of the Nicolsons. He went on to track down their Cihangir home.

'Vita wrote a book of poems titled *Constantinople*,' he tells me. 'One, "The Muezzin", describes the call to prayer from Cihangir Cami. In *Sweet Waters* Nicolson mentions a wooden house with a magnolia tree in the garden that was probably their home. While living in Cihangir Caddesi, I worked out that it must have been the house at the end of the street. For years there were attacks on it, probably by people who wanted to pull it down and build on the site. Now it's owned by the father of [pop superstar and actress] Hülya Avşar's ex-boyfriend. The house has been replaced, but the magnolia tree is still there.'

In *Passenger to Tehran*, Vita described Gertrude arriving to visit 'straight out of the desert, with all the evening dresses and cutlery and napery that she insisted on taking with her on her wanderings'. Later I stroll past the mosque in whose garden it is not perhaps too fanciful to imagine the two women pausing to soak up the panorama of domes and minarets marking the historic peninsula. But the substitute for the wooden house is disappointingly mundane. Its owners may have bagged one of the city's most awe-inspiring vistas, but the banality of the building from which they choose to admire it speaks volumes for how low architectural beauty tends to come in local priorities.

Most early travellers to Constantinople raved about their visits to Hagia Sophia but betrayed their inner Grand Tourist in the cursory attention they paid to the city's magnificent purpose-built mosques. Like them, Gertrude tended to gloss over the city's Islamic monuments, although in *Persian Pictures* she spoke approvingly of Muslim ritual, noting how the mosques displayed 'a friendly and a homelike air which is absent from Western churches'. Unusually, it was the life within them rather than the structures themselves that most struck this architectural obsessive:

> At every hour of the day you may see grave men lifting the heavy curtain which hangs across the doorway, and, with their shoes in their hand, treading softly over the carpeted floor, establishing themselves against one of the pillars which support a dome bright with coloured tiles, reading under their breath from the open Koran before them, meditating, perhaps, or praying, if they be of the poorer sort which meditates little, but, however poor they may be, their rags unabashed by glowing carpets and bright-hued tiles.

The relics of Byzantium were another matter. Over the course of her many trips to Constantinople, Gertrude visited almost all the churches that had survived the fall of the city in 1453, her diaries reflecting the limitless energy invested in the task. In just one day in the May of 1905 she not only visited Küçük Ayasofya but also the Bodrum Cami (chapel of the Myrelaion Palace); the Kalenderhane Cami (originally Theotokos Kyriotissa); the Vefa Kilise Cami (probably St Theodore Tyrone); the Eski İmaret Cami (originally St Saviour Pantepoptes); and the Zeyrek Cami (originally the Church of the Pantocrator) as well as the Sokollu Mehmet Paşa Cami, whose previous incarnation as the Church of St Anastasia she concluded could be taken only 'with the eye of faith'. In an itinerary calculated to exhaust people half her age, the next day she also knocked off the Hazreti Cabir Cami (originally Sts Peter and Mark); the remains of St Thecla (since lost); the Gül Cami (probably the Church of St Theodosia); and the Kariye Cami (originally Chora Church), at that time completely free of the residential development now penning it in.

But there was one church above all to which she returned again and again. The introverted neighbourhood of Küçük Ayasofya lies just inland from the ruins of the old Byzantine Bukoleon Palace. Hunkered down within the walls of the later Ottoman mosque complex, it takes its name from an almost circular church that predates Hagia Sophia. Its great age mesmerized Gertrude, who described it as 'most interesting, like a Ravenna church (the one with the mosaics of J[ustinian] and Theodora*)'. Her eyes were particularly drawn to the inscription circumnavigating the architrave, 'which the Turk has carefully preserved and picked out in white and blue wash', since removed. I climb onto the platform that makes it possible to examine the deep-set Greek lettering more closely, but tourism has taken its toll on the patience of worshippers. Where Gertrude once walked freely, a barrier now keeps intruders well away from the mihrab.

As the ferry glides into the Eminönü terminal my eyes alight on a building bestriding a bluff whose architecture would look more at home on the Beyoğlu side of the city. In 1882 the first stones were laid for the office that was to house the Düyun-u Umumiye (Ottoman Public Debt Administration), more commonly known as 'The Debt'. Designed by the Levantine architects Alexandre Vallaury and Raimondo d'Aronco, this eclectic edifice was where the payments required to settle the late Ottoman Empire's crippling debts were administered.

With the founding of the Republic, the debt was cancelled and the building became the Istanbul Boys High School, Atatürk reasoning that it would be salutary for the youthful citizens of the new Turkey to reflect on the horrors from which they had been liberated. It was here that Gertrude was shown a 'wonderful view' by a young family friend, Hugh Poynter. As I mount the stairs with their fine marble balustrades beneath domes of blue and gold, co-ed teens stream past me (the school has admitted girls since 1964), chatting to each other with the urgent intensity of youth, completely oblivious to any lessons to be learned from their surroundings.

When Cafer Bey unlocks the door of the Noble Salon, which juts out towards the Golden Horn, a whiff of undusted wood rises to greet me. I stop dead on the threshold and for a fleeting second see

*San Vitale

Chora Church (now Kariye Cami) in Istanbul in 1905

Gertrude doing likewise, one hand flying to her mouth, the other coming to rest on Hugh's arm as her eyes took in the sweeping panorama. The room is octagonal, the wall of windows on its water-facing side scanning a view that takes in everything from the new Haliç Bridge over the Golden Horn to the distant first Bosphorus Bridge*. Beneath me lie the trams of the Galata Bridge and the pigeon-filled square in front of the Yeni Cami. Off to the right are the towers and minarets of the Topkapı Palace and Hagia Sophia. Across the bridge is the Galata Tower, the distinctive witch's hat post-dating Gertrude's visit. Beyond it, melting into the distance, loom the tower blocks of 'Mashattan', the thriving modern business district.

It was with Hugh Poynter and his father, Sir Edward – the society artist who had painted a portrait of her as an eight-year-old girl with curls tumbling down her back – that Gertrude finally got round to exploring the 'cracking bastions and dismantled towers' of the Theodosian land walls, which had held so many would-be invaders at bay right up until the Ottoman victory in 1453. Completing their party was Alexander van Millingen, 'a distinguished and delightful archaeologist' and a leading authority on Byzantium.

*In 2016 the first Bosphorus Bridge was renamed 15 July Martyrs Bridge in memory of those killed during the failed coup attempt of that year.

Their expedition kicked off at Yedikule (Seven Towers), the great castle where the Ottomans used to imprison traitors, near the Mermerkule (Marble Tower), then standing on the shore, 'its golden feet washed by the blue water' of the Marmara. But Gertrude's favourite find was much closer to the Golden Horn, where a reclusive cemetery hugs the tomb of Toklu İbrahim Dede, believed to have been killed during the assault on the city in 1453 and buried alongside two companions of the Prophet. 'There were red roses growing in the tiny garden among the graves and eagles and kites in the towers above,' she wrote.

Time has not been kind to the land walls, after Hagia Sophia surely the greatest surviving monument to Byzantium. Effective as they may have been in protecting Constantinople from its enemies right up until 1453, they have proved defenceless in the face of modernity. Where poverty had shielded them from anything worse than time and tempest, prosperity has inflicted a plethora of insults, from the crass restoration that has left the Belgrade Gate looking like a child's toy castle to the running of the Metrobus right in front of them, eradicating at a stroke the dignity of their setting.

Hanging on by a thread are the *bostans*, the allotments that have probably existed in their shadow since Byzantine times. Retracing the walls on a fine summer day, I find a river of neatly tended greenery flowing through the old moat, injecting an unexpected air of rural serenity into an otherwise frenetically busy urban setting. Men are selling figs from makeshift stalls, fat green figs and pointed purple ones, luscious fruits that make you itch to pinch them. A farmer is scything hay. Another is raking the soil into plots that resemble an unwrapped bar of Dairy Milk chocolate. Smoke billows from a collapsing tower, faint echo of that momentous day in 1453 when the twenty-one-year-old Mehmet II brought the once invincible Byzantine Empire to its knees.

I pause to chat to Fatma and Hatice, a mother-and-daughter fig-packing team whose family relocated here from the Black Sea. Not figuring me for a fig-buyer, they're curious to know what I'm up to. When I tell them that I'm walking from Ayvansaray to Mermerkule their eyes fill with alarm.

'*Sakat* [Bad idea],' states Fatma firmly. '*Burası Türkiye* [This is

Turkey]' – the common explanation for anything out of the ordinary.

'*Sakat*,' is what a diminutive, cross-eyed gardener also shouts at me when I venture down a track to take a closer look at the Golden Gate that once opened onto the Via Egnatia. Fatma is fretting over the fact that I'm a woman unaccompanied by a man to safeguard me and guarantee my respectability. The gardener is fretting over two ferocious guard dogs who lunge towards me, teeth bared. Hobbled by their chains, they're all bark and no bite, but many Turks are terrified of dogs. To run such a risk for the sake of a few old stones! Only a foreigner would be so crazy.

In *Persian Pictures* Gertrude made much of the Merkezefendi Cemetery, 'the great city of the dead' that lay outside the walls. There, amid 'acre upon acre of close-packed graves, regiment upon regiment of headstones', it was the cypress trees that particularly enthralled her. They are 'like mutes', she wrote, 'who follow the funeral procession clothed in mourning garments but with sleek and well-fed faces. They rear their dark heads into the blue sky and beckon to their fellows in Scutari across the Bosphorus.'

Those fellows adorned the great Karacaahmet Cemetery, between Kadıköy and Üsküdar, where

> the surface of the ground is broken and heaped up as though the dead men had not been content to sleep, but had turned and twisted in their shallow covering of earth, knocking over their tombstones in the effort to force a way out of the cold and dark into the beautiful world a foot or two above their heads 'Remember us – remember us!' they cried, as we passed under the cypress-trees.

It was easier to remember – or at least to recognize – those buried in the less showy English cemetery behind Haydarpaşa Station on the Asian side of the city. In May Gertrude found it full of 'roses, lilac trees, Judas trees [and] tamarisk in full flower'. Beneath the shade of the cypresses and stone pines 'the ground [was] thick with the graves of men who died fighting, who died of cold and hunger in bleak Crimea', and as I read the epitaphs I'm struck by the fact that it would of course have been the Crimean War of 1853 to 1856 that would have been uppermost in the mind of a late-nineteenth-century British visitor, the battles of Inkerman and Sebastopol the names that resonated rather than those of the Somme and Gallipoli.

From Scutari (modern Üsküdar), Gertrude ascended Çamlıca Hill, a beauty spot renowned for its view, where

> the eye is greeted by one of the most enchanting prospects the world has to show – the blue waters of Marmora traversed by greener Bosphorus currents, light mists resting along the foot of the hill-bound coast of Asia, a group of islands floating on the surface of the water, the Golden Horn glimmering away northwards, with the marble walls of the Seraglio stretching a long white finger between it and the sea, Stamboul crowned with minarets and domes. Flocks of gray birds flit aimlessly across the water – the restless souls of women, says Turkish legend – the waves lap round the Tower of Leander (Kızkulesi), the light wind comes whispering down between the exquisite Bosphorus shores, bringing the breath of Russian steppes to shake the plane-leaves in Scutari streets.

Now a new multi-minareted mosque is colonizing the hilltop. Like the great Sinan mosques of the sixteenth century, whose silhouette it mimics in concrete, the Çamlıca Cami is to be the largest mosque in Turkey, visible from all over the city. Soon it will be worshippers rather than tourists who enjoy the stunning view*.

Gertrude's later visits to Constantinople took place in troubled times. As early as 1905 her diary records that 'the Sultan spends all the revenues on spies. They are everywhere, in every house and hotel and no man is safe from being taken up and exiled at a moment's notice.' That was the year in which she saw the sultan for the second time, on one of his routine Friday prayer trips to the Hamidiye Cami, so close to the gates of the Yıldız Palace that he could fulfil his religious obligations in a matter of minutes. Foreign visitors were permitted to view the *Selamlık*, the sultan's procession to the mosque, from a platform in the palace grounds. For Gertrude this was 'a fine, impressive sight'.

> The road was lined with soldiers in their summer uniforms, marines and a regiment with a triple green aghal on their heads … Then arrived an imam – the Sheikh al Islam – in a black cloak and yellow slippers, much welcomed and salaamed. Two or 3 carriages with women or little princes, these surrounded by black palace slaves in frock coats … As the Sultan appeared at the top of the slope the muezzin on the minaret began his

*Çamlıca Cami opened for worship in 2019.

chants ... He came in a carriage drawn by 2 huge chestnuts with a man in front of him riding the largest chestnut Arab I have ever seen. A crowd of officials and slaves ran behind .... He ... passed in silence, a worn, watchful phantom of royalty ... There was one very swell negro in a long gold embroidered cloak whom all the slave boys greeted, kissing his hand. I think he must have been the Abyssinian envoy – or the head of the Eunuchs.

By the time she returned in 1909 the city had been placed under martial law following the overthrow of the sultan. 'Personal liberty here is much restricted,' she wrote, 'newspapers supervised, teskerehs [travel documents] asked for' since 'at heart the town is not with the new govt'. The sultan had been ejected from Yıldız Palace, which was thrown open to the public. Looking round was a disappointing experience. For all the grandeur of his title and lineage, the sultan was revealed as a man of little taste who displayed on his walls 'a lithograph advertisement of a German manufactory of machinery'. The furniture was hideous and European. Much of it was in any case being evicted. 'Through the gates file bullock carts loaded with pink and green satin covered armchairs, dilapidated wire jardinières, jimcrack [sic] cupboards, journeying mournfully to the second hand furniture dealers.' The menagerie was little better. Most of the cages that once held animals stood empty, although some were 'still occupied by unhappy little beasts of the genus badger, sitting uncomfortably in the sun'.

Abruptly exposed to the common gaze, Yıldız Palace was revealed as a monument to paranoia, its views obstructed by trees thanks not to the blunder of a myopic landscaper but to the directive of a sultan who lived in fear of assassination. Even today the palace is not easy to explore. It was a compartmentalized residence, deliberately designed to impede swift progress from one quarter to another, with a high wall separating the guesthouse from the sultan's private space. 'It is not a palace at all. It is a labyrinth. It has the air of having been constructed with the unique object of rendering pursuit along the endless corridors impossible,' concluded one of the deputies whose task it was to make an inventory of its contents.

I take a turn around the guesthouse with a guide named Abdullah whose object is clearly to have me in and out again within the space of fifteen minutes. We whisk past a dining room almost entirely decorated in mother-of-pearl. We ogle a painting of Kaiser

Wilhelm II arriving at the Dolmabahçe Palace in 1889. We nod approvingly at a chair carved by the sultan himself, a man who might have been happier with a career in joinery. Only in the sprawling, personality-free Ceremonial Hall does Abdullah pause to draw breath. 'This is the largest Hereke carpet in the world,' he says, before reeling off the mind-boggling statistics.

Then I'm outside again, admiring a serpentine pool beside which a little kiosk once held a restaurant in which Gertrude took refreshment 'by the dirty pond on which the Sultan's ladies used to be rowed about by black slaves ... if anyone had told me two years ago that I should be lunching that day in Yildiz Harem, I should have set him down for a lunatic'. Of the unhappy little beasts of the genus badger there are no longer any traces, their place having been taken by much happier birds of the genus Aylesbury duck and a solitary cat sunning itself on the gravel.

The end when it came was both as abrupt and as simultaneously inconsequential as endings so often are. On 22 May 1914 Gertrude boarded the Orient Express to return to England after a short stay as a guest of the new British ambassador, Sir Louis Mallet, in Pera House. She and Mallet had bonded over a shared love of gardening. He was 'perfectly delightful', she wrote, adding that 'it isn't often that you find ambassadors so deeply interested in the country to which they are accredited'. They had explored the mosques and shopped together in the bazaars. It was a relationship she no doubt imagined striding on into a sunny future.

For all the background beating of war drums in 1914, she can have had no inkling that she was turning her back on Sirkeci Station for the last time; nor in her wildest dreams can she have imagined that just five years later the British would be marching into Constantinople as occupiers. As she tossed her hat onto the rack above her seat and settled down to take a last affectionate look at the city walls as the train steamed westwards, she must have assumed it was business as usual; that this was au revoir rather than farewell. But less than three months later Britain would be at war with Germany. Shortly afterwards the Ottoman government would

Gardening in the lee of Byzantine land walls in Istanbul; 2015

throw in its lot with the Germans, just days after Dorina Clifton de-scribed Sir Louis Mallet's undignified retreat from Sirkeci Station 'ensconced in his motor-car in the luggage van, surrounded by dis-patch boxes, diplomatic pouches, trunks and boxes, and a dog perched on his knee'.

For Gertrude, as for so many others, the war that was originally predicted to last only months turned into a partition, severing the continuity of her life and creating a before and after as absolute as the loss of a limb. Summoned to Cairo to share her knowledge of the Middle East with the Arab Bureau, she travelled on to Iraq, where, after hostilities ended, she made a home for herself in Baghdad. Had there been no war, it's hard to believe that there would not have been more books about Turkey: an account, perhaps, of the churches of Cappadocia or a more detailed telling of the time spent in Constan-tinople. But Anatolia turned out to belong to her pre-war existence, that brief 1914 visit the unexpected swansong for a relationship that had endured for a quarter of a century.

A Lonesome Gallipoli Grave

SEDDÜLBAHİR

'...my life, my breath, my hope, my heaven.'
Letter, 20 March 1915

There's one more trip I must make, one more trip that will be not so much in Gertrude's footsteps as on her behalf. It's one on which I embark with a heavy heart.

In 1915 the First World War was in full swing. Like so many of her contemporaries, Gertrude found herself caught up in the behind-the-scenes work, first sorting out paperwork in London, then sailing for France, where she was put in charge of the Red Cross Office for the Wounded and Missing, tasked with contacting relatives of the dead and injured. She had thrown herself into this unedifying work with her habitual zest and flair for organization, inheriting a mess and imposing order on it. No doubt her urgent busyness was in part to keep from focusing on what must have been gnawing away at the back of her mind: the knowledge that not only her brother, Maurice, but also her great love, Dick Doughty-Wylie, were out there amongst the combatants.

In 1915 she and Dick had a brief reunion in London. Then he sailed back to Turkey for the last time to join the fighting at Gallipoli.

The saga of Gallipoli needs little rehearsing; how the Australian and New Zealand troops came ashore in the wrong place; how they battled on for months despite an appalling death toll; how ultimately their efforts came to nothing as the Turks, led by Mustafa Kemal, the great war leader who would go on to become Atatürk, gained the ascendancy.

Most of the fighting took place in the northern part of the Gallipoli peninsula. It was Doughty-Wylie's fate, however, to lead his men into battle at Seddülbahir, some way to the south. On 26 April 1916 he went ashore, marching straight towards a small hill. As he reached the summit a sniper lined him up in his sights. He was killed by a single bullet through the head and buried on the spot where he had fallen.

It wasn't until five days later that Gertrude heard the news. Like so many of those who love without the legal right to do so, she was not on the list of people to be notified of his death, so it was while sitting around a London dinner table that she learnt of it, casually dropped into the conversation, just one more tragedy to be mulled over with the dessert. Only those who have found themselves in such a situation can possibly imagine the pain she must have felt, made all the worse by the need to conceal her feelings long enough to escape.

Gertrude and Dick were certainly well enough on in years to have known their own minds when their romance blossomed, although the cynical might wonder about the likely durability of what had always been a furtive love affair conducted primarily on paper. Despite the occasional snatched meeting, Gertrude had been unable to overcome her inhibitions (and fear of pregnancy) to consummate the relationship, leaving it one of longing rather than fulfilment. Would Doughty-Wylie have mustered the determination to leave his forceful wife? Would Gertrude have been able to face the stigma of scandal and a high-profile divorce? And how credible was it anyway that a woman who had thrived for more than a decade on desert exploration would have been able to swap the tents and campfires for a quiet urban life of childless domesticity?

But in thinking back over her life, I can't help but sense that something of Gertrude also died on that lonely hillside; that she was never really able to recover from the loss of Doughty-Wylie; that from the day she heard that crushing news there would always have been a gaping hole in her life that could never be filled.

These are the thoughts running through my head as I sail across the Dardanelles from Çanakkale to Kilitbahir and hail a taxi to take me to the cemetery. As I huddle on the back seat my heart starts to pound, my palms to sweat. In choosing to retrace the story of someone else's youth, I've acquired a godlike omniscience, the dubious gift of knowing how the story concludes. Day-to-day human existence is made bearable by ignorance of the future, permitting us to wake up each morning confident that we'll make it through to nightfall. But now the ghost of the future sits beside me in the taxi. Throughout the months that I've been following Gertrude I've been haunted by the knowledge of how her story would end; conscious that ultimately none of her great achievements could entirely compensate for her loneliness; knowing that nothing could save her from a premature end induced by a handful of sleeping pills downed in the heat of a Baghdad summer night. Now my mind is full of thoughts of the young Gertrude, the enthusiastic, curious, optimistic Gertrude, arriving in Çanakkale to seek out Frank Calvert, then rushing to explore the ruins of Troy, even as I sit here in the miserable knowledge that I am on the way to pay homage at the grave of the man she loved and lost. The sharpness of that contrast is momentarily too much for me and I have to bite my lip against burning tears.

In the small seaside village of Seddülbahir I embark for the last time on a ritual that is by now second nature. Since Doughty-Wylie was buried alone rather than in one of the peninsula's crowded cemeteries it's hardly surprising that his grave is unknown to the taxi driver, so I mount the steps to a teahouse where men are engaged in the usual lazy Sunday rituals: sipping *çay*, playing *okey*, skimming the newspaper headlines or just plain staring out to sea. I draw a blank at the first table. No, they know of no grave of an Englishman; no one of that name here. But at the second a wavering 'no' soon trips over into an assertive 'yes' as one man waves his hand back towards the village.

'Up there, by the water tower,' he says.

The taxi driver nods along. Yes, yes, up there on the right, by that tree, by that tower, and off we go again. Of course the Commonwealth War Graves Commission has been here ahead of us and a small signpost reads 'Doughty-Wylie'. We drive up, we park in the shade, and I walk over to pay my respects.

Like all the CWGC graves, Doughty-Wylie's is austere in its simplicity. There are no details of birth or residence, no mention of family, no flowery sentiments. Just a curt surname and initials, a list of decorations, a naming of regiment (Royal Welsh Fusiliers), a date of death. Georgina Howell's biography of Gertrude describes the grave as surrounded by lavender bushes and framed by cypresses, but modern Turkey, with its penchant for conjuring ugliness from beauty, has erased the trees. The site feels simply forgotten, the grave of some unknown and unknowable foreigner resting amid loose chippings just steps from someone's front gate.

Grave of Bell's great love, Dick Doughty-Wylie, at Seddülbahir; 2015

Gazing down on it, I'm ambushed by a confusing mixture of emotions. Here lies a man from my homeland, buried now in foreign soil, and it's hard not to feel a natural empathy with him. Yet at the same time here lies a man whose country had invaded the Ottoman Empire. I am a citizen of its successor state, Turkey, so at the same time I see him as partially responsible for the terror and misery inflicted on this part of the world during the First World War. But Doughty-Wylie himself seems to have felt the same emotional turmoil. He had, after all, spent many years in Anatolia and had played an active role in opposing the violent events preceding the war. So when posted here to fight against the Turks precisely because of his specialist knowledge of the country, he too must have felt these same contrarian pulls: loyalty to the land of his birth versus loyalty to a country and people that had come to mean everything to him. Contemporary accounts of what happened on that day at Seddülbahir suggest that he left his pistol on the boat, that he marched uphill as if anticipating death. Amongst the decorations listed on the grave is the Victoria Cross, awarded to him for his services during the Gallipoli campaign. But there, too, is the Order of the Mecidiye, bestowed on him after his death in recognition of his services to the Ottomans.

Like so many of the soldiers dying then, Doughty-Wylie was robbed of the chance to know which side would ultimately triumph. Glancing up, I can make out the tip of the peninsula and, bestriding it, the gaunt table of a monument named simply '*Abide* [Memorial]' that now provides the focal point for an ostentatious celebration of Turkish victory, a very twenty-first-century war memorial, presiding over a line-up of graves but devoid of any sense of sacrifice; a place

369

where visitors get to dress up as soldiers and have their picture taken well away from the mud and misery of real trench warfare.

Belatedly, I realize that I should have brought flowers. I look around frantically. Just one plant is still resisting winter, a purple cranesbill. I snap off the last blooms, twist their stems together and place them on the gravestone. It's the least I can do.

On the way back to Kilitbahir I chat to the taxi driver, whose name, as ever, is Mehmet. 'My grandfather fought here,' he tells me. 'His name was İbrahim, but, as you know, at that time we had no surnames. He was just İbrahim, son of İbrahim. So now we have no idea where he is buried.' And as I listen to him I wonder: was it memory of the carnage he had witnessed at Gallipoli and the awful anonymity of the thousands of Turks who died there that inspired Atatürk to insist in 1934 that henceforth every Turk must carry an identifying surname?

Was Gertrude ever able to visit her lover's grave? Howell's biography contains a story that has an air of wishful thinking about it. In November of 1915 she says that soldiers reported seeing a veiled woman placing a wreath there. The most likely candidate would have to have been his wife, Judith, although the date doesn't match with her known movements at the time. In which case, could the mysterious visitor have been Gertrude? In late November she had been summoned to report to the War Office in Cairo, landing at Port Said on 26 November. Just enough uncertainty shrouds her whereabouts over the next few days to make it conceivable that she could have headed to Turkey and back again before settling down to work in Egypt.

It's a pretty story that has something of the ring of Gertrude's determined character about it. But to believe it means accepting that she was able to make a frankly incredible string of sea connections between the two countries, in winter, at a time of war, in a tightly condensed timeframe. Janet Wallach finds no space for the story in her later biography.

Of course I'd love to think that Gertrude had a chance to say a proper goodbye to her beloved Dick.

But do I really believe that?

Probably not.

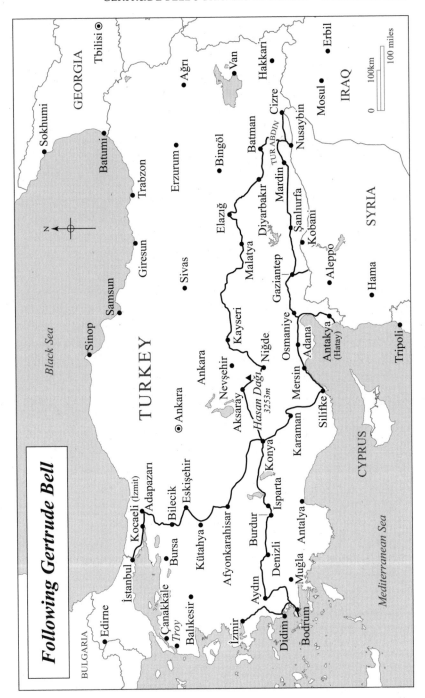

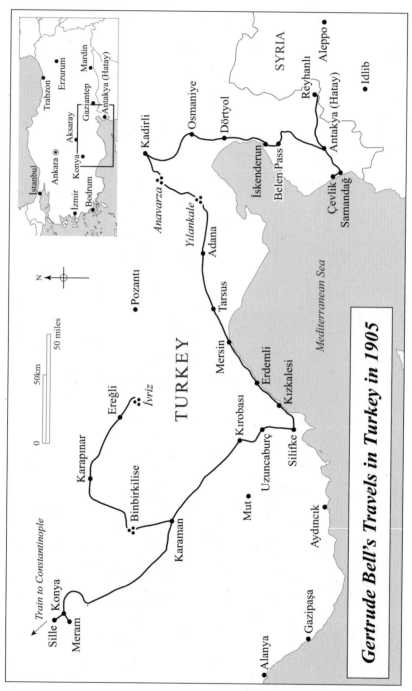

Gertrude Bell's Travels in Turkey in 1905

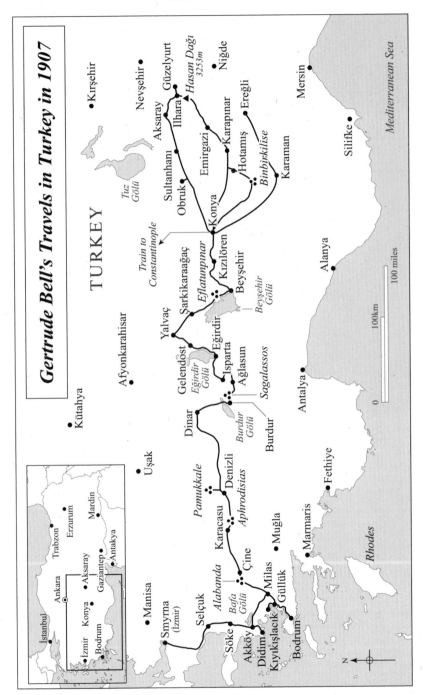

Gertrude Bell's Travels in Turkey in 1907

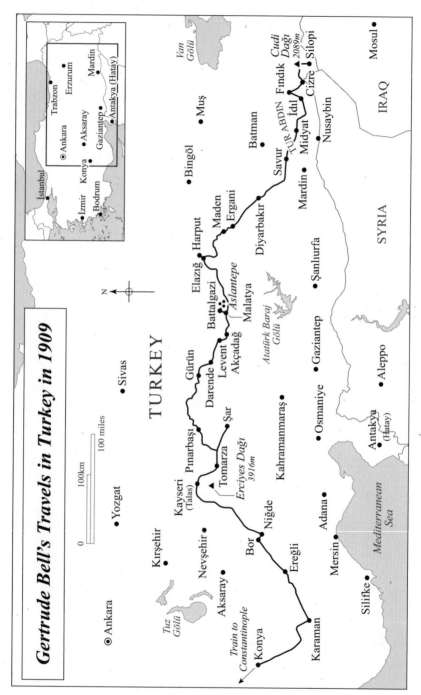

Gertrude Bell's Travels in Turkey in 1909

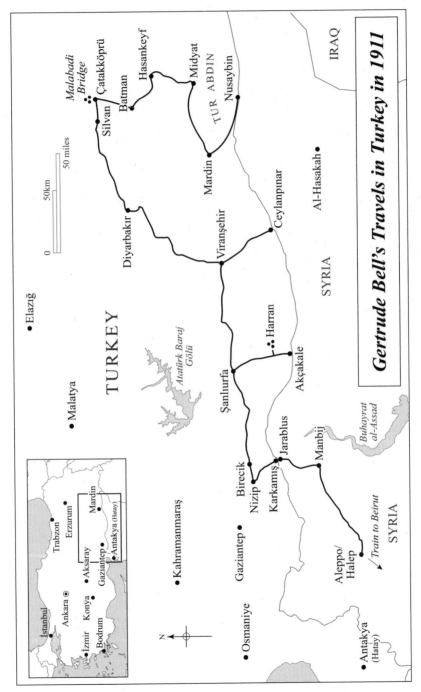

Acknowledgements

Long voyages of discovery such as this are heavily dependent on the input of others and I'm immensely grateful for the kindness and generosity offered by countless individuals who helped me track down possible campsites, pinpoint the sites of lost hotels, decipher no-longer-acceptable place names and grapple with local history. Amongst them I'd especially like to thank: Ken Dakan, Julie Dowdall, Gencer Emiroğlu, Caroline Finkel, Jennifer Gaudet, Jen Hattam, Susanne Güsten, Hüseyin Karagöz, Trici Venola and Lucy Wood in Istanbul; Catherine Yiğit in Çanakkale; Kalliopi Amygdalou, Nesim Bencoya, Elguz Pereira, Andrew Simes and Barbara Touews in Izmir; Craig Encer, Görkem Daskan, and Brian and Vanessa Giraud in Bornova; Şaban and Ali in Bulgurca; Mehmet Dincer in Değirmendere; Özgür Çağdaş and Ali Can in Selçuk; Zeki Acem in Söke; Natalie Sayın in Didyma; Erkin İlgüzer in Akköy; Chris Drum Berkaya, Marion James and Charlotte McPherson in Bodrum; Aydın Cihanoğlu in Aydın; Mehmet Özalp in Dinar; Mehmet Bedel in Burdur; İbrahim Ağartan in Eğirdir; Mustafa and Mehmet in Kireli; Asim Kaplan, İbrahim Kaplan, Mustafa Korasan and Nurettin Özkan in Konya; Cemal, Veysel, Döndü and Halit in Binbirkilise; Bora Gür in Silifke; Ali and Arzu Uysal at Cennet Cehennem; Bülent Akbaş and Latif Bolat in Mersin; Jonathan Beard, Hind Kuba and Mahmut Zeytinoğlu in İskenderun; Arie Amaya-Akkermans, Harun Cemal, Süleyman Çoban and Mehmet Tekin in Antakya; Sylvia di Christina, Kevin Ferrari, Gianpaolo Luglio, Nicolò Marchetti and Hasan Peker in Karkamış; Müzaffer Bey, Ahmet Polat, Sabri and Cihat Kürkçüoğlu, Yusuf Sabri Dişli, Ömer and Alison Tanık, and Zeynep Yılmaz in Urfa; Nurullah Parlakoğlu and Tacettin Toparlı in Mardin; Hamza Kaya in Dara; Niven and Nezihe Öztürk in Savur; Veli Güneş and Feyzi Şahin in Midyat; Father Aho Bilecen at Mor Yakup; Abdullah and Nisani Kurt in Mercimekli; Father Dale Johnson and Father Joachim Rabban at Mor Augen; Süleyman Ağalday and John Crofoot in Hasankeyf; Father Yusuf Akbulut in Diyarbakır; Abbas

Yılmaz in Ergani; İshak Tanoğlu in Harput; Bülent Korkmaz in Malatya; Hamit Ataş in Darende; Stuart Hughes in Güzelyurt; Danielle North and Ginna Narvaez in Ihlara; and Laura Prusoff in Viranşehir. Particular thanks are owed to Mevlüt Demir and the late Osman Diler, my wonderful, uncomplaining companions on the difficult ascent of Hasan Dağı.

Pınar Timer of the Pera Palace Hotel in Istanbul was kind enough to host me in the one Turkish hotel still in business on the same site under the same name as when Gertrude stayed in it. Former British consul to Turkey Leigh Turner facilitated access to the site of the old British summer embassy in Istanbul. Stephen Griffith kindly ironed out several ecclesiastical issues and answered random late-date questions. And Ellen Jewett and Hüsam Süleymangil loaned me a quiet place by the Bosphorus in which to finalize the manuscript.

Thanks, too, to Kate Macdonald, Nancy Öztürk, Nicole Pope and Jeremy Seal for reading and commenting on earlier versions of the text.

I am immensely grateful to Bryn Thomas of Trailblazer for his many helpful suggestions and for steering this project to its conclusion, and also to Lucy Ridout for digging me out of linguistic holes and suggesting some of the chapter headings. Nick Hill was the man behind the mapping; Jane Thomas drew up the index. Their talents were greatly appreciated.

My research would have been impossible without Newcastle University's Gertrude Bell Archive, but I would particularly like to thank Gertrude's archivist, Dr Mark Jackson, for his help in answering queries and providing contacts. *Cornucopia* magazine generously awarded me a grant towards the cost of the journey.

Finally, I couldn't end without thanking Edhem Eldem, whose *Nazlı'nın Defteri* exhibition at the Koç Research Centre for Anatolian Civilisations unexpectedly set my course for the next six years.

Of course all errors of fact or interpretation remain mine. One or two names have been changed for reasons of privacy.

Further Reading

The vast majority of Gertrude Bell quotes used in this book are from her letters and diaries, which, along with her photographs, have been placed online by Newcastle University and can be accessed via the Gertrude Bell Archive: http://gertrudebell.ncl.ac.uk.

A Handbook for Travellers in Turkey, John Murray, 1891

Allen, Susan Heuck *Finding the Walls of Troy: Frank Calvert and Heinrich Schliemann at Hisarlık,* University of California Press, 1999

Ash, John *A Byzantine Journey,* I.B.Tauris, 1995

Ballian, A, Panteleaki, N and Petropoulou, I *Cappadocia: Travels in the Christian East,* Adam Editions, 1994

Bean, George E *Turkey Beyond the Meander: An Archaeological Guide,* Ernest Benn, 1971

Bell, Florence (ed.) *The Letters of Gertrude Bell (Vol. I) 1874–1917,* Echo Press, 2006

Bell, Gertrude *Amurath to Amurath,* William Heinemann, 1911

Bell, Gertrude *Persian Pictures,* Ernest Benn, 1894

Bell, Gertrude 'Notes on a Journey through Cilicia and Lycaonia (Second Article)', *Revue Archéologique,* Vol. 7. Presses Universitaires de France, 1906

Bell, Gertrude and Mango, Marlia Mundell *The Churches and Monasteries of the Tur Abdin,* Pindar Press, 1982

Bell, Gertrude *The Desert and the Sown,* William Heinemann, 1907

Bell, Gertrude and Ramsay, William Mitchell *The Thousand and One Churches,* Cambridge University Press, 1909

Can, Ali *Ephesus in Old Postcards,* Selçuk Belediyesi, 2010

Çetin, Fethiye *My Grandmother: A Memoir,* Verso, 2008

Cooper, Lisa *In Search of Kings and Conquerors: Gertrude Bell and the Archaeology of the Middle East,* IB Tauris, 2016

Courtois, Sebastian de *The Forgotten Genocide,* Gorgias Press, 2004

Dalrymple, William *From the Holy Mountain,* HarperCollins, 1997

Eldem, Edhem *Nazlı's Guestbook,* Homer Kitabevi, 2014

Erdoğan, Nihat *The Ancient City of Dara*, Mardin Museum, 2014

Ertuğrul, Erman 'Ara Güler'in Gözünden Tüm Ayrıntılarıyla Aphrodisias 1958', *Arkeofili*, March 2015

Fraser, David *The Short Cut to India: The Record of a Journey Along the Route of the Baghdad Railway*, William Blackwood and Sons, 1909

Freely, John *The Eastern Mediterranean of Turkey*, SEV, 1998

Griffith, Stephen *Nightingales in the Mountain of Slaves*, Christians Aware, 2013

Güsten, Susanne *The Syriac Property Issue in Tur Abdin*, Istanbul Policy Center, 2015

Haslip, Joan *The Sultan: The Life of Abdul Hamid II*, Weidenfeld & Nicholson, 1958

Hill, Stephen 'The Early Christian Church at Tomarza, Cappadocia: A Study Based on Photographs Taken in 1909 by Gertrude Bell', *Dumbarton Oaks Papers*, Vol. 29, 1975

Hollerweger, Hans *Living Cultural Heritage: Tur Abdin*, Freunde des Tur Abdin, 1999

Howell, Georgina *Daughter of the Desert: The Remarkable Life of Gertrude Bell*, Pan, 2006

Johnson, Dale A *Visits of Gertrude Bell to Tur Abdin*, New Sinai Press, 2007

Kelsey, Tim *Dervish*, Penguin, 1996

Maner, Çiğdem *A Traveler's Guide to Mardin*, MAREV, 2006

Mansel, Philip *Levant*, John Murray, 2010

McCullagh, Francis 'What was Found in the Lair of Abdul Hamid', *New York Times*, 6 June 1909

Milton, Giles *Paradise Lost*, Sceptre, 2008

Montagu, Lady Mary Wortley *The Turkish Embassy Letters*, Virago, 1994

Neave, Dorina Lady *Romance of the Bosphorus*, Hutchinson & Co, 1949

Nicolson, Harold *Sweet Waters*, Sickle Moon Books, 1999

Ousterhout, Robert G *A Byzantine Settlement in Cappadocia*, Harvard University Press, 2012

Payet, Thierry *Narration: Mardin Stories*, 2014

Poynter, Mary A *When Turkey Was Turkey: In and Around Constantinople*, George Routledge & Sons, 1921

Richmond, Elsa *The Earlier Letters of Gertrude Bell*, Ernest Benn, 1937

Russell, Gerard *Heirs to Forgotten Kingdoms*, Simon & Schuster, 2014

Sackville-West, Vita *Passenger to Tehran* Hogarth Press, 1926

Sahakyan, Lusine 'Turkification of the Toponyms in the Ottoman Empire and the Republic of Turkey', Armenian Folia Anglistika, 2010

Sattin, Anthony *Young Lawrence: A Portrait of the Legend as a Young Man*, John Murray, 2014

Seal, Jeremy *Meander: East to West Along a Turkish River*, Chatto & Windus, 2012

Sinclair, TA *Eastern Turkey: An Architectural and Archaeological Survey*, Pindar Press, 1990

Sumner-Boyd, Hilary and Freely, John *Strolling Through Istanbul*, Redhouse Press, 1972

Taşkıran, Celal *Silifke and Environs: Lost Cities of a Distant Past in Cilicia*, 1993

Uysun, Mustafa *Guide to Iconography in the Rock-Cut Churches of Cappadocia*, 2014

Wallach, Janet *Desert Queen: The Extraordinary Life of Gertrude Bell*, Phoenix, 1996

Williams, Roger *The Fisherman of Halicarnassus*, Bilgi Yayınevi, 2013

Winstone, HVF *Gertrude Bell*, Quartet Books, 1980

Yoltar-Yıldırım, Ayşin 'Seljuk Carpets and Julius Harry Löytved-Hardegg: A German Consul in Konya in the early twentieth century' in Dávid, G and Gerelyes, I (eds.), *Thirteenth International Congress of Turkish Art: Proceedings*, Hungarian National Museum, 2009

Glossary

abi big brother

abla big sister

ağa chief, landowner

bakkal corner shop, grocery

bayram holiday, religious or secular

Belediye(si) municipality, town hall

beys powerful warlords who established regional fiefdoms all over Anatolia in the *beylik* period (between the collapse of the Selçuk Sultanate of Rum and the takeover of the Ottomans)

cadde(si) street

caique long, low boat, once standard Bosphorus transportation

cami mosque

caravanserai waystation on major roads where travellers and animals could stay overnight

çay Turkish tea usually served in tulip-shaped glass

dağ(ı) mountain; **dağları** mountains

dolmuş minibus shared 'taxi'

dragoman translator / interpreter

eski old

ev(i) house

ezan call to prayer

gavur infidel

gecekondu very basic housing, slum

göbektaşı marble slab for relaxation in centre of hamam

gület wooden yacht

hacı one who has been on the Haj; general term of respect

hamal porter

hamam Turkish bath

han urban equivalent of a caravanserai, where travellers and animals could stay overnight

GLOSSARY

hanımefendi polite term of address for woman

haremlik female/family section of house

iftar Ramadan break-of-fast evening meal

kahve literally, coffee; also name for old-fashioned village teahouses

kale(si) castle

kapı(sı) gate

karışık mixed up, troubled

kavass body guard

Kaymakam district governor

kerpiç mud-brick architecture

kervansaray see *caravanserai*

khan see *han*

kilise church

köfte meatballs

konak mansion

köprü(sü) bridge

köşk(ü) pavilion

köy village

külliye(si) mosque complex

kuruş small Ottoman coin

liwan open-fronted arched portal

lokanta no-frills restaurant serving Turkish staples

lokum Turkish delight

mahalle(si) neighbourhood

medres(si) Islamic school

mescit Muslim chapel

mihrab niche in mosque wall indicating direction of Mecca

mimber pulpit in mosque

misafir odası guestroom

mor saint (Syriac)

muhtar headman, a local official in towns and villages

nargile(h) water pipe for smoking tobacco

ney flute associated with whirling dervishes

oda(sı) room

okey popular Turkish tile game

örenyeri ruins

pardesü ankle-length women's overcoat

pekmez grape molasses

pide oblong-shaped Turkish version of pizza

poyraz northeasterly wind

Ramazan Ramadan

şadırvan ablutions fountain

sahur special early-morning breakfast during Ramadan

şalvar baggy cotton trousers mainly worn by rural women but also by some men

saray(ı) palace

sayyid men descended from the Prophet Mohammed

saz lute-like stringed instrument

selamlık (1) male/public part of house; (2) sultan's ceremonial procession to Friday prayers

simit bread roll studded with sesame seeds

tandır clay oven

tekke(si) dervish lodge

Ulu Cami literally, Great Mosque; a town's main mosque, particularly used for Friday prayers

vadi(si) valley

Vali local governor

yabancı foreigner

yalı waterside mansion

yasak forbidden

yayla upland summer meadows

yörük nomad

yufka paper-thin unleavened bread

Zabita specialist market police

Index